'Arabiyyat al-Naas fii Maṣr (Part One)

'Arabiyyat al-Naas fii Maṣr (Part One) offers a ground-breaking introduction to Arabic as it is written and spoken by native speakers.

It combines a progressive and rigorous grounding in Modern Standard Arabic (MSA), the form employed for reading, writing, and formal speaking, with an innovative integration of the dominant Egyptian variety. Introducing the two simultaneously and seamlessly building on their shared features, *'Arabiyyat al-Naas fii Maṣr (Part One)* uses each in its proper context: Egyptian dialect for conversations and MSA for reading and writing activities. In this way, the course efficiently prepares students for the practical realities of learning and living Arabic today.

A companion website with extensive materials accompanies the book at www.routledge.com/cw/weatherspoon.

Munther Younes is Reis Senior Lecturer of Arabic Language and Linguistics and Director of the Arabic Program at Cornell University, USA. He is the co-author of the *'Arabiyyat al-Naas* textbook series and the author of the following books: *The Routledge Introduction to Qur'anic Arabic, Kalila wa Dimna for Students of Arabic, The Integrated Approach to Arabic Instruction,* and *Charging Steeds or Maidens Performing Good Deeds: In Search of the Original Qur'an,* all published by Routledge.

Makda G. Weatherspoon is Senior Lecturer of Arabic at Cornell University, USA, where she is the Coordinator of the Elementary Arabic Program. She has also taught at Middlebury Language Program and worked as a curriculum developer of online Arabic materials at the University of Cambridge, Language Centre, UK. Prior to that, she worked as an English instructor with immigrants who were preparing to take their American citizenship tests. Makda is the co-author of *'Arabiyyat al-Naas (Part One)*.

Jonathan Featherstone is Senior Teaching Fellow of Arabic at the University of Edinburgh where he leads on an intensive master's degree in Arabic. Prior to this he taught Arabic at the Defence School of Languages in the UK and then at the Foreign and Commonwealth Office. Jonathan is also the author of *BBC Talk Arabic.*

Elizabeth (Lizz) Huntley is a current doctoral student in Second Language Studies at Michigan State University. She holds master's degrees in Teaching Arabic as Foreign Language and in Middle Eastern and North African Studies from the University of Michigan. She has taught Arabic at the college level at Cornell University and the University of Michigan, and at the high-school level with the Concordia Language Villages, the Middlebury-Monterey Language Academy, and the STARTALK Arabic Summer Academy of the Boston Public Schools.

Titles in the 'Arabiyyat al-Naas series:

'Arabiyyat al-Naas (Part One): An Introductory Course in Arabic
Munther Younes, Makda Weatherspoon, and Maha Saliba Foster
978-0-415-51693-8

'Arabiyyat al-Naas fii Maṣr (Part One): An Introductory Course in Arabic
Munther Younes, Makda G. Weatherspoon, Jonathan Featherstone, and Elizabeth Huntley

'Arabiyyat al-Naas (Part Two): An Intermediate Course in Arabic
Munther Younes and Hanada Al-Masri
978-0-415-50908-4

'Arabiyyat al-Naas (Part Three): An Advanced Course in Arabic
Munther Younes and Yomna Chami
978-0-415-50901-5

"'Arabiyyat al-Naas is a game-changing series that embodies a pioneering approach to Arabic language teaching and learning. By integrating formal and colloquial Arabic, 'Arabiyyat al-Naas presents the language as it is used in real life. The demand for this approach is now increasing exponentially around the world. 'Arabiyyat al-Naas is the result of years of creative thinking and innovative teaching."

– Jeremy Palmer, *American University of Sharjah, UAE*

'Arabiyyat al-Naas fii Maṣr (Part One)

An Introductory Course in Arabic

Munther Younes
Makda G. Weatherspoon
Jonathan Featherstone
Elizabeth Huntley
Zeinab A. Taha (Academic Consultant)

Routledge
Taylor & Francis Group
LONDON AND NEW YORK

First published 2020

by Routledge
2 Park Square, Milton Park, Abingdon, Oxon OX14 4RN

and by Routledge
52 Vanderbilt Avenue, New York, NY 10017

Routledge is an imprint of the Taylor & Francis Group, an informa business

British Library Cataloguing-in-Publication Data
A catalogue record for this book is available from the British Library

Library of Congress Cataloging-in-Publication Data
A catalog record for this book has been requested

ISBN: 978-1-138-06515-4 (pbk)
ISBN: 978-1-315-15994-2 (ebk)

Typeset in Scala
by Apex CoVantage, LLC

Visit the companion website: www.routledge.com/cw/weatherspoon

Contents

Acknowledgments

Much of the material and ideas in this book appeared in the first edition of *'Arabiyyat al-Naas* Levantine version (Routledge, 2013). We are grateful to all who contributed to the earlier version.

'Arabiyyat al-Naas fii Maṣr (Part One): An Introductory Course in Arabic has been designed to provide a comprehensive curriculum which integrates Egyptian Colloquial Arabic (ECA) with Modern Standard Arabic (MSA) in a way that reflects important aspects of the Arabic language and culture in context. This effort required the active involvement and participation of many colleagues and friends without whom this project would not have been possible. We would like to thank Dr. Zeinab Taha (American University in Cairo) for overseeing the recording and filming of the dialogues, which serve as the backbone and the main storyline of the book. We are also extremely grateful to Dr. Taha's expertise and advice with the appropriate usage of ECA throughout the textbook.

We would also like to acknowledge the crew members who did a fantastic job playing the different roles in the video and audio materials that accompany this book: Maya Mundell, the protagonist who played the role of Maya, and through whom we hope our students will vicariously experience Egypt and other Arab countries; Sarah Abou El-Goukh, who played the role of Salma, Maya's roommate; Ahmed Mostafa Saleh, Sound Engineer and owner of the audio studio; Amal Ishak, Director of Photography; Rami Courdi, Camera Man; and Faris Kerim, Video Editor.

We would also like to express our sincere gratitude to our colleagues and friends Dr. Abdellah Chekayri (Al Akhawayn University, Morocco) and Dr. Nancy Coffin (Princeton University, U.S.) for their suggestions and feedback.

Words fail to describe the dedication, professionalism, patience, and efficiency of the Routledge team who have worked with us tirelessly on this project. In particular we are very grateful to the following people who have been supporting us all along: Andrea Hartill, Publisher; Claire Margerison, Editorial Assistant; and Samantha Vale Noya, Editor.

Last but not least, we would like to thank our students who have patiently worked with the earlier versions of this book and for their positive feedback and comments throughout the project.

Visual tour of the textbook

Throughout the textbook you will see icons in the margin, which indicate where further multimedia resources are available. These stimulating online exercises are exclusive to purchasers of the textbook and provide a rigorous grounding in Modern Standard Arabic (MSA) while also seamlessly integrating the spoken Egyptian variety.

Multimedia resources include:

Video material
Video material can be found on the companion website.

Audio material
Audio recordings, including songs, can be found on the companion website.

Writing demonstrations
These videos demonstrating written Arabic can be found on the companion website.

Introduction

'Arabiyyat al-Naas fii Maṣr is an introductory comprehensive Arabic-as-a-foreign-language textbook designed for absolute beginners. The textbook integrates Modern Standard Arabic (فصحى) with Egyptian colloquial Arabic (مصري) in a way that reflects the use of the language by native speakers.

The organization of instructional materials in *'Arabiyyat al-Naas fii Maṣr* reflects native language usage. As the textbook progresses, the ratio of the فصحى material increases relative to the مصري material. Emphasis in the first part of the book is on the familiar, concrete, and informal, for which مصري is particularly appropriate. The فصحى material occupies an increasingly more prominent role with the progression towards the less familiar, less concrete, and more formal. The material is fully integrated in a way that reflects the practices of native speakers; reading passages are presented in فصحى and discussed in مصري. This balance helps to simultaneously develop the skills of the two varieties. It is important to note that the مصري presented in this book reflects the speech of educated native speakers, or عامية المثقفين.

The texts, activities, exercises, and accompanying media of the textbook have been designed with the goal of developing and integrating all four language skills. Humor, illustrations, pictures, maps, and different types of vocabulary-building activities are used to help make the acquisition and retention of language both enjoyable and effective.

The structure of the *'Arabiyyat al-Naas fii Maṣr* curriculum

The complete *'Arabiyyat al-Naas fii Maṣr* curriculum consists of the textbook and the companion website.

'Arabiyyat al-Naas fii Maṣr is designed to be covered in two 15-week academic semesters at university level or about 120 to 140 hours of classroom instruction. Each lesson is designed to be covered in one contact hour, but can be adjusted according to the pace of the curriculum. The materials are designed to bring students from the *novice low level* to the *intermediate low level* on the ACTFL scale (American Council on the Teaching of Foreign Languages), and from A1 to A2/B1 on the CEFR scale (Common European Framework Reference).

Please see the visual introductions/videos 1a and 1b on the companion website for a detailed overview of the textbook and website materials.

Structure of the textbook

'Arabiyyat al-Naas fii Maṣr consists of 19 units. Unit 1 contains 10 lessons, introducing students to the Arabic alphabet, numbers, and vocabulary for daily life.

Units 2–19 are theme based, following the story of an American student, Maya, who travels to Egypt and experiences situations that the foreign learner of Arabic is likely to encounter. Each unit is divided into 5 lessons, following the general structure below:

- Lesson 1: introduction to thematic vocabulary
- Lesson 2: video passage of Maya's experiences in Egypt
- Lesson 3: audio or reading passage
- Lesson 4: reading passage from Maya's diary
- Lesson 5: consolidation and wrap-up activities

Additionally, at the back of the book are comprehensive vocabulary and grammar glossaries.

Contents of the companion website

The *'Arabiyyat al-Naas fii Maṣr* curriculum requires the use of the companion website, which operates in tandem with the printed textbook. Online materials include:

- Video and audio passages
- Interactive activities and self-correcting drills
- Writing demonstrations
- Songs with lyrics
- Audio-recorded vocabulary flashcards
- Extra instructional materials

Access to materials is available at: www.routledge.com/cw/weatherspoon.

Culture

There are no separate sections dealing with Arab culture in the textbook, but culture is an integral part of it. In addition to the notes on Arab geography and descriptions of some Arab cities, culture is reflected in Maya's dealings with Arabic speakers of different ages and backgrounds and her experiences with airport officials, hotel employees, restaurant waiters, taxi drivers, a roommate and the roommate's family, and Arab friends.

Unit 1 الوحدة الأولى
Arabic alphabet and numbers

(I am a student.) أنا طالِب. : (Lesson 1) الدرس الأوّل

Exercise 1

Look at the pictures and listen to the recording of each word, starting from the right.

Exercise 2

Watch the following 4 short video clips and repeat each phrase you hear. On a separate piece of paper, write down in English the meaning of each phrase you recognize:

Exercise 3

Watch the following 2 short video clips and repeat each phrase you hear. Then say the appropriate phrase by inserting your own name (be sure to use the correct gender!).

Exercise 4

Watch the following 4 short video clips and translate them into English on a separate piece of paper.

Arabic numbers 1–10

These are the numbers as they are commonly written in Arabic. The English numbers are written below them as a reference.

١٠	٩	٨	٧	٦	٥	٤	٣	٢	١
10	9	8	7	6	5	4	3	2	1

Exercise 5 (Listening and memorizing)

With the help of the audio recording, memorize the Arabic numbers 1–10 and then practice reading them out loud. Note that Arabic is read from right to left.

١٠	٩	٨	٧	٦	٥	٤	٣	٢	١

Exercise 7 (Reading)

Practice reading the numbers out loud with your partner. You should start on the right as in the number line above:

١٠	٩	٨	٧	٦	٥	٤	٣	٢	١	١.
٣	٨	٦	٢	١٠	١	٤	٧	٩	٥	٢.
١	٧	٥	١٠	٣	٨	٤	٢	٩	٦	٣.

The Arabic alphabet

Before introducing the Arabic alphabet, here are a few important facts to keep in mind:

1. As we saw in the above exercise, Arabic is written and read from right to left.
2. There are 28 letters in the alphabet. Letters generally connect to the following letter in a word, like in cursive writing in English. There are, however, six letters that do not connect to the following letter. These letters, called "one-way connectors", will be identified as they are introduced.
3. The shape of a letter may change slightly according to its position in the word (whether it is at the beginning, middle, or the end of the word). You will learn all the different shapes for each letter as they are introduced. For the majority of letters, these differences in shape are minimal.
   As you learn each letter, focus on its basic shape regardless of position.
4. Arabic and English share a lot of common sounds for letters. For shared sounds, the English equivalent will be shown in the alphabet tables. For the sounds which are not shared, this space will be left blank. You will learn them by listening to your teacher or to the audio recording.

Exercise 8 (Reading)

Learn the letters below by listening to your teacher or the audio recordings.

English equivalent	*Other shapes* Final/*Medial*/*Initial*	*Basic shape*
(long) *a* as in *cat* and *car*	ـا/ـا/ا	ا
b	ـب/ـبـ/بـ	ب
	ـط/ـطـ/طـ	ط
l	ـل/ـلـ/لـ	ل
n	ـن/ـنـ/نـ	ن
s	ـس/ـسـ/سـ	س

Note: Shaded letters are one-way connectors (connect on the right only)

Secondary letters

English equivalent	*Other shapes* Final/*Medial*/*Initial*	*Basic shape*
a (found at the end of words only)	ـة/ة	

In the table below, you can see how the letters connect to form words. The words are presented as they are normally written in the top row, and with the letters separated below. As you read, can you guess what the words mean?

words as normally written	طالب	انا
words with letters separated	ط ا ل ب	ا ن ا

as normally written	طالبة	انا
letters separated	ط ا ل ب ـة	ا ن ا

Now read the following two words. Can you guess their meanings?

بطاطس	لبنان
ب ط ا ط س	ل ب ن ا ن

Notes about reading : ـة/ة

This letter is called *taa' marbuuTa* in Arabic. It is found only at the end of words, and generally marks feminine gender. ـة follows connecting letters, and ة follows non-connecting letters.

Exercise 9 (Listening and reading) (in class with the teacher)

Circle the word you hear.

١. انا/باب	٢. لبنان/طالب	٣. طالب/باب	٤. طالب/بطاطا	٥. طالب/طالبة

Exercise 10 (Listening and reading) (in class with the teacher)

Circle the letter you hear.

١. ب/ن	٢. ط/ل	٣. ا/ل	٤. ا/ن	٥. ل/ن

Exercise 11

Circle the letters you recognize in each of the following words:

١. باب	٢. طالب	٣. طالبة	٤. انا	٥. مرحبا	٦. بطاطا
٧. لبنان	٨. بريطانيا	٩. مدينة	١٠. أمريكا	١١. ليبيا	

Writing Arabic

Exercise 12 (Writing) (in class or at home)

Watch the writing demo or your teacher and practice writing the numbers 1–10 in your notebook until you can write them without looking.

١	٢	٣	٤	٥	٦	٧	٨	٩	١٠

Exercise 13 (Writing)

Write down each of the letters above the table under its other form in the space provided.

ن ب ة س ل

بـ	نـ	ســ	لـ	ـة

Exercise 14 (Writing)

Watch the writing demo or your teacher and practice writing the following pairs of words in your notebook until you can write them without looking.

انا	طالب

انا	طالبة

Mabruuk! Congratulations! You have written your very first complete sentences in Arabic! Can you guess what they mean?

Exercise 15 (Writing)

Label the following pictures in Arabic.

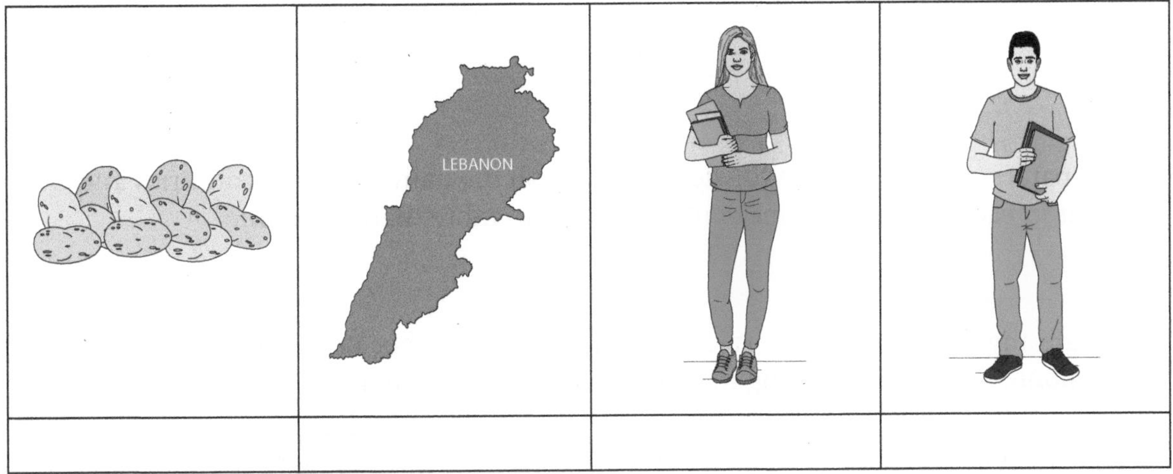

Exercise 16 (Listening) (in class or at home)

Listen to the following short conversation and answer the comprehension questions below.

Comprehension questions

1. How many male students are in the class?
2. How many female students?
3. How many teachers?

الدرس الثاني (Lesson 2) : انا من . . . (I am from . . .)

Exercise 1

You will hear three words numbered 1–3. Write the Arabic number under the map that corresponds to the word with that number.

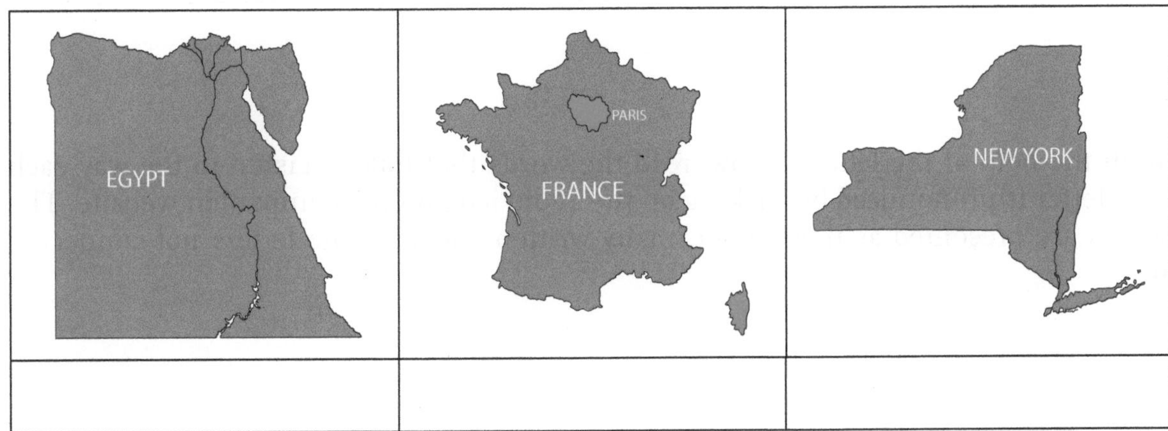

Exercise 2

Watch the following 4 short video clips and write down in English what each person is saying on a separate piece of paper:

1. Leila 2. Dan 3. Louise 4. Kathy

Now, introduce yourself to others in class following the same format.

Exercise 3 (Listening)

On a separate piece of paper, write down in English the names of Arab countries and cities you hear in each sentence. Some sentences contain more than one name.

Arabic numbers 11–20

Below are the Arabic numbers 11–20. Listen to your teacher or the audio recording and follow along. Remember reading in Arabic goes from right to left.

٢٠	١٩	١٨	١٧	١٦	١٥	١٤	١٣	١٢	١١

Exercise 4 (Listening and memorizing)

With the help of the audio recording, memorize the Arabic numbers 11–20 and then practice reading them out loud.

Exercise 6 (Reading)

The following are the numbers 11 through 20. They are in the correct order in the first line, and scrambled in the following three lines. Read each number out loud.

٢٠	١٩	١٨	١٧	١٦	١٥	١٤	١٣	١٢	١١	.١
١٣	١٨	١٦	١٢	٢٠	١١	١٤	١٧	١٩	١٥	.٢
١١	١٧	١٥	٢٠	١٣	١٨	١٤	١٢	١٩	١٦	.٣
١١	١٩	١٧	١٥	١٣	٢٠	١٨	١٦	١٤	١٢	.٤

Exercise 7 (Reading)

With the help of the letters below, read the words that follow. Listen to the way each new letter is pronounced by clicking on the audio icon on the companion website. The words are presented as they are normally written and with the letters not connected below.

Review letters

ة/ـة	س	ن	ل	ط	ب	ا

New letters

Remember that shaded letters are one-way connectors: they connect on the right only.

English equivalent	*Other shapes* *Final/Medial/Initial*	*Basic shape*
t	تـ/ـتـ/ـت	ت
d	د/ـد/ـد	د
r	ر/ـر/ـر	ر
f	فـ/ـفـ/ـف	ف
m	مـ/ـمـ/ـم	م
w *or* uu	و/ـو/ـو	و
y *or* ii	يـ/ـيـ/ـي	ي

Shaded letters = one-way connectors (connect on the right only)

New vocabulary

من (from)	في (in)	مدينة	دولة
م ن	ف ي	م د ي ن ة	د و ل ة

Now read the following names of cities and countries. Can you guess their equivalents in English?

بريطانيا	فلوريدا	بيروت	طرابلس	اليمن
ب ر ي ط ا ن ي ا	ف ل و ر ي د ا	ب ي ر و ت	ط ر ا ب ل س	ا ل ي م ن

سوريا	ليبيا	السودان	فرنسا
س و ر ي ا	ل ي ب ي ا	ا ل س و د ا ن	ف ر ن س ا

Exercise 8 (Listening and reading) (in class with the teacher)

Circle the word you hear.

١. دولة/مدينة	٢. ليبيا/سوريا	٣. السودان/اليمن	٤. بيروت/بريطانيا
٥. في/من	٦. طرابلس/بيروت	٧. طالب/طالبة	٨. فلوريدا/فرنسا

Exercise 9 (Listening and reading) (in class with the teacher)

Circle the letter you hear.

١. ب/د	٢. ل/م	٣. ت/د	٤. ا/ي	٥. م/ن
٦. ف/ط	٧. ط/د	٨. د/ر	٩. و/ر	١٠. س/ت

Exercise 10

Circle the letters you recognize in each of the following words:

١. كبير	٢. صغيرة	٣. شمال	٤. جنوب	٥. شرق
٦. غرب	٧. مصر	٨. دمشق	٩. أمريكا	١٠. كندا

Exercise 11 (Writing) (in class or at home)

Watch the writing demo or your teacher and practice writing the numbers 11–20 in your notebook until you can write them without looking.

١١	١٢	١٣	١٤	١٥	١٦	١٧	١٨	١٩	٢٠

Exercise 12 (Writing)

Write down each of the letters above the table under its other shape in the space provided.

ت د ر س ف م و ي

ـت	ـر	ـمـ	ـد	ـيـ	ـمـ	ـو	ـسـ	ـف

Exercise 13 (Writing)

Watch the writing demo or your teacher and practice writing the following words in your notebook until you can write them without looking.

السودان	من	في	مدينة	دولة
سوريا	ليبيا	بيروت	طرابلس	اليمن

Distinguishing between د ، ر ، ل

It is sometimes difficult to distinguish between ل and د and between د and ر.

ل and د

Notice that ل is a two-way connector while د is a one-way connector. Look again at Exercise 13 above. What other differences do you notice between د and ل?

ر and د

ر is generally flatter and goes below the bottom line while د is a bit more angular and sits above the bottom line. Both are one-way connectors.

With this in mind, circle the examples of ر ,ل, and د in the two words below. Then practice reading the words out loud.

فلوريدا	لندن

Exercise 14 (Writing)

Label each of the following words as دولة or مدينة.

٣. سوريا	٢. فرنسا	١. ليبيا
٦. طرابلس	٥. اليمن	٤. السودان
٩. لندن	٨. لبنان	٧. بيروت
١٢. سياتل	١١. باريس	١٠. بريطانيا

Exercise 15 (Writing)

Connect the following letters.

ا ل ي م ن	ا ل س و د ا ن	س و ر ي ا	ل ي ب ي ا	ل ب ن ا ن

ف ر ن س ا	ب ر ي ط ا ن ي ا	ف ل و ر ي د ا	ب ي ر و ت	ط ر ا ب ل س

Exercise 16 (Listening and writing) (in class or at home)

On a separate piece of paper, write down in Arabic the names of Arab countries and cities you recognize in each sentence. Some sentences contain more than one name.

Exercise 17 (Reading and writing) (in class or at home)

Match each of the following sentences to the corresponding picture by writing the sentence under it. Then translate the Arabic sentences into English in the space below.

بيروت في لبنان.
لندن في بريطانيا.
باريس في فرنسا.

Exercise 18 (Listening and writing)

Dictation – (in class or at home) Listen to the audio recording and complete each of the following sentences by writing the missing words.

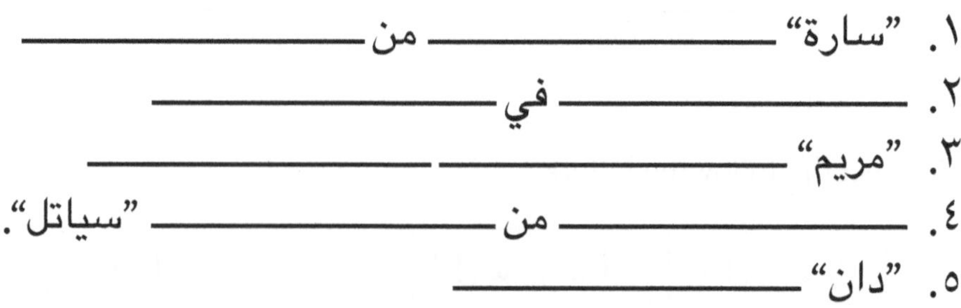

١. ”سارة“ ________ من ________
٢. ________ في ________
٣. ”مريم“ ________ ________
٤. ________ من ________ ”سياتل“.
٥. ”دان“ ________

الدرس الثالث: مدينة . . . كبيرة ولاّ صغيرة؟
(Lesson 3: The city of . . . is big or small?)

Exercise 1

Look at the picture and listen to the recording of each word.

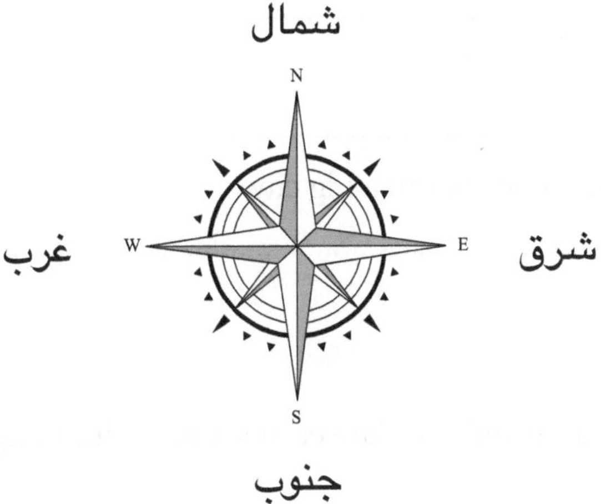

Exercise 2

Watch the following dialogue and answer the questions that follow.

First listening

Make a list of the names of people and places you recognize.

Second listening

1. Where is Dan from?

   ....

2. Where is Salma from?

   ....

3. According to the passage, is Los Angeles a big city? Is Alexandria a big city?

....

Exercise 3 (Listening)

Listen to the following short dialogue and answer the questions that follow.

First listening

1. What are the names of the two people speaking?

....

2. What do they do?

....

Second listening

1. Where is Nadia from?

....

2. Where is Aswan?

....

3. According to the passage, is Aswan a big city?

....

Exercise 4

Listen to the audio recording and translate each sentence into English in your notebook.

The Arabic numbers counting by tens: 10–100

Below are the Arabic numbers from 10 to 100, counting by tens. Listen to your teacher or the audio recording and follow along.

١٠٠	٩٠	٨٠	٧٠	٦٠	٥٠	٤٠	٣٠	٢٠	١٠

Exercise 5 (Listening and memorizing)

Listen to the audio recording and memorize counting by tens up to 100. Then practice reading the numbers above.

Exercise 6 (Listening and reading)

Circle the number you hear.

٥. ١٠/١٠٠	٤. ٧٠/٨٠	٣. ٦٠/٩٠	٢. ٢٠/٣٠	١. ١٠/٢٠
١٠. ٣٠/٨٠	٩. ٤٠/٢٠	٨. ٣/٣٠	٧. ٦٠/٣٠	٦. ٨٠/٨

Exercise 7 (Reading)

Read the following numbers.

١٠	٩	٨	٧	٦	٥	٤	٣	٢	١	١.
١٠٠	٩٠	٨٠	٧٠	٦٠	٥٠	٤٠	٣٠	٢٠	١٠	٢.
٧٠	١٠٠	٥٠	٣٠	١٠	٨٠	٢٠	٩٠	٤٠	٦٠	٣.
١٤	٢٠	١٨	١٣	١٧	١٢	١٠	١٥	١٩	١١	٤.

Exercise 8 (Reading)

With the help of the letters below, read the words that follow. Listen to the way each new letter is pronounced by clicking on the audio icon on the companion website. The words are presented as they are normally written and with the letters separated below.

Review letters

ة/ـة	ي	و	ن	م	ل	ف	ط	س	ر	د	ت	ب	ا

New letters

English equivalent	*Other shapes*	*Basic shape*
	Final/Medial/Initial	
j	جـ/ـجـ/ـج	ج
sh	شـ/ـشـ/ـش	ش
	صـ/ـصـ/ـص	ص
	غـ/ـغـ/ـغ/غ	غ
	قـ/ـقـ/ـق	ق
k	كـ/ـكـ/ـك	ك

New vocabulary

Small	
صغيرة	صغير
ص غ ي ر ة	ص غ ي ر
(feminine)	(masculine)

Big	
كبيرة	كبير
ك ب ي ر ة	ك ب ي ر
(feminine)	(masculine)

Reading

Using the compass in Exercise 1 above, write down in English the meaning of the following phrases:

١. شمال شرق ٢. شمال غرب ٣. جنوب شرق ٤. جنوب غرب

The following are the names of an Arab country and an Arab city. Can you guess their equivalents in English?

دمشق	الصومال
د م ش ق	ا ل ص و م ا ل

Exercise 9 (Listening and reading)

Circle the word you hear. (In class with the teacher.)

٥. شمال/ السودان	٤. مصر/ صغير	٣. غرب/شرق	٢. صغير/ سوريا	١. كبير/ امريكا
١٠. بريطانيا/ طرابلس	٩. جنوب/ لبنان	٨. فرنسا/ شرق	٧. كندا/كبير	٦. اليمن/ليبيا

Exercise 10 (Listening and reading)

Circle the letter you hear. (In class with the teacher.)

٥. ك/ق	٤. ا/ك	٣. ب/ت	٢. ا /غ	١. ف/ق
١٠. غ/ق	٩. ق/ج	٨. ش/س	٧. س/ص	٦. ط/ت

Exercise 11

Circle the letters you recognize in the following words.

٥. بغداد	٤. الصيف	٣. ثلج	٢. العراق	١. بارد
١٠. السعودية	٩. شمس	٨. الربيع	٧. مطر	٦. جورج
١٥. حار	١٤. جوّ	١٣. الخريف	١٢. الشتاء	١١. الربيع

Exercise 12 (Writing) (in class or at home)

Watch the writing demo or your teacher and practice writing the numbers 10–100 by tens in your notebook until you can write them without looking.

١٠٠	٩٠	٨٠	٧٠	٦٠	٥٠	٤٠	٣٠	٢٠	١٠

Exercise 13 (Writing)

Fill in the missing numbers from memory and read them out loud.

٨٠	٥٠	٣٠	٢٠	١٠

Exercise 14 (Writing)

Write down each of the letters above the table under its other shapes in the space provided.

ك ق غ ص ش ج

ـصـ	ـجـ	ک	ـق	ـشـ	ـغ	ـج	ـغـ	صـ

Exercise 15 (Writing)

Connect the letters to make up words.

ا ل س و د ا ن
ب غ د ا د
م ص ر
ش م ا ل
ش ر ق
ا ن ا

ط ا ل ب ة
غ ر ب
ج ن و ب
ص غ ي ر ة
ك ب ي ر ة
م د ي ن ة

Exercise 16 (Writing)

Fill in the missing words from the word bank below to complete each sentence.

غرب   شرق   جنوب   شمال

١. مصر ________________ السودان.
٢. امريكا ________________ كندا.
٣. العراق ________________ سوريا.
٤. المغرب ________________ تونس.

In some Arabic word processing programs, when ل is followed by م, the two letters combine into the following shape: لم, thus ال+مغرب → المغرب.

Exercise 17 (Listening and reading comprehension)

With the help of the words above and the audio recording on the companion website, read out loud the sentences below. Then, translate them into English.

١. انا سليم. أنا من مدينة بيروت. بيروت في غرب لبنان. لبنان دولة صغيرة.

....

٢. انا سارة. أنا من مدينة دمشق. دمشق في جنوب سوريا.

....

٣. ليبيا دولة كبيرة في شمال إفريقيا.

....

٤. مصر شمال السودان وشرق ليبيا.

....

٥. ليبيا غرب مصر وشمال غرب السودان.

....

٦. دمشق في جنوب غرب سوريا.

....

٧. مصر دولة كبيرة ولبنان دولة صغيرة.

....

Grammar/pronunciation note

Notice that the pronunciation of the letter ة (*taa marbuuTa*) changes to a "t" in phrases such as "the city of Beirut – مدينة بيروت madiinat beirut" and "the city of Damascus – مدينة دمشق madiinat dimashq". This is due to a grammatical construction called the *iDaafa Construct* (إضافة)', which you will learn more about in the tenth lesson of this unit. For now, memorize the pronunciation of the "t" as part of the complete phrase. Now, read each of the following words out loud separately and then together as a phrase, then translate the phrase into English.

بيروت	مدينة
دمشق	مدينة

←

مدينة بيروت
مدينة دمشق

Exercise 18 (Writing)

Complete the following sentences, translate into Arabic in your notebook, and then read them out loud.

1. I am (your name) ....
2. I am a student ....
3. I am from (name of city) ....
4. The city is in (north/south/east/west) (your state) ....
5. The city of...is big/small.......................................

Exercise 19 (Writing)

Look at the map below and write four or more sentences using the following words:

كبير/ة، صغير/ة، شمال، جنوب، شرق، غرب

Example

مصر شرق السودان.

(Lesson 4: The weather) الدرس الرابع – الجو

Exercise 1

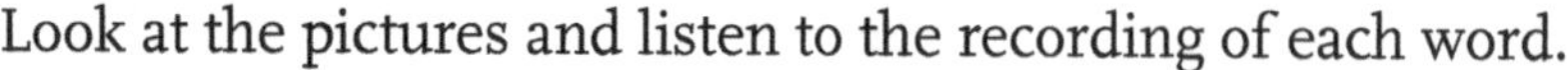

Look at the pictures and listen to the recording of each word.

 الشتاء	 الصيف	 الخريف	 الربيع
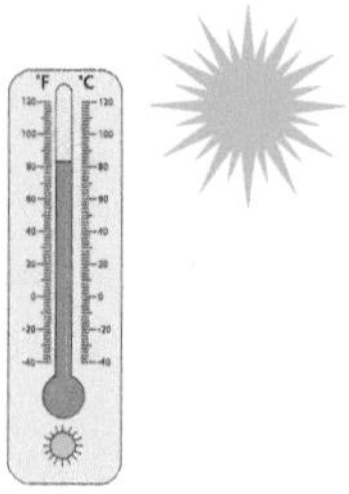 حار	 شمس	 بارد	 ثلج
 مطر			

Exercise 2

Listen to the audio recording and complete the English sentences below.

1. The weather in New York is .... in the ....
2. There is a lot of .... in ....
3. Is there .... in ....?

4. The weather in the city of Riyadh is .... in the .... and .... in the ....

5. How is the .... in .... today?

Exercise 3

Watch the following short video clips and answer the questions. Then carry out a similar conversation with your partner in class with information pertaining to you.

Clip 1: Questions

1. What is the girl's name?
2. Where is she from?
3. How did she describe the weather in her city?

Clip 2: Questions

1. What are the names of the speakers?
2. Where are they from?
3. In which city is the weather described? How is it described?

Exercise 4 (Listening)

Listen to the recording and answer the questions.

First listening

What is the topic of the conversation?

Second listening

According to the dialogue,

1. Is Iraq a big or a small country?
2. What types of weather are there in Iraq?
3. Which areas are hot?
4. What is the weather like in northern Iraq?
5. Which areas get rain?

Third listening

On the map below, circle the geographical areas discussed in the conversation and indicate what the weather is like in each area.

Exercise 5 (Listening)

Listen to the recording and answer the questions.

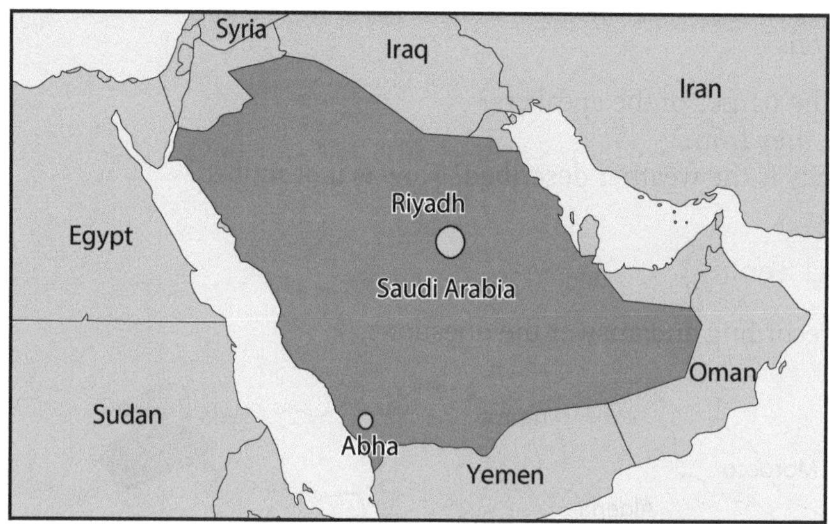

First listening

What is the topic of the passage?

Second listening

1. What is the weather like in Riyadh?
2. What is the weather like in the north and west?
3. Where is Abha?
4. What is the weather like in Abha?

Third listening

What is the weather like in each season for the different areas? Fill out the table below according to what you hear. Cross out the boxes where no information has been provided.

الشتاء	الصيف	الخريف	الربيع	
				مدينة الرياض
				مدينة ابها
				شمال السعودية
				غرب السعودية

Arabic numbers 21–30

Below are the Arabic numbers from 21 to 30. Listen to your teacher or the audio recording and follow along.

٣٠	٢٩	٢٨	٢٧	٢٦	٢٥	٢٤	٢٣	٢٢	٢١

Exercise 6 (Listening and memorizing)

Listen to and memorize the numbers 21–30 above.

With the help of the audio recording, practice reading the Arabic numbers 21–30 out loud.

Now count from 31 to 41 on your own following the same pattern above.

Exercise 7 (Reading)

Read the following numbers.

٣٠	٢٩	٢٨	٢٧	٢٦	٢٥	٢٤	٢٣	٢٢	٢١	.١
٢١	١٠	١٠٠	٢٩	٦٠	٢٠	٦	٩	١٥	١١	.٢
٢٢	٧٨	٨٧	٩٧	٨٦	٧٥	٦٤	٥٣	٤٢	٣١	.٣

The Arabic alphabet

Table 1 (review letters)

ص	ش	س	ر	د	ج	ت	ب	ا
ي	و	ن	م	ل	كـ/ك	ق	ف	ط
							ـة/ة	

Table 2 (new letters) Listen to the way each new letter is pronounced by clicking on the audio icon.

English equivalent	*Other shapes*	*Basic shape*
	Final/Medial/Initial	
th (as in *three*)	ـث/ـثـ/ثـ	ث
	ـح/ـحـ/حـ	ح
	ـخ/ـخـ/خـ	خ
	ـع/ـعـ/عـ/ع	ع

Note on the glottal stop (*Hamza*)

The letter *hamza* represents the sound that you make when you pronounce a vowel at the beginning of English words like *apple* and *orange*. Although not technically part of the 28 letters of the Arabic alphabet, the *hamza* is represented by its own letter, which comes in six shapes depending on adjacent vowels. Two of the most common shapes are أ and ء. Arabs often write أ as ا, which we have done so far to make things easier for you. But, technically, the two symbols should be differentiated, which we will do from now on. The words you have already seen with أ are أنا, أمريكا and أبها. The second *hamza* shape you saw is ء at the end of the word الشتاء "winter".

Arabic diacritical marks

The letters we have learned so far represent consonants and long vowels. There is a set of other symbols, called "diacritics" or "diacritical marks", that help with pronunciation. Because native speakers know the correct pronunciation of words, diacritics are not normally written except in children's books and religious texts such as the Qur'an.

Below are four common diacritical marks. They represent the short vowel sounds and the doubling of letters in Arabic.

Example	*Sound*	*Symbol (as they appear above the letter* ب*)*	*Diacritic Name*
مَدينة	Short ا	بَـ	*fatHa* فَتحة
لُبنان	Short و	بُـ	*Damma* ضَمّة
طالِب	Short ي	بِـ	*kasra* كَسرة
جَوّ	Doubling of letters in pronunciation	بّـ	*shadda* شَدّة

As your Arabic skills progress and you learn to recognize familiar words, you will gradually see fewer and fewer diacritical marks printed in this book.

Exercise 8 (Reading)

With the help of Tables 1 and 2 and diacritics above, read the following words. The words are presented as they are normally written and with the letters separated below.

الصَيف	الرَبيع	الشِتاء	الخَريف
ا ل ص ي ف	ا ل ر ب ي ع	ا ل ش ت ا ء	ا ل خ ر ي ف

شَمس	مَطَر	ثَلج	حار	بارِد	جَو
ش م س	م ط ر	ث ل ج	ح ا رّ	ب ا ر د	ج وّ

عُمان	عَمان	بَغداد	العِراق	السَعودية
ع م ا ن	عَ مّ ا ن	ب غ د ا د	ا ل ع ر ا ق	ا ل س ع و د ي ة

Exercise 9 (Listening and reading)

Circle the word you hear. (In class with the teacher.)

٥. بارد/بريطانيا	٤. شتاء/شمال	٣. خريف/صغير	٢. ربيع/طرابلس	١. صيف/جو
١٠. كبير/بارد	٩. مصر/مطر	٨. غرب/ربيع	٧. شمس/شرق	٦. حار/مطر

Exercise 10 (Listening and reading)

Circle the letter you hear. (In class with the teacher.)

٥. ـع/غ	٤. ت/ث	٣. ب/ت	٢. ج/ح	١. ص/س
١٠. ح/خ	٩. ف/ق	٨. ي/و	٧. ح/ـع	٦. ش/س

Exercise 11

Circle the letters you recognize in each of the following words.

الأحد	السبت	يوم	أسبوع	سنة	شهر
	الجُمعة	الخميس	الأربعاء	الثلاثاء	الإثنين

Exercise 12

Match each letter on the left column with its basic shape on the right column.

ـجـ	ك
ـحـ	ع
ـثـ	غ
ـع	ل
ـغـ	ش
ـفـ	ا
ـكـ	ث
ـلـ	ح
ـل	ف
ـشـ	خ

Exercise 13

Read the following words and write down their meaning in English.

بارِد	حار	تَلج	مَطَر	شَمس	رَبيع	شِتاء	خَريف	صَيف

Grammar: the definite article الـ

To make nouns and adjectives definite, Arabic attaches the article الـ to the beginning of the word:

a city, one city	مدينة
the city	المدينة

student	طالب
the student	الطالب

Just like in English, some countries and cities in Arabic have the definite article as a part of their name, while others do not have it.

Countries and cities without the definite article	Countries and cities with the definite article
بريطانيا	السودان
بيروت	اليمن
أمريكا	The United States
ليبيا	The Netherlands

Pronunciation of the ل of the definite article: the sun and moon letters

Listen to your teacher pronounce the following words and phrases. What do you notice about the pronunciation of the ل in the two tables?

Sun letters

الشتاء والربيع والصيف
صباح النور
السودان

Moon letters

الخريف
صباح الخير
الكويت

The pronunciation (but not spelling) of the ل in the definite article الـ changes depending on the letter that follows it. Arabic letters are divided into two groups according to where in the mouth they are pronounced: sun letters and moon letters.

Sun letters are pronounced with the tongue placed close to the front of the mouth, like the letter ش in شمس. When the definite article الـ is placed in front of a sun letter, the ل assimilates to (i.e. becomes the same as) that letter, which is pronounced twice as long: شمس (shams) → الشمس (ash-shams).

The rest of the letters, those pronounced with the lips only or farther back in the mouth, are called moon letters. When ال is placed in front of a moon letter, the ل keeps its normal pronunciation: قمر (qamar) → القمر (al-qamar).

Listen to your teacher or the audio recording reading the definite words below and repeat. Pay special attention to where your tongue is placed in your mouth as you pronounce each word:

Sun letters شمسية

التركيّة	ت
الثلج	ث
الدولة	د
الربيع	ر
السودان	س
الشرق	ش

Moon letters قمرية

الأمريكي	ا
الباب	ب
الجنوب	ج
الخريف	خ
الحار	ح
العراق	ع

ص	الصيف
ط	الطالبة
ل	الليبي
ن	النور

غ	الغرب
ف	الفرنسيّة
ق	القمر
ك	الكبير
م	المدينة
و	الولاية
ي	اليمن

Exercise 14 (Reading)

Read the following sentences and answer the English questions.

الجوّ في لبنان بارد في الشتاء وحارّ في الصيف.

1. What is the weather like in Lebanon?

البصرة مدينة كبيرة في جنوب العراق. الجوّ في البصرة بارد في الشتاء وحارّ في الصيف والخريف والربيع.

1. Where is Basra located?
2. What is the weather like in Basra in the summer?

Exercise 15 (Writing at home)

On a separate piece of paper, write down the numbers 1–30 from memory and then read them out loud.

Exercise 16 (Writing)

Connect the letters to form words and then pronounce the words.

ا ل ص ي ف
ا ل ر ب ي ع
ش م س
ا ل خ ر ي ف
ح ا ر
ا ل ش ت ا ء
ب ا ر د

Exercise 17 (Writing)

Translate the following into Arabic on a separate piece of paper.

Tripoli (طرابلس) is a big city in north Lebanon. The weather in Tripoli is cold in the winter and hot in the summer.

الدرس الخامس: الجوّ بارد في شهر أبريل؟
(Lesson 5: Is the weather cold in the month of April?)

Exercise 1 (Listening)

Listen to the recording of the words below.

Sunday	الأَحَد
Monday	الإثنين
Tuesday	الثلاثاء
Wednesday	الأربعاء
Thursday	الخَميس
Friday	الجُمعة
Saturday	السَبت

day – days	يوم – أيام
week – weeks	أُسبوع – اسابيع
month – months	شَهر – شُهور
year – years	سَنة – سَنوات

Exercise 2 (Listening)

In your notebook, write down in English the day of the week you hear in each sentence.

Months of the year

In many parts of the Arab world, people often use numbers to refer to the months of the year. So instead of "April – أبريل", people say "month four". For a day in a month, only numbers are often used, so May 20th will be simply عشرين – خمسة (literally "twenty – five"). Note that the day is said before the month, unlike in in English where this date would be expressed as 5/20.

Exercise 3

Watch the following short video clip and answer the questions in English. Then have a similar dialogue with your partner in class.

Comprehension questions

First listening

1. What greetings did the speakers use to start their conversation?
2. How did the speakers end their conversation?

Second listening

According to the video,

1. What day of the week is today?
2. What is today's date?

Now create a similar dialogue with your partner, based on what you just heard.

Exercise 4 (Listening)

Listen to the recording and answer the questions below

seasons فُصول	two seasons فصلين	(one) season فَصل

Comprehension questions

First listening

1. What countries are mentioned in the recording?

Second listening

1. How many seasons does each country have?
2. Which months are considered the "summer" in each country?

Arabic numbers 100 and above

Below are the Arabic numbers from 100 to 1000, counting by hundreds. Listen to your teacher or the audio recording and follow along.

١٠٠٠	٩٠٠	٨٠٠	٧٠٠	٦٠٠	٥٠٠	٤٠٠	٣٠٠	٢٠٠	١٠٠

In this next table are the Arabic numbers from 1000 to 10,000, counting by thousands. Listen to your teacher or the audio recording and follow along.

١٠٠٠٠	٩٠٠٠	٨٠٠٠	٧٠٠٠	٦٠٠٠	٥٠٠٠	٤٠٠٠	٣٠٠٠	٢٠٠٠	١٠٠٠

Reading numbers out loud

Arabic numbers are read out loud the way that English numbers are, meaning that you start with the largest number and make your way to the smallest. The only exception is that the ones place is read out before the tens place, as you learned in Lesson 3. Each number is separated by the word و (and). For example, this is the way the number 1965 would be read in Arabic:

Arabic	١٠٠٠ و ٩٠٠ و٥ و٦٠ ألف وتسعميّة وخمسة وستّين
English translation	One thousand and nine hundred and five and sixty

Exercise 5 (Reading)

Read the following numbers.

١٠٠٠	٩٠٠	٨٠٠	٧٠٠	٦٠٠	٥٠٠	٤٠٠	٣٠٠	٢٠٠	١٠٠	.١
١٠٠٠٠	٩٠٠٠	٨٠٠٠	٧٠٠٠	٦٠٠٠	٥٠٠٠	٤٠٠٠	٣٠٠٠	٢٠٠٠	١٠٠٠	.٢
٢٠٠١	٢٠٢٠	٢٠١٨	١٧٧٦	١٩٨١	١٩٩٥	٢٠٠	٥٠٠٠	٥٠٠	٧٠٠	.٣

Exercise 6 (Reading)

Read the following years and write down their English equivalent in your notebook.

١٨١٨	١٩٩٩	٢٠٠٤	٢٠٠٠	١٧٧٦	١٩٩١	١٩٩٥	.١
٦٣٢	٢٠٠١	١٤٩٢	١٢٨٠	١٨٦٥	٢٠٠١	٢٠١٨	.٢

The Arabic Alphabet

Table 1 (review letters and diacritics)

ش	س	ر	د	خ	ح	ج	ث	ت	ب	ا

ي	و	ن	م	ل	كـ/ك	ق	ف	غـ/ـغـ/ـغ/غ	عـ/ـعـ/ـع/ع	ط	ص

◌ِ (كسرة)	◌ُ (ضمّة)	◌َ (فتحة)	اً	ـة/ة	أ/ء

Table 2 (new letters) Listen to and repeat the pronunciation of the following new letters and diacritics.

English equivalent	*Other shapes*	*Basic shape*
	Final/Medial/Initial	
h	هـ/ـهـ/ـه/ه	هـ

Secondary letters

	إ (found only at the beginning of a word)	إ
This letter, called *alif maqsuura* (shortened *alif*), is pronounced exactly like the letter ا *(a)*	ـى/ى (found only at the end of a word)	ى
pronounced *laa*	ـلا/ـلا/لا	لا (ل + ا)
pronounced *an*	ـاً/اً (found only at the end of a word)	اً

Shaded letters = one-way connectors (connect on the right only)

Now read the following words:

أيّام	يوم	سَنة	شُهور	شَهر
أ يّ ا م	ي و م	س ن ة	شُ ه و ر	ش ه ر

السبت	الجُمعة	الخميس	الأربعاء	الثلاثاء	الإثنين	الأحد
ا ل س ب ت	ا ل جُ م ع ة	ا ل خ م ي س	ا ل أ ر ب ع ا ء	ا ل ث ل ا ث ا ء	ا ل إ ث ن ي ن	ا ل أ ح د
	شُكراً	عفواً	غداً	كُبرى	صُغرى	"ليلى"
	شُ ك ر اً	ع ف و اً	غ د اً	كُ ب ر ى	صُ غ ر ى	ل ي ل ى

Exercise 7 (Listening and reading)

Circle the letter you hear. (In class with the teacher.)

٥. ـغـ/ف	٤. ـعـ/ـغـ	٣. ـهـ/و	٢. لا/ا	١. عـ/غـ
١٠. ـهـ/ح	٩. ـهـ/عـ	٨. ت/ط	٧. خ/ح	٦. ـغـ/ق

Exercise 8 (Listening and reading)

Circle the word you hear.

Part 1 (in class)

١.شهر/شمس	٢.سنة/شتاء	٣.الأربعاء/أربعة	٤.السبت/ سبعة	٥.أربعة/ربيع
٦.شهر/شُهور	٧.اليوم/اليمن	٨.شرق/شهر	٩.عشرة/ شمال	١٠.خريف/خمسة

Part 2 On Companion Web site

Exercise 9

Circle the letters you recognize in each of the following words.

١. ساكن	٢. بيت	٣. شقّة	٤. غرفة	٥. طلبة
٦. جامعة	٧. صفّ	٨. بعيد	٩. واجب	١٠. قريب

Exercise 10 (Writing)

Write down each number below next to its equivalent in the table.

١٠٠٠، ٥، ٢١، ٠، ٣، ٢٠، ٥٠، ٢٠٠٠، ١٠٠٠٠٠٠، ٧٠

عشرين	
سبعين	
خمسين	
ألف	
مليون	
ألفين	
خمسة	
صفر	
واحد وعشرين	
ثلاثة	

Exercise 11

Ask your classmates about their birth dates (عيد ميلاد) and write each one down in Arabic following this format: اليوم/الشهر/السنة (day, month, year, in numbers). Report your dates to the class and figure out which month has the most birthdays!

you (feminine, singular) انتِ	you (masculine, singular) انتَ

- امتى عيد ميلادك؟ (When is your birthday?)
- عيد ميلادي في . . . (My birthday is on . . .)

Exercise 12 (Writing)

Copy the Arabic word under its English equivalent in the table.

السبت، الجمعة، الإثنين، الأحد، الأربعاء، الخميس، الثلاثاء

Sunday	Monday	Tuesday	
Wednesday	**Thursday**	**Friday**	**Saturday**

Exercise 13 (Writing)

Watch your teacher or the writing demo online. Then, practice writing the following words and phrases on a separate piece of paper. Write them as many times as necessary until you can write them from memory.

يوم أيام سنة سنوات شهر شهور

اسم اسمها أهلاً وسهلاً في هولندا

Exercise 14 (Writing)

Connect the letters to form words then say the words out loud and give their English meanings.

ا ل ص ي ف

ا ل ر ب ي ع

ش م س

ا ل خ ر ي ف

ح ا ر
ا ل ش ت ا ء
ب ا ر د

Grammar: negation in Egyptian Arabic

So far, you have learned two types of negation in spoken Egyptian Arabic.

1) For negating adjectives and nouns: مش

Negated statement	Statement	Word type
الجو مش بارد The weather is not cold	الجو بارد The weather is cold	adjective
سارة مش طالبة Sarah is not a student	سارة طالبة Sarah is a student	noun

2) For negating "there is/ there are" statements: ما فيش

Negated statement	Statement
ما فيش ثلج There isn't snow	فيه ثلج There is snow
ما فيش درس There isn't a lesson	فيه درس There is a lesson

Drill: With a partner, describe the picture below using as many statements and negated statements possible for both types of negation.

Helpful words: شمس، مطر، صيف، جوّ، حار، بارد، شتاء، كويّس

أغنية: ازاي الجو في أبريل؟

ازاي الجو في أبريل؟
الجوّ كويّس في لبنان،
مطر كثير في إربيل،
حَرّ شويّة في عمّان،
شمس كثير بوادي النيل.

الدرس السادس: أنا ساكن في شقّة.
(Lesson 6: I live in an apartment.)

Exercise 1 (تمرين رقم ١) (Listening)

Listen to the recording and practice pronouncing the words below.

ساكن (living, resident)

أنا سَاكِن في بيت الطلبة (I am a resident in the dorm, I live in the dorm)

Exercise 2 (تمرين رقم ٢)

Part 1

Watch the following short video clip and answer the questions below (refer to Exercise 1 above as needed).

First listening

1. What are the names of the people speaking?
2. What part of the day is it?
3. What types of housing are mentioned?

Second listening

Fill in the blanks in the following:

"دان" ساكن في .... "سارة" ساكنة في ....

Part 2

Now have a similar dialogue with your partner to learn about where they come from (city/town, state/country) and where they live now (دِلوَقت). When you are done, report what you've learned back to the class.

Helpful words

she هيَ	he هُوَ
this (feminine) دي	this (masculine) ده
this is Xiao = دي شاو	this is Marcus = ده ماركوس

ده "باتريك". هو من مدينة .... في ولاية .... دِلوَقتِ هو ساكن في ....

Exercise 3 (تمرين رقم ٣) (Listening)

Listen to the short passage and answer the questions that follow.

1. What are the names of the people introduced?
2. Where do they live?
3. Which of them lives far and which lives close by?

Review Letters and Diacritics

ص	ش	س	ر	د	خ	ح	ج	ث	ت	ب	ا

ي	و	هـ/ـهـ/ـه/ه	ن	م	ل	كـ/ك	ق	ف	غـ/ـغـ/ـغ/غ	عـ/ـعـ/ـع/ع	ط

ّ (شدّة)	ِ (كسرة)	ُ (ضمّة)	َ (فتحة)	اً	لا	ـة/ة	أ/ء/إ

New letters

English equivalent	*Other shapes*	*Basic shape*
	Final/Medial/Initial	
	ضـ/ـضـ/ـض	ض

One more diacritical mark: *sukuun*

You learned in Lesson Four that there is a set of special symbols, called diacritics, that are generally not written except in special texts. The first set you learned was the short vowels *fatHa* ◌َ, *kasra* ◌ِ, *and Damma* ◌ُ, and the doubling diacritic *shadda* ◌ّ.

The diacritic *sukuun* سكون looks like a small circle and is placed above a letter. It indicates that the letter to which it is attached is neutral, i.e. has no vowel sound.

Example	Sound	Symbol	Name
شمْس، الجُمْعة، السبْت	(above a letter) marks the absence of a vowel	بْ	سكون

Exercise 4 (تمرين رقم ٤)

Read the following words out loud paying special attention to the diacritics.

١. طالِب ٢. غَرْب ٣. مِن ٤. بارِد ٥. بَيت

٦. بَيت طلبة ٧. ساكِن ٨. بَعيد ٩. قَريب ١٠. شُكراً

١١. انتَ ١٢. انتِ ١٣. الجُمْعة ١٤. عَمّان ١٥. عُمان

Exercise 5 (تمرين رقم ٥) (Listening and reading)

Circle the word you hear. (In class with the teacher.)

١. بيت/بُيوت	٢. شهر/شُهور	٣. ثلاثة/الثلاثاء	٤. شقّة/شرق	٥. ثلج/الجمعة
٦. قريب/كبير	٧. بعيد/بارِد	٨. طالِب/طَلَبة	٩. شمس/شمال	١٠. أربعة/الأربعاء

Exercise 6 (تمرين رقم ٦) (Listening and reading)

Circle the letter you hear. (In class with the teacher.)

١. ت/ث	٢. س/ص	٣. ت/ط	٤. ء/ع	٥. ي/و
٦. خ/ح	٧. ح/ع	٨. غ/ر	٩. هـ/ح	١٠. لا/هـ

Exercise 7

Circle the word that does not belong in each row.

١.	بيت	شقّة	لُبنان	أوضة
٢.	ليبيا	السودان	أمريكا	الصيف
٣.	قريب	مِن	بعيد	كبير
٤.	شَمال	شَهر	سَنة	يوم
٥.	عَمّان	عُمان	بيروت	لندن
٦.	مَرحبا	أهلاً وسهلاً	مع السلامة	ساكِن
٧.	الصيف	الخريف	ولاية	الربيع
٨.	سان فرانسيسكو	باريس	المغرب	الخرطوم
٩.	حارّ	بارِد	مُشمِس	الشتاء

Shortcuts: For the sake of speed, most Arabs use shortcuts when writing by hand. Here are the most common shortcuts:

1. The two dots of ت and ي and تاء مربوطة are written as a short line.
2. س and ش are written with a straight line instead of the three "teeth".
3. The three dots of ش and ث are replaced by a "circumflex" sign (ˆ).
4. ـهـ (medial ـهـ) is simplified to ـٮـ when writing by hand. The top half is not written.

This is shown in the following table:

ت	ت
ي	ي
ة	ة
س	س
ش	ش
ث	ث
ـهـ	ـهـ

Exercise 8 (تمرين رقم ٨) (Writing)

Connect the letters to form words, then give their English equivalents. Use the shortcuts you've just learned. Follow the examples.

house	بيت	ب ي ت
big house	بيت كبير	ب ي ت/ك ب ي ر
		ش قّ ة
		غُ ر ف ة/ص غ ي ر ة
		ب ي ت/طَ ل ب ة
		ج ا م ع ة
		صَ فّ/ك ب ي ر
		ش ق ة/ق ر ي ب ة
Hint: This is a full sentence!		ا ل ج ا م ع ة/ ب ع ي د ة

Grammar: nouns, adjectives, and agreement

Unlike English, adjectives in Arabic come after the noun they modify.

Nouns and adjectives must also agree in gender, which is normally indicated by the presence or absence of the final ـة.

Look at the example noun-adjective phrases below, and verify for yourself that they follow the rules stated above:

big house	بيت كبير
big apartment	شقّة كبيرة

Exercise 9 (تمرين رقم ٩) (at home or in class)

Part 1

Below is a list of nouns. Translate them into English, then determine their gender. The easiest way for you to differentiate masculine from feminine gender is to look for ـة (*taa marbuuTa*).

Gender	Translation	Nouns
		طالب
		طالبة
		دولة
		مدينة
		ولاية
		بيت

		شقّة
		أوضة
		جَوّ

Part 2: Writing

In your notebook, write 10 noun-adjective phrases using all the nouns in the table above and the adjectives below and translate your phrases into English.

Adjectives
كبير صغير بارد حارّ مُشمِس بعيد قريب

الدرس السابع: عندي أخ واحد.
(Lesson 7: I have one brother.)

Exercise 1 (تمرين رقم ١)

Listen to the recording and practice pronouncing the words below.

brother – brothers	أخ – إخوة
sister – sisters	أُخت – أَخَوات

Exercise 2 (تمرين رقم ٢)

Watch the following short video clip and complete the table about Sarah and her siblings.

First listening

1. What names do you hear?
2. Two types of questions are asked? What are they?

Second listening

Listen to the dialogue again and fill in the empty cells in the following table.

العُمر	الاسم
٢٢ سنة	
	"كمال"
	"ليلى"

Bonus question: How does Sarah describe herself at the end?

Exercise 3 (تمرين رقم ٣) (Listening)

Comprehension questions

1. How many brothers and sisters does Yousif have?
2. How many brothers and sisters does the other speaker have? How did she describe her family?

Exercise 4 (تمرين رقم ٤) (Listening)

Comprehension questions

1. Who is Yousif?
2. How many houses does Yousif have?
3. Where is Yousif now?

Grammar (القَواعِد)

1. Possession in Arabic (my, your, his, her)

To express possession in Arabic, possessive endings are attached to nouns, as shown in the following table:

(a) name	اسم
my name	اسمي
your name (masculine)	اسمَك
your name (feminine)	اسمِك
his name	اسمُه
her name	اسمها

Exercise 5a (تمرين رقم ٥ أ)

With reference to the table above, fill in the empty cells in the following table.

age	عُمر
my age	عُمري
your age (masculine)	
your age (feminine)	
his age	
her age	

When we add the possessive endings to feminine words ending in the ـة/ة, this letter turns into a ت so that it can connect to the letters that follow it. The ـة (*taa marbuuTa*, which translates literally as "tied-up *taa*") is "untied" and turns into a regular ت so that it can connect to the possessive endings.

(an) apartment	شقّة
my apartment	شَقّتـي
your (masculine) apartment	شقّتـكَ
your (feminine) apartment	شقّتـكِ
his apartment	شقّتـهُ
her apartment	شقّتـها

Exercise 5b (تمرين رقم ٥ ب)

Now fill in the empty cells in the following table.

city	مَدينة
my city	
your (masculine) city	مَدينتَك
your (feminine) city	
his city	
her city	

2. Possession with عند (I have, you have, he has, she has)

To express ownership in Arabic, we add the same possessive endings to the word عند. Compare the phrases below.

my sister I have a sister	أختي عندي أخت
your sister you have (masculine) a sister	أختَك عندَك أخت
your sister you have (feminine) a sister	أختِك عندِك أخت
his sister he has a sister	أختُه عندُه أخت
her sister she has a sister	أختها عندها أخت

Although "to have" is a verb in English, in Arabic the word عند acts like a preposition.

3. كم + the singular

Unlike English, the question word كم (how much or how many) is always followed by a singular noun. For example, كم طالب في الصفّ literally means how many *student* (is) in the classroom?

Now translate the following questions into Arabic, then take turns with your partner to ask them.

1. How many states are in America?
2. How many doors are in the room?
3. How many days are in a week?

The Arabic alphabet

Review letters and diacritics

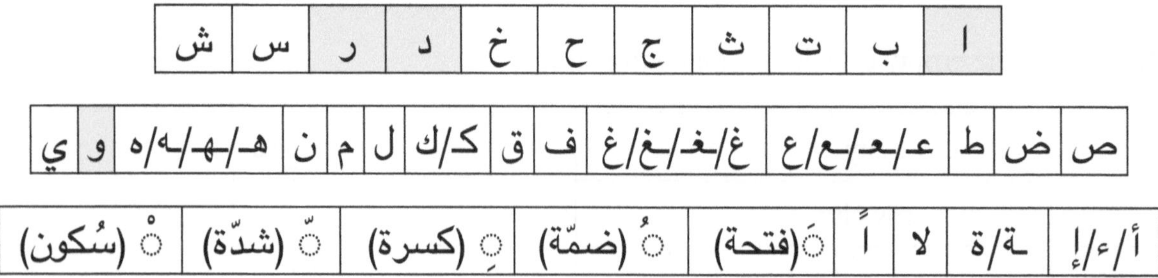

ش	س	ر	د	خ	ح	ج	ث	ت	ب	ا

ي	و	ه/ـه/ـهـ/هـ	ن	م	ل	كـ/ك	ق	ف	غ/ـغ/ـغـ/غـ	ع/ـع/ـعـ/عـ	ط	ض	ص

◌ْ (سُكون)	◌ّ (شدّة)	◌ِ (كسرة)	◌ُ (ضمّة)	◌َ(فتحة)	اً	لا	ـة/ة	أ/ء/إ

New secondary letter

English equivalent	Other shapes	Basic shape
	Final/Medial/Initial	
This is the shape *hamza* (ء) takes next to a ي or the diacritic كسرة	ئـ/ـئـ/ـئ	ئ

Shaded letter = one-way connector (connects on the right only)

Exercise 6 (تمرين رقم ٦) (Reading)

Read the following words and write down their meanings in English.

اسمي	اسمها	اسمه	اسم	أُخت	أَخ	أُمّ	أَب	عائِلة
	عُمر	كَم	عندِك	عندَك	عندها	عنده	عِندي	اسمَك

Exercise 7 (تمرين رقم ٧) (Listening and reading)

Circle the word you hear. (In class with the teacher.)

٥. عُمر/أمّ	٤. عُمر/غرب	٣. اسم/السبت	٢. أخ/أخت	١. أب/أم
		٨. عند/بعيد	٧. سنة/ساكن	٦. عائلة/ربيع

Exercise 8 (تمرين رقم ٨) (Listening and reading)

Circle the letter you hear. (In class with the teacher.)

٥. ج/ح	٤. ص/س	٣. ر/غ	٢. لا/ر	١. ئـ/ع
١٠. س/ش	٩. د/ر	٨. ل/د	٧. ض/د	٦. ث/ب

Exercise 9 (تمرين رقم ٩) (Reading and writing)

Match the words below with their English translation by rewriting them in the space provided below.

أخ، أُمّ، أسبوع، أُخت، جامِعة، عائِلة، أب، شقّة، صفّ، دَرس، طالب، شتاء، صيف، شهر، سنة، يوم

mother	summer	apartment	family

sister	father	lesson	classroom

brother	month	university	day

winter	year	student	week

Exercise 10 (تمرين رقم ١٠) (Reading)

Read the passage below and answer the questions that follow.

اسمي سعيد. أنا من مدينة بيروت عاصمة لبنان. عندي بيت في بيروت وبيت في عمان. عائلتي كبيرة؛ عندي أب وأم وأخ واحد وثلاث أخوات، يعني كلنا سبعة. أبي اسمه يوسف وأمي اسمها جميلة.

Comprehension questions

1. Where is Sa'eed from?
2. How many houses does he have? Where?
3. How many people are in his family?
4. What is Sa'eed's mother's name?

Exercise 11 (تمرين رقم ١١) (Reading and writing)

Part 1: Read the table below. What do you think it is?

عائلة مايا

الأب والأُم	هنري ٥٦		إليزابث ٥٨
الأولاد	ميشيل ٢٧	مايا ٢٥	ماثيو ١٧

Part 2

Use the information from Part 1 and the word bank below to fill in the blanks.

عُمرها	عُمره	أُخت	أُم	واحد	سنة	عائلة

هذه .... مايا. اسم أبو مايا هنري و .... ٥٤ سنة،
واسم .... مايا إليزابث، و .... ٥٣ سنة. عند
مايا .... وأخت. اسم أخو مايا ماثيو، وعمره ١٧ .... ،
واسم .... مايا ميشيل وعمرها ٢٧ سنة.

Exercise 12 (تمرين رقم ١٢) (Writing)

Complete each word using one of the following letters: خ، غ، م، ة، ئ. Remember to use the correct shape for the letter position in the word. When you are done, translate the words into English. One letter is used twice.

عا . . . لة

أ . . . ت

إس . . .

عُ . . . ر

شقّ . . .

. . . رفة

Exercise 13 (تمرين رقم ١٣) (Writing)

Translate the following into Arabic:

1. I have one brother.
2. I have one sister.
3. My name is. . . . . .
4. My brother's name is . . . . .
5. My mother's name is . . . . . and my father's name is . . . . .

Exercise 14 (تمرين رقم ١٤) (Writing)

Working with a partner, first write in Arabic and then share the following information about yourself:

1. Your age (... عُمري)
2. Your birthday (... عيد ميلادي)
3. Number of siblings (عندي أخ واحد/أخوين/٣ إخوان وأخت واحدة/أختين/٣ أخوات)
4. Your telephone number (... رقم تلفوني)
5. Number of days in the current month (في الشهر ده ... يوم)
6. Number of days in a year (... عدد أيّام السنة)
7. Population in your city (... عَدد سُكّان مدينتي)
8. Number of countries you have visited (أنا زُرت . . . دولة)
9. Number of your friends on social media (عندي . . . صاحب على "فيسبوك")
10. Number of years you have studied in university (درست في الجامعة . . . سنوات)

الدرس الثامن: أختي مهندسة وعندها ثلاث أولاد
(Lesson 8: My sister is an engineer and has three children)

Exercise 1 (تمرين رقم ١) (Listening)

Listen to the recording and practice pronouncing the words below.

Exercise 2 (تمرين رقم ٢) (Listening)

Listen to the passage and answer the questions below. Some new words are listed to help you out. Note that the word جمع, abbreviated as ج. means plural.

boy, son, child	وَلَد (ج. أولاد)
girl, daughter	بِنت (ج. بَنات)
husband	جوز

First listening

1. Which words for family members are used?
2. Which professions are mentioned?
3. Who has these professions?

Second listening

Where does the family live?

Third listening

How many children are in the family? What are their ages?

Table 1 (review letters and diacritics)

ش	س	ر	د	خ	ح	ج	ث	ت	ب	ا

ي	و	هـ/ـهـ/ـه/ه	ن	م	ل	كـ/ك	ق	ف	غـ/ـغـ/ـغ/غ	عـ/ـعـ/ـع/ع	ط	ض	ص

سكون ـْ	شَدّة ـّ	كَسرة ـِ	ضَمّة ـُ	فَتحة ـَ	اً	لا	ـة/ة	أ/ء/إ/ى

Table 2 (new letters)

English equivalent	*Other shapes* *Final/Medial/Initial*	*Basic shape*
th (as in *weather*)	ذ/ـذ/ـذ	ذ
	ظـ/ـظـ/ـظ	ظ

Shaded letter = one-way connector (connects on the right only)

Exercise 3 (تمرين رقم ٣)

Read the following words and write down their English equivalents.

	طَبيب
	مُهَندِسة
	كُمبيوتر
	أُستاذ
	سِكرتير
	مَكتَب
	مَدرسة
	بَنك
	جامِعة
	مُستشفى

Exercise 4 (تمرين رقم ٤) (Listening and reading)

Circle the word you hear. (In class with the teacher.)

٥. سكرتير/أستاذ	٤. بنك/كندا	٣. مكتب/مطعم	٢. مهندس/شهور	١. طبيب/طالب
١٠. مستشفى/شتاء	٩. كبير/مكتب	٨. مدرسة/مدينة	٧. طبيبة/طالبة	٦. كمبيوتر/بيوت

Exercise 5 (تمرين رقم ٥) (Listening and reading)

Circle the letter you hear. (In class with the teacher.)

٥. ل/ك	٤. ك/ق	٣. ذ/د	٢. هـ/ظ	١. م/هـ
١٠. ح/ع	٩. ك/خ	٨. ك/ح	٧. ب/ن	٦. ذ/ث

Exercise 6 (تمرين رقم ٦) (Listening and reading)

Listen to the short dialogue and answer the questions that follow.

Helpful words

One sister, a sister	أُخت واحدة
Two sisters	أُختين

Circle the correct answer(s):

1. The occupation of Yousif's father is

مُهندس　　طبيب　　دكتور

2. Yousif's father works in

مدرسة　　جامعة　　مستشفى

3. How many siblings does Yousif have?

أُخت واحدة　　أُختَين　　أخ واحد

4. Where does/do his sibling(s) work?

بنك　　مكتب　　مُستشفى

Grammar قَواعِد: singular, dual, plural

You have seen that Arabic nouns can be singular, dual, or plural. As you look at the examples below, what relationship do you see between the singular and dual forms?

Plural (جمع)	Dual	Singular
seasons فُصول	two seasons فصلَين	season فَصل
sisters أَخَوات	two sisters أختَين	sister أُخت
offices مَكاتِب	two offices مكتبَين	office مَكتَب
universities جامعات	two universities جامعتَين	university جامعة

Plural forms follow several different patterns. You will learn the most common plural patterns later on in this book. For now, try to learn the plural form of a noun along with its singular counterpart.

Remember from the previous lesson that when possessive endings are added to feminine words, the final ة/ـة turns into a ت. This allows the letters to connect as normal. The same change occurs for adding any suffix (or ending) to a noun.

Exercise 7 (تمرين رقم ٧)

Fill in the empty cells with the singular, dual, or plural form and translation of each word in the following table:

Plural	Dual	Translation	Singular
طُلّاب		student	
			يَوم
شُهور			

سَنَوات			
دُوَل	دَولَتَين	country	
مُدُن	مَدينتَين		

Exercise 8a (تمرين رقم ٨ أ) (Reading)

مريم طالبة في الجامعة الأمريكيّة في القاهرة. عائلة مريم كبيرة: أب وأُمّ وأَخَين وأُختين. مريم ساكنة مع عائلتها في بيت كبير. أبو مريم مُهندس وأُمّها أُستاذة في مدرسة بنات. أخو مريم الكبير يعمل في بنك وأخوها الصغير طالب في المدرسة. أُخت مريم الكبيرة سكرتيرة في مكتب وأُختها الصغيرة تعمل في مطعم.

Mariam's brother أخو مريم	Mariam's dad أبو مريم
he works يَعمَل = يشتغل	two brothers أَخَين
restaurant مَطعَم	she works تَعمَل = تشتغل

أسئلة

1. What does Mariam do? Where?
2. How many people are in Mariam's family?
3. What do Mariam's brothers do and where?
4. What do Mariam's sisters do and where?
5. What do Mariam's parents do?

Exercise 8b (تمرين رقم ٨ ب) (Reading)

Now draw a line connecting each person's name with their occupation based on the above reading.

مُهندس	مريم
يعمل في بنك	أبو مريم
طالبة	أُم مريم
سكرتيرة	أخو مريم الكبير
أستاذة	أخو مريم الصغير
تعمل في مطعم	أُخت مريم الكبيرة
طالب	أُخت مريم الصغيرة

Exercise 9 (تمرين رقم ٩) (Writing)

Form complete sentences by rearranging the following words and then read them out loud.

١. القاهرة/مريم/الجامعة/في/الأمريكيّة في/طالبة
٢. عائلة/كبيرة/مريم
٣. أبو مريم في/بنات/مُهندس/مدرسة/وأُمّها/أستاذة
٤. أخو/الكبير/بنك/في/مريم/يعمل
٥. مريم/في/طالب/المدرسة/الصغير/أخو

Exercise 10 (تمرين رقم ١٠) (Dictation – writing at home)

Listen to the following eight sentences and write down the occupation and/or workplace you hear in each sentence. The first sentence is given as an example.

Occupation المهنة	Place of work مكان العمل	
أستاذ	جامعة	١.
		٢.
		٣.
		٤.
		٥.
		٦.
		٧.
		٨.

الدرس التاسع: عندي درس عربي الساعة عشرة!
(Lesson 9: I have an Arabic lesson at 10 o'clock!)

Exercise 1 (تمرين رقم ١)

Listen to the recording and practice pronouncing the words below.

Chemistry	كيمياء
Physics	فيزياء
Mathematics	رياضيات
Economics	اقتصاد
Biology	احياء
Arabic	عَربي
English Literature	أدَب إنجليزي
History	تاريخ
Engineering	هندسة

Exercise 2 (تمرين رقم ٢)

Watch the short video clip and answer the questions that follow.

1. What time is it according to the dialogue?
2. Ask your partner what time it is now? (Greet him/her, ask about the time, and then thank him/her.)

Exercise 3 (تمرين رقم ٣) (Listening)

Listen and answer the questions below.

1. What subject/class is Nadia asking about?
2. Who did Nadia ask?
3. Where is the class held?

Exercise 4 (تمرين رقم ٤) (Listening)

Listen and answer the comprehension questions below.

First listening

1. What names are mentioned?
2. What subjects are mentioned?

Second listening

1. How many classes does Waleed have today? What are they?
2. What time is the English class?
3. When is Waleed's economics class?
4. How many classes does Nadia have today? What are they?
5. What time is her math class?

The Arabic alphabet

Table 1 (review letters and diacritics)

<table>
<tr><td>ظ</td><td>ط،</td><td>ص،</td><td>ض،</td><td>ش</td><td>س</td><td>ر</td><td>ذ</td><td>د</td><td>خ</td><td>ح</td><td>ج</td><td>ث</td><td>ت</td><td>ب</td><td>ا</td></tr>
<tr><td>ي</td><td>و</td><td>هـ/ـهـ/ـه/ه</td><td>ن</td><td>م</td><td>ل</td><td>كـ/ك</td><td>ق</td><td>ف</td><td>غـ/ـغـ/ـغ/غ</td><td>عـ/ـعـ/ـع/ع</td></tr>
</table>

Secondary letters, diacritics, and symbols

<table>
<tr><td>سكون ـْ</td><td>شدّة ـّ</td><td>كسرة ـِ</td><td>ضمّة ـُ</td><td>فتحة ـَ</td><td>اً</td><td>لا</td><td>ـة/ة</td><td>أ/ء/إ/ئ</td></tr>
</table>

Table 2 (new letters and diacritics)

English Equivalent	*Other Shapes*	*Basic Shape*
	Final/*Medial*/*Initial*	
z	ز/ـز/ـز	ز

Shaded letter = one-way connector (connects on the right only)

Exercise 5: **Reading:** With the help of Tables 1 and 2 above, read the words below and write down their meanings in English.

إلّا خمسة	نُصّ وخمسة	تُلت	رُبع	نُصّ
دقيقة	ساعة	أدَب إنجليزي	عَربي	اقتصاد
رياضيّات	فيزياء	كيمياء	تاريخ	تاريخ
			هندَسة	أحياء (بيولوجيا)

Exercise 6 (تمرين رقم ٦) (Listening and reading)

Circle the word you hear. (In class with the teacher.)

٥. فرنسي/فرنسا	٤. فيزياء/صَفّ	٣. رياضيّات/طيّارة	٢. الأحد/واحد	١. كيمياء/كمبيوتر
١٠. مطعم/مكتب	٩. ساعة/السبت	٨. تُلت/تلاتة	٧. دقيقة/قريب	٦. مهندسة/مهندس

Exercise 7 (تمرين رقم ٧) (Listening and reading)

Circle the letter you hear. (In class with the teacher.)

٥. ض/ط	٤. ض/د	٣. ض/ص	٢. ز/س	١. ز/ر
١٠. ب/ي	٩. ز/ن	٨. ـئـ/ن	٧. هـ/ح	٦. ذ/د

Exercise 8 (تمرين رقم ٨) (Reading and writing)

Match the time phrases with the times on the clock by writing the phrase under the correct time.

تلاتة إلّا رُبع – تلاتة إلّا عشرة – تلاتة ورُبع – سبعة إلّا عشرة –
سبعة وعشرة – ستّة وعشرة

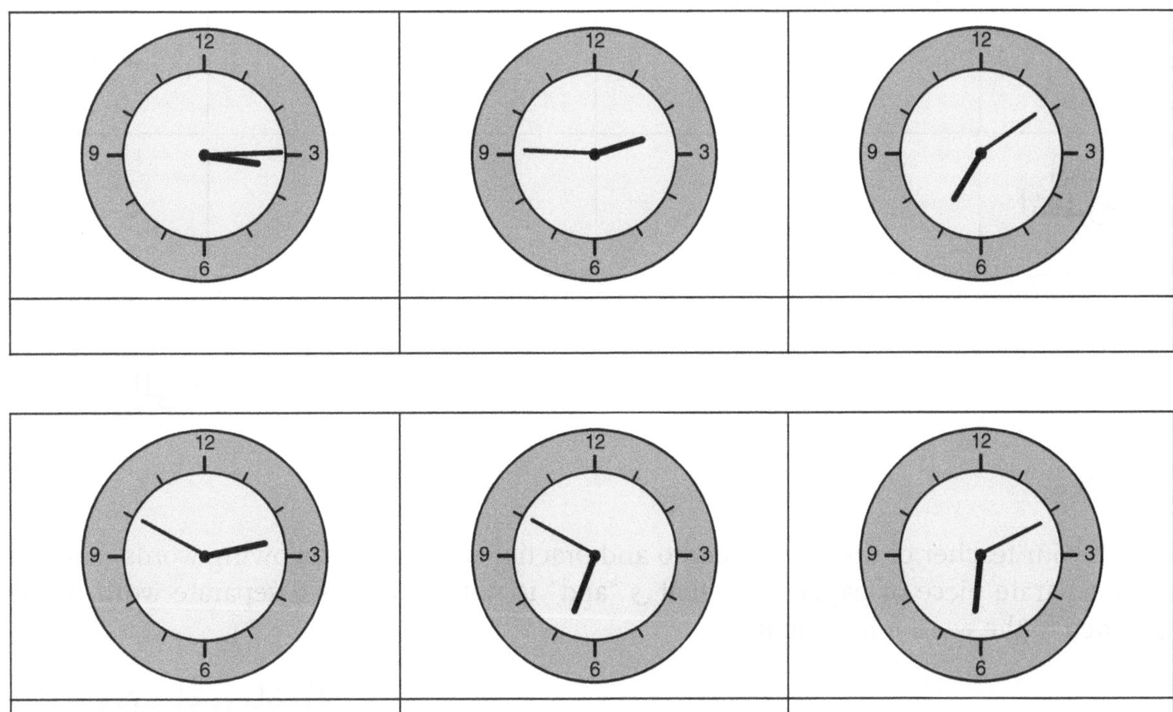

Exercise 9 (تمرين رقم ٩) (Reading and writing)

Help Sarah finish filling out her class schedule (الجدول الدراسي) based on the information below (follow the examples on the table). She has the following classes:

1. Economics 101 three days a week on Sunday, Tuesday, and Thursday 9–11 am.
2. Physics 220 on Monday and Wednesday from 11 am to 12 pm.
3. Arabic Language 420 on Sunday, Tuesday, and Thursday from 1–2 pm.
4. Math 140 on Monday and Wednesday from 1–2 pm.
5. English Literature 240 on Sunday, Tuesday, and Thursday 3–4 pm.
6. Physics test (امتحان فيزياء) on Thursday 2–3 pm.

جدول سارة الدراسي

	الأحد	الإثنين	الثلاثاء	الأربعاء	الخميس
٨–٩					
٩–١٠			اقتصاد ١٠١		
١٠–١١					
١١–١٢					
١–٢		رياضيّات ١٤٠			

					٢–٣
أدب إنجليزي ٢٤٠					٣–٤

كلمات جديدة (new words)

مِن . . . إلى (لِ) from . . . to

Exercise 10 (تمرين رقم ١٠) (Writing)

Watch your teacher or the writing demo and practice writing the following words/phrases on a separate piece of paper. Note that و "and" is not written as a separate word but is attached to the word following it.

فيزياء وكيمياء ورياضيّات.
عربي وإنجليزي وفرنسي وإسباني.

أيّام الأسبوع هي السبت والأحد والإثنين والثلاثاء والأربعاء والخميس والجمعة.

Grammar (قَواعِد)

Number–noun (dis-)agreement

You have learned many nouns and their plurals, as well as the numbers. But what if you want to count nouns, i.e. say "three days", "ten cities", or "a university"?

The singular

To express "a book" or "one book" in Arabic, you can simply say كتاب or كتاب واحد. For the singular, the number "one" never comes before the noun.

The dual

As you have learned, the dual is formed by attaching the suffix ين to the noun. This gives the meaning of two, as in كتابين (two books) or طالبتين (two female students).

It is redundant to say the number اتنين after using the dual, but it is sometimes used for emphasis, as in "not one but two": مش كتاب واحد، كتابين اتنين.

The plural (الجمع)

Arabic has special agreement rules with plural nouns. Here are the rules:

a. With the numbers 3–10 the *plural* form of the noun is used:

٣ بُيوت، ٤ طُلّاب، ٦ طالِبات، ١٠ ساعات.

b. With the numbers 11 and above the *singular* form is used:

١٢ ساعة، ٦٠ دقيقة، ٤٠ طالب، ٢٠٠ طالبة، ١٢٠٠ بيت

Counted nouns summary

Number	1	2	3–10	11 and up
Noun form used	Singular	Dual	Plural	Singular
Example	كتاب واحد or كتاب	كتابين	٧ كُتُب	٩٩ كتاب

Exercise 10 (تمرين رقم ١٠) (Writing at home)

Write a paragraph of 40–50 words that describes your class schedule for the current term/semester. For example,

عندي درس رياضيات يوم الإثنين والأربعاء والجُمعة، ودرس .... يوم ....
....

الدرس العاشر: الدول العربيّة وعواصمها
Lesson 10: The Arab countries and their capitals

Exercise 1 (تمرين رقم ١) (Reading and writing)

Match the numbers (written out in words) with the digits they correspond to by copying the words in the spaces provided. The first one is given as an example.

ثلاثة وعشرين
خمسة وخمسين
واحد وعشرين
ثمانية
سبعة وستّين
ألف وتسعمئة وسبعة وستّين
ستّة وسبعين
واحد
ثمانية وثمانين
إثنين

واحد	١
	٢
	٨
	٢١
	٢٣
	٥٥
	٦٧
	٧٦
	٨٨
	١٩٦٧

Exercise 2 (تمرين رقم ٢)

Working in pairs, orally answer the following questions:

١. كم أسبوع في السنة؟
٢. كم شهر في السنة؟
٣. كم يوم في الأسبوع؟
٤. كم يوم في السنة؟
٥. كم يوم في الشهر؟
٦. كم أسبوع في الشهر؟
٧. اليوم ايه؟
٨. بُكره ايه؟ بعد بكره؟
٩. امبارح كان ايه؟
١٠. كم ساعة في اليوم؟
١١. كم دقيقة في الساعة؟
١٢. كم دقيقة في نُصّ ساعة؟ رُبع ساعة؟ تُلت ساعة؟
١٣. الساعة كم دلوقتِ؟

Exercise 3 (تمرين رقم ٣) (Reading and writing)

Write down each of the following words next to its opposite in column أ.

بعيد   حار   جنوب   شتاء   صغير   غرب   لأ

ب	أ
	كبير
	شمال
	شرق
	ايوه
	صيف
	بارد
	قريب

v

Grammar (قَواعِد): the *iDaafa Construct* – الإضافة

When two or more nouns are placed next to each other in Arabic, they show another type of possession or special relationship with each other. Look at the following examples:

The city of Cairo	مدينة القاهرة
The math lesson (literally: the lesson of math)	درس الرياضيات
Maya's family (literally: the family of Maya)	عائلة مايا
The dorm (literally: the house of the students)	بيت الطلبة

This relationship is called the *iDaafa Construct* إضافة. Two things to remember about إضافة are:

1. If the phrase is definite, definiteness is shown on the second word, either with ال or if the word is a proper noun like "مايا". The first word in an إضافة phrase can never have ال.
2. If the first word of إضافة ends in التاء المربوطة, the تاء مربوطة is pronounced like a regular ت, as in مدينة بيروت "the city of Beirut".

Exercise 4 (تمرين رقم ٤) (Reading and writing)

Arab countries and their capitals (الدول العربيّة وعواصمها)

Study the following table which lists the Arab countries and their capitals and complete the sentences that follow and read them aloud. Pay particular attention to the pronunciation of the تاء مربوطة in construct (إضافة) phrases as in مدينة القاهرة (*madiinat al-qaahira*, etc.):

The Arab countries الدول العربية			
العاصمة	الدولة	العاصمة	الدَولة
الخَرطوم	السودان	القاهِرة	مصر
الرَباط	المَغرِب	الجزائر	الجَزائِر
الرِياض	السعوديّة	بغداد	العِراق
صَنعاء	اليَمَن	دمشق	سوريا
عَمّان	الأردن	تونس	تونِس
القُدس	فلسطين	طرابلس	ليبيا
مَسقَط	عُمان	بيروت	لُبنان
الكويت	الكُويت	أبو ظبي	الإمارات
مُقديشو	الصومال	الدَوحة	قَطَر
جيبوتي	جيبوتي	نواكشط	موريتانيا
المنامة	البحرين	موروني	جزر القَمَر

Complete the following sentences and read them out loud. The first sentence is given as an example.

١. مدينة الجزائر عاصمة الجزائر.

٢. مدينة .... عاصمة مصر.

٣. مدينة .... عاصمة العراق.

٤. .... دمشق ....

٥. .... تونس ....

٦. .... ليبيا.

٧. .... بيروت ....

٨. .... السودان.

٩. .... الرباط ....

١٠. .... السعوديّة.

١١. .... صنعاء ....

١٢. .... عمّان ....

١٣. .... القدس ....

١٤. .... مسقَط ....

١٥. .... الكويت.

١٦. .... البحرين.

Exercise 5 (Reading and writing)

Write the names of the following Arab countries on the map.

العراق، سوريا، السعوديّة، اليمن، السودان، مصر، جيبوتي، ليبيا، تونس، الجزائر، المغرب، الصومال، موريتانيا

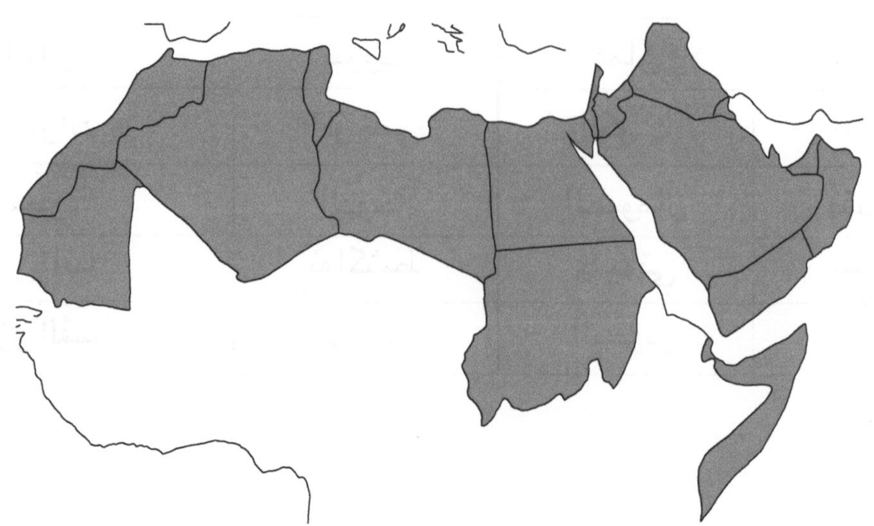

The Arabic alphabet: review

Listen to the audio recording and memorize the names of the letters (not the diacritics and other symbols) and their order.

Shape(s)	Letter name
ا	ألف
بـ/ب	باء
تـ/ت	تاء
ثـ/ث	ثاء
جـ/ج	جيم
حـ/ح	حاء
خـ/خ	خاء
د	دال
ذ	ذال
ر	راء
ز	زاي
سـ/س	سين
شـ/ش	شين
صـ/ص	صاد
ضـ/ض	ضاد
ط	طاء
ظ	ظاء
عـ/ـعـ/ع/ـع	عين
غـ/ـغـ/غ/ـغ	غين
فـ/ف	فاء
قـ/ق	قاف
كـ/ك	كاف
لـ/ل	لام
مـ/م	ميم
نـ/ن	نون

هـ/ـهـ/ـه/ه	هاء
و	واو
يـ/ي	ياء

Exercise 6 (تمرين رقم ٦)

As you have noticed, many letters have similar shapes and are only distinguishable by the number and placement of dots. Review the alphabet table above with a partner, and group the letters into "families" based on their shapes. When you are done, share and compare your "families" with the class.

Secondary letters, diacritics, and symbols

Examples	Shape(s)	
الشتاء، أنا، إنجليزي، عائلة	ء، أ، إ، ئـ	همزة
طالبة، سكرتيرة، مدينة، عربيّة	found only at the end of a word ة، ـة	(تاء مربوطة)
الأحد، الإثنين، الثلاثاء، إلّا	When ل is followed by ألف (or همزة on الف) they are combined into لا or لأ	(لام ألف)
مُستشفى، على، إلى، "لَيلى"	pronounced like ا, found only at the end of a word	(ألف مقصورة) ى
اليَمَن	◌َ	فتحة
طالِب	◌ِ	كسرة
عُمان	◌ُ	ضمّة
عَمّان	◌ّ	شدّة
بِنْت	◌ْ marks the absence of a vowel	سُكون
شُكراً، عفواً	pronounced *an*, found only at the end of a word	اً

Note on writing non-Arabic names

When Arabs write foreign words with sounds that have no correspondences in their language, they generally use the Arabic letter that represents the Arabic sound closest to the foreign one. The following table shows some of the English sounds that have no Arabic equivalents and what Arabic speakers generally substitute for them.

What Arabic speakers generally perceive as short vowels are not normally written:

Bill	بل
Rebecca	ربكا

They represent what they perceive as an *o* (as in *cold*) sound with و:

Theodore	ثيودور
Morgan	مورغان
Paul	بول/پول
Robert	روبرت

They represent what they perceive as *ay*-sounds (as in *way*) with ي:

Casey	كيسي
Rachel	ريتشل

Now write down your full name! ______________________________

Exercise 7 (تمرين رقم ٧) (Reading and writing)

The following list includes the names of Arab countries and cities with the letters scrambled. Rearrange the letters and connect them to match the correct spelling of these names. The countries and cities listed are:

بغداد، مصر، بيروت، تونس، لبنان، اليمن، عُمان، الخرطوم، جدّة، دمشق.

	ا خ ر ط ل م و
	س ن ت و
	م ا ي ن ل
	ا ب د غ د
	ص ر م
	ة دّ ج
	ت ر ب و ي
	ش ق د م
	مّ ن ا ع
	ن ب ل ن ا

Unit One Vocabulary كلمات الوحدة الأولى

father أَب
Abu Dhabi أَبو ظبي
biology أحياء
brother أَخ
sister أُخت
English literature أدَب إنجليزي
how إزّاي
How are you (feminine) إزّايِك
How are you (masculine) إزّايَّك
teacher, professor أستاذ
name اسم
economics اقتصاد
except, to إلّا
Monday الإتنين
Sunday الأحد
Wednesday الأربعاء
Jordan الأُردن
الإمارات العَرَبيّة المُتَّحدة
the United Arab Emirates
Tuesday الثلاثاء
Algeria الجَزائِر
Friday الجُمعة
Khartoum (the capital of Sudan) الخَرطوم
fall, autumn الخَريف
Thursday الخميس
Doha (the capital of Qatar) الدَوحة
Rabat (the capital of Morocco) الرَباط
spring الربيع
Riyadh (the capital of Saudi Arabia) الرِياض
Saturday السبت
Saudi Arabia السعودية
Sudan السودان
winter الشتاء
summer الصيف
Iraq العِراق
Cairo القاهرة
Jerusalem القُدس
Kuwait الكُويت
God (Allah) الله
Morocco المَغرِب
today النهاردَه
Yemen اليمن
yesterday امبارح
America أمريكا
mother أم
I أنا
you, feminine انتِ
you, masculine انتَ
or أو
what إيه
yes أيوه
cold بارِد

Britain بريطانيا
potatoes بطاطِس
far بَعيد
Baghdad بَغداد
tomorrow بُكره
bank بَنك
house بيت
dormitory, student hostel بيت طلبة
Beirut بيروت
history تاريخ
Tunis, Tunisia تونِس
one-third ثُلث
snow ثَلج
university جامعة
south جَنوب
weather جَوّ
hot حارّ
lesson دَرس
minute دَقيقة
doctor, physician دُكتور
Damascus دِمشق
this (masculine) دَه
country دَولة
this, feminine دي
quarter, one-fourth رُبع
math رِياضيّات
hour, clock, watch ساعة

living ساكِن
secretary سِكرتير
year سنة (ج. سنين، سَنَوات)
Syria سوريا
east شرق
apartment شقّة
thank you شُكراً
north شَمال
sun شَمس
month شهر (ج. شُهور)
good morning (greeting) صباح الخير
good morning (answer) صباح النور
low (temperature) صُغرى
small صَغير
San'aa (the capital of Yemen) صَنعاء
student طالِب
physician طبيب
Tripoli طرابلس
family عائلة/عيلة
capital عاصِمة
(Arab, Arabic) عَرَبي
you're welcome عَفواً
Oman عُمان
Amman عَمّان
age عُمر
you have, feminine عندِك
you have, masculine عندَك

he has عندُه

she has عندها

I have عندي

west غَرب

room غُرفة

France فَرنسا

Palestine فِلِسطين

Florida فلوريدا

in في

physics فيزياء

where فين

there is, there are فيه

close, near قريب

Qatar قَطَر

big كبير

how much, how many كَم

Canada كَندا

Chemistry كيمياء

no لأ

Lebanon لُبنان

Libya ليبيا

I don't know ماعرفش

there isn't, there aren't ما فيش

school مَدرَسة

city مدينة

hello, hi مَرحبا

hospital مُستشفى

Muscat (the capital of Oman) مَسقَط

not مِش

Egypt مَصر

rain مَطَر

restaurant مَطعَم

office مكتَب

from مِن

computer engineer مُهندس كُمبيوتر

engineer مُهندس

half نُصّ

engineering هَندَسة

he هُوّ

she هِيّ

or وَلّا

state وِلاية

day يوم (ج. أيّام)

Exercise 8 (تمرين رقم ٨) (في البيت)

Look at the vocabulary list above and write down as many words as possible under each of the following categories.

وَظيفة (job)	الجَوّ	العائلة
الوَقت (time)	مدينة/عاصمة	الجهات (directions)
مادّة (subject)	مَكان (place)	ضمير (pronoun)

Exercise 9 (في الصف) (تمرين رقم ٩)

Engage in mini-dialogues with your partner in class on the following topics:

1. Basic greetings and farewells (مرحبا، أهلاً وسهلاً، إزايك، مع السلامة، الخ)
2. Self-introductions (أنا . . .، أنا طالب، أنا من)
3. Describe your city (انت من أي مدينة؟ مدينة . . .كبيرة/صغيرة، كيف الجوّ؟ الخ)
4. Your family (كم أخ وأخت عندك، أختي اسمها . . . . .، الخ)
5. Place of residence (أنا ساكن في بيت/شقّة، بيتي بعيد/قريب، الخ)

Exercise 10 (تمرين رقم ١٠) (in class then at home)

Part 1: Speaking (in pairs)

Ask your partner his/her name, where he/she is from, is it a big/small city/state, where he/she lives now, how many brothers and sisters he/she has, what are their names, what his/her parents do, what classes he/she is currently taking. Make notes as you hear the answers. Then introduce your partner to the rest of the class.

ده . . . ، هو/هي طالب/طالبة في جامعة . . . ، هو/هي من مدينة . . . ، هو/هي ساكن/ساكنة في . . ., في الفصل (السمستر) ده عنده/عندها . . . ، الخ.

Part 2: Writing (at home)

Write a paragraph of about 50 words about yourself, where you live, your family, where you are from, the weather in your city, classes you are currently taking, etc.

Exercise 11 (تمرين رقم ١١) (Reading handwritten Arabic)

Read the following handwritten words.

الشمس والقمر، شمال العراق، مكتب
الجامعة، سوريا واليمن، الخميس والجمعة

اختبر معلوماتك (Jeopardy)

(In Teacher's Book)

Sociolinguistic Corner

In the introduction to this textbook, it was pointed out that different varieties of Arabic are used side by side in daily life. For formal situations and written language, Modern Standard Arabic (فصحى) is generally used. For informal situations and spoken language, a colloquial dialect is used.

The dialect used in this book is Egyptian Colloquial Arabic (مصري). Thanks to Cairo's position as a cultural and artistic center within the Arab world, مصري is one of the most widely understood dialects.

One difference you may have noticed so far is that certain letters are often pronounced differently depending on the register used. Below is a table with some of the most common changes:

Examples	المَصري	الفُصحى
ثلاثة، ثالث، تلج	ت، س	ث
جامعة	Pronounced like English g	ج
أستاذ	د، ز	ذ
أبو ظبي، وظيفة	ض، ز	ظ
دلوقتي	همزة (أ / ؤ / ئ / ء)	ق

Note that there are some exceptions to these general changes. For example, the word for Cairo القاهرة retains its ق sound like in فصحى.

As you continue your Arabic studies, you will gain a sense of what pronunciation changes generally occur between فصحى and مصري. For now, simply try to note where the differences are, and train your ear to "hear" them as the same letter.

الوحدة الثانية
أهلاً وسهلاً في القاهِرة!

الدرس الأوّل

تمرين رقم ١

Listen to the recording of the following words and repeat them out loud.

date تاريخ

grandfather جَدّ

nationality, citizenship جِنسيّة

international دَولي

trip رِحلة

number رَقَم

visit زِيارة

سِنّ = عُمر

company شَرِكة

month شَهر (ج. شُهور)

to fly, take off طار/طارت

address عُنوان

coming (from) قادِم (مِن)

station, terminal مَحَطّة

period, duration مُدّة

Egyptian (f.) مصرية

place مَكان

profession مِهنة

employee مُوظّف

time, appointed time مَوعِد

والِد = أب

والِدة = أم

birth وِلادة

تمرين رقم ٢

Circle the word that does not belong.

١. مَطار	قاعة استقبال	مَطَر	مَحَطّة
٢. والِد	أُمّ	جَدّ	وصول
٣. مكان	مَحَطّة	قاعة استقبال	مِهنة
٤. شَرِكة	بَنك	مُستشفى	مُدّة
٥. شهر	أسبوع	سَنة	سِنّ

تمرين رقم ٣

Complete each sentence by choosing the correct word and then translate the sentence into English.

١.......................... (جنسيّة/رقم/ولادة) أبي أُردنيّة وجنسيّة أُمي مصريّة.

٢.......................... (مكان/سافر/مُدّة) إلى مصر قبل أسبوع.

٣. الطائرة .... (سافرت/ساكنة/طارت) من المطار الساعة ٨:٣٠ في الصباح.

٤. .... (أهلاً وسهلاً/عنوان/شُكراً) فيك في مصر!

٥. .... (فُندُق/عنوان/زيارة) البيت: ١٥٤ شارع الجامعة.

٦. الطائرة .... (وُصول/موعِد/قادمة) من مدينة لندن.

٧. .... (مكان/جواز سفر/تأشيرة) الولادة القاهرة.

٨. .... (مُدّة/قاعة استقبال/تاريخ) الزيارة شهرين.

٩. كانت الرحلة من نيويورك لمصر .... (كبيرة/طويلة/موظّفة) جدّاً (very).

١٠. ما هو .... (تاريخ/رقم/عنوان) تليفون شركة الطيران؟

تمرين رقم ٤

Match each of the words below by writing it next to its English translation.

رِحلة، مَطار، مُوظف طيران، زيارة، موعِد، جنسيّة، شنطة، شركة طيران، جَواز سَفر، أهلاً وسهلاً

passport	
appointment	
airline company	
visit	
airport	
nationality	
suitcase	
Welcome!	
journey	
airline employee	

تمرين رقم ٥

Unscramble the letters to form words and give the English meaning of each word. All the words are found in the list above.

١. ا م ر ط ....

٢. ة ش ك ر ....

٣. ا ة ز ر ي ....

٤. ر ا ي ن ط ....

٥. ح ة ل ر ....

٦. ع و د م ....

تمرين رقم ٦

Complete a travel itinerary below for a journey you have taken or wish to take and share it with the class.

الاسم:...........		
التاريخ:...........	شَرِكة الطيران:..........	رقم الرِحلة:..........
من مدينة:..........	الى مدينة:..............	المطار:...............
الساعة:...........	مُدّة الرحلة:..............	موعد الوصول:.........

الدرس الثاني: عنواني في مصر ولّا في أمريكا!

النص الأول: مشاهدة

كلمات جديدة

ثاني second

مُشاهَدة viewing, watching

عُنوان address

وَلّا or

عيلة = عائلة family

تَمام good, perfect

تاريخ date

ميلاد birth

بَعدين then, and then

فُندُق hotel

يَعني it means, in other words

مُدّة period of time, length of time

زِيارة visit

كِده thus, this way

خَلاص done, finished

اتفضّل please, go ahead, take

تعبير (expression)

تاريخ ميلاد date of birth

أسئلة (questions)

تمرين رقم ١

Part 1

1. Did the man ask Maya about her address in Egypt, in America, or both?
2. When was Maya born?
3. What's her profession?
4. How long is she staying in Egypt?

Part 2

Watch the video of Maya in the airport again. Which of Maya's responses in the box below answer the man's questions? Write each response next to its question.

مدينة إثاكا في ولاية نيو يورك - ١٣/٤/١٩٩٥ - مايا - جونسون - طالبة .. كايرو إن

ردّ مايا (Maya's response)	أسئلة الرجل (the man's questions)
	اسمِك؟
	اسم العائلة (العيلة)؟
	العنوان في أمريكا؟
	تاريخ الميلاد؟
	العنوان في مصر؟
	المِهنة؟

قَواعِد (Grammar)

Plural pronouns

So far you have learned the singular pronouns for first person (أنا), second person (انتَ، انتِ), and third person (هُوّ، هِيّ). Below are the most commonly used plural pronouns in Egyptian Arabic.

We	إحنا
You (plural)	إنتو
They	هُمّ

Possession

You learned in Unit 1 that possession is expressed by attaching possessive suffixes (endings) to nouns. Below is the full set of possessive suffixes. Note that that m.s. refers to "masculine singular", f.s. refers to "feminine singular", and pl. refers to "plural".

لُغة Language	اسم Name	Possessive suffix	Pronoun
لُغتي	اسمي	my ـي	أنا
لُغتنا	اسمنا	our ـنا	إحنا
لُغتَك	اسمَك	your ـَك	إنتَ
لُغتِك	اسمِك	your, f.s. ـِك	إنتِ
لُغتكُم	اسمكُم	your, pl. ـكُم	إنتو
لُغتُه	اسمُه	his ـُه	هُوّ
لُغتها	اسمها	her ـها	هِيّ
لُغتهُم	اسمهُم	their ـهُم	هُمّ

تمرين رقم ٢

Part 1

Add possessive suffixes to the nouns in the table below. Some have been given as examples.

مِهنة Profession	عنوان Address	شنطة Bag	Pronoun
		شنطتي	أنا
	عنواننا		إحنا
		شنطتَك	إنتَ
مهنتِك			إنتِ
	عُنوانكُم/عُنوانكو		إنتو
	عنوانه		هو
مهنتها			هي
		شنطتهُم	هُم

Part 2

The table below is similar to the table in Part 1, except that now the possessed nouns are part of an *iDaafa* (إضافة) phrase.

Look at the examples given to you – which noun does the possessive suffix get added to? Once you have figured it out, fill out the rest of the table.

اسم عائلة Family name	تاريخ ميلاد Date of birth	جواز سفر Passport	Pronoun
	تاريخ ميلادي		أنا
اسم عائلتي			إحنا
		جواز سفرَك	إنتَ
اسم عائلتِك			إنتِ
	تاريخ ميلادكُم		إنتو
		جواز سفرِك	هو
		جواز سفرها	هي
اسم عائلتهم			هُم

تمرين رقم ٣

Classmate interviews

Part 1

Make up questions and answers using the key words with the possessive pronouns. Key words: أسم، تاريخ ميلاد، عيلة، عنوان، مهنة

Example

ط١ اسمِك ايه؟

ط٢ كرستن. وانتَ اسمك ايه؟

ط١ مايك.

Part 2

Pick a celebrity and write a profile about him/her. Then in class the next day describe your celebrity and students guess who it is.

الدرس الثالِث–استماع: جواز السفر، لو سمحتِ!

النصّ الأوّل

كلمات جديدة

لُغة language

دِراسة study, studying

عَشان for the purpose of

تعابير (expressions)

أهلاً وسهلاً welcome

أهلاً بيك welcome to you

جَواز سفر passport

لَو سمحتِ if you please

أسئلة (questions)

1. Why is Maya in Egypt?
2. Where is she going to study?
3. What is she going to study?

النص الثاني

كلمات جديدة

ثالِث third

مُوظّف (ج. مُوَظَّفين) employee

بَنك bank

شَرِكة company

مَدرسة ثانَويّة secondary school, high school

مَع with

عائِلة (ج. عائلات) = عيلة family

سافرَت she traveled

أغُسطُس August

طَيّارة = طائرة airplane

طَبعاً of course

رِحلة (ج. رحلات) trip

كانَت she, it was

طَويل long

وَصَلت she arrived

مَطار airport

بَعد الظُهر afternoon

جواز (ج. جَوازات) = جواز السفر (ج. جوازات السفر) passport

سأل he asked

سؤال (ج. أسئلة) question

كَثير many

تَعبان (ج. تعبانين) tired

قَوي a lot

أسئلة

1. What is Maya's brother's name?
2. How old is Maya's father?
3. Who is Michelle? How old is she?
4. What does Michelle do?
5. How old is Matthew? What does he do?
6. How did Maya travel to Egypt?
7. What time did she arrive in Cairo?
8. Who asked Maya a lot of questions?

النصّ الثاني: قراءة

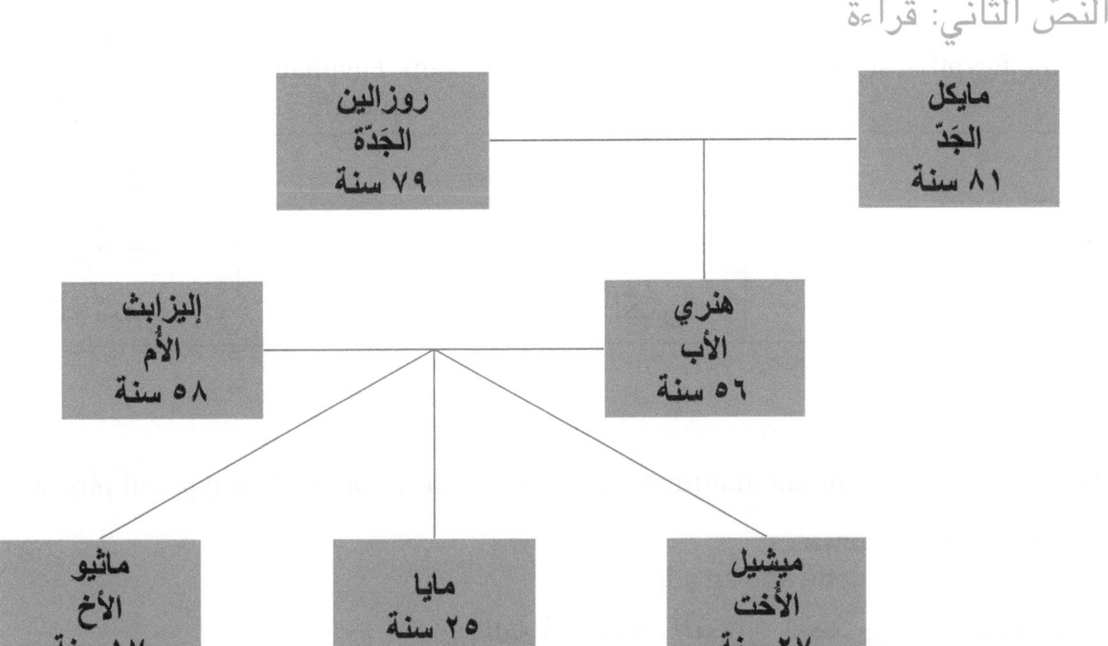

كلمات جديدة

جَدّ grandfather

جَدّة grandmother

أسئلة

1. What is Maya's grandmother's name? How old is she?
2. What is Maya's mother's name? How old is she?
3. What is Maya's father's name?

قَواعِد

Noun-adjective agreement

As was shown in the sixth lesson of Unit 1, adjectives agree with the nouns they modify in gender, as was shown in the examples بيت كبير and شقّة كبيرة. In addition to agreeing in gender, adjectives also agree with nouns in definiteness, as shown in the following examples:

Definite phrases
الطالبة الأمريكية
العنوان المصري

Indefinite phrases
طالبة أمريكية
عنوان مصري

تمرين رقم ١: أكمل الجدول (Complete the following table)

the Egyptian student		(an) Egyptian student	طالب مصري
			جامعة بريطانيّة
			فُندُق قَريب
	العائلة الكبيرة		عائلة كبيرة

Review of إضافة phrases and noun-adjective phrases

Among the most common grammatical structures in Arabic are two types of phrases:

- Noun-adjective phrases
  - Consist of a noun and an adjective
  - Examples: طالبة أمريكيّة ـ العنوان المصري
- إضافة phrases
  - Consist of two or more nouns
  - Examples: اسم الأم ـ ولاية نيويورك

تمرين رقم ٢

Of the following phrases eight are إضافة phrases, including the example, and three are noun-adjective phrases. Give an English translation of each one and indicate which category it belongs to. The first phrase is given as an example.

Type	Translation	Phrase
إضافة	The name of the family, family name	اسم العائلة
		تاريخ الميلاد
		أدب عربي
		مدة الزيارة
		جواز السفر

Type	Translation	Phrase
		جامعة القاهرة
		طالبة أمريكية
		مدينة أوستن
		مدينة صغيرة
		المدرسة الثانويّة

Non-human plurals

In addition to agreement in gender and definiteness, Arabic adjectives agree with the nouns they modify in number.

(an) Egyptian student	طالب مصري
Egyptian students	طُلّاب مَصريّين

There is, however, one exception to this rule. Arabic distinguishes between nouns that are "human" and nouns that are "non-human", as shown in the following table:

Non-human nouns	**Human nouns**
دَرس	طالب
سؤال	بِنت
عائلة	مُهندس

Non-human nouns in the plural act like feminine singular nouns, as shown in the phrase أسئلة كثيرة (many questions). Because أسئلة is a **non-human plural noun**, it "acts" like a feminine singular noun and takes a feminine singular adjective كثيرة. See the examples below:

Feminine singular adjective	**Non-human plural noun**
كثيرة	أسئلة
كبيرة	عائلات
طويلة	رحلات

Remember that this *only* occurs in the plural – in the singular form, non-human nouns show regular agreement (مدينة صغيرة – عنوان مصري).

الدرس الرابِع: قراءة

النصّ الأوّل

جمهورية مصر العربية وزارة الداخلية تأشيرة دخول	
الاسم: مايا	اسم الأب: هنري
اسم الأم: اليزابث	اسم العائلة: جونسون
تاريخ الميلاد: ١٣/٤/١٩٩٥	مكان الولادة: نيويورك، أمريكا
الجنسية: أمريكية	رقم جواز السفر: ٣٥٢٦٧
المهنة: طالبة	تاريخ ومكان الصدور: ٦/٧/٢٠١١، واشنطن دي سي
العنوان في مصر: فندق كايرو ان، القاهرة	مدّة الزيارة: ٣ شهور

كلمات جديدة

رابِع fourth

جمهورية مصر العربية Arab Republic of Egypt

تأشيرة دخول entry visa

تاريخ date

وِلادة = ميلاد birth

مَكان place

جِنسيّة nationality, citizenship

رَقَم number

جواز سفر = جواز passport

صُدور issue

زيارة = visit

أسئلة

1. When was Maya born?
2. Where is her place of birth?
3. What is the number of her passport?
4. Where was her passport issued?
5. How long is her visit to Egypt?

النصّ الثاني

شركة الطيران	رقم الرحلة	موعد الوصول	قادمة مِن	المحطّة	قاعة الاستقبال
مطار القاهرة الدولي مواعيد وصول الطائرات في ١٠ /١١					
مصر للطيران	م.س. ٧٩٢	١٧:٥٠	روما	٣	١
القطريّة	ق.ر. ١٣٠١	٢٠:١٦	الدوحة	٣	١
المصريّة	يو.ج. ٨٢٦	١٨:١٠	العَين	١	١
السعوديّة	س.ف. ٣١٣	١٨:١٥	الرياض	١	٣
الفرنسيّة (إير فرانس)	ا.ف. ٥٠٨	١٨:٢٠	باريس	١	٣
النيل للطيران	ن.ب. ١٠٢	١٨:٤٥	الطائف	١	١
مصر للطيران	م.س. ٧٥٢	١٨:٥٠	بودابست	٣	١
الألمانيّة (لوفتهانزا)	ل.هـ. ٥٨٠	١٨:٥٠	ميونخ	٣	١
طيران الشرق الأوسط	م.إي. ٣٠٦	١٩:١٥	بيروت	١	٣
مصر للطيران	م.س. ٦٧٢	١٩:٤٥	جدّة	٣	١
طيران الخليج	ج.ف. ٠٧٩	١٩:٥٠	البحرين	١	١
الملكيّة الأردنيّة	ر.ج. ٥٠٥	٢٠:١٥	عمّان	٢	١
مصر للطيران	م.س. ٧٥٤	٢٠:٢٥	مدريد	٣	١
طيران الإمارات	إي.كي. ٩٢٥	٢٢:١٥	دُبيّ	١	١
طيران الاتّحاد	إي.واي. ٦٥٥	٢٣:٣٥	أبو ظبي	١	١

كلمات جديدة

دَولي international

شَركة طَيَران airline (company)

مَوعد (ج. مواعيد) time, appointed time

وُصول arrival

قادِم (مِن) coming (from)

مَحَطّة station, terminal

قاعة استِقبال reception hall, lounge

النيل the Nile

الخليج the Gulf

أسئلة

1. What is the arrival time of the following flights?
   - Egypt Air coming from Rome
   - Air France from Paris
   - Lufthansa from Munich
   - Middle East Airlines from Beirut
   - Ettihad Airlines from Abu Dhabi
2. Which terminal are the following flights arriving at?
   - Qatar Airlines from Doha
   - Saudia Airlines from Riyadh
   - Egypt Air from Al-Ayn
   - Gulf Airlines from Bahrain
   - The Emirates Airlines from Dubai

قواعِد: النسبة (The *Nisba* adjective)

How would you translate the following sentences?

مايا جونسون طالبة أمريكيّة.

مايا جونسون طالبة من أمريكا.

Notice that the feminine word for American أمريكية is derived from the name of the country أمريكا. This is called the *Nisba* Adjective (صفة النسبة). Now consider the following examples. Can you see a pattern?

Human Plural Adjective	Feminine Adjective	Masculine Adjective	Original Noun
أمريكيين	أمريكيّة	أمريكي	أمريكا
مصريين	مصريّة	مصري	مصر
عراقيين	عراقيّة	عراقي	العراق
سودانيين	سودانيّة	سوداني	السودان
سوريين	سوريّة	سوري	سوريا/سورية

تمرين رقم ١

Part 1 (at home)

Fill in the blank for each sentence, by changing the country name to the صفة النسبة. Remember the rules of noun-adjective agreement in Arabic: pay attention to whether the noun is definite or indefinite, as well as its gender.

1. هو طالب ______________ (اليمن).
2. "لفربول" مدينة ______________ (بريطانيا) كبيرة.
3. أنا من مصر، لكن (but) عندي جنسية ______________ (السودان).
4. أنتِ الأستاذة الـ______________ (المغرب)؟
5. "لوفتهانزا" شركة (company) ______________ (ألمانيا Germany).
6. "اير فرانس" شركة ______________ (فرنسا).

Part 2 (in class)

With a partner, translate your sentences. What do you notice about the difference between nouns and adjectives in Arabic and nouns and adjectives in English?

Part 3 (in class)

Extra practice: This method of forming adjectives can be applied to almost any noun in Arabic. How would you translate the following?

translation الترجمة	النسبة	الاسم the noun
	يومي/يوميّة	يوم
	صيفي/صيفيّة	الصيف
	جنوبي/جنوبيّة	جنوب
	اقتصادي/اقتصاديّة	اقتصاد

The verb "to be" in Arabic and equational sentences

You may have noticed by now that sentences in Arabic seem to be missing the verb "to be". This is because the verb "to be" is implied. Look at the examples below:

عنواني في أمريكا مدينة إثاكا في ولاية نيويورك
My address in America [is] the city Ithaca in New York State.

إنتِ في مصر ليه يا مايا؟
Why [are] you in Egypt, Maya?

This type of sentence is called an "equational sentence". Rather than having an obvious verb "to be", you can think of there being an equals sign between both parts of the sentence. The equals sign in the sentences below is where the verb "to be" is implied.

Original sentence	مدة الزيارة ثلاث شهور
Sentence with equal sign	مدة الزيارة = ثلاث شهور
Translation	The length of visit *is* three months.

Original sentence	مايا جونسون طالبة أمريكية في جامعة تكساس
Sentence with equal sign	مايا جونسون = طالبة أمريكية في جامعة تكساس
Translation	Maya Johnson is an American student at the University of Texas.

تمرين رقم ٢

The sentences in تمرين ١ are all *equational sentences*. With a partner, reread the sentences in the تمرين and determine where the verb "to be" should go by drawing in an equals (=) sign.

الدرس الخامس

كلمات الوحدة

جَدّة grandmother

جمهورية مصر العربية
Arab Republic of Egypt

جِنسيّة nationality, citizenship

جواز (ج. جَوازات) = جواز السفر
(ج. جوازات السفر) passport

جَواز سفر passport

خَلاص done, finished

دِراسة study, studying

دَولي international

رابِع fourth

رِحلة trip

رَقَم number

زِيارة visit

سافرَت she traveled

سأل he asked

سؤال (ج. أسئِلة) question

أغُسطُس August

الخليج the Gulf

the Nile النيل

welcome أهلاً وسَهلاً

welcome to you أهلا بيك

afternoon بَعد الظُهر

then, and then بَعدين

bank بَنك

date تاريخ

date of birth تاريخ ميلاد

entry visa تأشيرة دخول

tired تَعبان

please, go ahead, take اتفضّل

good, perfect تَمام

third ثالِث

second ثاني

grandfather جَدّ

language لُغة

if you, f.s., please لَو سمحتِ

station, terminal مَحَطّة

period of time مُدّة

مَدرسة ثانَويّة
secondary school, high school

viewing, watching مُشاهَدة

airport مَطار

with مَع

place مَكان

employee مُوظّف (ج. موظفين)

time, appointed time مَوعد

she arrived وَصَلت

arrival وُصول

or وَلّا

birth وِلادة = ميلاد

it means, in other words يَعني

company شَرِكة

airline (company) شَركة طَيَران

issue صدور

to fly/take off طار–يطير

of course طَبعاً

long طَويل

airplane طَيّارة = طائرة

family عائِلة (ج. عائلات) = عيلة

for the purpose of عَشان

address عُنوان

hotel فُندُق

coming (from) قادِم (مِن)

reception hall, lounge قاعة استِقبال

a lot قَوي

she, it was كانَت

many كَثير

thus, this way كِده

تمرين رقم ١– قراءة: شركات الطيران

مطار القاهرة الدولي مواعيد وصول الطائرات في ١٠ /١١					
شركة الطيران	رقم الرحلة	موعد الوصول	قادمة مِن	المحطّة	قاعة الاستقبال
مصر للطيران	م.س. ٧٤٨	١٧:٥٠	أثينا	٣	١
البريطانيّة (برتش إيرويز)	بي.إي. ١٥٥	٢٣:٥٩	لندن (هيثرو)	١	١
السودانيّة	س.د. ١٠٢	٠١:٣١	الخرطوم	١	١
الهولنديّة (كي إل إم)	ك.ل. ٥٥٣	٠٢:٠٥	أمستردام	١	٣
الإيطاليّة (أليتاليا)	ا.ز. ٨٩٤	٠٢:٣٥	روما	١	١
مصر للطيران	م.س. ٨٣٤	٠٦:١٠	أسوان	٣	١
العراقيّة	إي.ا. ١٠١	١١:٣٠	بغداد	١	١

1. What is the arrival time of the following flights?
   - Egypt Air coming from Athens
   - KLM from Amsterdam
   - Iraqi Airlines from Baghdad
2. Which terminal are the following flights arriving at?
   - British Airways from London (Heathrow)
   - Sudanese Airlines from Khartoum
   - Alitalia from Rome
   - Egypt Air from Al-Ayn

تمرين رقم ٢: استماع

تُعلِن مِصر للطيران عن وصول رحلتها رقم ٧٤٨ والقادمة من أثينا. يتمّ استقبال المسافرين في قاعة الاستقبال رقم ١.

يُعلن طيران الشرق الأوسط عن تأخّر رحلته رقم ٣٠٦ القادمة من بيروت. الموعد الجديد لوصول الطائرة هو الساعة الثامنة والنصف. وسيتمّ استقبال المسافرين في قاعة الاستقبال رقم ٣.

يُرجى من المسافرين الكرام عدم ترك أمتعتهم الشخصيّة. . .

1. Where is Egypt Air Flight 748 coming from?
2. Which reception hall will it be arriving at?
3. What is the new arrival time of Middle East Airlines flight 306 from Beirut?

Sociolinguistic Corner

In the Sociolinguistic Corner sections of this book, you will learn about the more salient changes that occur between مصري and فصحى. The purpose of this section is to raise your awareness about these differences. As you progress in your studies, you will gain a sense of what to expect in each variety.

In addition to changes in the way some individual letters are pronounced, there are sometimes different words used in the two varieties.

While some words are only used in either فُصحى or مَصري, the majority of words and grammatical structures are shared by the two varieties. In many instances the only difference between فُصحى and مَصري is in the pronunciation of a word. You have already seen this with the pronouns and the two words عائلة/عيلة and طائرة/طيّارة.

	فُصحى	مَصري
I	أنا	أنا
We	نَحنُ	إحنا
You (m.s.)	أنتَ	إنتَ
You (f.s.)	أنتِ	إنتِ
You (pl.)	أنتُم	إنتو
He	هُوَ	هُوَّ
She	هِيَ	هِيَّ
They	هُم	هُمَّ
Family	عائلة	عيلة

طائرة/طيّارة

The difference between the two versions of the word for "airplane" is not simply a pronunciation difference. Both words are used in both Arabic varieties, مصري and فصحى, but طائرة is generally found in written and formal contexts, while طيّارة occurs in less formal communication.

تمرين رقم ٣: (تكلّم في الصفّ) (Speak in class)

Take turns interviewing your partner and then report the information about him/her to the class.

Example

ط ١ اسمك ايه؟

ط ٢ دان.

ط ١ بيتك فين؟

ط ٢ في لندن...

ط ١ ده دان. بيته في لندن...

Some key words and expressions:

عيد ميلاد، تاريخ، اسم، جنسيّة، رَقم، جواز سفر، بيت، مَوعِد، أيّ ساعة

تمرين رقم ٤: كتابة (writing) (في البيت)

Pretend that you are traveling to Egypt to take an Arabic summer course that will last two months. Fill out the following form accordingly. Remember that in order to make a noun "dual", you just add the suffix ين: شهر "one month", شهرين "two months". The plural of شهر is شُهور.

جمهورية مصر العربية وزارة الداخلية تأشيرة دخول	
الاسم:	اسم الأب:
اسم الأم:	اسم العائلة:
تاريخ الولادة:	مكان الولادة:
الجنسية:	رقم جواز السفر:
المهنة:	تاريخ ومكان الصدور:
العنوان في مصر:	مدّة الزيارة:

الوحدة الثالثة
التاكسي

الدرس الأوّل

تمرين رقم ١

Learn the following words by listening to them and repeating them out loud.

قِطار (ج. قِطارات)	سَوّاق	تاكسي
صباح	مُغادَرة	تَذكَرة (ج. تذاكِر)

more than أكثر مِن

afternoon بعد الظُهر

nearly, about, approximately تقريباً

Egyptian pound (currency) جنيه مصري

you (formal way to address a man), sir حَضرتَك

you (formal way to address a woman), ma'am حَضرتِك

train, bus (line) خَطّ

first class درجة أولى

he studied درَس

she studied درست

by the way عَلى فِكرة

pleasant, nice لطيف

air-conditioned مُكَيّف

downtown وَسط البَلَد

(arrival time وقت الوصول) time وقت

January يَنايِر

تمرين رقم ٢: استماع

Listen to the audio recording and translate each sentence into English on a separate piece of paper.

تمرين رقم ٣

Copy each of the following words/phrases under its appropriate category.

أهلاً وسهلاً، جواز سفر، شركة طيران، صباحاً، غداً، طيّارة، بعد الظُهر، مُغادرة، فُندُق، شهر، مساءً، تاكسي، مَوعِد، سوّاق، تذكِرة، شهر، عَلى فِكرة، قِطار، تقريباً

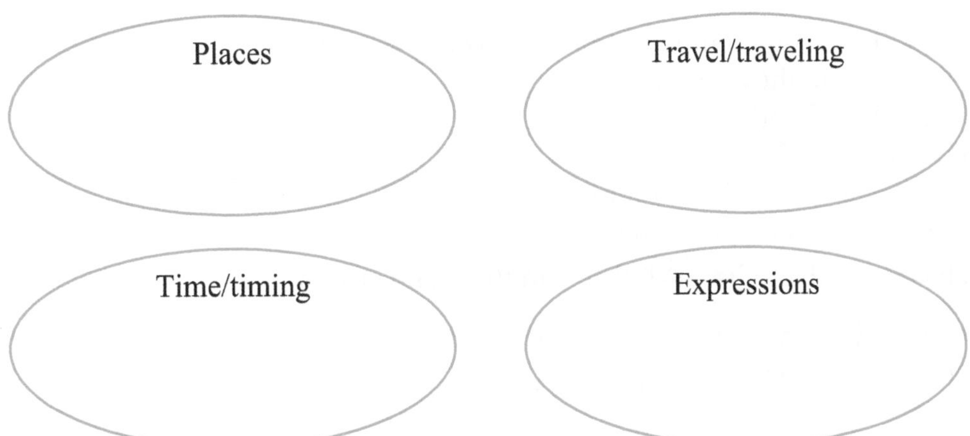

تمرين رقم ٤

Fill in the blanks using words from the word bank below.

تقريباً - مُكَيَّف - مُغادرة - ركب - حَضرِتَك - صباحاً - ثمن - مصري

١. الجو حارّ اليوم، لكن البيت ....

٢. ....أُستاذ في الجامعة؟

٣. عندي موعِد بعد ساعة ....

٤. ....التاكسي الساعة ٦:٣٠ صباحاً.

٥. موعد ....الطيّارة من مطار "هيثرو" هو الساعة عشرة............

٦. ....تذكرة القطار ١٢٠ جنيه.....................

تمرين رقم ٥

Part 1

Matching (companion website)

Part 2

Translate the matched phrases into English on a separate piece of paper.

تمرين رقم ٦

At home (في البيت): With the help of the new words above, translate the questions below into Arabic.

In class (في الصفّ): Obtain information from your partner in class by asking them the questions below and then report your findings to the class.

1. Who (مين) has an appointment this week (الأسبوع دَه)?
2. Who has work in the evening?
3. Who has a lot of work?
4. Who is tired today?
5. Who has an air-conditioned room?
6. Who rode a bus in the morning?
7. Who has more than (أكثر مِن) three brothers and sisters?
8. Who knows (يعرف) where the taxi driver is?
9. Who has a plane ticket to Egypt?

الدرس الثاني–مشاهدة: على فين في القاهرة؟

كلمات جديدة

Note that abbreviation *lit.* stands for the word "literally".

taxi تاكسي

to where عَلى فين

you (lit. your presence) حَضرتِك

but لَكِن

you speak بتتكلّمي

you learned تعَلّمتِ

in it, it has فيها

more than أكثر مِن

by the way عَلى فِكرة

your name (polite) اسم حضرتك

welcome to you too (response to أهلاً وسهلاً)

أهلاً بيك

if you want لَو عايز

card كارت

cell phone (mobile) موبايل

here هِنا

أسئلة

1. Which hotel is Maya going to?
2. Where did Maya say she is from?
3. Where did she learn Arabic?
4. How many students are at the University of Texas?
5. What did the taxi driver give Maya?
6. (companion website) صحّ أو خطأ؟

قَواعِد

Expressing "to want" in Egyptian Arabic (مَصري)

Instead of using a verb like "to want", مصري uses the "active participle" عايز to express the same idea.

مايا عايزة تاكسي.	أحمد مش عايز تاكسي.
Maya wants a taxi.	Ahmad doesn't want a taxi.

What is an active participle?

An active participle in Arabic is a noun derived from a verb to indicate the doer of an action. The English equivalent is the word *writer*, derived from the verb "to write". Another participle you have seen is ساكن "(a person) living".

Like عايِز, ساكن has three forms: *masculine singular*, *feminine singular*, and *plural* as can be seen below.

Plural	Feminine singular	Masculine singular
'ayziin عايزين	*'ayza* عايزة	*'aayiz* عايِز
sakniin ساكنين	*sakna* ساكنة	*saakin* ساكِن

تمرين رقم ١

Part 1

Read the following Egyptian Colloquial Arabic (مصري) phrases and then translate them into English:

.1	مايا عايزة تاكسي.
.2	أحمد وأمجد مش عايزين شقّة.
.3	إنتَ عايز ايه؟
.4	أنا مش عايز رقم موبايلك!
.5	أنا مش عايزة رقم موبايلك!
.6	هيّ عايزة بيت كبير.

Part 2

1. What is the difference between #4 and #5?
2. Based on the sentences above, explain how عايز/ عايزة/عايزين are negated.

تمرين رقم ٢ (قراءة ومُحادثة)

Part A. Below is a list of some of the phrases from the video. With a partner, read them out loud and try to figure out who said which phrase, مايا ولا أمجد؟.

تاكسي! تاكسي!

على فين؟

فندق "كايرو إن" لو سمحت.

اتفضّلي.

حضرتك من أمريكا؟

أنا من مدينة صغيرة.

تعلمتِ عربي فين؟

جامعة تكساس كبيرة قوي.

على فكرة، أنا اسمي أمجد.

أهلاً وسهلاً يا مايا.

اهلاً بيك.

شكراً. مع السلامة.

Part B. With your partner, come up with a small skit based on the phrases above. You will need to add your own lines to make sure it makes sense!

الدرس الثالِث

النصّ الأوّل: استماع

كلمات جديدة

tired تَعبان

coming جاي

also كَمان

she took أخذَت

she entered دخلَت

she rode, got on ركبت

about, approximately تقريباً

driver سَوّاق

she studied درسَت

he said قال

originally أصلاً

now دِلوقتِ

because لأنّ

work شُغل

he spoke تكَلّم

many كِتير

he was كان

nice لَطيف

أسئلة

1. List three things the passport employee asked Maya?
2. Did Maya get a visa to enter Egypt?
3. How long did the trip from the airport to the hotel take?
4. What type of questions did the taxi driver ask Maya?

5. Who is Amgad?
6. Where is Amgad originally from?
7. Why does he live in Cairo now?

النصّ الثاني: استماع

كلمات جديدة

like زَيّ
because (of) عَشان
this, that كِده
old, older كَبير
he went راح
there هِناك

أسئلة

Listen to the passage and complete the missing information in the following table:

الاسم	العمل	السكن
أمجد	سوّاق تاكسي	
		السعوديّة
عزّة		

قَواعِد

The past tense (الفعل الماضي)

The past tense الفعل الماضي in Egyptian Arabic is conjugated by attaching different endings (suffixes) to the basic form of the verb. Listen to the audio recording while you read the past tense verb conjugations below for the verb "to study" درس.

Pronoun	Suffix		Translation
أنا	ـت -	درست	I studied
إحنا	ـنا -	درسنا	We studied
إنتَ	ـت -	درست	You (m.s.) studied
إنتِ	ـتِ -	درستِ	You (f.s.) studied
إنتو	ـتوا -	درستوا	You (pl.) studied
هو	(none) -	درس	He studied
هي	ـِت -	درسِت	She studied
هُمّ	ـوا -	درسوا	They studied

Note the following:

1. The هو conjugation does not have any suffixes attached to it. Because of this, the past tense هو conjugation is considered to be the most basic form.
2. The conjugations of انتَ and أنا sound and look identical in spoken Arabic.
3. The ا at the end of the هُمّ and إنتو conjugations is silent.

تمرين رقم ١ (كتابة في البيت) Writing at home

With reference to the table above, fill in the gaps in the following table:

Part 1

entered	learned	arrived	traveled	
			سافرت	أنا
	تعلّمنا			إحنا
	تعلّمت			إنتَ
دخلتِ		وصلتِ		إنتِ
دخلتوا				إنتو
	تعلّم		سافر	هو
		وصلِت		هي
		وصلوا		هُمّ

Part 2

asked	rode	took	spoke	
				أنا
	ركبنا			إحنا
سألت		أخذت		إنتَ
			تكلّمتِ	إنتِ
		أخذتوا		إنتو
			تكلّم	هو
سألِت	ركبِت			هي
		أخذوا		هُمّ

تمرين رقم ٢ (تصريف أفعال بالماضي)

Oral drill: Use the verbs in the table above in meaningful sentences. Be sure to use all of the pronouns. Follow the example.

مثال: سافر
الطالب: أنا سافرت لفرنسا. أنتِ سافرتِ لفرنسا؟

تمرين رقم ٣

Part 1

Matching (companion website)

Part 2

Translate the matched phrases into English on a separate piece of paper.

Verb stems

As you learned above, the هو conjugation, which has no suffixes, is the basic form. This هو form will be referred to from now on as the "verb stem". Learning how to identify the verb stem is important – if you know the verb stem, then you know how to conjugate that verb for all pronouns in the past tense.

تمرين رقم ٤

For the verbs in the following table, give a full English translation and then identify the verb stem. Some cells in the table have been filled in.

Verb stem	Translation	Verb
سافر	She traveled	سافرِت
		كانِت
		وَصَلت
تكلّم	You speak	بتتكلمي
		تعلمتِ
سأل	And he asked her	وسألها
		أخذت

		ودخلت
		ركبت
		درست
		تكلّم
		وسأل
		كان

From now on, new verbs will listed according to the verb stem. For example, a verb like سافرت "I traveled" will be listed as "سافَر" (which translates literally as "he traveled").

الدرس الرابِع: قراءة

النصّ الأوّل

مواعيد قطارات وتذاكر خط القاهرة ـ أسوان ليوم غد السبت ١٧ يناير ثمن التذكرة بالجنيه المصري درجة أولى مُكيّفة: ١١٣،٥٠ درجة ثانية مُكيّفة: ٥٧		
القاهرة ـ أسوان		
رَقَم القِطار	وقت المُغادَرة	وقت الوصول
٩٨٠	٨ صباحاً	١٠ مَساء
٩٨٢	١٢ مساء	٢:٣٠ صَباحاً
٩٨٨	٧ مساء	٨ صَباحاً
٩٩٦	١٠ مساء	١١:٢٠ صَباحاً
٩٨٦	١١:١٥ مساء	١٢:٣٠ مَساء

أسوان – القاهرة		
٩٨١	٥:٣٠ صباحاً	٧:٥٠ مَساء
٩٨٣	٧ صباحاً	٩:٢٥ مَساء
٩٨٧	٣ مساء	٤:١٥ صباحاً
٩٨٩	٩:٣٠ مساء	١٠:٤٥ صباحاً

كلمات جديدة

قِطار (ج. قِطارات) = قَطر (ج. قُطُرات) train

تَذكَرة (ج. تذاكِر) ticket

خَطّ line

غَد = بُكرة tomorrow

يَنايِر January

ثَمَن price

جِنيه مَصري the currency of Egypt (Egyptian pound)

دَرَجة class

أولى first

مُكَيّف air-conditioned

مُغادَرة departure

صباحاً in the morning

مَساءً in the evening

أسئلة

Indicate whether each of the following statements is صحّ (correct) or خطأ (incorrect) according to the information in the table.

١. قطار الدرجة الثانية مكيّف.

٢. حسب الجدول (according to the table) اليوم هو يوم السبت.

٣. ثمن تذكرة الدرجة الأولى ١١٣ ونصّ جنيه مصري.

٤. وقت وصول القطار رقم ٩٨٨ إلى أسوان هو الساعة ثمانية في الصباح.

٥. وقت مُغادرة القطار رقم ٩٨٦ من القاهرة الساعة ١٢ ونصّ في المساء.

٦. يسافر (it travels) القطار رقم ٩٨٣ من أسوان إلى القاهرة.

٧. وقت مغادرة القطار رقم ٩٨٧ من أسوان هو الساعة أربعة وربع في الصباح.

النصّ الثاني: المُدن المصريّة

	الإسكندريّة	أسوان	القاهرة	دَهَب	الأقصُر	بور سَعيد	شَرم الشيخ	واحة سيوة	السُويس	طابا
الإسكندريّة	٠									
أسوان	١١٣٣	٠								
القاهرة	٢١٦	٩٢٦	٠							
دَهَب	٧٥٤	١٤٥٩	٥٣٣	٠						
الأقصُر	٩١٥	٢٢٩	٧٠٨	١٢٤١	٠					
بور سَعيد	٢٧٣	١١٤٥	٢٢٠	٥٥٣	٩٢٨	٠				
شَرم الشيخ	٧١٦	١٤٢٩	٥٠٣	٩٣	١٢١١	٥٣٦	٠			
واحة سيوة	٦٢٣	١٢٧٤	٧٥٢	١٢٩٣	١٠٥٦	٨٩٦	١٢٠٠	٠		
السُويس	٣٤٨	١٠٦١	١٣٥	٣٩٨	٨٤٣	١٦٨	٣٦٨	٨٣٢	٠	
طابا	٧٦١	١٤٦٦	٥٤٠	١٤٩	١١٠٨	٤٢٠	٢٤٢	١٢٩٣	٢٦٥	٠

أسئلة

واحة oasis

What are the distances between the following Egyptian cities or locations according to the table?
Alexandria to Cairo
Port Said to Aswan
Sharm el-Sheikh to Taba
Luxor to Cairo
Alexandria to the Siwa Oasis
Suez to Luxor

تمرين رقم ١ (كتابة في البيت)

Write four or more sentences describing the distances between eight or more Egyptian cities/areas, as in the example below.

طابا قريبة من السويس، لكن بعيدة عن واحة سيوة. المسافة (the distance) بين (between) طابا والسويس ٢٦٥ كيلومتر (kilometer)، لكن المسافة بين طابا وواحة سيوة ١٢٩٣ كيلومتر.

الدرس الخامس

كلمات الوحدة

أخَذ he took
اسم حضرتك your name (polite)
أصلاً originally
أكثر مِن more than
أهلاً وسهلاً welcome
أهلاً وسهلاً بيك welcome to you (response to أهلاً وسهلاً)
أولى first
تاكسي taxi
تَذكَرة (ج. تذاكِر) ticket
تَعبان tired
تعَلّم he learned
تقريباً about, approximately
تكلّم he spoke
ثَمَن price
جاي coming
جِنيه مَصري Egyptian pound
حَضرتِك you (lit. your presence)
خَطّ line
دخل he entered
دَرَجة class
درس he studied
دِلوقتِ now
راح he went

ركِب he rode
زَيّ like
سَوّاق driver
شُغل work
صباحاً in the morning
عَشان because (of)
عَلى فِكرة by the way
عَلى فين to where
غَد = بُكرة tomorrow
فيها in it, it has
قِطار (ج. قِطارات) train
كارت card
موبايل cell phone (mobile)
كان he was
كَبير old, older
كِثير many
كده this, that
كَمان also
لأنّ because
لَطيف nice
لكِن (لاكِن) but (pronounced
لَو عايز if you want
ما فيهاش (she, it) does not have
مَساءً in the evening

departure مُغادَرة

air-conditioned مُكَيِّف

here هِنا

there هِناك

oasis واحة

January يَنايِر

قراءة

دخلت خِدمة التاكسي "أوبر" (أو "يوبر") مدينة القاهرة، عاصمة مصر، وبالتحديد مناطق الزمالك والمهندسين والجيزة. وستدخل بعض المُدن المصريّة الأخرى في المستقبل. وخِدمة أوبر موجودة في عدد من المُدُن العربيّة مثل دُبَيّ وأبوظبي في الإمارات العربيّة المتّحدة، وجَدّة والرياض في السعوديّة وبيروت في لبنان.

Make a list of the six Arab cities that have Uber taxi service.

Review of negation in مصري

You have learned that the word مش is used in مصري to negate sentences as in:

He is not a student.	هو مش طالب.
That is not big.	ده مش كبير.
She does not want a ticket.	هي مش عايزة تذكرة.
Maya is not from Egypt.	مايا مش من مصر.
I am not living in Cairo.	أنا مش ساكن في القاهرة.

Existential expressions are negated with ما and ش. You have seen this in expressions of *there is not* or *there are not*, as in:

There isn't snow (there is no snow).	ما فيش ثلج.
There aren't buses in the street.	ما فيش أوتوبيسات في الشارع.

In such expressions فيه "there is" is "sandwiched" between ما and ش. (The presence of the ـه in فيه and its disappearance in ما فيش is a matter of spelling that you shouldn't worry about at this point.) The word **فيها** "in it" or "it has" is negated in the same way. Now translate the following two sentences into English:

1. السويس ما فيهاش شغل كثير.
2. أمجد راح القاهرة عشان فيها شغل أكثر من السويس.

تمرين رقم ١: كلمات متقاطعة

١٠	٩	٨	٧	٦	٥	٤	٣	٢	١	
										١
										٢
										٣
										٤
										٥
										٦
										٧
										٨
										٩
										١٠

أفقي

١. واحد من الفصول؛ أكبر دولة عربيّة بعدد السكّان (population)
٣. ندرسه في المدرسة والجامعة
٤. عكس (opposite) "شرق"
٥. دولة عربيّة كبيرة في أفريقيا
٦. فيه ٣٠ أو ٣١ يوم
٧. عكس "غربي"
٨. عكس "بعيد"
١٠. عكس "حارّ"؛ من اليمن

عمودي

١. عاصمة المغرب؛ ... في السيّارة
٣. يعمل في مكتب
٥. واحد من ستّين من الساعة
٦. ضمير (pronoun)
٧. من ليبيا
٩. عكس "كبير"
١٠. عاصمة لبنان

Sociolinguistic Corner

Note that, in general, "train" is referred to in فصحى as قِطار but in مصري as قَطْر.

تمرين رقم ٢: حضّر في البيت، تكلّم في الصفّ

Create a dialogue with another student in which one is the driver and the other a passenger. Tell where you are going, talk about everyday things, then negotiate the price.

تمرين رقم ٣: اكتب في البيت

Write a few sentences describing a trip you took by plane, train, or taxi. Describe where you went, when, how you traveled, with (مع) whom, etc. Use the words you've learned in this and the two previous units.

الوحدة الرابعة
الفندق

الدرس الأوّل

أخذ he took

اوضة room

تَرك he left

تَوصيل delivering, transporting

حَجَز he reserved

حَمّام bathroom

خاصّ private

خِدمة (ج. خَدَمات) service

سِعر (ج. أسعار) price

شارِع street

شَنطة/حقيبة suitcase

صندوق المفقودات lost and found

ضاع he (it) got lost

طَريق road

طَلَب he asked for, requested

عَدَد number

فتّش (عَلى) he looked for

فُطور breakfast

كَارت card

مَجّاني for free, no charge

مَرّة time

مُشكِلة problem

مَطعَم (ج. مَطاعِم) restaurant

مَقبول acceptable

مُمتاز excellent

مُمكِن possible, perhaps

مَوقِع location

نَجمة (ج.نُجوم) star

يَعمل (he, it) works, operates

تعابير (expressions)

أيّ خدمة؟ Can I help you? (lit. Any service?)

صَباح الخير good morning

صَباح النور good morning (response)

لو سمحتِ = من فضلِك if you please

آسف sorry

Note: آ, called madda (مَدّة), is a combination of ا + ء, and is pronounced as a long ا

الله أعلم! God knows!

ان شاء الله God willing

تمرين رقم ١: وافق بين الكلمة والصورة

Match the pictures with the Arabic words written below.

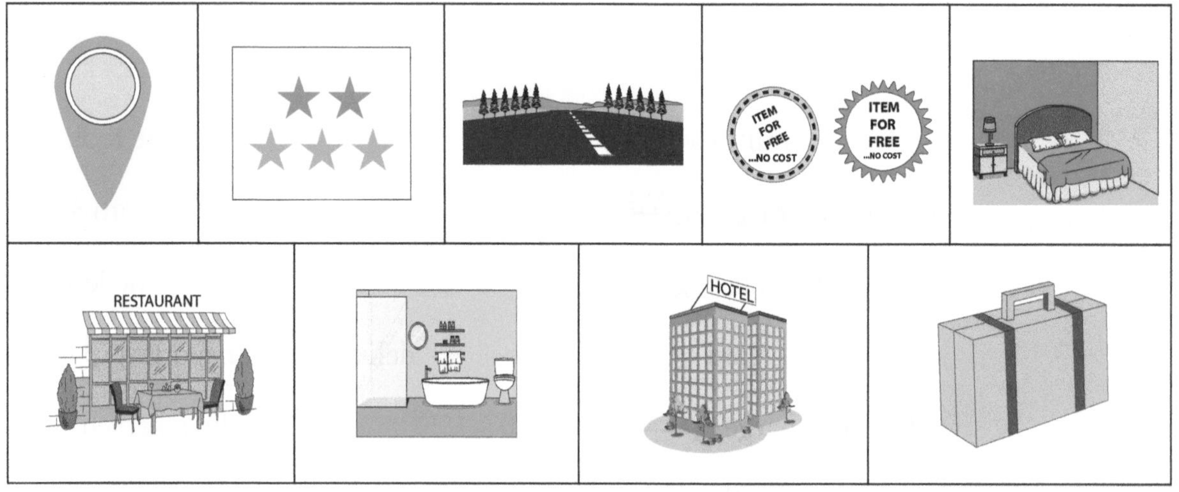

حمّام، فندق/اوتيل، مَجّاني، موقع، شَنطة/حقيبة، نُجوم، أوضة، شارع/طريق، مَطعم

تمرين رقم ٢

Identify the word that does not belong in the group.

صندوق المفقودات	ضاع	سِعر	وجد
شارع	حمّام	تكسي	ركِب
ساعَد	حَجز	فندُق	نُوم
كثير	كبير،	لطيف،	طريق
مَطار	مُشكلة	مصر الجديدة	مَطعم

تمرين رقم ٣: املأ الفراغات

سِعر، موقع، أوضة، مجّاني، فتشت، شارع، صندوق المفقودات، حجزت، أخذت، يعمل

١. الموظف .... في الفُندُق.

٢. .... الفُندُق مُمتاز.

٣. طلب .... بحمّام "جاكوزي".

٤. .... على الشنطة في المطار.

٥. جواز السفر في ....

٦. .... تاكسي من المطار إلى الفُندُق.

٧. الفُندُق على أي .... ؟

٨. .... الأوضة ١٥٠ دولار في الليلة لكن الفطور ....

٩. أنا .... غرفة بحمّام.

تمرين رقم ٤ (كتابة وشفهي في الصف)

Copy each of the phrases below next to its appropriate expression and then practice them with a classmate.

في الجامعة في أمريكا، طبعاً عندي جواز سفر، صباح النور، شكراً، حجزت أوضة في الفندق، أنا آسف، إسمي مايا

انت بتتكلّمي عربي كويّس	
أيّ خدمة	
اسم حضرتك ايه؟	
جواز سفري ضاع	
عندك جواز سفر	
فين تعلّمت عربي	
صباح الخير	

الدرس الثاني–مشاهدة: أوضة بحمّام طبعاً!

كلمات جديدة

room أوضة

bathroom حَمّام

good morning صَباح الخير

good morning (response) صَباح النور

Can I help you? (lit. Any service?) أيّ خدمة

he reserved حَجَز

if you please لو سمحتِ = من فضلك

(he spoke تكلّم) you speak بتتكلمي

(he learned تعلّم) you learned تعلمتِ

with you مَعاك

with me معايَ

(he left خَلّى) I leave أخلي

suitcase شَنطة

(he went راح) I go أروح

problem مُشكِلة

possible مُمكِن

must, necessary لازِم

(he went راح) you (f.) go تِروحي

أسئلة

1. What did Maya tell the hotel receptionist about the room she wanted?
2. Where did Maya learn Arabic?
3. Why did Maya have to go back to the airport?
4. Why did Maya not need a taxi?

قَواعِد

Possession continued: عندي versus معي

In Unit 1, you learned that possession is expressed in Arabic with the preposition عند and the possessive endings (عندي، عندَك، عندك، عندُه، عندها). In this dialogue, you heard a slightly different way of expressing ownership:

You don't have your passport with you?	مش مَعاك جواز سفرك؟
I had it (it was with me) in the airport.	كان معاي في المطار.
No, I've got a phone number for a taxi (right here).	لأ، معاي رقم تاكسي.

The preposition مع ("with") is used with the possessive endings to express having something with you at the moment, on your person, whereas عند just means "to have". Of course,

Maya *has* عندها a passport, but the problem is that she doesn't have that passport *with her* معاها at that moment. Luckily, she has the card for the taxi driver *with her* معاها! Note the addition of ا to مع when a suffix is attached to it.

Listen to the recordings for عند and مع.

مَع	عند	Pronoun
معايَ	عندي	أنا
معانا	عندِنا	إحنا
معاك	عندَك	إنتَ
معاكِ	عندِك	إنتِ
معاكُم	عندُكم	إنتو
معاه	عندُه	هو
معاها	عندها	هي
معاهُم	عندُهم	هُمّ

You have seen other examples of prepositions and possessive endings, as in the response to the greeting أهلا وسهلا – أهلا بيك. In fact, these endings can be added to any preposition.

تمرين رقم ١

Part 1

Do you own the following items Are they currently with you? Use عندي or معاي as appropriate. You can add more items to the list.

جواز سفر، كتاب، شنطة، موبايل، عربية (car)، ٥٠ دولار، ١٥ جنيه مصري

Part 2

Interview your partner to find out if he or she has the same items above. You will report back your results to the class when you are done.

تمرين رقم ٢: حوارات قصيرة (Mini dialogues)

At home في البيت : Match each phrase in column أ with its appropriate response in column ب and practice reading it aloud. Refer to the video as needed.

In class في الصف : Take turns practicing the phrases in columns أ and ب with a partner. For example, if your partners says صباح الخير your response should be صباح النور. Be sure to pay special attention to gender agreement.

ب	أ
حجزت أوضة على الانترنت.	صباح الخير.
جواز السفر ......؟. يا الله فين جواز سفري؟	أهلاً وسهلاً
صباح النور	أي خدمة؟
طبعا، مش مشكلة.	طيب، اسم حضرتك، لو سمحت.
أهلا بيك.	دقيقة، من فضلك، أوضة بحمام؟
طبعاً!	انت بتتكلم عربي كويس.
كان معايَ في المطار.	جواز السفر، من فضلك.
اسمي..........................	ممكن أخلي الشنطة هنا وأروح المطار؟
شُكراً!	مش معاك جواز سفر؟

Now play the role of Maya and the hotel employee using your own words and phrases.

الدرس الثالِث-النصّ الأوّل: استماع: زعلانة ليه؟

كلمات جديدة

كثير (ج. كُتار) many

أوّل first

مَرّة (ج. مَرّات) time, instance

باتكلّم I speak (he spoke تكلّم)

ياه Oh, what's the matter?

حاجة thing

زعلان (ج. زعلانين) upset

عَمَل he did

آسِف sorry

ضاع he (it) got lost

ان شاء الله God willing

صَندوق المفقودات lost and found box

أسئلة

1. Why wasn't Amgad the taxi driver there? Who was driving instead?
2. What made the driver think that Maya was upset?

3. Why was Maya upset?
4. Where could the passport be according to the taxi driver?

تمرين رقم ١: حوارات قصيرة (Mini dialogues)

1. At home (في البيت) Translate the following words/expressions taken from the listening passage into English using full sentences:
   - على فين؟ ....
   - انت من فين؟ ....
   - دي اول مرة انت في مصر؟ ....
   - فيه حاجة، انت زعلان ليه؟ ....
   - انا آسف/آسفة. جواز سفري ضاع ....
   - ان شاء الله يكون في صندوق المفقودات: ....
2. Roleplaying (في الصفّ): Working with a partner, pretend you are upset because you lost something/someone at the airport. Use as many vocabulary words and expressions from the audio as possible.

النصّ الثاني: قراءة

اسم الفندق	الموقع	عدد النجوم	السعر بالجنيه المصري	خدمات الفندق
ماريوت القاهرة وكازينو عمر الخيام	١٦ شارع الجزيرة، الزمالك	٥ (ممتاز)	١٨٣٠ ج. م.	٧ مطاعم ميني بار في كُلّ غرفة
فندق نوفوتيل المطار	طريق المطار مصر الجديدة	٤ (جيّد جدّاً)	١٣٧٢ ج. م.	٥ مطاعم خدمة توصيل من وإلى المطار
فندق المعادي	١٩ طريق مصر– حلوان المعادي	٤ (جيّد جدّاً)	١٠٩٨ ج. م.	مطعم وكوفي شوب حمام خاص بكل غرفة

فندق بيروت	٢١ شارع إسماعيل محمد الزمالك	٣ (جيّد)	٧٤٧ ج. م.	فطور مجاني حمام خاص بكل غرفة
فندق السفير	٢٢ ميدان المساحة االدقي	٣ (جيّد)	٦١٠ ج. م.	بنك يعمل ٢٤ ساعة تلفزيون وستالايت
فندق آمون	ميدان السفينكس المهندسين	٢ (مقبول)	٥٩٨ ج. م.	حمام خاص بكل غرفة تلفزيون وستالايت
فندق كليوباترا بالاس	١ شارع البستان وسط البلد	٢ (مقبول)	٤٥٧ ج. م.	٨٤ غرفة موقع ممتاز

كلمات جديدة

مَوقِع location

عَدَد number

نُجوم star

سِعر (ج. أسعار) price

خِدمة (ج. خَدَمات) service

شارِع street

مَطعَم (ج. مَطاعِم) restaurant

كُلّ every

مَجّاني for free, no charge

تَوصيل delivering, transporting

مِن from

إلى to

طَريق road

جيّد = كويّس good

جِدّاً very

مِصر الجَديدة Heliopolis (lit. New Egypt)

خاصّ private

فُطور breakfast

يَعمل (he, it) works, operates

مَقبول acceptable

مُمتاز excellent

أسئلة

اكتب صحّ أو خطأ

١. ماريوت القاهرة أحسن مِن (better, more highly ranked than) فندق بيروت.

٢. فندق المعادي أغلى (more expensive) مِن فندق السفير.

٣. فندق ماريوت القاهرة وفندق بيروت في نفس المنطقة (same area).

٤. هُناك (there is) فطور مجّاني في فندق بيروت.

٥. هناك حمّام خاصّ بكلّ غرفة في ثلاثة فنادق.

٦. هناك خدمة توصيل من وإلى المطار في ثلاثة فنادق.

7. The hotels that have a مقبول designation are cheaper than the hotels that have the جيّد designation.
8. What variable or variables are the hotels ranked by from top to bottom?

قَواعِد

Root types

The great majority of Arabic words are derived from three basic letters, called "roots". In the following table, the words on the right are derived from the three-letter roots on the left. The three root letters have been highlighted in each word.

Roots	Words
ط - ل - ب	طالب
ط - ل - ب	طلبنا
س - ف - ر	سافرَت
س - ف - ر	(جوار) سفر
س - أ - ل	سألوا
س - أ - ل	سؤال
ق - ر - ب	قريب
ق - ر - ب	تقريباً

Roots in Arabic are categorized by whether they are made up of vowels, consonants, or both. You will learn about two different root types in this unit.

Sound roots

Sound roots are made up entirely of consonants. All of the examples above are sound roots. Note that, in Arabic, the *hamza* ء (and all of its forms أ إ ئ ؤ) is considered a consonant.

Hollow roots

Hollow roots have a long vowel for the second root letter. Below are some examples of hollow roots:

Roots	Words
ك-و-ن	كان
ر-و-ح	راح
ض-ي-ع	ضاع

Note that vowels in Arabic can change from vowel to another. You can see this in the examples above, where the past tense verbs all have the letter ا in the middle but the roots have either a و or a ي as their second root letter.

These vowels changes are predictable, and follow regular patterns. You will eventually learn these patterns as you continue to progress in your language skills. For now, just be aware that vowel changes *can* occur.

تمرين رقم ٢

Complete the following table. Remember that *hamza* and all of its forms (ء أ إ ئ ؤ) is considered a consonant in Arabic, and that vowel changes can occur!

Root type	Root	Translation	Verb stem
		he took	أخذ
	ك-و-ن		كان
			ترك
sound			درس
	ع-ل-م		تعلّم
			سأل
	ض-ي-ع		ضاع
	س-ف-ر		سافر

الدرس الرابِع: مذكّرات مايا

اسمي مايا جونسون. عُمري ٢٥ سنة. أنا طالبة في جامعة تكساس في أوستن. عائلتي من مدينة صغيرة في ولاية نيويورك.

اسم والدي هنري، واسم والدتي إليزابث. عُمر والدي ٥٦ سنة وهو أستاذ جامعة، وعُمر والدتي ٥٣ سنة وهي مُوظّفة في بنك.

عندي أخ واحد اسمه ماثيو وأخت واحدة اسمها ميشيل. عُمر ماثيو ١٧ سنة وهو طالب في المدرسة الثانويّة، وعُمر ميشيل ٢٧ سنة وهي موظّفة في شَرِكة.

قبل رحلتي إلى القاهرة بشهرين، حجزت غرفة في فندق على الانترنت. حجزت غرفة فيها حمّام خاصّ، والفُطور في الفندق مجّاني. موقع الفندق ممتاز لكن بعيد قليلاً عن المطار.

وصلت القاهرة يوم الأربعاء الماضي. كانت الرحلة طويلة، وما نِمت كثيراً. أخذت سيّارة تاكسي من المطار الى الفندق.

سائق التاكسي كان لطيفاً جداً وساعدني في حمل حقيبتي الكبيرة. في الفندق طلبت الموظّفة جواز سفري. بحثت عن جواز سفري في حقيبتي الصغيرة ولكن ما وجدته، ثُمّ بحثت في حقيبتي الكبيرة، ولكن ما وجدته أيضاً. ماذا حدث لجواز سفري؟ الله أعلم... تركت الحقيبة في الفندق وأخذت سيّارة تاكسي إلى المطار.

كلمات جديدة

مُذكّرات diary

قبل رِحلتي بشهرين two months before my trip (lit. before my trip by two months)

غُرفة = أوضة room

مَجّاني for free, no charge

قليلاً = شويّة a little

ما did not

نَمت I slept

كَثيراً a lot

ساعَدني he helped me (ساعَد he helped)

حَمل carrying

حقيبة = شَنطة suitcase

طَلَب he asked for, requested

بَحَث (عَن) he looked for

وجدته I found it (وَجَد he found)

ثُمّ = بَعدين then

ماذا = ايه what

حَدث he (it) happened

الله أعلم! God knows!

تَرَك he left

أسئلة

١. أكمل الجدول (Complete the table)

العمَل	العُمر	
طالبة		مايا
		هنري
	٥٣ سنة	إليزابث
		ماثيو
موظّفة في شركة		ميشيل

2. Answer the following questions in English.
   1. When did Maya reserve the room?
   2. How does she describe the location of the hotel?
   3. When did Maya arrive in Cairo?
   4. How does Maya describe the taxi driver?
   5. Where did Maya look for the passport?
   6. What did Maya leave at the hotel?

Arrange the following statements in the order they are found in the passage. The first one is given as an example.

--- – تعمل أخت مايا في شركة.

..١.. – تعمل والدة مايا في بنك.

--- – حجزت مايا غرفة في الفندق.

--- – سائق التاكسي ساعد مايا.

--- – موقع الفندق ممتاز.

--- – وصلت مايا إلى الفندق يوم الأربعاء.

قَواعِد

1. Hollow verb conjugation in the past tense

In Unit 3 we learned how to conjugate sound verbs in the past tense. Hollow verbs conjugate using the exact same endings, but with a different pattern for the middle vowel. Look at the conjugations below – can you see this pattern?

Past tense verb	
كُنت	أنا
كُنّا	إحنا
كُنت	إنتَ
كُنتِ	إنتِ

كُنتوا	انتو
هو	كان
هي	كانت
هُمّ	كانوا

Notice that, for the third-person pronouns in the shaded section (هو/هي/هم), the middle letter ا is not deleted.

For all other pronouns, the middle long vowel changes to a short vowel. This short vowel is sometimes a ُ like in the example above (كان/كُنت). For other verbs like نام (he slept), it is a ِ (نِمت = I slept). For each new hollow root that you learn, try to memorize the vowel change as a part of the verb.

تمرين رقم ١: تصريف الفعل راح في الماضي

Oral (في الصفّ): Conjugate the verb راح – *to go* in the past tense for each pronoun and use it in complete sentences.

مثال (example): أنا - أنا رُحت للمطار

تمرين رقم ٢

With reference to the above discussion, complete the following conjugation table for the two hollow verbs كان and ضاع. Below each verb is its root.

	ضاع ض-ي-ع	نام ن-و-م
أنا	ضِعت	
إحنا	ضِعنا	
إنتَ		نِمت
إنتِ		
إنتو		
هو		
هي		نامِت
هُمّ		

2. Definiteness, possession, and noun-adjective agreement

In Unit 1, we learned that the definite article الـ makes nouns definite. We also learned that proper nouns are considered definite. Check your understanding of this concept by reviewing the table below. Do these categories make sense to you?

Definite noun	Indefinite noun
الفندق	فندق
مايا	طالبة
القاهرة	مدينة

A noun is also considered definite if it is "possessed" (has a possessive ending). Think about the difference between شنطة (a bag) and الشنطة (the bag) and شنطتي (my bag). Both الشنطة and شنطتي refer to specific bags, where شنطة could be any bag. This means that both الشنطة and شنطتي are considered grammatically definite nouns.

This distinction is important, because you learned earlier that adjectives must agree with the nouns they modify in terms of definiteness. If a noun is considered definite – for any reason – then the adjective modifying it must be definite as well.

Definite noun-adjective phrase	Indefinite noun-adjective phrase
الفندق الصغير the small hotel	فندق صغير a small hotel
شنطتي الكبيرة my large bag	شنطة كبيرة a large bag

تمرين رقم ٣

Translate the following noun-adjective phrases into Arabic. Remember that nouns and adjectives agree in gender as well as definiteness.

1. An Egyptian company ....
2. My large family ....
3. The English language ....
4. Our older (bigger) sister ....
5. The new restaurant ....
6. A private bathroom ....

الدرس الخامس

كلمات الوحدة

آسِف sorry
أخلي I leave (خَلّى he left)
أروح I go (راح he went)
الله أعلم! God knows!
إلى to
ان شاء الله God willing
أوّل first
أيّ خدمة Can I help you? (lit. Any service?)
باتكلّم I speak (تكلّم he spoke)
بتتكلمي you speak (تكلّم he spoke)
بَحَث (عَن) he looked for
تَرك he left
تِروحي you (f.) go (راح he went)
تعلم he learned
تَوصيل delivering, transporting
ثُمّ = بَعدين then
جِدّاً very
جيّد = كويّس good
حاجة thing
حَجَز he reserved
حَدث he (it) happened
حقيبة = شَنطة suitcase
حَمّام bathroom
حَمل carrying
خاصّ private
خِدمة (ج. خَدَمات) service
ساعَدني he helped me (ساعَد he helped)
سِعر (ج. أسعار) = ثَمَن (ج. أثمان) price
شارِع street
شَنطة suitcase
صَباح الخير good morning
صَباح النور good morning (response)
صندوق المفقودات lost and found box
ضاع he (it) got lost
طَريق road
طَلَب he asked for, requested
عَدَد number
عَمَل he did
غُرفة = أوضة room
فُطور breakfast
قَبل رِحلتي بشهرين
two months before my trip
(lit. before my trips by two months)
قليلاً = شويّة a little
كثير (ج. كُثار) many

كُلّ every

لازم must, necessary

لو سمحتِ = من فضلِك if you please

ما did not

ماذا = ايه what

مَجّاني for free, no charge

مُذكّرات diary (memoirs)

مَرّة time

مُشكِلة problem

مِصر الجَديدة Heliopolis (lit. New Egypt)

مَطعَم (ج. مَطاعِم) restaurant

مَعاك with you

معايَ with me

مَقبول acceptable

مُمتاز excellent

مُمكِن possible

مِن from

مَوقِع location

نُجمة (ج. نُجوم) star

وجدته I found it (he found وَجَد)

ياه Oh, what's the matter?

يَعمل (he, it) works, operates
(he worked عمَل)

يكون it is, will be (he, it was كان)

قراءة

يقع بيت الشباب "ميراميس" (ميراميس هوستل) في وسط القاهرة، بين نهر النيل ومحطة القاهرة. وهو قَريب مِن سوق "خان الخليلي" ومن المَتحف المِصري. يُمكن الوصول لميراميس بسهولة من مَوقف نجيب وموقف السادات للمترو.

- ١٣ غُرفة نَظيفة ومُكيّفة
- غُرَف عائليّة
- غُرَف لغير المدخّنين
- مَطعَم وخدمة نقل لِمطار القاهرة الدولي

يمكن الحجز في بيت شباب ميراميس عن طريق الإنترنت

أسئلة

1. What type of housing is "ميراميس"?
2. Where is it located?
3. What is it close to?

4. How can one get to "ميراميس"?
5. Describe the different accommodations found in "ميراميس".
6. What does الحجز mean?
7. What non-Arabic words do you recognize?

تمرين رقم ١

Below are excerpts of Maya telling her story. Change the pronouns, possessive endings, and verbs so that you are retelling her story, like in the example below.

١. أنا سافرت لمصر يوم ٢٩ أغسطس.
مايا (هي) سافرت لمصر يوم ٢٩ أغسطس.
٢. بعد الرحلة الطويلة كُنت تعبانة.
٣. أنا تكلمت مع موظف الجوازات.
٤. أخذت تاكسي ورحت للفندق.
٥. لما وصلت الفندق فتّشت على جواز سفري في شنطي.

تمرين رقم ٢

For each of the verbs in the following table, all taken from the texts of this unit, provide a full English translation and identify the stem, the root, and the root type. Some cells have been filled in to help you fill in the rest. All the verbs are in the past tense.

Root type	Root	Stem	Translation	Verb
Sound	أ-خ-ذ	أخذ	and I took	وأخذت (أنا)
				بحثت (أنا)
				تركت (أنا)
	ع-ل-م		you (f.) learned	تعلّمتِ (أنتِ)
				حجَزت (أنا)
	ح-د-ث	حدث	he (it) happened	حدث
			he (it) got lost	ضاع
				طلبت (هي)
				عَملت (أنا)
				كان
	ك-و-ن			كانَت (هي)

				وَتعلّمت (أنا)
				وصلت (أنا)
			and I was	وكُنت (أنا)

Grammar review

You have learned three common constructions in Arabic: the noun-adjective phrase, the إضافة phrase, and the equational sentence. Below are brief summaries of each type of phrase or sentence:

الاسم والصفة (Noun-adjective phrases)

The noun اسم comes first, followed by the adjective صفة. Both must agree in gender, number, and definiteness.

	Adjective	Noun
A big apartment	كبيرة	شقة
The big apartment	الكبيرة	الشقة
Our big apartment	الكبيرة	شقتنا

الإضافة

The إضافة phrase is made up of two or more nouns. Only the last noun can be definite (and don't forget that possessed nouns are considered definite in Arabic!).

	Final noun (definite or indefinite)	Initial noun(s) (indefinite)
My friend's apartment	صاحبي	شقة
A dorm (a house of students)	طلبة	بيت
The door of the bathroom of the apartment	الشقّة	باب حمّام

Equational sentences

The verb "to be" is implied, but not written.

	Noun or indefinite adjective	Initial noun (definite)
Maya is a student.	طالبة.	مايا
The sentence is long.	طويلة.	الجملة

For the following phrases and sentences:

1. Indicate whether each one is إضافة ,اسم وصِفة, or جُملة (sentence).
2. Translate the phrase or sentence into English.

		Phrase or sentence type اسم وصفة، إضافة، جُملة	الترجمة
.١	عائلة كبيرة		
.٢	العائلة كبيرة		
.٣	عائلتي كبيرة		
.٤	عائلتي الكبيرة		
.٥	حقيبتها الكبيرة		

Sociolinguistic Corner

You read in the Sociolinguistic Corner of Unit 2 about some of the differences between مصري and فصحى, like إحنا/نحن and the pronunciation of certain sounds, particularly consonants such as ق، ث، ظ, and so on.

Such a difference is found in the pronunciation of the preposition "with" مع. When a suffix is attached to مع an ا is added in مصري but not in فصحى. This is reflected in the spelling of the preposition in this book:

	فُصحى	مصري
أنا	مَعي	مَعايَ
إحنا	معنا	معانا
إنتَ	مَعَك	مَعاك
إنت	مَعَك	مَعاكِ
إنتو	معكُم	معاكُم
هو	مَعَهُ	مَعاه
هي	معها	معاها
هُمّ	معهُم	معاهُم

تمرين رقم ٣: حضّر في البيت وتكلّم في الصفّ

Create a dialogue with another classmate in which one of you is a hotel receptionist and the other a guest at the hotel.

الوحدة الخامسة
جواز السفر

الدرس الأوّل

تمرين رقم ١

Listen to and repeat the following words out loud.

لون (ج. ألوان) color
أبيض
أسوَد
أحمَر
أخضر
أزرق
بُنّي

اسم الوالِد father's name

اسم الوالِدة mother's name

الاسم الكامِل full/complete name

العُمر age

تاريخ الصدور date of issue

تاريخ الوِلادة date of birth

صندوق المفقودات lost and found box

ضاع he, it got lost

ضَيّع he lost (something)

غير معروف not known

مُدير manager, director

مكان الصدور place of issue/issuance

nationality جنسيّة

passport جواز سفر

number رَقم

place of birth مكان الوِلادة

clothes مَلابِس

passport (office) employee موظف الجوازات

أغنية: البيت الأبيض بابه أحمر

The white house	البيت الأبيض
Its door is red	بابه أحمر،
The red house	البيت الأحمر
Its door is green.	بابه أخضر،
The green house	البيت الأخضر
Its door is brown.	بابه بنّي،
The brown house?	البيت البنّي؟
. . .	. . .
Its door is round.	بابه مدوَّر.

تمرين رقم ٢ (استماع) – Listening

Listen to the audio recording and translate each sentence into English on a separate piece of paper.

تمرين رقم ٣ (القراءة) – Reading

Circle the word that does not belong.

١. والد   أب   والِدة   أخ   وِلادة

٢. جواز سفر   شنطة   طيّارة   مُدير   مطار

٣. أبيض   أخضر   أزرق   أولاد   بُنّي

٤. صندوق المفقودات   أوضة   حمّام   فُندق   شقّة

٥. موظف الجوازات   مُدير   سوّاق   مَطعم   مُهندس

تمرين رقم ٤ (قراءة وكتابة) – Reading and writing

Copy each of the following words/phrases under its appropriate category.

أخضر - موظف الجوازات - مُدير - تاريخ الصدور - أستاذ - أحمر - طالب - أخ - والدة - أزرق - مكان الصدور - والد - أحمر - تاريخ الولادة - أُمّ - جدّ - مطار

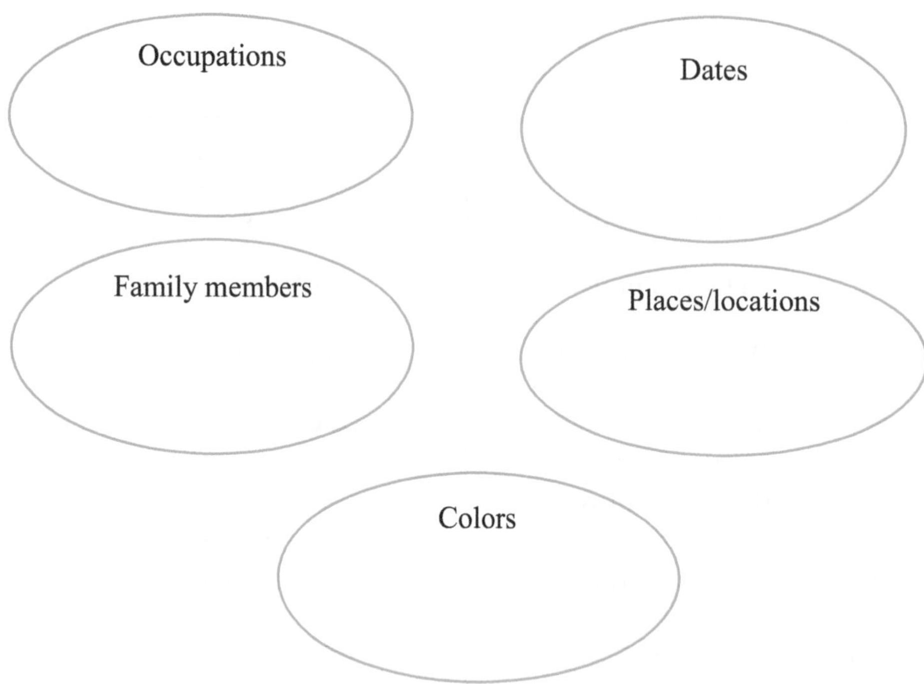

تمرين رقم ٥ (تحضير في البيت وحوار في الصفّ)

Prepare at home and come ready to share your answers with the class.

١. ايه ألوان العَلَم (flag) المصريّ؟ العَلَم الأمريكيّ؟ العَلَمَ البريطاني، علم دولتك؟

٢. ايه لون جواز السفر البريطاني؟ جواز سفر دولتك؟

٣. ايه لون شنطتك؟

٤. ايه لون جاكيتتك؟

٥. ايه لونك المُفضل (favorite)؟ (لوني المُفضل ....)

تمرين رقم ٦ (كتابة)

Fill out the following ID card about yourself and come ready to share it in class.

الاسم الكامِل:	اسم العائلة:
الاسم الأوّل:	الاسم الثاني/الوسط:
اسم الوالِد:	اسم الوالِدة:

تاريخ الولادة:	مكان الولادة:
المِهنة:	الجنسيّة:
لون العُيون (eyes):	لون الشَعر (hair):

الدرس الثاني–مشاهدة: جواز سفري ضاع!

كلمات جديدة

النهاردَه today

غير مَعروف = مِش معروف not known

مِش فاكِر (I) don't remember

أسئلة

صحّ أو خطأ؟

١. جواز سفر مايا ضاع اليوم (النهار ده).
٢. موظّف المطار سأل مايا عن اسم أبوها. (سأل عَن he asked about)
٣. موظّف المطار سأل مايا عن اسم أمّها.
٤. موظّف المطار سأل مايا عن اسم جدّها.
٥. مايا تذكّرت (she remembered) رقم جواز السفر.
٦. مايا تذكّرت مكان صدور جواز السفر.

قَواعِد

More on the active participle

In Unit 3 you learned that words like عايز/عايزة/عايزين and ساكن/ساكنة/ساكنين are called active participles. It's important to remember that active participles behave as nouns in Arabic; they have feminine and masculine forms as well as plural and singular forms. They are not conjugated like verbs.

In مصري, active participles convey the meaning of present tense verbs, as you saw with انتِ عايزة "you (f.) want" and هو ساكِن "he lives".

In this lesson Maya says "آسفة مش فاكرة". Although فاكرة is a feminine singular noun (meaning "one who remembers"), the whole phrase would be translated as "sorry, I don't remember".

With this in mind, translate the following sentences into English.

English translation	Arabic phrase
	نعم، أنا فاكر.
	انتِ ساكنة لوحدِك (alone) في الشقّة؟
	حضرتِك عايزة مُساعَدة؟ (help)
	هي رايحة فين؟

تمرين رقم ١ (تحضير في البيت وحوار في الصفّ)

Write each answer below next to its appropriate question based on the video. Then practice the Q and A with a partner in class.

النهار ده - أمريكيّة - مِش فاكر/ة - مدينة واشنطن - سنة ٢٠١٤ - ايوه لو سمحت

١. نعم؟ حضرتك عايز/عايزة مُساعدة؟ ....
٢. امتى ضاع جواز سفرك؟ ....
٣. الجنسية؟ ....
٤. رقم جواز السفر؟ ....
٥. مكان صدور جواز السفر؟ ....
٦. سنة صدور جواز السفر؟ ....

تمرين رقم ٢

Speaking practice 1 (groups of 3)

You have just arrived at Cairo Airport and are helping a fellow English-speaking passenger communicate with the passport officer who can only speak Arabic. You act as interpreter.

		وصلت منين النهار ده؟ وجنسيتك ايه؟ جواز سفرك لو سمحت.	ضابط الجوازات:
Passenger	I have arrived from Sydney. I am Australian.		
		بس عندك اسم عربي	
	My father is Lebanese but has Australian nationality.		
		والدك راح استراليا امتى؟	
	I don't remember when he went to Australia.		
		وجنسية والدتك إيه؟	

	She is from Palestine but her nationality is unknown.		
		طيب شكراً – اتفضّل الجواز أهلاً وسهلاً في مصر!	

Speaking practice 2

Below is a dialogue between an Irish student in Cairo, who has lost his passport and a local police officer (ضابط شرطة). This dialogue has been jumbled up. Working with a classmate and reading the dialogue aloud, try to match the police officer's questions with the Irish student's replies. The first pair have been done for you (highlighted).

طالب إيرلندي		ضابط شرطة	
لو سمحت؟	a	اسم حضرتك ايه؟	.١
جواز سفري ضاع مني.	b	جنسيتك ايه؟	.٢
اسمي جون سميث.	c	انت فاكر رقم الجواز؟	.٣
أنا إيرلندي.	d	أيوه – أي خدمة؟	.٤
لا مش فاكر رقم الجواز.	e	مش فاكر فين؟ مش كويس!	.٥
ضاع مني امبارح ولكن مش فاكر فين!	f	جواز سفرك ضاع إمتى وفين بالضبط؟	.٦

الدرس الثالِث–استماع: اسمك بالكامل لو سمحتِ!

كلمات جديدة

الحمدُ لِلّه! Thank God!

بالكامِل in full, complete

ناس people

أكيد certainly

طيّب ok

استني! Wait!

مُدير manager

أسئلة

1. Why was the airport employee confused?
2. Where is the father's name according to Maya?
3. Whom does the airport employee need to talk to?

4. What did Maya ask the airport employee at the end?
5. What was the employee's response?

تمرين رقم ١- كتابي (في البيت)

(Complete the following table) أكمل الجدول

	he said	كان he was	
		كان	
	قُلت		أنا
			اِحنا
		كُنت	إنتَ
نِمتِ			إنتِ
			إنتو
			هو
			هي
			هُمّ

تمرين رقم ٢ – شفهي (في الصفّ): تصريف أفعال

Oral: Use the verbs below in complete sentences. Be sure to use as many different pronouns as possible.

تكلّم:
كان:
قال:
درس:
نام:
راح:

قواعِد

Plural patterns

Arabic has many different ways to make singular nouns plural. As you have increased your vocabulary, you may have noticed certain patterns emerging. Arabic plural patterns are generally categorized into two types: *sound plurals* and *broken plurals*.

Sound plurals

One common sound plural pattern is the *feminine sound plural.* You have learned that the *taa' marbuuta* ـة often indicates female gender. Singular nouns ending in ـة are often made plural by replacing the *taa' marbuuta* with the ending – ات. See the examples below:

Feminine sound plural pattern	
Plural (الجمع)	Singular (المُفرَد)
عائلات	عائلة
طيارات	طيارة
جنسيات	جنسية
شركات	شركة
حاجات	حاجة

Broken plurals

Broken plurals are formed by changing the vowels of the word (generally, the consonants are not affected). Broken plurals get their name because the basic letters in the singular noun are "broken apart" in order to form the plural. The English equivalent of broken plurals are words like *goose – geese, man – men,* and *woman – women.*

Below are two common broken plural patterns. As you read the patterns out loud with your teacher or the audio recording, try to identify the pattern you hear.

Broken plural pattern 2		Broken plural pattern 1	
Plural	Singular	Plural	Singular
أيام	يَوم	شُهور	شَهر
أَولاد	وَلَد	دُروس	دَرس
أَلوان	لَون	نُجوم	نِجمة
أَسعار	سِعر	خُطوط	خَطّ

Below are three more plurals. Match each one to the plural pattern number above.

Plural Pattern Number	الجمع	المفرد
	أَرقام	رَقَم
	أَعمار	عُمر
	بُنوك	بَنك

As you continue to learn more vocabulary, you will develop a sense for what type of plural pattern nouns take. For now, try to memorize singular nouns and their plural forms together as a unit.

تمرين رقم ٣ (مُحادثة)

You have forgotten your suitcase (شنطة) at Cairo Airport. Answer the following questions in order to locate your شنطة.

	لون شنطتك إيه؟
	أكيد (are you sure) لونها أحمر؟
	وصلت القاهرة أمتى؟
	اسمك بالكامل لو سمحت؟
	عندك ثلاث اسماء؟
	جنسيتك ايه؟
	طيب - لازم اتكلم مع المُدير (manager)؟

الدرس الرابع: قراءة

النصّ الأوّل

مطار القاهرة الدولي

صندوق المفقودات

١. حقيبة كبيرة لونها اسود باسم السيد احمد سلمان.
العنوان: السالمية، الكويت، مكتوب عليها ملابس للأولاد.
٢. حقيبة يد صغيرة لونها بنّي.
٣. جواز سفر أمريكي باسم مايا هوب جونسون.
٤. تلفون موبايل آي فون لونه احمر.
٥. جاكتة رجالي لونها أسود.
٦. كتاب بعنوان جمهورية افلاطون باسم سليم عبدالله الشافعي.
٧. ساعة يد اوميغا رجّاليّة.

كلمات جديدة

لون color
أسوَد black
مَكتوب written
عَليها on it
مَلابِس clothes
للأولاد (ل + الأولاد) for (the) boys
يَد hand
رِجّالي for men
بُنّي brown
أحمَر red
عُنوان title (also address)

Guess the meanings of the following words and expressions:

مَطار القاهرة الدولي، حقيبة يد، جمهورية أفلاطون، ساعة يَد

أسئلة

١. أكمل الجدول التالي

1. Fill in the empty cells in the following table. Ignore those marked with x's.

الشيء thing, object	اللون	الاسم name (of owner)
حقيبة كبيرة		أحمد سلمان
حقيبة يد صغيرة		xxx
	xxx	مايا هوب جونسون
	بُنّي	xxx
	أحمر	xxx
جمهورية أفلاطون	xxx	

النصّ الثاني: مذكّرات مايا

في المطار ذهبت الى مُوظَّف في قسم المفقودات وقلت له إنّني فقدت جواز سفري. سألني عن اسمي واسم أبي واسم جدّي واسم أمّي واسم عائلتي، ثمّ قال: "إذا المصري ضيّع جواز سفره، دي مشكلة صغيرة، لكن إذا الأمريكي ضيّع جواز سفره، دي مشكلة كبيرة."

جلست، وبحث مُوظَّف المطار في صندوق المفقودات. كان جواز السفر في الصندوق، ولكن كانت هناك مشكلة: اعتقد المُوظَّف أنّ الاسم الثاني هو اسم أبي. ولكن في النهاية أعطاني جواز السفر، وقال لي "أهلاً وسهلاً في مصر".

فرحتُ كثيراً عندما وجدت جواز سفري في المطار. رجعت الى الفندق ونِمت حتّى الساعة الثانية بعد الظهر. كُنت تعبانة جِدّاً.

كلمات جديدة

he went ذَهَب	he thought فكّر
he said قال	end نِهاية
that I إنّني	he gave me أعطاني
he lost ضَيّع (مصري) = فَقَد (فُصحى)	he became happy فرِح
he asked me سَألني	very جداً
if إذا	when عِندَما
this دي	until حَتّى
he sat جَلَس	

أسئلة

1. What is a "big problem", according to the passport employee?
2. Where did the passport employee look for the passport?
3. Why was there a problem after finding the passport?
4. What did the policeman invite Maya for?
5. How long did Maya sleep? Why?

أكتب صحّ (✓) أو خطأ .(✗)

١. الموظّف سأل مايا عن اسم جدّها.

٢. حسب (according to) الموظّف، إذا الأمريكي ضيّع جواز سفره، هذه مشكلة كبيرة.

٣. فكّر الموظّف أنّ الاسم الأوّل هو اسم أب مايا.

٤. في النهاية مايا أخذت جواز السفر.

٥. مايا نامت كثيراً لأنّها وجدت جواز السفر.

قَواعِد

Direct object suffixes

The following three words are complete sentences consisting of a verb, a subject, and an object. Can you break them into their three elements?

I found it وجدته

He asked me سألني

He helped me ساعدني

As you can see, the direct objects ("it" and "me") are suffixes ("-ـه" and "-ـني") which attach to the end of the verb. Because they stand in place of the direct object, they are another type of pronoun in Arabic.

Direct object suffixes look and act almost exactly the same as possessive suffixes, which you learned in Unit 1. The only difference is for the pronoun أنا (my/me) as shown in the table below:

Direct object suffix	Possessive suffix	
he helped me ساعَدني	my age عمري	– ي/– ني
he helped you (m.s.) ساعَدَك	your (m.s.) age عمرَك	– كَ
he helped you (f.s.) ساعَدِك	your (f.s.) age عمرِك	– كِ
he helped him ساعَدُه	his age عمرُه	– هُ
he helped her ساعَدها	her age عمرها	– ها
he helps us ساعَدنا	our age عمرنا	– نا
he helped you (pl.) ساعَدكُم	your (pl.) age عمركُم	– كُم
he helped them ساعَدهُم	their age عمرهُم	– هُم

Now translate the following sentences into English on a separate piece of paper:

(أنا) سألتها أسئلة كثيرة.

(هي) سألتني أسئلة كثيرة.

(هي) سألتنا أسئلة كثيرة.

سألكم أسئلة كثيرة.

(أنا) سألتَك عن (about) عنوان بيتك.

أعطاها جواز السفر.

أعطاني جواز السفر.

أعطانا جواز السفر

وجدني في المطار.

(أنا) وجدته في المطار.

And now translate the following sentences into Arabic on a separate piece of paper:

I asked him about the address.
I asked them many questions.
He gave me the address of his house.
He found it (him) in the suitcase (حقيبة).
I asked you (pl.) many questions.
She found her at (in) the airport.
He gave him her address.
He gave us the address.

الدرس الخامس

كلمات الوحدة

white أبيض	Thank God! الحمدُ لِلّه!
red أحمَر	today النهار دَه
green أخضَر	that I إنّني
if إذا	in full, complete بالكامِل
blue أزرَق	brown بُنّي
wait استنّي	very جِداً
black أسوَد	he sat جَلَس
he gave me أعطاني	until حَتّى
certainly أكيد	this دي

he went ذَهَب	he thought فكّر
for men رِجّالي	he said قال
he asked me سَألني	for (the) boys للأولاد (ل + الأولاد)
he lost ضَيّع	color لون
ok طيّب	manager مُدير
on it عَليها	I don't remember مِش فاكِر
when عِندَما	written مَكتوب
they have عِندهُم	clothes مَلابِس
title (also address) عُنوان	people ناس
not known غير مَعروف = مِش معروف	he slept نام
he became happy فرِح	end نِهاية
he lost فَقَد	hand يَد

تمرين رقم ١: املأ الفراغات (Fill in the blanks)

Following is the entry in Maya's diary that you read in Lesson 4 with a number of words and phrases taken out and placed above it. Copy these words and phrases into the appropriate blanks without looking at the original entry.

أبي، الشاي، الصندوق، المطار، بعد الظهر، مصر، جواز سفري، صغيرة، عائلتي

في المطار ذهبت الى مُوظَّف الجَوازات وقلت له إنّني فقدت . . . .، سألني عن اسمي واسم والدي واسم جدّي واسم والدتي واسم . . . .،
ثمّ قال: "إذا المصري ضيّع جواز سفره، دي مشكلة . . . .،لكن إذا الأمريكي ضيّع جواز سفره، دي مشكلة كبيرة."

جلست، وبحث مُوظَّف الجوازات في صندوق المفقودات. كان جواز السفر في . . . . .، ولكن كانت هناك مشكلة: فكّر المُوظَّف أنّ الاسم الثاني هو اسم . . . .
ولكن في النهاية أعطاني جواز السفر، وقال لي: " أهلا وسهلا في . . . .
فرحتُ كثيراً عندما وجدت جواز سفري في . . . . رجعت الى الفندق ونِمت. نِمت حتّى الساعة الثانية . . . . كُنت تعبانة جداً.

تمرين رقم ٢: كلمات متقاطعة

١٠	٩	٨	٧	٦	٥	٤	٣	٢	١	
										١
										٢
										٣
										٤
										٥
										٦
										٧
										٨
										٩
										١٠

أفقي

١. منطقة (area) في القاهرة

٣. عكس "قليل" أو "شويّة"

٤. الشهر الثامن (eighth) في السنة

٦. تحتاجها (need it) لدخول دولة أجنبيّة (foreign)

٧. موجود في كلّ بيت

٨. مُفرد "أسئلة"

١٠. فيه ١٥ دقيقة؛ من فُصول (seasons) السنة

عمودي

١. تكتبها مايا كلّ يوم؛ ثَمَن

٣. من فصول السنة، بين الشتاء والصيف؛ جمع "شارع"

٥. لون البحر

٦. عكس "بعد"

٨. جمع "مطعم"

٩. ندرسه في الجامعة مع الفيزياء والأحياء والرياضيّات

Sociolinguistic Corner

The past tense (الفعل الماضي) in فصحى and مصري

The past tense conjugations are pronounced slightly differently in مصري and in فصحى. Listen to the audio recording while you read the past tense verb conjugations below for both registers of Arabic. Circle the differences that you notice.

فُصحى		مصري	
درستُ	أنا	درسْت	أنا
درسنا	نَحنُ	درسنا	إحنا
درستَ	أنتَ	درسْت	إنتَ
درستِ	أنتِ	درستِ	إنتِ
درستُم	أنتُم	درستوا	إنتو
درسَ	هو	درس	هو
درسَت	هي	درسِت	هي
درسوا	هُم	درسوا	هُمّ

Remember that مصري is generally spoken, but not written. This means that you will likely see the فصحى versions in writing, but hear the مصري versions in conversation.

تمرين رقم ٣

For each of the verbs in the following table, all taken from the texts of this unit, provide a full English translation and identify the stem, the root, and the root type. Some cells have been filled in to help you fill in the rest. All the verbs are in the past tense.

Root type	Root	Stem	Translation	Verb
hollow	ق–و–ل	قال	You (f.s.) said	قُلتِ
sound				سألني
				قال
	ض–ي–ع	ضيّع		ضيّع
				جلست
			And he searched	وبحث
	ع–ق–د	اعتقد		اعتقَد
			I was	كُنت
				أعطاني
			I was happy	فرحت
				رجعت
	ن–و–م			نِمت

تمرين رقم ٤ (حضّر في البيت وتكلّم في الصفّ)

1. **At home (في البيت)**: Pretend you lost something (passport, book, suitcase, etc.). Prepare a list of useful vocabulary words and questions that you plan to use to help you find the missing item.

Expressions/phrases التعابير	Vocabulary words المفردات

2. **In class (في الصفّ)**: Refer to #1 above and create a dialogue with another classmate in which one of you lost something and the other one is helping to find it.

الوحدة السادسة
المطعم

الدرس الأوّل

تمرين رقم ١

أسيوي Asian
أكل food
أكلة/وجبة food, dish
بَحري from the sea
توصيل delivery
ثلّاجة refrigerator
ثمن cost/price/value
سَريع fast, quick
سَندويشة (ج. سندويشات) sandwich
شِمال left
صيني Chinese
طلب to order, ask for something
مَأكولات foods, dishes
مَشوي baked, grilled

مقلي fried
نوع (ج. أنواع) type
هِندي Indian
يَمين right
ادّيني give me
إزّاي how
تِسلم ايدَك thank you (lit. may your hand be safe)
في رأيَك in your opinion
مُمتاز excellent
مِن عينيّ I'd be happy to, it would be my pleasure (lit. from my eyes)
مِن غير without

Meaning	Comparative (-er, more than)	Adjective
far	أبعَد	بعيد
inexpensive, cheap	أرخص	رخيص
expensive	أغلى	غالي
close by, near	أقرب	قريب
many, a lot	أكثر	كثير

تمرين رقم ٢ (استماع)

Listen to each sentence and write down on a separate piece of paper in English the food/drink item you hear. Some sentences have more than one item.

تمرين رقم ٣ (قراءة وكتابة)

Part 1

Matching (companion website)

Part 2

Translate the matched phrases into English on a separate piece of paper.

تمرين رقم ٤ (قراءة وكتابة)

اكتب عكس كلّ من الكلمات التالية.

Write the opposite of each of the following words.

١. رخيص	٢. بعيد ....
٣. يمين	٤. أبيض ....
٥. كبير	٦. ضيّع ....

تمرين رقم ٥ (محادثة في الصفّ)

Working with a partner, take turns playing the role of a customer and a server. Order as many foods and drinks as possible. Use the following words and phrases in your dialogues.

إِزّاي - ادّيني - من غير - في رأيَك - مُمتاز - مِن عينيّ - تِسلم ايدَك - شُكراً - عفواً

تمرين رقم ٦ (كتابة)

ترجم الجمل التالية إلى العربيّة (Translate the following sentences into Arabic.)

1. The Indian restaurant is cheap but far.
2. In your opinion, how is the fish (dish)?
3. I ordered chicken with rice.
4. He ate cheese and fruit and drank green tea in the morning.
5. In my opinion, grilled chicken is better than (احسن من) fried chicken.

الدرس الثاني–مشاهدة: فيه مطعم قريب؟

كلمات جديدة

أقرب closer

جَعان (ج. جَعانين) hungry

إِزّاي how

غالي expensive

ثاني other (also second)

أرخص cheaper

نوع (ج. أنواع) type
أكتَر more
مِتر meter
روحي go (f.)!
على طول straight
ادخُلي enter (f.)!
يَمين right
حَتوصَلي you will reach, arrive at
شِمال left
مُمتاز excellent
تِعرَفي you (f.) know
ليكِ to you

أسئلة

1. What are the names of the three restaurants mentioned?
2. How is the food at مطعم أمّ حسن described?
3. Which restaurant is cheaper مطعم أمّ حسن or مطعم العُمدة?
4. Which restaurant has more types of food?
5. How far is مطعم أمّ حسن?
6. Is مطعم أمّ حسن on the right or left of the street?
7. How many streets does Maya know in Cairo?

قَواعِد

The comparative

Look at the following sentences from this lesson's dialogue:

Is there a restaurant nearby?	فيه مطعم قريب؟
Umm Hasan's restaurant is closer than the other restaurants.	مطعم أم حسن أقرَب من المطاعم الثانية.

Is the El Umda restaurant cheap?	معطم العمدة رَخيص؟
El Umda is cheaper.	معطم العمدة أرخَص.

These are two examples of how to form the comparative in Arabic. If we are comparing things, such as "closer than", we use the comparative plus the preposition من. Look at the examples below – can you see a pattern?

Comparative	Adjective
أكبَر (من)	كبير
أصغَر (من)	صغير

أَبعَد (من)	بعيد
أَطوَل (من)	طويل
أَغلى (من)	غالي

Just like in English, the adjective "good" and its comparative "better" look nothing alike!

better than	good
أحسَن (مِن)	كويّس

تمرين رقم ١: أكمل الجدول التالي

Meaning	Comparative	Adjective
inexpensive, cheap		رخيص
	أقرب	
		كثير
	أسرَع	

تمرين رقم ٢ (مُحادثة) (pair work and group activity)

In your opinion, what is the best restaurant in town? With a partner, compare your choices – which one has better food? Which one is cheaper? The more creative you are, the more likely you'll be able to convince your classmates that your restaurant really is the best! (أحسن مطعم).

تمرين رقم ٣: فيه مطعم قريب؟

Conversation activity : فيه مطعم قريب؟

Your أستاذ or أستاذة will hand out maps to you. With a partner, take turns playing the roles below to navigate your way to a tasty restaurant.

Person 1

You are جَعان قَوي/جَعانة قَوي and want to find somewhere قريب to eat! Ask your partner if there is a restaurant close by. You might say:

فيه مطعم قريب؟

You can also specify the type of restaurant you want. You might say:

فيه مطعم كويس قريب؟ مطعم غالي؟ رخيص؟ عربي؟ صيني ؟

You will need to listen carefully to the directions that your partner gives you to find your way to the restaurant.

Person 2

Your picky partner needs directions to a specific restaurant. Use the map provided by your teacher to give directions. You can use direction words like:

على طول

أول شارع على اليمين/ثاني شارع على الشمال

المطعم على اليمين/الشمال

Your partner is going to listen to your directions and try to follow along on the map.

الدرس الثالِث-استماع: كل حاجة موجودة في مطعم أم حسن!

كلمات جديدة

تحبّي you like

عندُكو = عندكم you (pl.) have

كُله all, everything

مَوجود present, found

قَهوة coffee

عَصير juice

عَطشان (ج. عَطشانين)

مَية ساقعة cold water

والله by God . . . , the truth is . . .

ثلّاجة refrigerator

مَكسور broken

مَعَلش! don't worry!

عادي ordinary, usual

تِسلم ايدَك thank you (lit. may your hand) be safe

تِطلُبي you ask for, order

وجبة food, dish

في رأيَك in your opinion

فِراخ chicken

مَشوي baked, grilled

خُضار vegetables

لَحمة meat

سَمَك fish

رُزّ rice

مافيش there is not

إدّيني give me

حلو sweet

أَمّ علي، رز بلبن names of desserts

مِن غير without

كَافين caffeine

لبن milk

مِن عينيّ will be happy to (lit. from my eyes)

أسئلة

1. How do you translate the phrase كلّه موجود؟
2. Is there cold water at the restaurant? Why?
3. What did Maya order to drink?
4. Does the restaurant have meat with vegetables?
5. What does Maya order for her main meal?
6. What does she order for dessert?
7. Does the restaurant have decaffeinated coffee?
8. What did Maya order to drink besides the water?

The present tense (المُضارِع)

The present tense in Arabic is conjugated by attaching prefixes (and sometimes both prefixes and a suffixes) to the verb as shown in the following table. Listen to the audio recording as you read the conjugations out loud. What patterns do you notice?

Prefixes and suffixes	Verb: شرب	Verb: حبّ	Pronoun
أ -	I drink أشرب	I like أحبّ	أنا
ن -	we drink نشرب	we like نحبّ	إحنا
ت -	you (m.s.) drink تشرب	you (m.s.) like تحبّ	انتَ
ت - ي	you (f.s.) drink تشربي	you (f.s.) like تحبّي	انتِ
ت - وا	you (pl.) drink تشربوا	you (pl.) like تحبّوا	انتو
ي -	he drinks يشرب	he likes يحبّ	هو
ت -	she drinks تشرب	تحبّ	هي
ي - وا	they drink يشربوا	they like يحبّوا	هُمّ

تمرين رقم ١: كتابي (في البيت)

With reference to the table above, fill in the empty cells in the following table.

تكلّم - يتكلّم		ركب - يركَب	طَلَب - يطلُب	سأل - يسأل	
	أدرُس				أنا

					إحنا
					انتَ
تتكلمي					انتِ
			تطلُبوا		انتو
					هو
		تِركَب			هي
				يسألوا	هُمّ

Now that you have seen the past and present conjugations, verbs will be listed in word lists in their simple past and present forms, i.e. the "he" conjugations, and the English equivalent will be the simplest form of the English verb, the infinitive. So a verb like بتتكلّمي (you (f.s.) speak) will be listed as تكلّم-يتكلّم "to speak".

تمرين رقم ٢: شفهي (في الصفّ)

تصريف الأفعال في المضارِع.

سافر-يسافِر، تكلّم-يتكلّم، وصل-يوصَل، تعلّم-يتعلّم، راح-يروح، خلّى-يخلّي، حَبّ-يحِبّ

الأستاذ: أنا-سافر

طالب: أنا أسافر

الأستاذ: هي

طالب: هي تسافِر، الخ

أغنية سافر دان لبيروت يحكي عربي وياكل توت

تمرين رقم ٣

Part A. Below is a list of some of the phrases from the video. With a partner, read them out loud and try to figure out who said which phrase, مايا ولا الجارسون؟

- اتفضّلي... تحبي تشربي ايه؟
- عندكم ايه؟

- أنا عطشانة.

- والله آسف ما فيش.

- ممكن ميّة عادي لو سمحت.

- تسلم ايدك.

- تحبي تطلبي ايه؟

- طيّب ادّيني خضار باللحمة، ورُزّ.

- في ايه حلو؟

- كل حاجة موجودة: حلويات شرقية، أم علي، رز بلبن . . .

- اديني أم علي لو سمحت . . . فيه قهوة؟

- طبعاً فيه قهوة.

- من عينيّ.

Part B. With your partner, come up with a small skit based on the phrases above. You will need to add your own lines to make sure it makes sense!

الدرس الرابِع: مطاعم القاهرة

وسط البلد/جاردن سيتي

- **جاد** (مأكولات سريعة، مصري) (نجمتين) *خدمة توصيل
- **كشري التحرير** (كشري) (٣ نجوم)
- **مؤمن** (مأكولات سريعة، مصري) (نجمتين) *خدمة توصيل
- **تبولة** (لبناني) (٤،٥ نجوم)
- **كوك دور** (مأكولات سريعة) (نجمتين) *خدمة توصيل
- **تسيباس** (حلويات) (٥ نجوم) *خدمة توصيل

الدُقي/المُهندسين

- **جريل استاشن** (أمريكي) (٣ نجوم)
- **مطعم أسماك قدّورة** (مأكولات بحرية) (٥ نجوم)
- **أبو يوسف السوري** (سوري) (٤ نجوم)
- **الدمياطي** (حلويات) (٤ نجوم)
- **كوك دور** (مأكولات سريعة، سندويشات) (نجمتين) *خدمة توصيل

مدينة نصر/مصر الجديدة

- **باندا هاوس** (أسيوي) (٣ نجوم) *خدمة توصيل
- **سيفود هاوس** (مأكولات بحرية) (٣ نجوم)
- **استاكوزا** (مأكولات بحرية) (٣ نجوم)
- **كوك دور** (مأكولات سريعة) (نجمتين) *خدمة توصيل
- **تشيليز** (أمريكي) (٣ نجوم) *خدمة توصيل
- **مطعم مهراجا الهندي** (أسيوي) (٤ نجوم)

المعادي

- **لوسيلز** (أمريكي) (٤ نجوم)
- **مطعم جوي لاك الصيني** (أسيوي) (٤ نجوم)
- **جوّه البحر** (مأكولات بحرية) (٤،٥ نجوم) *خدمة توصيل
- **أبو شقرة** (مأكولات مصرية) (نجمتين) *خدمة توصيل
- **جاد** (مأكولات سريعة، مصري) (نجمتين) *خدمة توصيل
- **مؤمن** (مأكولات سريعة، مصري) (نجمتين) *خدمة توصيل

الزمالك

- **ساباي ساباي** (أسيوي) (٥ نجوم)
- **اسماك الجمهورية** (مأكولات بحرية) (نجمة واحدة)
- **أبو السيد** (مصري) (٣ نجوم)
- **سبكترا** (إيطالي، مكسيكي) (٣ نجوم) *خدمة توصيل
- **ديدوس** (إيطالي) (٤ نجوم)

كلمات جديدة

مَأكولات foods, dishes

سَريع fast

نجمة (ج. نُجوم) star

توصيل delivery

كُشَري name of an Egyptian dish

تَبّولة name of a dish, typically Lebanese

سَمَك (ج. أسماك) fish

بَحري from the sea

سَندويشة (ج. سندويشات) sandwich

أسيوي Asian

هِندي Indian

صيني Chinese

تمرين رقم ١: أكمل الجدول

Complete the table by writing down the type of restaurant and country as shown in the example.

اسم المطعم	نوع المأكولات
كشري التحرير	مأكولات سريعة، مصري
تبّولة	
تسيباس	
أبو يوسف السوري	
باندا هاوس	
جوّه البحر	
أسماك الجمهوريّة	
ديدوس	

تمرين رقم ٢

The restaurant guide above has many examples of non-human plural nouns.

a. Circle all of the examples you can find, along with any adjectives that modify them.

b. In your own words, what is the rule for non-human plural nouns and agreement?

:النصّ الثاني
مذكّرات مايا

يوم السبت الماضي كنت جوعانة جدّاً. كنت أريد أن آكل كشري في دُكّان الكُشري القريب من الفندق، لكن صديقتي "بريجيت" كانت تريد أن تأكل في مطعم مصري جَيّد وليس في دُكّان الكشري.

بريجيت طالبة بريطانيّة، درست اللغة العربيّة في جامعة إدنبره الاسكتلندية، والآن تدرس العربيّة في القاهرة.

قرّرنا أن نأكل في مطعم "فلفلة" المشهور في وسط البلد. وسط البلد بعيد عن الفندق لذلك ركبنا المترو إلى المطعم.

في المطعم أنا طلبت شاورما دجاج وطلبت بريجيت سمك مشوي مع خضار. كلّمنا الموظّف بالإنجليزيّة واستغرب عندما كلّمناه بالعربيّة. كان يفكّر أنّ كلّ الأجانب يتكلّمون الإنجليزيّة أو لغة أخرى غير العربيّة. ثمّ سألنا أين تعلّمنا العربيّة وهل اللغة العربيّة صعبة. كان لطيفاً جِدّاً.

كلمات جديدة

ماضي past, last

كنت أريد I wanted (lit. I was wanting, desiring)

أنْ to

صَديق friend

لَيْسَ = مِش not

قرّر-يُقرّر to decide

مَشهور famous, well-known

كلّم-يُكلِّم to speak to

استغرب-يستَغرِب to find (something) strange

كان يُفكّر he thought, he was thinking

أنّ that

أجنَبي (ج. أجانِب) foreigner

لُغة language

غَير other than

أخرى = ثانية other, another

ثُمّ = بَعدين then, and then

أيْنَ = فين where

صَعب difficult

أسئلة

1. Who is Bridget?
2. Where did Bridget want to eat?
3. How did they go downtown?
4. What did they eat?
5. What did the restaurant employee find strange?
6. What did he ask Maya and her friend?
7. Arrange the following statements according to their occurrence in the reading passage. The first statement is already indicated with the number ١.

______ مطعم فلفلة مشهور.

______ سأل موظّف المطعم مايا أين تعلّمت اللغة العربيّة.

______١ هناك دكّان كشري قريب من الفندق.

______ ذهبت مايا وصديقتها إلى المطعم بالمترو.

______ درست بريجيت في اسكتلندا

______ تكلّم موظّف المطعم باللغة الإنجليزيّة.

______ تدرس بريجيت في القاهرة.

______ أكلت مايا شاورما دجاج.

قَواعِد

The particle أنْ in فصحى

Look at the sentences and their translations below. What do you notice about the word أنْ and the words around it?

I wanted to eat	كنت أريد أن آكل
She wanted to eat	كانت تريد أن تأكل
We decided to eat	قرّرنا أن نأكل

The word أن is a "particle". A particle is a word that serves a grammatical purpose, but doesn't really have any meaning on its own. In the sentences above, the particle أن comes in between two verbs.

The verb that *follows* أن must always be in the present tense. Reread the examples above to verify that for yourself. As you read, can you figure out which tenses the verb *before* أن can be?

تمرين

With your partner, go back through the text and find all examples of the particle أن. Circle the particle along with the verbs surrounding it, then translate them into English.

Adjectives with إضافة phrases

You have already learned that the noun comes before the adjective in Arabic noun-adjective phrases. But where does the adjective go if the noun being modified is part of an إضافة construct? Look at the following example:

دُكّان الكشري القريب

دكّان الكشري "the *koshary* shop" is a construct phrase and القريب is the adjective that modifies it. Because دكّان الكشري is definite, the adjective is definite.

There are four more such phrases (construct + adjective) in Maya's diary of this lesson. Can you find them?

الدرس الخامس

كلمات الوحدة

أجنَبي (ج. أجانِب) foreigner

أخرى = ثانية other, another

ادخُلي! enter (f.)!

ادّيني give me

أرخص cheaper

إزّاي how

اِستغرب-يستَغرب to find (something) strange

أسيوي Asian

أقرب closer

أكتَر more

أمّ علي، رز بلبن names of desserts

أنْ to

أنّ that

أيْنَ = فين where

بَحري from the sea

تَبّولة name of a dish, typically Lebanese

تسلم ايدَك thank you (lit. may your hand be safe)

توصيل delivery

تاني other (also second)

تلّاجة refrigerator

ثُمّ = بَعدين then, and then

جَعان (مصري) = جَوعان (فُصحى) hungry

حَبّ-يحِبّ to like, to love

حلو sweet

خُضار vegetables

رُزّ rice

روحي go (f.)!

سَريع fast

سَندويشة (ج. سندويشات) sandwich

شِمال left

صَديق friend

صَعب difficult

صيني Chinese

طَلَب-يطلُب to ask for, order

عادي ordinary, usual

عِرف-يعرِف to know

عَصير juice

عطشان (ج. عطشانين) thirsty

على طول straight on

عندُكو = عندكُم you (pl.) have

غالي expensive

غَير other than

فَرخة (ج. فِراخ) chicken

في رأيَك in your opinion

قرّر-يُقرّر to decide

قَهوة coffee

كافين caffeine

كان يُفكّر he thought, he was thinking

كُشَري name of an Egyptian dish

كلّم-يُكلِّم to speak to

كُله all, everything

كنت أريد
I wanted (lit. I was wanting, desiring)

لبن milk

لَحمة meat

لُغة language

لَيْسَ = مِش not

ليكِ to you

ماضي past, last

مافيش there is not

مَأكولات foods, dishes

مِتر meter

مَشهور famous, well-known

مَشوي baked, grilled

مَعَلش! don't worry!

مَكسور broken

مُمتاز excellent

مِن عينيّ
will be happy to (lit. from my eyes)

مِن غير without

مَوجود present, found

مَية ساقعة cold water

نجمة (ج. نُجوم) star

نوع (ج. أنواع) type

هِندي Indian

والله . . . by God . . . , the truth is . . .

وجبة food, dish

وِصِل-يوصَل to reach, arrive at

يَمين right

مَطعَم قدّورة

السندوتشات

الثَمَن بالجنيه

فول/فلافل ٣
فول/فلافل + بيض مَقلي ٥
فول/فلافل + بطاطس مَقلية ٤
فول + فلافل ٤
جِبنة مقليّة .... ٤،٥
برجر مايونيز وكاتشب .... ٨،٥
برجر جِبنة وبيض ١٠

الشاورما

شاورما لحم .... الوسط: ١٣ ، الكبير ١٧
شاورما فراخ .... الوسط: ١٤ ، الكبير ١٨
شاورما مِكس .... الوسط: ١٤ ، الكبير ١٨

الوجبات

ربع فراخ + أرز بسماتي + خبز سلطة + كولا ٢٩
نص فراخ + أرز بسماتي + خبز + سلطة + كولا ٣٩
صوابع كفتة + أرز بسماتي + خبز + سلطة + كولا ٣٨

الحلويات

كريم كراميل ١٠
سلطة الفَواكه ١٧
أُمّ علي بالمُكَسّرات ١٩

المشروبات

كولا – سفن أب – بيبسي – فانتا ٧
عَصير فريش: برتقال – تفاح – فراولة – مانجو ١٠
شاي–شاي أخضر – شاي بالنعناع ٧
نسكافيه – قهوة تركي – كابشيونو ١٠

أسئلة

1. What are the main categories that the menu of مَطعم قدّورة consists of?
2. Which words do you recognize as borrowed from English or another Western language? (There are at least 16 words.)
3. Can you guess the meanings of
   a. الوَجَبات
   b. المَشروبات
   c. عَصير فريش
4. What is the least expensive item on the menu? What is the most expensive item?
5. How many kinds of dessert are there? What are they?

Sociolinguistic Corner

1. The Present Tense (الفعل المضارع) in فصحى

The present tense in فصحى is similar to the present tense in مصري. The only difference is that the verb conjugations for أنتِ – أنتم – هم can have an additional ـن ending. Listen to the recording as you look at the examples below:

The present tense in فصحى	
أشرب	أنا
نشرب	نَحنُ
تشرب	أنتَ
تشربين/تشربي	أنتِ
تشربون/تشربوا	أنتُم
يشرب	هو
تشرب	هي
يشربون/يشربوا	هُم

There are grammatical rules for when these conjugations have the additional -ن ending and when they don't. You will eventually learn these rules as you continue your Arabic studies. For now, simply note that both options (with the ـن and without it) have the same meaning.

2. Expressing "to want" in both فصحى and مصري

You have learned that مصري uses the active participle عايز to express "wanting". In فصحى, the regularly conjugated verb أرادَ – يُريد is used. Here is the full conjugation of the verb in the past and present tenses.

Present Tense	Past Tense	Pronoun
أُريد	أَرَدتُ	أنا
نُريد	أَرَدنا	نحن
تُريد	أَرَدتَ	أنتَ
تُريدين	أَرَدتِ	أنتِ
تُريدون	أَرَدتُم	أنتم
يُريد	أَرادَ	هو
تُريد	أَرادَت	هي
يُريدون	أَرادوا	هم

You learned in Lesson 4 that the particle أن is used in فصحى to separate two verbs like أريد أن آكل "I want to eat". No such particle is used in مصري. Compare فصحى and مصري in this respect.

	مصري	فُصحى
I wanted to eat	كنت عايز آكل	كنت أريد أن آكل
She wanted to eat	كانت عايزة تاكُل	كانت تريد أن تأكل
We decided to eat	قرّرنا ناكُل	قرّرنا أن نأكل

تمرين (حضّر في البيت وتكلّم في الصفّ)

Create a dialogue with another classmate in which

a. one of you asks directions to a place and the other gives those directions, or
b. one is a waiter and the other a customer in an Arab restaurant.

الوحدة السابعة
السكن

الدرس الأوّل

تمرين رقم ١

Listen to the recording and practice pronouncing the words below.

بيت	شقّة	أُوضة (ج. أُوَض)
اسانسير	فُندق	بيت طلبة

بَلكونة
مَطبَخ
ANNOUNCEMENT
GARAGE SALE
$50
إعلان
شَقّة (ج. شُقَق) فندقيّة
سرير (ج. سَرايِر)
دولاب (ج. دَواليب)
كُرسي (ج. كَراسي)
طبق (ج. أطباق)
$$
رخيص
$$$$
غالي
ترابيزة (ج. ترابيزات)
بوتاجاز
كوب (ج .أكواب)

اتّصَل-يتّصِل to contact, get in touch with

اِشتَرى-يَشتَري to buy

اعتقَد-يعتَقِد to believe

أنتقل-يَنتَقِل to move

دَفَع-يدفَع to pay

رِكِب-يركَب to ride

سَأَل-يسأَل to ask

سَكَن-يسكُن to live

عرَف-يَعرِف to know

قال-يَقول to say

قرأ-يَقرأ to read

نَظَّف-يُنَظِّف to clean

تكييف air-conditioning

جاهِز ready

جَديد new

خُصوصاً especially

شَهريّاً monthly

فاضي empty, unfurnished

فَخم luxurious

كَهرَباء electricity

مَدخل entrance

مَفروش furnished

نَظيف clean

للاتّصال (ل + ال + اتّصال) for contacting, calling

للاستعلام (ل + ال + استِعلام) for information

للإيجار (ل + الإيجار) for rent

للسكن (ل + ال + سَكَن) for living, residence

للبيع (ل + ال + بيع) for sale

تمرين رقم ٢ (استِماع)

Each of the following sentences has at least one of the vocabulary words above. Listen carefully and write down on a separate piece of paper the meaning of each word in English.

تمرين رقم ٣ (قراءة)

Circle the word that does not belong in each row.

١. سكن	كهرباء	اشترى	انتقل
٢. كُرسي	سرير	دولاب	فُندُق
٣. إعلان	سيّارة	مِترو	اوتوبيس
٤. نظيف	غالي	طبق	فَخم
٥. مطبخ	إيجار	حمّام	أوضة

تمرين رقم ٤ (قراءة وكتابة)

Give the singular of each of the following words and its English equivalent.

Plural – الجمع	Singular – المُفرد	Translation – الترجمة
١. أُوَض		
٢. شُقق		
٣. سراير		
٤. كراسي		
٥. أطباق		

تمرين رقم ٥ (قراءة وكتابة)

Part 1

Matching (companion website)

Part 2

Translate the matched phrases into English on a separate piece of paper

تمرين رقم ٦ (قَواعِد)

Notice the construction of the word للاتّصال – *"to call"* below, which literally means *"for the contacting"*. This word is made up of two parts: لِـ + الاِتّصال. When الـ follows the preposition لِ, the *alif* is not written.

ل + ا ل + اتّصال = للاتّصال

Now complete the following equations and translate to English as shown in the examples:

for information لـ + الـ + استِعلام = للاستعلام

to, for the house لـ + الـ + بيت = للبيت

١. لـ + الـ + إيجار =

٢. لـ + الـ + سَكَن =

٣. لـ + الـ + شقة =

٤. لـ + الـ + مطبخ =

٥. لـ + الـ + جامعة =

تمرين رقم ٧: (كتابة) ترجِم إلى العربيّة

1. Cost: 2,500 Egyptian pounds (جنيه مصري) monthly.
2. An apartment ready for living.
3. House for rent.
4. Apartment close to the metro.
5. New and luxurious hotel apartment for rent.
6. A house for sale.

تمرين رقم ٨ (كتابة ومحادثة)

First label the different rooms and items in the following diagram and then discuss your findings with a partner in class.

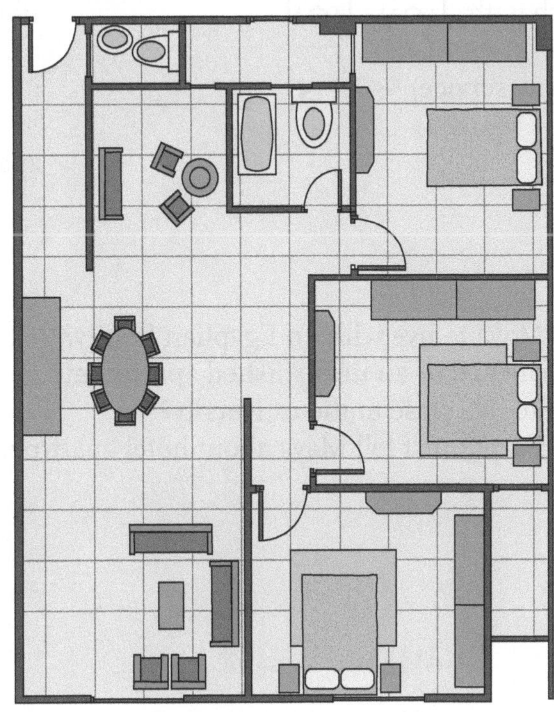

الدرس الثاني-مشاهدة: حَتسكني ف ين؟

كلمات جديدة

سَكَن-يسكُن to live

فكّر-يِفَكَّر to think

اعتقَد-يعتَقِد to believe

صَعب difficult

عادةً usually

حَد one, someone (with negation, anyone)

غَريب stranger

مَفروش furnished

فاضي empty, unfurnished

مِشي-يِمشي to walk

رِكِب-يِركَب to ride

مِترو subway, underground

وَلّا or

شَقّة (ج. شُقَق) apartment

شقة فندقيّة hotel apartment

رخيص cheap

لاقى-يِلاقي to find

مُمكن possible

إعلان (ج. إعلانات) ad, announcement

للإيجار (ل + الإيجار) for rent

استنّى-يِستنّى to wait

خلّيني let me

شاف-يشوف to see

كَلِّم-يِكَلِّم to speak to

شُكراً جَزيلاً thanks a lot

اتّصَل-يِتّصِل to contact, get in touch with

أي خدمة don't mention it (lit: any service)

أسئلة

1. Why is it difficult for Maya to live with an Egyptian family?
2. Does Maya want a furnished or an unfurnished apartment?
3. Why does Maya want to live close to the university?
4. What does the hotel receptionist tell Maya about hotel apartments?
5. What is a good idea?
6. What did the ad say?

قَواعِد

1. Expressing the future (المُستقبَل) in مصري

The future tense in مصري is created by attaching the prefix حَ directly to the present tense verb. The following table shows the conjugation of the verb راح-يروح with all subject markers.

حاروح	أنا
حَنروح	إحنا
حَتروح	إنتَ
حَتروحي	إنتِ
حَتروحوا	إنتو
حَيروح	هو
حَتروح	هي
حَيروحوا	هُمّ

تمرين رقم ١: تصريف أفعال في المستقبل (شفهي في الصفّ)

Speaking (in class): Convert the following verbs to the future tense in مصري and then use them in complete sentences.

يسكُن، يشرَب، يتكلِّم يسافِر

تمرين رقم ٢: ترجم للمصري (شفهي في الصفّ)

a) Maya will live with Salma in an apartment in Cairo.
b) I will travel to Cairo tomorrow.
c) My brother will work in Beirut next year (السنة الجاية).
d) I will visit (زار–يزور) my mother next month.

More on the present tense in مصري: the prefix بـ

The prefix بـ is commonly attached to present tense verbs in مصري. You heard this in the استِماع.

بافكّر أسكن مع عيلة.

ما بتحبّش حَد غريب يسكن معاها.

باحبّ أمشي.

Note that not every present tense verb has a بـ prefix. Can you tell which verbs have the بـ prefix and which ones do not? You will learn more about how to use بـ later in this book.

Verb negation

You have learned that the word *mish* is used in مصري to negate sentences as in,

I am not a student. أنا مش طالب.

مش is the equivalent of English *not*. Other examples of its use are:

not big	مش كبير	big	كبير
not here	مش هِنا	here	هنا
not from Egypt	مش من مصر	from Egypt	من مصر
not living in Egypt	مش ساكن في مصر	living in Egypt	ساكن في مصر

You have also learned that in order to express the idea of *there is not* or *there are not*, مصري uses ما فيش, as in,

There isn't any snow. ما فيش ثلج.

There are no buses in the street. ما فيش أوتوبيسات في الشارع.

ما فيش is the negative equivalent of فيه "there is, there are", with ما placed before the word to be negated and ش after it.

عند and مع, which are used for possession, are negated the same way:

I don't have (own) ما عنديش	I have (own) عندي
I don't have (with me) ما معيش	I have (with me) معي

The "ما-ش "sandwich" is used to negate verbs, with ما before the verb and ش after it.

he doesn't travel	ما بيسافرش	he travels	بيسافر
we didn't arrive	ما وصلناش	we arrived	وصلنا
I didn't study	ما درستش	I studied	درست
she doesn't ask	ما بتسألش	she asks	بتسأل

تمرين رقم ٣

Answer the following questions in the negative. The first one has been done for you.

لا - أنا ما سألِتش أختي امبارح.	انت سألت أختك امبارح؟	١.
	أمّك بتأكل لحم؟	٢.
	أخوك أخذ التأشيرة؟	٣.
	مايا بتدرس رياضيّات؟	٤.
	انت سافرت مصر يوم السبت؟	٥.
	هي بتحبّ حد يسكن معاها في الشقّة؟	٦.

تمرين رقم ٤ (تكوين جُمل قصيرة)

Use the following words in short sentences and come ready to share them with the class.

١. انا بافكّر اسكن في..

٢. انا بافكّر..

٣. اعتقد..

٤. ايه رأيك..

٥. خليني اشوف..

٦. هي حتتصل بـ..

الدرس الثالث–استماع: عندك أوضة للإيجار؟

النصّ الأوّل

كلمات جديدة

تَكَلِّم–يِتكَلّم to speak

نَظيف clean

رَئيسي main

لَوَحدِك by yourself

كُرسي (ج. كَراسي) chair

ترابيزة (ج. ترابيزات) table

سرير (ج. سَرايِر) bed

دولاب (ج. دَواليب) cupboard

بوتاجاز cooker

تكييف air-conditioning

أسئلة

1. How does Salma (the woman Maya speaks to over the phone) describe the apartment?
2. How far is it from the university?
3. Who lives with Salma?
4. What furniture does the apartment have?
5. What does it not have?

النصّ الثاني

كلمات جديدة

دَفَع–يِدفَع to pay

كَهرَبا electricity

كلُّنا all of us

مَع بَعض together

weak ضَعيف	I came جيت
last أخير	the whole time طول الوَقت
seriously بِجَدّ	friend صاحِب (ج. أصحاب)
to think افتَكَر-يِفتِكِر = فكّر-يِفَكَّر	except الّا
I thought you . . . . . . افتَكَرتِك	word كِلمة
to come جِه-ييجي	

أسئلة

1. How much is the monthly rent?
2. Who pays for electricity?
3. Does the apartment have internet?
4. What did Salma tell Maya about her Arabic?
5. What is the problem that Maya mentions?
6. What was Salma's reaction?

تمرين رقم ١: ترجم إلى الإنجليزيّة (Translate into English)

١. العائلات المصريّة عادة ما بتحبّش حَد غريب يسكن معاها في نفس البيت.

٢. باحبّ أمشي.

٣. فيها كراسي وسرير ودولاب، بس ما فيهاش ترابيزة.

٤. لكن الانترنت مش غالي قوي.

٥. وما بنعرفش من الإنجليزي الا كلمتين.

قَواعِد

Root types: doubled roots in مصري

You learned about sound and hollow roots in Unit 4. Another root type in Arabic is the doubled root, which has the same letter for its second and final root letters. One common doubled root is ح – ب – ب, from which the verb "to like, love" is derived.

Listen to the audio recording of the conjugation of حبّ in الماضي and المُضارِع.

	حَبّ (ماضي)	يحبّ (مُضارِع)
أنا	حَبّيت	باحِبّ (بَحِبّ)
إحنا	حبّينا	بِنحِبّ

أنتَ	حَبّيت	بِتحِبّ
أنتِ	حَبّيتِ	بِتحِبّي
أنتو	حَبّيتوا	بِتحِبّوا
هو	حَبّ	بيحِبّ (بِحِبّ)
هي	حَبِّت	بِتحِبّ
هم	حَبّوا	بيحِبّوا (بِحِبّوا)

As you have noticed, for doubled verbs المضارع is conjugated like regular sound verbs, with no spelling changes. In الماضي, however, some pronouns have an additional vowel added to their conjugations, as you can tell from the spelling.

تمرين رقم ٢ (شفهي في الصفّ)

A. Each pair will play the role of Maya and Salma talking over the phone and prepare a mini dialogue following these guidelines:

Pair #1: Answering the phone in Arabic (ألو؟ مين بيتكلّم . . . ؟)

Pair #2: Self introductions, purpose of call (انا اسمي . . . . ، عندك . . . . للإيجار؟)

Pair #3: Obtaining location details about rental (بعيد/قريب، عنوان، شارع . . . ؟)

Pair #4: Obtaining details about furniture (مفروشة، فاضيّة، ثلاجة، ترابيزة، . . .)

Pair #5: Rent and utilities (كم الأجرة، مع الكهربا، الميّة، الانترنت . . .)

Pair #6: Last question and farewells (سؤال أخير . . . .، شكراً، مع السلامة . . .)

B. Now form a continuous dialogue by starting from the beginning (Pair #1) to the end (Pair #6).

الدرس الرابِع

قراءة: النصّ الأوّل

للإيجار

بين فيصل والهرم شقه مفروشة، إيجار جديد، ١٥٠ متر، ٣ غُرَف، رسبشن، حمّامين ومطبخ سوبر لوكس، بُرج فخم، مَدخل شيك.

السعر ٢٥٠٠ شهريّاً

للاستعلام تلفون 01000269856

للإيجار
شقة، ١٩٥ متر، مفروشة بالكامل، ٣ غُرف نوم، منها غرفة ماستر، حمّامين، مطبخ كبير، ورسبشن. بلكونة كبيرة وفيو مُباشر لنادي الصيد في الدقّي. جاهزة للسكن
السعر ١٥٠٠٠ شهريّاً
للاتّصال تلفون 01000269856

للإيجار
شقّة سوبر لوكس مكيّفة، ١١٥ متر، غرفتين مع حمّام، بُرج، اسانسير على شارع زغلول الرئيسي
الإيجار ٢٥٠٠ جنيه شهريّاً
للاستعلام 0111456849 او 01015122771

كلمات جديدة

- غُرفة (ج. غُرَف) = أوضة
- جَديد new
- بُرج tower
- فَخم luxurious
- مَدخَل entrance
- شَهريّاً monthly
- مَطبَخ kitchen
- للاستعلام (ل + ال + استِعلام) for information
- بالكامل (ب + ال + كامِل) completely
- غُرفة (ج. غُرَف) نوم bedroom
- بَلكونة balcony
- مُباشِر direct
- جاهِز ready
- للسكن (ل + ال + سَكَن) for living, residence
- للاتّصال (ل + ال + اتّصال) for contacting, calling
- اسانسير elevator, lift

أسئلة

1. The apartment ad includes at least 11 words that are clearly borrowed from English or another European language. Make a list of these words.
2. The first apartment is located between Faysal and al-Haram. Where are the other two apartments located?
3. Which apartment is the most expensive?
4. Which is the least expensive?
5. Which two apartments are advertised by the same real estate office?

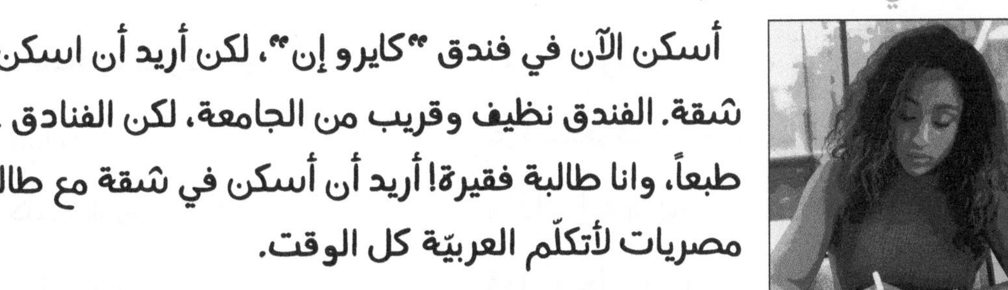

النصّ الثاني: مذكّرات مايا

أسكن الآن في فندق "كايرو إن"، لكن أريد أن اسكن في شقة. الفندق نظيف وقريب من الجامعة، لكن الفنادق غالية طبعاً، وانا طالبة فقيرة! أريد أن أسكن في شقة مع طالبات مصريات لأتكلّم العربيّة كل الوقت.

أريد شقّة قريبة من الجامعة. لا أريد أن أركب تاكسي كلّ يوم. طبعاً من الممكن أن أركب الأوتوبيس أو المترو. التذكرة رخيصة، وهناك أوتوبيس أو مترو كلّ خمس أو عشر دقائق، لكن أحبّ المشي، خصوصاً لأنّ الطقس هنا ممتاز في هذه الأيّام.

قرأت إعلاناً على الانترنت عن غرفة للإيجار في شقّة. كلّمت طالبة اسمها سلمى وسألتها عن الغرفة، فقالت إنّها تسكن في شقّة مع طالبة أخرى وهناك غرفة للإيجار وقالت إنّ الغرفة نظيفة ومفروشة وفيها سرير ودولاب. ذهبت إلى الشقّة والتقيت بسلمى وصاحبتها رانية، ورأيت الغرفة. قالت سلمى إنّها آسفة لأنّ الملابس والكُتُب والأطباق وأكواب الشاي في كلّ مكان. وقالت إنّها سَوفَ تنظّف الشقّة بعد يوم أو يومين.

أنا الآن لا أعرف ماذا افعل. أخاف أن تبقى ألأطباق وأكواب الشاي في كلّ مكان. ولكن . . .

كلمات جديدة

أراد-يُريد to want

فَقير poor

اِشتَرى-يَشتَري to buy

سَيّارة car

يُمكن is possible

أوتوبيس bus

مِترو metro

هُناك there is, there are

خُصوصاً especially

طَقس weather

هذه (هاذِه this, these (pronounced

يوم (ج. أيّام) day

قرأ-يَقرَأ to read

سَأَل-يسأَل to ask

قالت إنّها she said that she

أخرى another (f.)

التقى-يَلتَقي to meet	نَظَّف-يُنَظِّف to clean
رأى-يَرى = شاف-يشوف to see	الآن = دِلوَقتِ now
مَلابِس clothes	عرَف-يَعرِف to know
كِتاب (ج. كُتُب) book	ماذا = إيه what
طبق (ج. أطباق) dish	فعل-يفعل to do
كوب (ج. أكواب) drinking glass	خاف-يَخاف to be afraid
سَوفَ = حَ will	بَقي-يَبقى to remain

Note about آ

It was mentioned in Unit 4, Lesson 1, that the symbol آ, called *madda* (مَدّة), is a combination of hamza and ألف.

The reason مَدّة was not introduced in Unit 1 is that it is quite rare and you will not encounter many occurrences of it in this book. Some of the most common words with مَدّة are الآن, آسف and القُرآن. If you are not sure, ask your teacher or a native speaker to pronounce these words for you.

أسئلة

صحّ أو خطأ؟

١. مايا لا تريد أن تسكن في فندق لأنّها طالبة فقيرة.

٢. تريد مايا أن تسكن في شقّة مع طالبات عربيّات حتى تتكلّم الإنجليزيّة.

٣. مايا لا تريد أن تشتري سيّارة.

٤. هناك أوتوبيس أو مترو كلّ ساعة تقريباً.

٥. مايا تحبّ المشي.

٦. صاحبة مايا اسمها رانية.

٧. كانت الغرفة نظيفة.

٨. شربت مايا الشاي مع سلمى ورانية.

٩. رتّب الجمل حسب ورودها في النصّ.

Arrange the following statements in the order they are found in the passage. The first one is given as an example.

- التقت مايا بسلمى ورانية. ....
- الطقس ممتاز في القاهرة.
- مايا تريد أن تسكن في شقّة. ......١......

- مايا لا تريد أن تشتري سيّارة. ....
- مايا لا تعرف ماذا تفعل ....
- هناك ملابس أطباق وكتب وأكواب الشاي في كلّ مكان في شقّة سلمى. ....

قَواعِد

Negation of المُضارع in فصحى

المُضارع in فُصحى is negated with لا, which is placed before the verb as in لا أريد أن أركب تاكسي كلّ يوم "I do not want to ride (take) a taxi every day."

Now translate the following sentence into English:

أنا الآن لا أعرف ماذا افعل.

Expressing المُستَقبَل (the future) in فصحى

In فصحى the future tense is formed by using the word سَوفَ before the present tense verb. This is sometimes shortened to a simple prefix سَـ. Compare the فصحى and مصري versions in the table:

	فُصحى	مصري
She will clean	سَتنظّف، سَوف تنظّف	حَتنظّف

More uses of أنْ

In the last unit, you saw that the word أنْ is a particle that can come between two verbs in فصحى. You also learned that the verb following أنْ must always be in the present tense. Below is another example where أنْ is used. As you read, what do you notice about the words coming before and after أنْ? What is the difference between its use here and in the last unit?

طبعاً من الممكن أن أركب الأوتوبيس. Of course, it is possible to ride the bus.

One thing you should have noticed is that أنْ is still followed by a present tense verb. The difference between its use here and in Unit 6 is what comes before it: the expression من المُمكن.

There are a few expressions like من المُمكِن "it is possible, that, to", which require the use of أن such as من الصعب "it is difficult", من السهل "it is easy", and من اللازم "it is necessary".

تمرين (كتابة)

On a separate piece of paper, write four sentences in which you use the four expressions: من الممكن، من الصعب، من السهل، من اللازم and a fifth sentence where أن is preceded and followed by a verb.

The case system in فُصحى

In Maya's diary, you came across the sentence:

قرأت إعلاناً على الانترنت.

You may have noticed that the word إعلان has an additional اً ending to it. This ending is called a "case ending", and it is part of the case system of فُصحى.

Arabic is not the only language with a case system – if you have studied Russian or German, then you would be familiar with the concept of case. Case endings are simply additional suffixes on words which denote what role they play in the sentence. The Arabic case system, called إعراب, occurs in فصحى. In مصري and other Arabic dialects no such system exists.

There are many rules governing how to assign case endings to words, which you will learn as you progress in your Arabic studies. For now, just know that إعلان and إعلانا are two forms of the same word, with no difference in meaning. The same is true of صباح and صَباحا which you saw in Unit 3. As you continue to read, you will see other examples of case. Try to focus on the parts of the word that you recognize, and ignore any additional markings that are unfamiliar to you.

الدرس الخامس

كلمات الوحدة

اتّصَل-يِتّصِل to contact, get in touch with

أخذ-ياخُذ to take

أخرى another (f.)

أخير last

اسانسير elevator, lift

استنّى-يِستنّى to wait

اِشترى-يَشتَري to buy

اعتقَد-يعتَقِد to believe

إعلان (ج. إعلانات) ad, announcement

افتكَر-يِفتِكِر = فكّر-يِفكّر to think

افتكَرتِك... I thought you . . . .

الّا except

الآن = دِلوَقتِ now

التقى-يَلتَقي to meet

إنّها that she

أوتوبيس bus

أي خدمة don't mention it (lit. any service)

بالكامل (ب + ال + كامِل) completely

بِجَدّ seriously

بُرج tower

بَقي-يَبقى to remain

بَلكونة balcony

بوتاجاز cooker

ترابيزة (ج. ترابيزات) table

تَكَلّم-يِتكَلّم to speak

تكييف air-conditioning

جاهِز ready

جَديد new

جِه-ييجي to come

جيت I came

حَد one, someone (with negation, anyone)

خاف-يخاف to be afraid

خُصوصاً especially

خلّيني let me

دَفَع-يِدفَع to pay

دولاب (ج. دَواليب) cupboard

رأى-يَرى = شاف-يشوف to see

رَئيسي main

رخيص cheap

رِكِب-يِركَب to ride

سُؤال question

سَأَل-يسأَل to ask

سألتها I asked her

سرير (ج. سَرايِر) bed

سَكَن-يِسكُن to live

سَوفَ = حَ will

سَيّارة car

شاف-يِشوف to see

شَقّة (ج. شُقَق) فندقيّة hotel apartment

شُكراً جَزيلاً thanks a lot

شَهريّاً monthly

صاحِب friend

صَعب difficult

ضَعيف weak

طبق (ج. أطباق) dish

طَقس weather

طول الوَقت the whole time

عادةً usually

عرَف-يَعرِف to know

غُرفة (ج. غُرَف) نوم = أوضة (ج. أوَض) نوم bedroom

غَريب stranger

فاضي empty, unfurnished

فَخم luxurious

فعَل-يفعل to do

فَقير poor

فكّر-يِفَكَّر to think

قال-يَقول to say

قرأ-يَقرأ to read

كِتاب (ج. كُتُب) book

كُرسي (ج. كَراسي) chair

كَلِّم-يِكَلِّم to speak to

كِلمة word

كُلّنا all of us

كهرباء electricity

كوب (ج. أكواب) drinking glass

لاقى-يِلاقي to find

للاتّصال (ل + ال + اتّصال) for contacting, calling

للاستعلام (ل + ال + استِعلام) for information

للإيجار (ل + الإيجار) for rent

للسكن (ل + ال + سَكَن) for living, residence

لَوَحدِك by yourself

ماذا = إيه what

مُباشِر direct

مِترو subway, underground

مَدخَل entrance

مِشي-يِمشي to walk

مَطبَخ kitchen

مَع بَعض together

مَعايَ with me

مَفروش furnished

مَلابِس clothes

مُمكن possible

نَظيف clean

نَظَّف-يُنَظِّف to clean

هذه (هاذِه pronounced) = دي this, these

هُناك there is, there are

وَلّا or

يُمكن is possible

تمرين رقم ١: أملأ الفراغات

أسكن – الأيّام – التاكسي – الغرفة – دقائق – شقة – كل الوقت – كلّ مكان – للإيجار

أسكن الآن في فندق "كايرو إن"، لكن أريد أن اسكن في.......................
الفندق نظيف وقريب من الجامعة، لكن الفنادق غالية طبعاً، وانا طالبة فقيرة! أريد أن
.......................في شقة مع طالبات عربيّات حتى أتكلّم العربيّة
....

أريد شقّة قريبة من الجامعة. لا أريد أن أشتري سيّارة أو أركب.................. كلّ يوم. يمكن طبعاً أن أركب الأوتوبيس أو المترو. التذكرة رخيصة، وهناك أوتوبيس أو مترو كلّ خمس أو عشر............... ، لكن أحبّ المشي، خصوصاً لأنّ الطقس هنا ممتاز في هذه...............

قرأت إعلاناً على الانترنت عن غرفة للإيجار في شقّة. كلّمت طالبة اسمها سلمى وسألتها عن.................. ، فقالت إنّها تسكن في شقّة مع طالبة أخرى وهناك غرفة.............. ذهبت إلى الشقّة والتقيت بسلمى وصاحبتها رانية، ورأيت الغرفة. قالت سلمى إنّها آسفة لأنّ الملابس والكُتُب والأطباق وأكواب الشاي في ....وقالت إنّها سَوفَ تنظّف الشقّة بعد يوم أو يومين.

أغنية: حبّيتك وباحبّك وحاحبّك على طول (محمّد عبد المطّلب)

I loved you, I love you, and I will love you forever	حبّيتَك وباحبّك وحاحبّك على طول
I am not a betrayer and forgot you as you say	مش خاين ونسيتَك زَي انتَ ما بتقول
I loved you, I love you, and I will love you as long as I live	حبّيتَك وباحبّك وحَ احبّك على طول حبّيتَك وباحبّك وحَ احبّك طول عُمري
Be clear in your heart for me, I have given up myself to you	اصْفى لي من قلبَك؛ سَلّمت ليك أمري
I (swear) by your life and your eyes there is no one other than you on my mind	وحياتك وعيونَك ما في غيرك على بالي
To forget you or betray you, this never occurs to my imagination	كوني أنسى أو اخونك ده ما يخطُر بخيالي
I dream about you at night and in the day I am preoccupied with you	أنا ليلي أحلَم بَك ونهاري بيك مشغول

Plural patterns

In Unit 5 you learned that plurals in Arabic are "sound" when they can be made plural by simply adding an ending to the word. This was the case with feminine sound plurals (like عائلة – عائلات and شركة – شركات). Broken plurals are formed by changing the vowels of the word (like يوم – أيام and شهر – شهور). Below are some more common plural patterns.

Sound plurals: masculine sound plural

Masculine sound nouns are made plural by adding – ـين, as in the following examples:

Plural	Singular
موظفين	موظف
تعبانين	تعبان
زعلانين	زعلان
جوعانين	جوعان
عطشانين	عطشان

Broken plurals

Below are two more common broken plural patterns. As you read the patterns out loud with your teacher or the audio recording, try to identify the pattern you hear.

Broken plural pattern 4		Broken plural pattern 3	
Plural	Singular	Plural	Singular
أُوَض	أوضة	أَسابيع	أسبوع
شُنَط	شنطة	دَكاكين	دُكّان
شُقَق	شَقة	مَواعيد	مَوعِد

In your own words, how would you describe the way that these patterns are formed?

تمرين رقم ٢: أكمل الجدول التالي

المُفرَد	المعنى	الجمع
إعلان	advertisements	
		أوتوبيسات
		ترابيزة
دولاب		دَواليب
سُؤال		
		سَرايِر
		أصحاب

أطباق		طَبَق
كُتُب		
		كُرسي
أكواب		
مطابِخ		

تمرين رقم ٣: اختبر معلوماتك

(In Teacher's Book)

تمرين رقم ٤ (كِتابة في البيت)

Create your own rental ad (اعلان للإيجار) for an apartment, house, or room following the format in Lesson 4.

تمرين رقم ٥ (حضّر في البيت وتكلّم في الصفّ)

1. **At home (في البيت)**: You are looking for housing. Write down a list of "must-haves" in the place you are looking for.
2. **In class (في الصفّ)**: Create a dialogue with another classmate in which one of you is a potential tenant and the other is a landlord or a real estate agent. Be sure to use your list above.

الوحدة الثامنة
المواصَلات

الدرس الأوّل

تمرين رقم ١

Listen to the recording and practice pronouncing the words and expressions below.

smoking تدخين
public/governmental حُكومي
private خاصّ
always دائماً
passenger راكب (ج. رُكاب)
congestion, crowded traffic زَحمة
driver سائق = سَوّاق
owner (also friend) صاحِب
normal, standard عادي
counter, meter عَدّاد
difference فَرق
sign لافِتة

fast/fastest سريع/أسرع
small/smallest صغير/أصغر
big/biggest كبير/أكبر
cheap/cheapest رخيص/أرخص
far/farthest بعيد/أبعد
close/closest قريب/أقرب
expensive/most expensive غالي/أغلى
to like أحبّ-يُحِبّ
to use استعمَل-يستعمل
to stop تَوَقّف-يتوقّف
to smoke دخَّن-يُدخِّن
to think ظَنّ-يظُنّ

محطة (bus) stop/station

مَسؤول responsible, person in charge

مَمنوع prohibited

مُمَيَّز distinguished

مُواصلات transportation

مُواصَلات عامّة public transportation

ناس people

مَلَك-يَملك to own

وَضَع-يَضَع to put

وَقّف-يِوَقِّف to stop (someone)

أكيد certainly

قَد ايه؟ how much?

كَيف = اِزّاي how

مش عارف/عارفة I don't know

مش معقول no way, impossible

يَبدو it seems

تمرين رقم ٢

Circle the word that does not belong.

١. تاكسي   باص   سيّارة   سائق

٢. راكب   لافتة   مسؤول   سائق

٣. زحمة   أكبر   أقرب   أرخص

٤. سريع   صغير   محطة   بعيد

٥. أكيد   دخّن   استعمل   توقّف

تمرين رقم ٣

Label each picture using words/phrases from the list above.

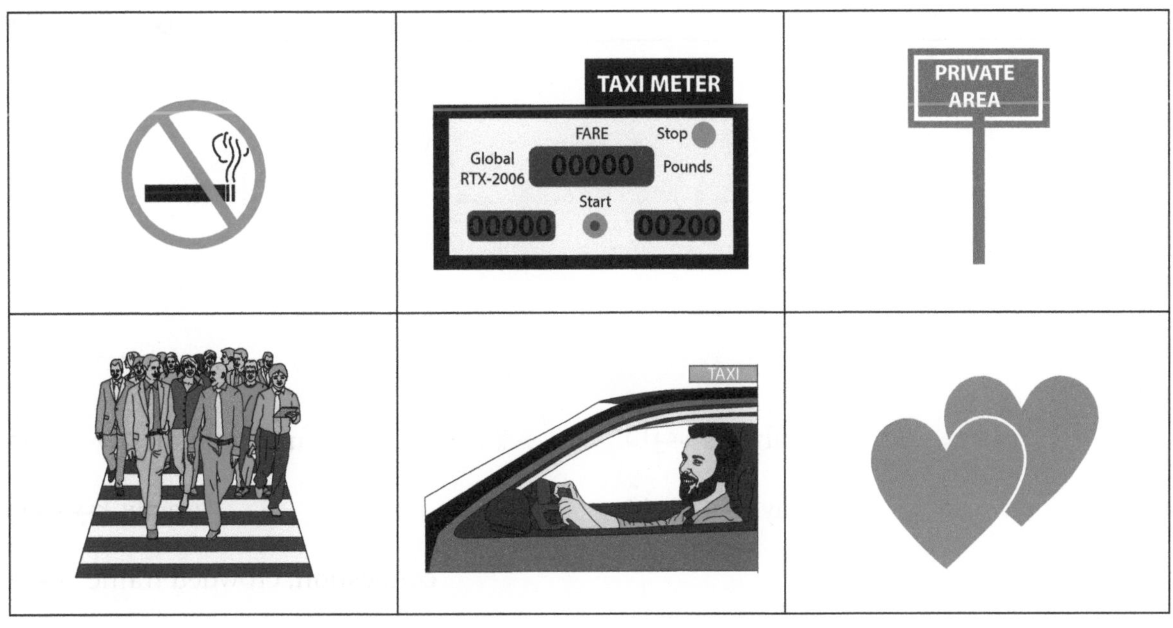

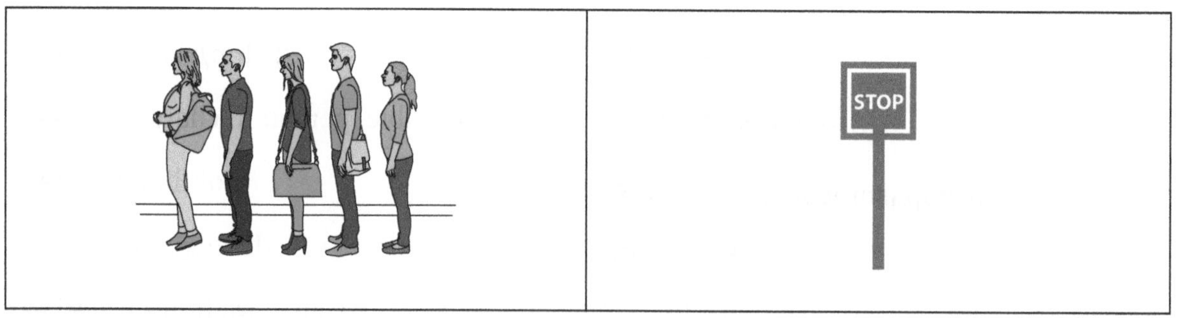

تمرين رقم ٤

Complete each sentence by choosing the correct word.

١. التدخين ________ (أكيد - ممنوع - مسؤول) في التاكسي.

٢. هناك ________ (زحمة - سيّارة - خاص) في القاهرة.

٣. أنا ________ (املك - أظن - استعمل) المواصلات العامّة كُل يوم.

٤. مايا ________ (صاحب - تدخين - دائماً) مشغولة في الجامعة.

٥. ما هو ________ (الفرق - حكومي - ناس) بين التاكسي المُميز والتاكسي العادي؟

تمرين رقم ٥ (كتابة)

Use the following words in meaningful sentences.

١. سريع/أسرع: ________________________________

٢. صغير/أصغر: ________________________________

٣. رخيص/أرخص: ________________________________

٤. نظيف/أنظف: ________________________________

٥. بعيد/أبعد: ________________________________

الدرس الثاني - مشاهدة: أروح وسط البلد إزّاي؟

كلمات جديدة

مُواصَلات transportation

بالضبط exactly

زَحمة congestion, crowded traffic

دايماً always

دَفَع-يدفَع to pay

تعابير

مش عارفة I don't know

أحسَن حاجة the best thing

قَد ايه؟ how much?

بالكثير (ب + ال + كثير) at most

ربّنا معاك God be with you, good luck!

سؤال

Make a list (in Arabic) of the types of transportation discussed by Maya and Salma.

الأوتوبيس، . . .

Then make a table of these types and indicate what are the advantages and disadvantages of each. You can use Arabic or mix English and Arabic.

قَواعِد

The particle إنّ

In the last unit, Maya wrote the following phrases in her diary:

قالت إنّ الغرفة نظيفة ومفروشة وفيها سرير ودولاب. She said that the room is clean and furnished with a bed and a dresser.
وقالت إنّها سَوفَ تنظّف الشقّة. And she said that she will clean the apartment.
قالت سلمى إنّها آسفة. She said that she is sorry.

The particle إنّ is used with the verb قال – يقول to form the phrase "say that (somebody or something. . .)".

The important thing to remember about إنّ is that it must always be followed by a noun. This noun can be a separate word, like in the first example sentence above (الغرفة), or it can be an attached pronoun like in the second and third example sentences (ـها-).

With separate noun	With attached pronoun
قلنا إنّ التكييف رخيص. We said that air-conditioning is cheap.	قلنا إنّه رخيص. We said that it is cheap.
قلتم إن الطلاب جاؤا. You all said that the students came.	قلتم إنهم جاؤا. You all said that they came.

تمرين رقم ١

What did Salma say to Maya about her transportation options? Pick three things that Salma said to Maya. You will write two versions of what Salma said: one with a separate noun, and one with its equivalent attached pronoun. Follow the example below:

Separate noun

(she said that the metro is fast) قالت إنّ المترو سريع

Attached pronoun

(she said that it is fast) قالت إنّه سريع

تمرين رقم ٢ (مُحادثة)

الجزء الأوّل

You are at the reception of the hotel Pension Roma in وسط البلد (downtown Cairo). Ask the receptionist what is the best way to get to Alexandria.

First, match the following Egyptian opening gambits with their English equivalents and then use them to complete the list of questions you have prepared for the receptionist:

فيه كام؟	لو سمحت!	إيه أسرع؟	قدّ إيه؟	إزاي؟	منين؟	إيه؟
What (is)?	How many is/are there?	Excuse me!	Which is quicker?	From where?	How?	How long?

- .... عاوز اروح اسكندرية.	1
.... الأوتوبيس ولا القطر؟	2
.... قطر كل يوم من مصر لاسكندرية؟	3
الرحلة بتاخذ............. ؟	4
ممكن تقول لي لازم أركب القطر .... ؟	5
اروح محطة رمسيس .... ؟ ممكن بالمترو؟	6
.... أرخص؟ القطر ولا الأوتوبس؟	7

الجزء الثاني

You play the role of the receptionist at Pension Roma. Try to answer the questions asked by your classmate in Egyptian Arabic using the information you have in front of you which is written in فُصحى.

معلومات عن السفر من القاهرة إلى الإسكندرية

السفر بالقطار

قطارات كل ساعة من محطة رمسيس – تستغرق الرحلة ساعتين ونصف

التذكرة (ذهاب وعودة) بين 54 و 142 جنيه

تقع محطة رمسيس على الخط الأول في مترو الأنفاق

السفر بالأوتوبيس

تغادر الأوتوبيسات الى الإسكندرية كل ساعة من ميدان التحرير – تستغرق الرحلة – اربع ساعات تقريبا

التذكرة (ذهاب وعودة) بين 55 و 142 جنيه

الدرس الثالِث–استماع: التاكسي المُميّز

كلمات جديدة

اتولِد–يتولِد to be born

أكيد certainly

عَدّاد counter, meter

أهوه here it is

شوفي look, see!

على الجَنب on the side

مش معقول no way, impossible

فَرق difference

مُمَيَّز distinguished

عَرَبيّة = سيّارة

وَقّف–يِوَقّف to stop (someone)

يَبدو it seems

لِسّه ما بتعرفيش حاجة you still don't know any thing

أسئلة

1. When did Maya arrive in Cairo?
2. What was Maya's first response when the driver asked her where she learned Arabic?
3. How much does Maya normally pay?
4. What is the difference between التاكسي المميّز and the التاكسي العادي?
5. What did the taxi driver say at the end about Maya's Arabic and knowledge of taxis in Egypt?

قَواعِد

Remember that in verbal negation, the verb is "sandwiched" between ما and ش.

تمرين رقم ١: ترجم إلى الإنجليزيّة

١. ليه ما قُلتش انّك أغلى من التاكسي العادي؟
٢. انتِ وقّفتيني وما سألتينيش.
٣. انتِ بتتكلمي عربي كويّس، لكن يبدو لسه ما بتعرفيش حاجة عن التاكسي في مصر.

The superlative

In Unit 6, you learned how to form the comparative in order to describe things as "better than", "bigger than", and "cheaper than".

Suppose you wanted to go beyond the comparative to describe an object as the "most" (something), i.e. "the most fun", "the biggest", "the tallest", etc. You would want to use the *superlative*. The superlative in Arabic is based on the comparative. Look at the examples in the chart below – what do you notice?

Superlative	Comparative
أنظف تاكسي the cleanest taxi	تاكسي أنظف a cleaner taxi
أحسن مطعم the best restaurant	مطعم أحسن a better restaurant
أغلى فندق The most expensive hotel	فندق أغلى a more expensive hotel
أطول طالب The tallest student	طالب أطول a taller student
أقصر طالب The shortest student	طالب أقصر a shorter student

As you can see, the comparative is formed like a regular noun-adjective phrase, with the noun coming before the adjective.

The superlative, on the other hand, is formed like an إضافة construct. In this case, the superlative adjective acts like a noun (the cleanest thing, the best thing). The superlative is formed by placing the superlative adjective before the noun.

تمرين رقم ٢: ترجم الى الانجليزيّة

١. التاكسي المميز أغلى مُواصلات في مصر.
٢. فندق الحياة أغلى فندُق في القاهرة.
٣. بيته أكبر بيت في المنطقة (area).

تمرين رقم ٣ (في الصفّ)

Line up in class from oldest to youngest by asking each other كام عمرك or امتى عيد ميلادك.
Then take turns making statements about yourself in relation to others. For example,

- انا اكبر من .... لكن انا أصغر من ....
- أكبر طالب هو ....
- اصغر طالب هو ....

Repeat the above exercise using طويل، أطول.

تمرين رقم ٤ (في البيت وفي الصفّ)

Although you've been studying with your classmates for quite a while now, there are probably some things you still don't know about them. Come up with three questions using the superlative that you can ask tomorrow in class.

For example, who has the biggest family? Who is the oldest (أكبر) student? Who has the most expensive car? Who still (لِسّه) lives with their family?

تمرين رقم ٥ (في الصفّ)

الجزء الأوّل

سؤال وجواب

Work with a partner asking and answering questions using the following question words:

- على فين؟
- الأخ/الأخت من . . . ؟
- إمتى . . . ؟
- فين . . . ؟
- إزّاي؟
- بكام؟
- ايه الفرق؟
- ليه؟

الجزء الثاني

Work with a partner asking and answering questions using the following answers:

- لوسط البلد.
- مِن أستراليا.

- قبل شهرين.
- في الجامعة في أستراليا، وكمان في الأردن.
- لأ، التاكسي ده أرخص من "أوبر".

الدرس الرابِع

قراءة: مذكّرات مايا

يملك الكثير من المصريّين سيّارات خاصّة، ولكن يستعمل أكثر الناس المواصلات العامّة. هناك ثلاثة أنواع من المواصلات في القاهرة وهي الأوتوبيس والميكروباص والمترو. كلّها أرخص من التاكسي طبعاً!

أكثر ركاب الأوتوبيسات والميكروباصات والمترو موظّفون حكوميّون وطلاب مدارس وجامعات. والميكروبَاصات أصغر من الأوتوبيسات طبعاً، وهي أسرع أيضاً! تتوقف الأوتوبيسات والميكروبَاصات كثيراً في الطريق، لكنها لا تتوقف لمدة طويلة.

لا أعرف أين محطة الأوتوبيس، ولا أظن أنّ هناك محطات ميكروبَاصات! لذلك أحبّ أن أركب المترو، لكن محطة المترو أبعد من محطة الأوتوبيس والتذكرة أغلى أيضاً. من اللازم أن أجرّب الأوتوبيسات والميكروباصات أكثر . . .

التدخين مشكلة كبيرة هنا! الأسبوع الماضي أخذت تاكسي من وسط البلد الى الشقّة، كان في التاكسي لافتة مكتوب عليها "ممنوع التدخين". ولكن السائق أخرج سيجارة وبدأ يدخّن. عندما سألته كيف يدخّن وهناك لافتة تقول التدخين ممنوع، قال إنّ هذه ليست سيّارته وإنّ صاحب السيّارة وضع اللافتة، وهو مسؤول عنها! جواب غريب لا أفهمه . . .

كلمات جديدة

مَلَك-يَملِك to own	مُواصَلات عامّة public transportation
خاصّ private	حُكومي governmental
استعمَل-يستعمل to use	مَدرَسة (ج. مَدارِس) school
ناس people	أسرع faster

تَوَقف-يتوقَّف to stop
عرَف-يعرِف to know
ظَنّ-يظُنّ to think
أحبّ-يُحِبّ to like
جَرَّب-يُجَرِّب to try
تَدخين smoking
أُسبوع week
ماضي last, past
لافِتة sign
مَمنوع prohibited
سائق = سَوّاق driver
أخرَج-يُخرِج to take out

بدأ-يَبدأ to start
دخَّن-يُدخّن to smoke
عندَما when
كَيف = اِزّاي
لَيست = مِش
صاحِب owner (What other meaning does this word have
وَضَع-يَضَع to put
مَسؤول responsible, person in charge
جَواب answer
غَريب strange

أسئلة

صحّ أو خطأ؟

١. التاكسي أرخص من المترو في القاهرة.
٢. يركب كثير من طلّاب المدارس في الأوتوبيسات والمترو.
٣. الميكروباصات أسرع من الأوتوبيسات.
٤. الأوتوبيسات تتوقّف مدّة طويلة في الطريق.
٥. المترو أغلى من الأوتوبيس.
٦. سائق التاكسي دخّن سيجارة.
٧. سائق التاكسي هو صاحب سيّارة التاكسي.

رتّب الجمل التالية حسب ورودها في النصّ.

- التدخين مشكلة كبيرة في مصر. ------------
- السائق يسوق تاكسي ليست سيارته. ------------
- المترو أغلى من الأوتوبيس. ------------

- الميكروباصات أسرع من الأوتوبيسات. ....
- هناك ثلاثة أنواع من المواصلات العامّة في القاهرة. ......١ ....
- يركب طلاب المدارس والجامعات في الأوتوبيسات والمترو. ....

قَواعِد

Verb-subject (dis)agreement in فُصحى

Look at the sentences below, taken from Maya's diary. For each sentence, circle the verb, and then draw an arrow to its subject.

يملك الكثير من المصريّين سيّارات خاصّة.

يستعمل أكثر الناس المواصلات العامّة.

You might have noticed that the subject for each verb is a plural noun (many Egyptians, most people). The verb, however, is conjugated for a singular pronoun. Go back and reread the sentences to double check that you see this for yourself.

What is going on here? You have already learned that فصحى has a flexible word order – a subject can go before or after its verb. If the subject is plural, but comes *after* the verb, then the verb remains singular as in the above two sentences. If the verb comes after the subject, then it agrees with its subject:

Many Egyptians own private cars.	الكثير من المصريّين يملكون سيّارات خاصّة.
Most people use public transportation.	أكثر الناس يستعملون المواصلات العامّة.
Salma owns a private car.	سَلمى تملك سيّارة خاصّة.
Ahmad uses public transportation.	أحمد يستعمل المواصلات العامّة.

More examples of إعراب (the case system in فُصحى)

In the last unit, you were introduced to the case system in Arabic. You learned that the cases are generally used to mark the function of the word in the sentence. Words which are marked by case may look slightly different, but still have the same meaning.

You were also introduced to sound masculine plurals which end in ـين. In this lesson, you can see that sound masculine plurals have case endings in فصحى, which means that they can end in either ـين or ـون depending on case.

employees = موظّفين = موظّفون

Egyptians = مصريّين = مصريّون

Remember that case endings are mainly a feature in فصحى, and that regardless of the ending the words have the same meaning.

Relative clauses modifying indefinite nouns

The three examples below are taken from Maya's diary. Each one consists of a noun and a sentence or "clause" that describes it. As you read each example, draw a circle around the noun being described, and draw brackets around the clause that describes it. The first one is given as an example:

١. (لافتة) [مكتوب عليها "ممنوع التدخين"]

٢. لافتة تقول التدخين ممنوع

٣. جواب غريب لا أفهمه . . .

As you can see, the nouns above are indefinite ("a sign", "an answer"). Rather than being described by a single adjective, each noun is described by a clause ("it says 'no smoking' ", "I don't understand it"). These clauses act like adjectives because they follow the noun which they describe.

Below are examples of indefinite nouns being described by an adjective, as well as by a whole sentence.

A governmental employee	حكومي	موظف
An employee who works for the government	يعمل في الحكومة	موظف
An Egyptian student	مصرية	طالبة
A student who rides the bus every day	تركب الباص كل يوم	طالبة

تمرين رقم ١

Part 1

Below are English sentences with indefinite nouns being described by either an adjective or a clause. As you read each sentence, draw a circle around the noun being described, and brackets around the adjective or the clause that modifies the noun.

- I know a Syrian girl.
- I know a girl who uses public transportation.
- We ride cheap buses (أوتوبيسات رخيصة).
- We ride buses that stop a lot.
- Do you have Arab friends?
- Do you have friends who smoke?

Part 2

Translate the sentences above into Arabic.

الدرس الخامس

كلمات الوحدة

to be born اتولِد-يِتوِلِد

to like أحبّ-يُحِبّ

to take out أخرَج-يُخرِج

week أُسبوع

to use استعمَل-يستعمل

faster أسرع

certainly أكيد

here it is أهوه

exactly بالضبط

at most بالكثير (ب + ال + كثير)

to start بدأ-يَبدأ

smoking تَدخين

to stop تَوَقف-يتوقّف

to try جَرَّب-يُجَرِّب

answer جَواب

governmental حُكومي

private خاصّ

always دايماً=دائماً

to smoke دخَّن-يُدخّن

to pay دَفَع-يدفَع

God be with you, good luck! ربّنا معاك

congestion, crowded traffic زَحمة

driver سائق = سَوّاق

look, see! شوفي

owner, friend صاحِب صاحِب (ج. أصحاب) does this word have

to think ظَنّ-يظُنّ

counter, meter عَدّاد

عَرَبيّة = سيّارة

to know عرَف-يعرِف

on the side على الجَنب

when عِندَما

strange غَريب

difference فَرق

how much? قَد ايه؟

كَيف = اِزّاي

sign لافتِة

لَيست = مِش

last, past ماضي

school مَدرَسة (ج. مَدارِس)

مَسؤول responsible

مِش عارِف I don't know

مش معقول no way, impossible

مَلَك-يَملِك to own

مَمنوع prohibited

مُمَيَّز distinguished

مُواصَلات عامّة public transportation

ناس people

وَضَع-يَضَع to put

وَقّف-يِوَقِّف to stop (someone)

يَبدو it seems

(تمرين رقم ١ (قراءة

تاكسي النيل

افتتح وزير النقل المهندس سعد الجيوشي مشروع التاكسي النهري (تاكسي النيل) في شهر مارس ٢٠١٦ بالاتفاق مع ثلاث شركات لتولي مهمة تشغيله وإنشاء وتطوير محطّات له.

ستكون هناك ثلاث محطات رئيسية وهي محطة منيل الروضة ومحطة جاردن سيتي ومحطة التحرير، على ان يتم انشاء محطات فرعية جديدة بين مرسى نادي اليخت بكورنيش المعادي والتحرير كمرحلة اولى.

وعن سعر تذكرة التاكسي النهري اعلنت وزارة النقل ان تكلفة تذكرة المحطة الواحدة خمسة جنيهات، بحيث تكون تكلفة الانتقال من محطة المعادي للتحرير ٢٠ جنيه. وتكون مواعيد التشغيل بداية من الساعة السادسة ونصف صباحاً حتى الساعة العاشرة مساءً.

ومن المتوقع ان يتم تعميم مشروع التاكسي النهري على القاهرة الكبرى خلال الشهور القادمة مع انشاء المزيد من محطات التوقف على كورنيش النيل، حيث يتم عمل مراسي للتاكسي في عدد من الاماكن بجانب محطات الاتوبيسات ووسائل النقل الأخرى.

أسئلة

صَحّ أو خطأ؟

On companion website
Grammar review: the comparative and superlative

You learned in Lesson 3 of this unit that both the comparative and the superlative take the same shape (أكبر، أصغر، أبعد، أغلى).

تمرين رقم ٢

Translate each sentence into English on a separate piece of paper and write whether the sentence contains a comparative or a superlative below each translation.

١. الأوتوبيس والميكروباص والمترو أرخص من التاكسي طبعاً.

٢. أكثر ركاب الأوتوبيسات والميكرو باصات والمترو موظّفون حكوميّون وطلاب مدارس وجامعات.

٣. الميكرو بَاصات أصغر من الأوتوبيسات طبعاً، وهي أسرع أيضاً!

٤. لكن خطّ المترو أبعد من محطة الأوتوبيس والتذكرة أغلى أيضاً.

٥. من اللازم أن أجرّب الأوتوبيسات والميكرو بَاصات أكثر!

Roots and families

جَذر (ج. جُذور) root
Here is a list of 12 different جذور:

ر – خ – ص	د – ر – س	ع – ر – ف	ب – ع – د
ك – ث – ر	ر – ك – ب	غ – ر – ب	ك – ت – ب
ج – م – ع	ق – ر – ب	س – ر – ع	س – أ – ل

Below is a list of words derived from those جُذور. On a separate piece of paper, make a chart matching all of the words to the correct جَذر. When you are done, look at all the words in each root "family" and make a guess for what general meaning each root conveys.

أبعد، الجامعة، أرخص، كتاب، أركب، غريب، أسرع، رخيص، درست، أعرف، سريع، اكتب، أكثر، بتعرفي، بعيدة، تقريباً، دروس، رُكّاب، سألت، الجمعة، سألنا، عارفة، قريب، كتاب، الكثير، مدرسة، مسؤول، المغرب، مكتوب، الجمع، مدارس، كِتابة، معروف

Sociolinguistic Corner

ليس/مش

You have learned that, in مصري, nouns and adjectives are negated with the particle مش.

In فصحى, nouns and adjectives are negated with the word لَيسَ. You saw this in the reading above in the sentence:

He said that this is not his car.	قال إنّ هذه ليست سيّارته.

Unlike other negation words, لَيسَ is special because it is "conjugated" like a past tense verb:

النفي (negation)	الضمير (pronoun)
لَستُ	أنا
لَسنا	نحن
لَستَ	أنتَ
لَستِ	أنتِ
لَستُم	أنتم
لَيسَ	هو
لَيسَت	هي
لَيسوا	هم

تمرين رقم ٣ (حضّر في البيت وتكلّم في الصفّ)

Create a dialogue with another classmate in which:

a. one of you asks for and the other gives directions for transportation from one place to another,
b. one is a taxi driver and the other a passenger.

الوحدة التاسعة
الجَوّ

الدرس الأوّل

تمرين رقم ١

Listen to the recording and practice pronouncing the words below.

warm دافئ	dry, arid جافّ	mountain جَبَل (ج. جِبال)
shore, bank شَطّ	coast ساحِل	humid رَطب
flower وَرد (ج. وُرود)	mild مُعتَدِل	season فَصل (ج. فُصول)

sometimes أحياناً

beginning بِداية

climbing تَسَلّق

to change تغيَّر-يتغيَّر

mountainous جَبَلي

dryness, drought جَفاف

beautiful جَميل = حِلو

weather جَوّ

to like حَبّ-يِحِبّ

it depends, according to حَسَب

cold سَقعة = بَرد

touristic سِياحي

coming, next قادِم

favorite مُفَضّل

area, region مَنطَقة (ج. مَناطِق)

air هَواء

تمرين رقم ٢

The sentences on the companion website each contain one word from the new vocabulary above. Listen carefully and translate the sentences into English on a separate piece of paper.

تمرين رقم ٣

Write each of the following words under its appropriate category.

– صحراويّة – الخريف – حارّ – رطب – الصيف – الربيع – دافئ بارد – مُعتدِل – ساحليّة – جبليّة – الشتاء

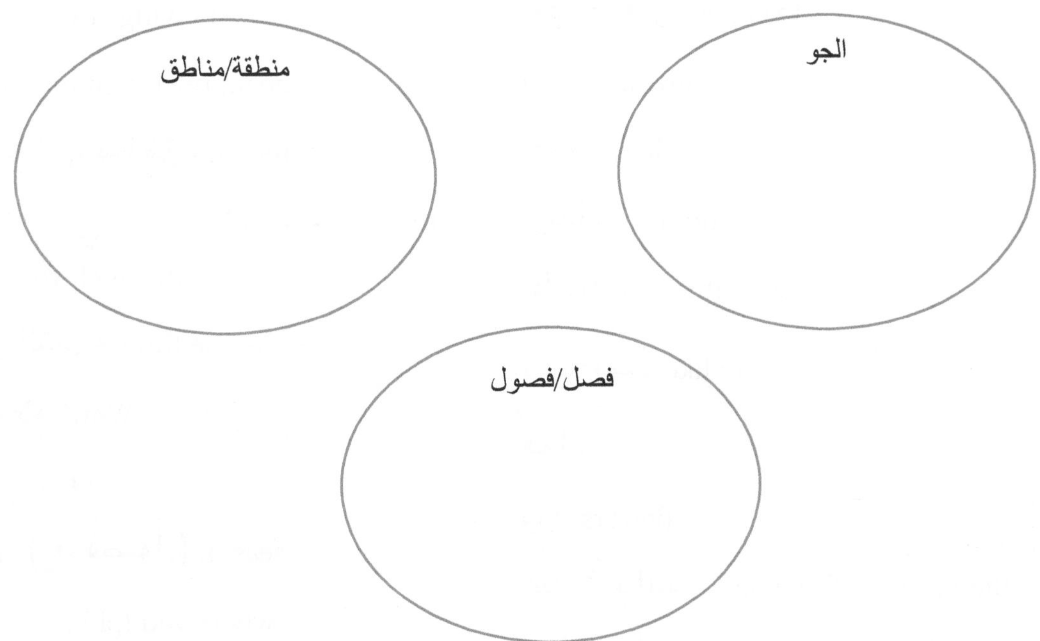

تمرين رقم ٤

Working with a classmate, take turns asking and answering the questions below.

١ . ايه فصلك المُفضّل؟ فصلي المُفضل . . . .

٢ . ازّاي الجو في مدينتك في الصيف؟ في الخريف؟ الشتاء؟ الربيع؟

٣ . فيه مناطق ساحليّة/جبليّة/صحراويّة قريبة من منطقتك؟

تمرين رقم ٥ (كتابة): ترّجم إلى العربيّة

1. The weather is moderate in the spring.
2. My favorite season is the fall (autumn).
3. The weather is beautiful today.
4. There are four seasons in my city.
5. I like climbing mountains.

الدرس الثاني–مشاهدة: إزّاي الجو في أمريكا؟

كلمات جديدة

جَوّ weather

رَطب humid

جافّ dry

عارِف knowing, aware

قَصدي I mean, my intention

مَنطَقة (ج. مَناطِق) area, region

المنطقة اللي إنت ساكنة فيها the area in which you live

نفس الشيء the same thing

يا سَلام! Wow!

ياه! O, wow!

فَصل (ج. فُصول) season

عِندُكم where you (pl.) are

حَسَب it depends, according to

مُعتَدِل moderate

أحياناً sometimes

مُفَضّل favorite

تغيَّر–يتغَيّر to change

أخضَر green

أصفَر yellow

بُرتُقالي orange

حِلو beautiful (sweet)

حَبّ–يحِبّ to like

هَواء air

ورد flowers

عيد شَمّ النَسيم the Festival of *shamm an-nasiim*

مَخصوص special

أسئلة

صحّ أو خطأ؟

١. هناك (= فيه) جوّ حارّ وجوّ رطب في أمريكا.

٢. مايا سكنت في ولاية كولورادو.

٣. في نيويورك وكولورادو الجوّ حارّ في الصيف.

٤. هناك شمس في نيويورك أكثر من كولورادو.

٥. في تكساس الجوّ بارد في الشتاء.

٦. في بعض (some) مناطق (areas) نيويورك هناك ثلج أكثر من أربعة شهور.

٧. الجوّ في الخريف معتدل في الخريف.

٨. فصل مايا المفضّل هو فصل الربيع.

٩. في مصر الفصل المفضّل هو فصل الربيع.

قَواعِد

Relative clauses modifying definite nouns

In the last unit, you learned about relative clauses modifying indefinite nouns, where an entire sentence acts like an adjective for an indefinite noun:

- موظف يعمل في الحكومة an employee (who) works for the government
- لافتة تقول التدخين ممنوع a sign (that) says "smoking is not allowed"

What if you want to describe a *definite* noun? In Arabic, you must use the connecting particle اللي. See the examples below:

The employee who works for the government	بيشتغل في الحكومة	اللي	الموظف
The student who rides the bus every day	بتركب الباص كل يوم	اللي	الطالبة
The cold and snow that you guys have	عندكم	اللي	السقعة والتلج

تمرين رقم ١

Part 1

Below are English sentences which contain definite nouns. As you read each sentence, draw a circle around the noun being described. If the sentence contains a definite relative clause, draw brackets around the clause describing the noun. If the sentence contains a regular adjective (الصفة), draw a square around it.

- Maya is the student who is studying Arabic in Egypt.
- Maya is the American student.
- Did he eat the expensive sandwich?
- Did he eat the sandwich that was on the table?
- We ride the bus that stops frequently.
- We ride the blue bus to school.
- I want to call the new hotel employee.
- I want to call the hotel employee who helped me.

Part 2

Translate the sentences above into Arabic.

The returning pronoun (الضمير العائد)

In her diary of the previous unit, Maya says: ...جواب غريب لا أفهمه, which literally translates as "a strange answer I don't understand it". A better English translation would be "a strange answer which I don't understand" or "a strange answer I don't understand". In the Arabic, the returning pronoun literally "returns" or refers back to the original topic noun in the sentence.

تمرين رقم ٢

Following are three sentences that contain returning pronouns. First, circle the returning pronoun and then draw an arrow back to the the noun it refers to. Provide two translations of the second and third sentences following the example of the first sentence.

١. دي هي العربيّة اللي اشتريتها.

Literal translation: This is the car that I bought it.
Idiomatic translation: This is the car that I bought.

٢. ده هو الأوتوبيس اللي ركبناه.

٣. قصدي الجوّ في المنطقة اللي انتِ ساكنة فيها.

فَصلي المُفضَّل (My favorite season)

In the dialogue above Salma asks Maya what her favorite season is:

ايه فصلك المُفضل؟ lit: *what is your season the favorite?*

Remember that the noun "season" is definite because it is possessed ("*your* season"). Therefore, the adjective that modifies it ("favorite") must also be definite.

تمرين رقم ٣

Matching (companion website)

تمرين رقم ٤

Ask a classmate or your أستاذ/أستاذة the following questions:

١	ايه لونك المفضل؟
٢	فين كانت أستاذتك القديمة (old, former)؟
٣	ايه فصل والدتك المفضل؟
٤	فين شقتك الجديدة؟

٥	ايه اسم استاذك الجديد؟	
٦	ايه مدينتك المُفَضَّلة؟	
٧	ايه مطعمك المفضل؟	
٨	ايه موسيقاك (music) المفضّلة؟	

تمرين رقم ٥: تصريف أفعال في الماضي والمضارع (شفهي في الصفّ)

سكن-يسكُن، نزِل-ينزل، حبّ-يحبّ، تغيّر-يتغيّر، قعد-يقعد

تمرين رقم ٦

Each phrase below is missing a word. Pick the correct matching word or words from the word bank, then translate the completed phrase into English.

السنة – أكثر من – يا – قوي – الشيء – معقول – حارّ – كلّ – المُفضّل – الشتاء

١. الصيف ________ قوي.

٢. الجو بارد في ________.

٣. مش ________!

٤. ايه فصلك ________؟

٥. طول ________.

٦. نفس ________.

٧. في كولورادو» فيه شمس ________ نيويورك.

٨. ________ سلام!

٩. حلو ________.

١٠. في ________ مكان.

الدرس الثالِث: استماع: هنا في مصر الشتاء يعني المطر!

كلمات جديدة

صَحراوي desert-like

خالِص at all

قبل ما = قبل أن before

صَحّ correct

sensible, possible, reasonable مَعقول

cold سَقعة = بَرد

the cold and السقعة والتلج اللي عندكم snow that you guys have

the Delta الدِلتا

coast شَطّ

أسئلة

1. What is the weather like in the Sinai in the spring?
2. Does snow fall in Egypt? If so, where?
3. Why does Maya say مش معقول? What is that a reaction to?
4. According to Maya, where is summer better, in Egypt or America?
5. Does Salma agree?
6. What is the weather like in desert areas of Egypt in the summer?
7. What is it like on the Mediterranean coast?
8. How would you translate Maya's statement:

بس أكيد الصيف عندنا في أمريكا أحسن من اللي عندكم هنا في مصر.

تمرين رقم ١ (شفهي في الصفّ): مراجعة عند (عنده، عندها، عندهم، عندَك، عندِك، عندكم، عندي، عندنا)

قَواعِد

قبل ما

Note that when the prepositions قبل and بعد (and a few others that you will see in time) come before verbs, they require ما to separate them from these verbs. ما in this position has no meaning at all.

تمرين رقم ٢: مُحادَثة (Conversation Activity)

With your partner, take turns interviewing each other about the weather in their area, who has better weather, and why.

أمثلة (examples)

– ازاي الجوّ في المدينة اللي انت ساكن فيها؟

– الجوّ حلو قوي في المدينة اللي ساكن فيها، خصوصاً في فصل الربيع . . .

– بينزل تلج (مطر) في مدينتك؟

– لأ، ما بينزلش تلج خالص، بسّ بينزل مطر كتير . . .

Some helpful words and phrases:

فصل الصيف/الخريف/الشتاء/الربيع، بارد، حارّ، صحراوي، جبلي، ساحلي، ثلج، مطر، خالص، خصوصاً، طبعاً، قبل ما، مش كثير، مش معقول، أحسن من، ممكن، أكيد، كلّ الناس، حلو قوي

الدرس الرابِع–قراءة: مذكّرات مايا

الجوّ هنا ممتاز هذه الأيّام. في أمريكا عِشت في ثلاث ولايات: نيويورك وكولورادو وتكساس. في هذه الأيّام الجوّ بارد في نيويورك وكولورادو، لكن دافئ في تكساس، ولكن لا أريد أن أفكّر في الصيف في تكساس، فهو حارّ جدّاً!

مصر دولة كبيرة طبعاً، يعيش أكثر السكّان في منطقة صغيرة هي منطقة وادي النيل. تقع أكثر المدن المصريّة الكبيرة مثل الإسكندريّة والقاهرة وأسيوط والأقصر في هذه المنطقة.

أكثر مناطق مصر صحراوية، الجوّ فيها حارّ جدّاً وجافّ في الصيف. قالت لي سلمى إنّ الشمس والجفاف في مصر أكثر من أيّ دولة في العالم. ما صدّقت في البداية ولكن هكذا تقول "ويكيبيديا". في الشتاء الجوّ دافئ في النهار وبارد في الليل (من اللازم أن تلبس لفصلَين مختلفَين في يوم واحد!)

طبعاً في مصر مناطق غير المناطق الصحراويّة. هناك مناطق جبليّة ومناطق على ساحل البحر.

سمعت الكثير عن منطقة شرم الشيخ وواحة سيوة ومرسى مطروح، وهي مناطق سياحيّة مشهورة في مصر. سأزور كلّ هذه المناطق طبعاً، ولكن منطقتي المفضّلة هي منطقة جبل موسى في سيناء. الجَوّ في هذه المنطقة معتدل وجميل في الربيع والخريف وأنا أحبّ تسلّق الجبال. سأتسلّق جبل موسى في الرحلة القادمة.

كلمات جديدة

عاشَ–يَعيش to live

دافِئ warm

سُكّان inhabitants

وَقع–يَقَع to be located (تَقَع (it, she) is located)

جَفاف drought, dryness

صَدّق–يُصَدِّق to believe (that someone is) telling the truth

ما صَدّقت I did not believe (see grammar note) below

بِداية beginning

هكَذا thus, this way (pronounced هاكَذا)

جَبَلي mountainous

ساحِل coastal

واحة oasis

سِياحي touristic

مَشهور famous

زار–يَزور to visit

جَبَل (ج. جِبال) mountain

جَميل = حِلو beautiful

تَسَلُّق climbing

قادِم coming, next

أسئلة

١. كيف الجَوّ في تكساس في هذه الأيّام، حسب مايا؟
٢. أين يعيش أكثر سكّان مصر؟
٣. كيف الجَوّ في المناطق الصحراويّة في مصر؟
٤. ماذا قالت سلمى لمايا عن الشمس والجفاف في مصر؟
٥. ما هي بعض المناطق السياحيّة المشهورة في مصر؟
٦. ما هي منطقة مايا المفضّلة؟
٧. كيف الجَوّ في الربيع والخريف في منطقة جبل موسى؟

1. What is the weather like (how is the weather) in Texas these days, according to Maya?
2. Where do most Egyptians live?
3. What is the weather like in the desert areas of Egypt?
4. What did Salma tell Maya about the sun and dryness in Egypt?
5. What are some of the famous tourist areas in Egypt?
6. What is Maya's favorite area?
7. How is the weather in the spring and autumn in the جبل موسى area?

صحّ أو خطأ؟ (companion website)

تمرين رقم ١: ترجم إلى الإنجليزيّة

المدن المصريّة الكبيرة	منطقة صغيرة
المناطق الصحراويّة	أكثر مناطق مصر صحراوية
مناطق سياحيّة مشهورة	مناطق جبليّة
الرحلة القادمة	منطقتي المفضّلة

قَواعِد

Root types: assimilated roots

You have learned three root types so far: sound roots (like ش-ر-ب), hollow roots (like ك-و-ن), and doubled roots (like ح-ب-ب).

A fourth root type is the *assimilated root*. Assimilated roots have a vowel as their first root letter. Examples of verbs from assimilated roots are وصل "to arrive", وجد "to find", and وقع "to be located".

Like other roots with vowels in them, assimilated roots undergo a spelling change where the vowel occurs. This spelling change only happens in فصحى and only in the present tense. As you read the فصحى conjugations below, try to identify the spelling change:

	ماضي	مُضارِع
أنا	وَجَدت	أَجِد
أنتَ	وَجَدت	تَجِد
أنتِ	وَجَدتِ	تَجِدين
أنتم	وَجَدتم	تَجِدون
هو	وَجَد	يَجِد
هي	وَجَدَت	تَجِد
هم	وَجَدوا	يَجِدون

As you have noticed, الماضي is conjugated like regular sound verbs, with no spelling changes. In المضارع, on the other hand, the initial vowel is deleted. This explains the form تقع "it, she is located", which is derived from the verb وقع.

Negation of the past tense in فصحى

You learned in Unit 7 that المُضارع (the present tense) is negated in فُصحى with لا, which is placed before the verb. The past tense (الماضي) is negated in one of two ways. One way is by placing the particle ما before the verb as in:

I did not believe at the beginning. ما صدّقت في البداية.

The second way of negating past tense verbs using لم will be discussed in Unit 13.

Dual agreement

You learned in Lesson 8 of Unit 1 that nouns can be singular, dual, or plural, as in شهر-شهرين-شهور. You also learned that adjectives agree with the nouns they modify in gender, definiteness, and number, with the exception of non-human plurals, which are modified by adjectives in the feminine singular.

Adjectives of dual nouns agree with them in gender, definiteness, and number as in فصلين مختلفين "two different seasons".

الدرس الخامس

كلمات الوحدة

sometimes أحياناً

yellow أصفَر

the Delta الدِلتا

that, which اِللي

beginning بِداية

orange بُرتُقالي

climbing تَسَلُّق

to change تغيَّر–يِتغَيّر

dry جافّ

mountain جَبَل (ج. جِبال)

mountainous جَبَلي

dryness, drought جَفاف

beautiful جَميل = حِلو

weather جَوّ

to like حَبّ–يِحِبّ

it depends, according to حَسَب

beautiful (sweet) حِلو

at all خالِص

warm دافِئ

humid رَطب

to visit زار–يَزور

coastal ساحِل

cold سَقعة = بَرد

inhabitants سُكّان

touristic سِياحي

coast شَطّ

correct صَحّ

desert-like صَحراوي

to believe (that someone is telling the truth) صَدَّق–يُصَدِّق

عارِف knowing, aware

عاش–يَعيش to live

عِندُكم where you (pl.) are

عيد الفِصح Easter

عيد شَمّ النَسيم the Festival of *shamm an-nasiim*

فَصل season

قادِم coming, next

قبل ما = قبل before

قَصدي I mean, my intention

مَخصوص special

مَشهور famous

مُعتَدِل moderate

مَعقول sensible, possible, reasonable

مُفَضّل favorite

مَنطَقة (ج. مَناطِق) area, region

نَفس الشيء the same thing

هكَذا (هاكَذا thus, this way (pronounced

هَواء air

واحة oasis

وَرد flowers

وَقع–يَقَع to be located

(تَقَع (it, she) is located)

يا سَلام Wow!

ياه O, wow!

تمرين رقم ١: املأ الفراغات

وواحة، والخريف، والجفاف، مشهورة، المنطقة، المفضّلة، الليل، الصيف، الصحراويّة، الشتاء

أكثر مناطق مصر صحراوية، الجَوّ فيها حارّ جدّاً وجافّ في ....

قالت لي سلمى إنّ الشمس .... في مصر أكثر من أيّ دولة في العالم. لم أصدّق في البداية ولكن هكذا تقول "ويكيبيديا". في .... الجَوّ دافئ في النهار وبارد في ....

طبعاً في مصر مناطق غير المناطق .... هناك مناطق جبليّة ومناطق على ساحل البحر.

سمعت الكثير عن منطقة شرم الشيخ .... سيوة ومرسى مطروح، وهي مناطق سياحيّة .... في مصر. سأزور كلّ هذه المناطق طبعاً، ولكن منطقتي .... هي منطقة جبل موسى في سيناء. الجَوّ في هذه .... معتدل وجميل في الربيع ....، وأنا أحبّ تسلّق الجبال. سأتسلّق جبل موسى في الرحلة القادمة.

Noun and adjective stems

You have been working on identifying verb stems. Remember that the verb stem represents the simplest form of the verb, which is the past tense conjugation for هو.

Nouns and adjectives also have stems. Noun and adjective stems are the most basic form of the word, which in this case is masculine, singular, and indefinite. There should also not be any possessive suffixes. Note that some words are grammatically feminine by default (such as مدرسة and جامعة) – for these words, there is no masculine equivalent and التاء المربوطة is part of the stem.

The table below walks you through the steps of what to look for when trying to find the stem for the words المصريين ,القادمة, and الرحلة. Read through the explanations for each word and make sure you understand each step.

	القادمة	المصريّين	الرحلة
Remove feminine ending ـة or plural marking	القادم	المصري	Nothing to remove, الرحلة is feminine by default
Remove definite article الـ or possessive suffixes	قادم	مصري	رحلة
Stem	قادم	مصري	رحلة

The following nouns and adjectives are all found in Maya's diary from Lesson 4 of this unit. First give an English translation of the word, then identify its stem. Use the steps above as a guideline. The first two words are given as examples.

Stem	الترجمة	Noun or صفة
منطقة	area	مِنطَقة
صحراوي	desert-like	الصحراويّة
		الأيّام
		وِلايات
		دولة
		الكبيرة
		لفصلَين
		المناطق
		جبليّة
		واحة

سياحيّة		
مشهورة		
المفضّلة		

تمرين رقم ٢: كلمات متقاطعة

	١	٢	٣	٤	٥	٦	٧	٨	٩	١٠
١										
٢										
٣										
٤										
٥										
٦										
٧										
٨										
٩										
١٠										

أفقي

١. فيه سبعة أيّام؛ عكس "سؤال"

٣. لون باسم فواكه؛ والدي

٥. دولة عربيّة شرق السعوديّة

٦. حرف جرّ (preposition)

٨. "يروح" بالفصحى؛ صديقة

١٠. ليس حارّاً وليس بارداً؛ "مش" بالفصحى

عمودي

١. "حبّ" بالفصحى؛ سيّارة بالمصري

٣. اسم فواكه في منطقة البحر الأبيض المتوسّط؛ ليس هناك

٦. اسم عيد مسيحي معروف في فصل الربيع

٨. منها خمسين في أمريكا؛ من البحر

١٠. عكس "قريب"؛ العربيّة والإنجليزيّة والفرنسيّة والإسبانيّة

Sociolinguistic Corner

جه – ييجي

As is the case in English and many other languages, the equivalent of the verb "to come" in Arabic has an irregular conjugation. While you will notice some patterning with the conjugations of other verbs, it is best at this stage to think of this verb as irregular and to remember the conjugation for each of the eight pronouns.

Listen to your teacher or the audio recording for the pronunciation of جه/ييجي of مصري and جاء/يجيء of فصحى and try to imitate the correct pronunciation as closely as possible.

فُصحى		مصري		
مضارع	ماضي	مضارع	ماضي	
أجيء	جئتُ	آجي	جيت	أنا
نَجيء	جئنا	نيجي	جينا	إحنا/نحنُ
تَجيء	جئتَ	تيجي	جيت	انتَ
تجيئي/تجيئين	جئتِ	تيجي	جيتِ	انتِ
تجيئوا/تجيئون	جئتُم	تيجوا	جيتوا	انتو/أنتُم
يجيء	جاء	ييجي	جَه	هو
تجيء	جاءت	تيجي	جَت	هي
يجيئوا/يجيئون	جاءوا	ييجوا	جُم	هم

تمرين رقم ٣ (حضّر في البيت وتكلّم في الصفّ)

1. **At home (في البيت)**: Create an outline in bullet point format about the types of weather found in your city.
2. **In class (في الصفّ)**: With the help of your outline above, discuss the weather in your hometown or your favorite weather with another student in the class.

الوحدة العاشرة
العائلة والمهن

الدرس الأوّل

اِشتَغَل–يِشتِغِل to work

بَقى–يِبقى to become

بَنك bank

تاريخ history

تِجارة business

تَعَرّف–يَتَعَرّف to get to know

حَياة life

خَبّاز/خَبّازة baker

دَرَس–يِدرِس to study

ذَكي smart, clever

رجل أعمال/سيدة أعمال business man/woman

سائق/سائقة driver

سِتّ بيت (ربة بيت) homemaker

شَرِكة company

طِبّ medicine

طَبّاخ/طبّاخة cook

طَبيب/طبيبة (دكتور/دكتورة) physician

طَيّار/طيّارة pilot

عَمَل work

فُرصة (ج. فُرَص) opportunity

قَرّر–يُقَرِّر to decide

لاقى–يِلاقي to find

مُحاسِب/مُحاسبة accountant

مُدَرِّس/مُدَرِّسة = أستاذ/أستاذة = مُعَلِّم/معلّمة

مَدرَسة school

مدرسة ثانوية high school, secondary school

مُدير/مُديرة manager

مُساعِد/مُساعِدة assistant

مُستَشفى hospital

مُمَرِّض/مُمرّضة nurse

مُوَظَّف/موظفة employee

ميكانيكي/ميكانيكية mechanic

هَندَسة engineering

تمرين رقم ١

On a separate piece of paper, organize the following words into three groups: profession (المهنة), place of work (مكان العمل), and subject of study (المادّة).

أستاذ، بَنك، تاريخ، تِجارة، جامِعة، خبّاز، ربة بيت، رجُل أعمال، سائق، شَرِكة، طالبة، طِبّ، طبّاخ، طبيبة، طيّار، فُندق، مُحاسِب، مُدرِّسة، مَدرَسة، مدرسة ثانوية، مُديرة، مُساعِد مُدير، مُستشفى، مطار، مطبخ، مطعم، مُمرّض، مُهندس، مُوظّفة، ميكانيكي، هندسة

تمرين رقم ٢ (استماع وترجمة) (companion website)

Translate the sentences you hear into English on a separate piece of paper.

تمرين رقم ٣

Circle the word that does not belong.

١. طبيب　مُمرض　طِبّ　تِجارة

٢. مَدرسة　هَندسة　جامعة　مُستشفى

٣. تاريخ　قرّر　درَس　تَعرّف

٤. مطبخ　طبّاخ　خبّاز　مَطار

٥. مُحاسِبة　طيّار　مُهندسة　مَدرسة

تمرين رقم ٤

Part 1

Matching (companion website)

Part 2

Incorporate each phrase into a meaningful sentence. Write the sentences in your notebook.
Ex. المحاسب يعمل في البنك

تمرين رقم ٥

Write down each Arabic word next to its English equivalent.

مدير - مُحاسب - مُساعد مدير - ربة بيت - شركة - تجارة - حياة - عمل - فُرصة - مدرسة ثانوية - مُوظّف - ذَكي

High school	
Commerce	
Director	
Assistant Director	
Employee	
Company	
Life	
Smart/clever	
Homemaker, housewife	
Opportunity	
Work	
Accountant	

تمرين رقم ٦

Translate the phrases and sentences you hear into English on a separate piece of paper.

الدرس الثاني- مشاهدة: كم أخ وأخت عندك يا مايا؟

النصّ الأوّل

كلمات جديدة

أكبر bigger, older

أصغَر smaller, younger

اشتغَل-يِشتِغِل to work

دَرَس-يِدرِس to study

مُساعِد assistant

مُدير manager

سِتّ بيت homemaker, housewife

قِصّة story

النصّ الثاني

كلمات جديدة

بَقى–يِبقى to become

دُكتور (ج. دَكاترة) = طبيب (ج. أطِبّاء) physician, doctor

مُدَرّس (ج. مُدرّسين) = أستاذ (ج. أساتذة) teacher

تِجارة business

مُحاسِب (ج. مُحاسِبين) accountant

تعرّف–يتعرّف to get to know

زار–يزور to visit

أحلى best (lit. sweeter, the sweetest) (from حِلو)

مَحشي stuffed (food)

أسئلة

١. صحّ أو غلط؟ (companion website)

٢. أكمل الجدول (complete the table)

الاسم	المهنة
أُخت مايا	تعمل في شركة
أبو مايا	
أبو سلمى	
أم سلمى	مُساعَدة مدير في بنك
	دكتور
أيمن	مُدَرِّس في الإمارات العربيّة المتّحدة
	مُحاسبة في بنك
ريم	

تمرين رقم ١

Below is a set of answers to a set of questions. On a separate piece of paper, write down a question for each given answer.

١. عندي أخ واحد.

٢. عندي أخت واحدة.

٣. أخوي أكبر مني.

٤. أختي أصغر مني.

٥. لا، أخوي لسه في المدرسة الثانوية.

In class (في الصفّ): Working with a classmate ask each other the questions above and report your findings to the class.

تمرين رقم ٢: استعمل الكلمات او العبارات في جُمل.

Use the words/phrases below in sentences of your own.

١. أنا لازم . . . .

٢. انا عايز/عايزة أدرس . . . . في الجامعة.

٣. بابا عايزني أدرس . . . . وماما عايزاني أدرس . . . .

٤. عيلتي كُلهم بيتكلّموا اللغة . . . .

٥. كلنا . . . . في الصفّ العربي.

٦. أنا . . . . كمان.

قَواعِد

More on the present tense (المُضارِع) in مصري

You learned in Unit 7 that the prefix بـ is attached to the present tense verb in مصري. The prefix بـ is added to a verb when it is the main verb in the sentence, as in the example below:

أختي بتشتغل في شركة.
My sister works in a company.

The prefix بـ is not used, however, on verbs that are not the main verb in the sentence. You heard examples of this in the dialogue:

لازم نقعد ونشرب شاي.
We should sit and drink tea.

بابا كان عايزنا كلّنا نبقى دكاترة ومهندسين.
My father wanted us to become doctors and engineers.

Do not worry too much about when to use the prefix بـ right now. You will learn through repeated exposure and practice!

تمرين رقم ٣

For the sentences below, draw a line around the main verb. If there is a بـ prefix, circle it.

١. هم بيشتغلوا ولا بيدرسوا ولا ايه؟

٢. والدك ووالدتك بيشتغلوا ايه؟

٣. لازم تيجي بيتنا في اسكندرية وتتعرّفي على العيلة كلّها.

٤. لازم أزوركم.

٥. وكمان ماما بتعمل أحلى مَحشي في مصر.

٦. أنا باموت في المحشي!

الدرس الثالث-استماع: أنا خايف ريم ما بتذاكرش كويّس!

كلمات جديدة

afraid خايف

to study at home, to do homework ذاكِر-يِذاكِر

intention, meaning قَصد

night ليل

daytime نَهار

to come out, go out خرَج-يخرُج

true, correct صَحيح

to fin لاقى-يلاقي

opportunity فُرصة (ج. فُرَص)

work عَمَل

outside, abroad برّه

ok ماشي

(one who is) understanding فاهِم

smart ذَكي

life حَياة

enough كِفاية

history (Can you think of another meaning for this word?) تاريخ

أسئلة

1. What is Reem's father worried about?
2. Does Reem eat with the family?
3. Why do they talk about her books?
4. What do they say about Ahmad and Mustafa?
5. Why does Reem's father (Mahmoud) think it's better for Reem to study medicine or engineering?
6. Why did Samira (Reem's mother) say: يعني اللي بيدرس تجارة مش ذكي?
7. What does Mahmoud want for his children?

تمرين رقم ١

You learned in Unit 9 that the "relative pronoun" اللي means "who", "that", or "which" in English. There are instances of اللي in which a better translation is "the one who", "that who", or "that which".

اللي occurs in the listening selection of this lesson four times as follows. Study these phrases and sentences and translate them into English in your notebook.

١. يعني اللي بيِدرس تجارة مش ذكي؟
٢. مش زي الفُرص اللي كانت عندي . . .
٣. اللي فات مات.
٤. احنا بنعمل اللي علينا والباقي على الله.

قَواعِد

Root types: final-weak roots

You have already been introduced to four different types of roots:

Sound roots, like درس

Hollow roots, like كان

Doubled roots, like حبّ

Assimilated roots, like وجد

The fifth and last root type you will learn about is the final-weak root, which has a long vowel as its third and final root letter. Examples of verbs derived from final-weak roots are:

اشترى (to purchase) – بَقى (to become) – استنى (to wait) – لاقى (to find)

These verbs follow the same pattern in the past tense but two different patterns in the present tense. This is illustrated by the verbs بقى–يبقى and لاقى–يلاقي. Study the table and answer the questions below. As you study the two patterns, pay close attention to what happens to the third root letter ي.

المضارع	الماضي	المضارع	الماضي	
ألاقي	لاقيت	أبقى	بَقيت	أنا
نِلاقي	لاقينا	نِبقى	بَقينا	إحنا
تلاقي	لاقيت	تِبقى	بَقيت	أنتَ
تِلاقي	لاقيتِ	تِبقي	بَقيتِ	أنتِ
تلاقوا	لاقيتوا	تِبقوا	بَقيتوا	أنتو
يلاقي	لاقى	يِبقى	بَقى	هو
تلاقي	لاقِت	تِبقى	بَقِت	هي
يِلاقوا	لاقوا	يِبقوا	بَقوا	هُم

أسئلة

1. Explain the difference in the vowel of the past and the present tense within each verb.
2. Explain the difference between the two patterns represented by the two verbs.
3. Now complete the following table:

المضارع	الماضي	المضارع	الماضي	
أشتَري	اشتَريت	أستَنّى	استنّيت	أنا
				إحنا
تشتري		تِستَنّى		أنتَ
تشتري		تِستَنّي	استنّيتِ	أنتِ
تشتروا			استنّيتوا	أنتو
يشتري	اشتَرى			هو
	اشترِت		استنِّت	هي
		يستنّوا		هُم

تمرين رقم ٢ (النفي negation): ترجم إلى الإنجليزيّة

١. مش عارف يا سميرة - خايف إنها ما بتذاكرش كويس.
٢. قصدك بنتنا ريم؟ ما بتذاكرش كويس إزّاي؟
٣. دي بتقعد في أوضتها ليل نهار تقرأ كُتُبها، ما بتخرجش حتى تاكل معانا.
٤. صحيح هي بتذاكر كويس، بس مش زي منى ومصطفى . . .
٥. لا، لا مش قصدي كده. بس كمان لو بقت دكتورة أو مهندسة ممكن تشتغل هنا في مصر. مش زي أيمن ورشا - درسوا عربي وتجارة وما لاقوش فُرص عمل إلا بَرّه.
٦. ماشي. أنا فاهم قصدك يا سميرة . . . بس كمان ريم ذكية. مش عايزها تدرس تجارة.
٧. يا سلام؟ يعني اللي بيدرس تجارة مش ذكي؟
٨. أنا عايز لهم أحسن حاجة - أحسن فُرَص - أحسن حياة! مش زي الفُرص اللي كانت عندي . . .

تمرين رقم ٣: تكلّم مع زميلك وكون جُمل او حوارات قصيرة

Working with a partner use the phrases/expressions below in sentences or mini dialogues of your own.

- مش عارف/عارفة:
- انا خايف/خايفة من:
- انا فاهم/فاهمة إنّه:
- هو دكتور في مستشفى؟ لا قصدي هو . . . .
- الكتاب معك او معه؟
- اللي عايز/عايزة . . . . لازم . . . .

الدرس الرابِع: مذكّرات مايا

عائلة سلمى كبيرة. أكثر العائلات المصرية كبيرة. أكبر من العائلات الأمريكيّة. عند سلمى ثلاث أخوات وأربعة إخوة. والد سلمى محمود عنده مطعم في الإسكندرية. ووالدة سلمى سميرة ربّة بيت.

كان محمود يُريد أن يُصبح أولاده وبناته أطبّاء ومهندسين، ولكن واحد فقط (مصطفى) أصبح طبيباً وواحد (أحمد) أصبح مهندساً.

هاني مساعد مدير في فندق في القاهرة، وأيمن مُعلّم لغة عربيّة في دولة الإمارات العربيّة المتّحدة.

أخت سلمى الكبيرة اسمها مُنى، وهي الآن ممرّضة في مُستشفى في الإسكندرية، ورشا تعمل محاسِبة في بنك. أصغر بنت في العائلة هي ريم، عمرها ١٨ سنة وهي طالبة في المدرسة الثانويّة.

سألتني سلمى عن عائلتي وماذا يعمل أبي وأمّي وأختي وأخي وكم أعمارهم. عندما قُلت لسلمى إنّ أخي "مات" عمره ١٨ سنة، قَفَزت وصاحت: "الله يرحمه! مات وعمره ١٨ سنة؟ إزّاي مات؟ بعيد الشرّ! مات في حادث ولّا مَرض ولا إيه؟" قلت لها إنّ اسمه "مات"، أي "ماثيو" أو "مَتّى" بالعربية.

عندما سمعت سلمى ذلك هدأت وشكرَت الله لأنّ أخي "مات" ما مات. في المستقبل لن أقول إنّ اسم أخي "مات"، ولكن ماثيو.

كلمات جديدة

ربّة بيت = سِتّ بيت homemaker, housewife

كان يُريد = he had wanted

طبيب (ج. أطِبّاء) = دُكتور (ج. دكاترة)

فَقَط = بَسّ only

قَفَز–يَقفِز to jump

صاح–يَصيح to shout

الله يرحمه! may God have mercy on him!

مات–يموت to die

بعيد الشرّ! God forbid! (lit. may bad! things be far

حادِث accident

مَرَض sickness

عِندَما = لمّا when

سَمِع–يَسمَع to hear

ذلك that

شَكَر–يَشكُر to thank

قَرّر–يُقَرِّر to decide

أسئلة

١. اعمل قائمة (make a list) بأسماء عائلة سلمى وعمل كلّ واحد منهم:

أب (والد) سلمى	عنده مطعم في الإسكندرية
أم (والدة) سلمى	
مصطفى	
أحمد	
هاني	
أيمن	
مُنى	
رَشا	
ريم	

٢. صحّ أو خطأ؟ (companion website)

٣. رتّب الجمل التالية حسب ورودها في النصّ.

(Arrange the statements according to their appearance in the text.)

١. العائلات المصريّة أكبر من العائلات الأمريكيّة.
٢. أيمن أخو سلمى معلّم.
٣. تعمل مُنى، أخت سلمى، في مستشفى.
٤. سلمى سألت مايا عن عمر أفراد (individuals, members) عائلتها.
٥. سلمى فكّرت أنّ ماثيو أخو مايا ميّت.
٦. قرّرت مايا أنّها لن تستعمل (use) الاسم "مات".
٧. مصطفى أخو سلمى طبيب.
٨. هاني أكبر ولد في عائلة سلمى.

قَواعِد

Negating the future tense in فصحى with لَن

The future tense in فُصحى is negated with لَن. You saw this above in Maya's diary when she wrote:

لن أقول إنّ اسم أخي "مات".
I will not say that my brother's name is Matt.

لن is used with a regular present tense verb.

Using إنّ and أنّ

In her diary of Unit 6 Maya wrote:

كان (الموظّف) يفكّر أنّ كلّ الأجانب يتكلّمون الإنجليزيّة أو لغة أخرى غير العربيّة.

The employee was thinking that all foreigners speak English or another language besides Arabic.

في المستقبل لن أقول إنّ اسم أخي "مات".

In the future I will not say that my brother's name is Matt.

As you can see, both إنّ and أنّ are translated in English as "that". The difference between them is

- The verb قال uses إنّ
- All other verbs use أنّ

قرّر أحمد أنّه لن ينام في النهار.	قرّر أنّ
Ahmed decided that he won't sleep during the day	
فكّرت أنّها الطبيبة!	فكّر أنّ
I thought that she was the doctor!	
سمعوا أنّ التجارة أصعب تخصّص في الجامعة.	سمع أنّ
They heard that business is the most difficult major on campus.	
كيف عرفتم أنّها تخرّجت؟	عرف أنّ
How did you guys know that she graduated?	

Part A

In the sentences below, circle all examples of verbs and the particle أنّ or إنّ that you see, and draw an arrow pointing to the noun that follows it.

١. لماذا قُلتَ لي إنّك لا تحبّني؟

٢. خافت والدتي أنّي لن أتخرج من الجامعة!

٣. قرأتُ أنّ الجزائر أكبر دولة في إفريقيا.

٤. سمعنا أنّه يتكلم ٦ لغات!

٥. يقول الطلّاب إنّ كلمتهم المُفضّلة في اللغة العربية هي كلمة "مُمكن" أو كلمة "دَجاج".

Part B

Translate the sentences above into English

الإعراب (case endings)

You read in Units 7 and 8 about إعراب in فصحى. You read that إعراب rules are quite complicated and that for now simply remember that pairs of words like إعلان/إعلاناً, موظّفون/موظّفين, and مصريون/مصريّين have the same meaning; the difference in the ending signifies a difference in the function of the word in the sentence.

In her diary, Maya uses the following words: طبيباً and مهندساً. These words mean the same thing as طبيب and مهندس. The case endings here do not change the meaning, they simply indicate what function each word performs. You will learn more about the rules of إعراب in the second textbook of this series.

الدرس الخامس

كلمات الوحدة

تعرّف–يتعرّف to get to know

حادِث accident

حَياة life

خايف afraid

خرَج–يخرُج to come out, go out

دَرَس–يدرِس to study

دُكتور (ج. دَكاترة) = طبيب physician, doctor

ذاكر–يذاكر to study at home, to do homework

ذَكي smart

ذلك that

ربّة بيت = سِتّ بيت homemaker

أحلى (from حِلو) best (lit. sweeter, the sweetest)

اشتغَل–يِشتِغِل to work

أصغَر smaller, younger

أكبر bigger, older

الله يرحمه! may God have mercy on him!

بَرّه outside, abroad

بعيد الشرّ! God forbid! (lit. May bad things!) be far

بَقى–يِبقى to become

تاريخ history (Can you think of another meaning for this word?)

تجارة business

قَفَز–يَقفِز to jump

كِفاية enough

لاقى–يِلاقي to fin

ليل night

مات–يَموت to die

ماشي ok

مُحاسِب (ج. مُحاسِبين) accountant

مَحشي stuffed (food)

مُدَرّس (ج. مُدرّسين) = أستاذ (ج. أساتذة) teacher

مُدير manager

مَرَض sickness

مُساعِد assistant

نَهار day (time)

زار–يزور to visit

سَمِع–يَسمَع to hear

شَكَر–يَشكُر to thank

صاح–يَصيح to shout

صَحيح true, correct

طبيب (ج. أطِبّاء) = دُكتور (ج. دكاترة) physician

عَمَل work

عِندَما when

فاهِم (one who is) understanding

فُرصة (ج. فُرَص) opportunity

فَقَط = بَسّ only

قَرّر–يُقَرِّر to decide

قِصّة story

قَصد intention, meaning

تمرين رقم ١: املأ الفراغات

Fill in the blanks in the following without looking at the reading passage of Lesson 4.

أستاذ في جامعة، ربّة بيت، طالب في المدرسة الثانويّة، طالبة في المدرسة الثانويّة، طبيباً، عنده مطعم، محاسِبة في بنك، مُساعد مُدير، مُعلّم لُغة عَربيّة، مُمرّضة، مُهندساً، مُوظّفة في بنك، مُوظّفة في شَركة في كاليفورنيا

عند سلمى ثلاث أخوات وأربعة إخوة. أبو سلمى (محمود) . . . .

في الإسكندرية. و"سميرة " أم سلمى. . . . .

كان محمود يُريد أن يُصبح أولاده وبناته أطبّاء ومهندسين، ولكن واحد فقط صار . . . . وواحد آخر صار . . . .

هاني . . . . في فندق في القاهرة، وأيمن . . . . في دولة الإمارات العربيّة المتّحدة.

أخت سلمى الكبيرة اسمها مُنى، وهي الآن . . . . في مستشفى في الإسكندرية، ورشا تعمل . . . .

أصغر بنت في العائلة هي ريم، عمرها ١٨ سنة وهي . . . .

هذه عائلة سلمى. أمّا عائلة مايا فَكما تعرِفون فيها خمسة أشخاص: أبو مايا وأمّها وأختها ميشيل وأخوها ماثيو ومايا طبعاً. أبو مايا . . . . ، وأمّها . . . . ، وأختها ميشيل . . . . وأخوها ماثيو . . . .

تمرين رقم ٢: أكمل الجدولين (Complete the two tables)

1.

Stem الصيغة المجرّدة	Translation الترجمة	Verb الفعل
اشتغل	they work	بيشتغلوا
		بيدرسوا
	we sit	نقعد
		ونشرب
	and she works	وبتشتغل
	and you (f.) get to know	وتتعرّفي
		بتعمل
	you (f.s.) die	بتموتي
	you will eat it	حَتاكليه
		(ما) بتذاكرش
لاقى		(ما) لاقوش

يُصبح		أصبح
قُلت	I said	
قفزت		
سمعَت		
وصاحت		
قرّرت	I decided	
أقول		

.2

Noun or adjective الاسم أو الصفة	Translation الترجمة	Stem الصيغة المجرّدة
مُساعِدة		
طويلة		
قصّتهم		قِصّة
دكاترة		
ومهندسين		
والثانيين		ثاني
الإمارات		إمارة
المُدَرّس		
المَدرسة		
الثانويّة		
الفُرَص		فُرصة
العائلات		
المصرية		
المُتّحدة		مُتّحِد
عائلتي		
أعمارهم		عُمر
	Extra credit	
عايزنا		

تمرين رقم ٣: اكتب مُفرد (singular) كلّ من الكلمات التالية:

دَكاترة، مهندسين، عائلات، موظّفين، أعمار، أطِبّاء، فُرَص، مُساعِدين، أخَوات

Sociolinguistic Corner

أنّ and إنّ across registers

You learned in this unit that أنّ and إنّ have slightly different uses in فصحى: إنّ is used with the verb قال, whereas all other verbs use أنّ:

١. لا أظن أنّ هناك محطات ميكروباصات.
٢. قال إنّ هذه ليست سيّارته وإنّ صاحب السيّارة وضع اللافتة، وهو مسؤول عنها!

In مصري , this distinction is not made: only إنّ is used.

تمرين رقم ٤: (حضّر وتكلّم ثمّ اكتب) Prepare, discuss in class, then write up

1. **At home (في البيت)**: Prepare an outline about the members of your family.
2. **In class (في الصفّ)**: With the help of the outline above, talk about your family with a classmate.
3. **At home (في البيت)**: Write a paragraph or two about the members of your family: their names, ages, where they live, and what they do.

الوحدة رقم ١١
الدراسة

الدرس الأوّل

الدين الإسلامي the Islamic religion

الشرق الأوسط the Middle East

امِتحان (ج. امتِحانات) test

امِتحان الثانويّة العامّة general secondary school examination

تأسّس–يَتَأسَّس to be founded

تَخرّج–يِتخَرَّج to graduate

تَخَصُّص specialization, major

تَعليم instruction, teaching, education

تَكلِفة (ج. تَكاليف) cost

جامِع mosque

حَسَّن–يحسّن to improve

حَصَل–يَحصُل (عَلى) to obtain

دراسة (ج. دِراسات) study

دَرَجة (ج. دَرَجات) grade, degree, extent

عالَم world

عالي high

عِلم (ج. علوم) science, branch of knowledge

عُلوم سِياسية political science

كُلّيّة college

كُلّيّة حُقوق law school

لُغة (ج. لغات) language

مادّة (ج. مَوادّ) subject

مَركَز (ج. مَراكِز) center

مَسجِد (ج. مَساجِد) = جامِع (ج. جَوامِع) mosque

مِنحة (ج. مِنَح) scholarship

مُهِمّ important

مَوضوع (ج. مَواضيع) subject

نَتيجة (ج. نتائِج) result

تمرين رقم ١ (استماع وقراءة)

Circle the word you hear.

١.	امتحان	تخرَّج	تخصّص	حسّن
٢.	جامعة	جامِع	الجُمعة	جَمع
٣.	عِلم	علوم	عالِم	عالَم
٤.	خرَج	تخرَّج	خُروج	خارِج
٥.	كلمة	كُلّهم	كُليّة	قليل

تمرين رقم ٢ (قراءة وكتابة)

Copy each of the following words and phrases next to its English translation in the table.

علوم الدين الإسلامي ـ دراسات الشرق الأوسط ـ جامِع ـ تكلفة التعليم ـ التعليم في المدارس العربيّة ـ كُلية طِبّ ـ علوم سياسيّة ـ درجة عالية ـ اللُغة العربيّة ـ جامعة "كورنيل" ـ مركز لُغات

١.		A high degree
٢.		College of Medicine
٣.		Cornell University
٤.		Education in Arab schools
٥.		Islamic Studies
٦.		Language center
٧.		Middle Eastern Studies
٨.		Mosque
٩.		Political Science
١٠.		The Arabic language
١١.		The cost of education

تمرين رقم ٣

Part 1

Matching (companion website).

Part 2

Translate the matched phrases into English on a separate piece of paper.

تمرين رقم ٤

Write in Arabic the word defined by each of the sentences below.

١. مادّة يدرسها المُهندس.______________________

٢. مادّة يدرسها الطبيب.______________________

٣. المكان الذي يصلي (pray) فيه المسلمون.______________________

٤. يحصل عليها الطالب إذا علاماته عالية.______________________

٥. يدرس فيها الطالب بعد المدرسة الثانويّة.______________________

٦. يتخرّج منها المُحامي.______________________

تمرين رقم ٥

(In class) Ask each other the questions below and then report your findings to the class.

١. مين عنده مِنحة؟

٢. مين بيدرس دراسات الشرق الأوسط؟

٣. مين بيدرس لُغة أجنبيّة (foreign)؟

٤. مين بيدرس هندسة؟

٥. مين بيدرس أكثر من ٤ موادّ؟

الدرس الثاني–مشاهدة: حتدرسي ايه بالضبط؟

كلمات جديدة

عَلَشان (عَلى شان) for the sake of, in order to

حَسِّن–يحسّن to improve

بتاع of, belonging to

مادّة (ج. مَوادّ) subject

تَخَصُّص specialization, major

دراسة (ج. دِراسات) study

تَخرّج–يتخَرَّج to graduate

لمّا = عِندَما when

مَحظوظ lucky

دَرَجة degree, extent

تعابير

الشرق الأوسط the Middle East

عَلى طول right away

بالنسبة ل . . . as for, as relates to . . .

وَجَع دماغ headache

أسئلة

1. What subjects is Maya going to study?
2. Why does she want to study Arabic?
3. Where did Maya get her BA degree?
4. What was her major?
5. What is she currently studying? Where?
6. How long has Maya been studying?
7. How does Salma view studying?

رتّب الجمل التالية حسب ورودها في الحوار.

- سلمى سألت مايا أين سَتدرس.
- سلمى لا تُحبّ الدراسة.
- مايا تدرس دراسات الشرق الأوسط.
- ستدرس مايا الأدب المصري
- مايا ستدرس في جامعة القاهرة.
- مايا درست أكثر من ٢٢ سنة.
- مايا درست التاريخ.
- مايا ما اشتغلت بعد البكالوريوس.

قَواعِد

Negating the future tense in مصري

In this listening, you heard an example of negation of future tense when Salma asked:

ومش حَتدرسي مادّة ثانية؟

To negate the future tense in مصري, simply add the word مش in front of the future tense verb.

Expressing possession in the past tense with كان

You have learned that possession is expressed in Arabic using the prepositions عند and مع with possessive endings, as عندي شقّة في إِسكندريّة "I have an apartment in Alexandria" and معي ثلاث شُنَط "I have three suitcases with me".

To express possession in the past, you use the verb كان with the same phrases:

Past tense	Present tense
كان عندي شقّة في اِسكندريّة. I had an apartment in Alexandria.	عندي شقّة في اِسكندريّة. I have an apartment in Alexandria.
كان مَعايَ ثلاث شُنَط. I had three suitcases with me.	مَعايَ ثلاث شُنَط. I have three suitcases with me.

To negate possession in the past tense, you negate the verb كان the same way you negate any past tense verb:

ما كانش عندي شقّة في اِسكندريّة. I did not have an apartment in Alexandria.	كان عندي شقّة في اِسكندريّة. I had an apartment in Alexandria.
ما كانش مَعايَ ثلاث شُنَط. I did not have three suitcases with me.	كان مَعايَ ثلاث شُنَط. I had three suitcases with me.

بتاع، بتاعة، بتوع

مصري, like all other spoken Arabic dialects, offers an alternative to adding possessive suffix endings to the end of nouns. The normal possessive suffixes are added to a "vehicle" meaning "belonging to". In the dialogue of this lesson Maya says: عايزة أحَسّن العربي بتاعي = *I want to improve my Arabic.*

بِتاع is the masculine singular form of the word. There is also a feminine singular (بِتاعة) and a plural form (بِتوع). It is important to keep in mind that the *possessed* noun must be definite. Here is the full conjugation of بِتاع/بتاعة/بتوع.

	Plural items	Feminine items	Masculine items
mine	بتوعي	بتاعتي	بتاعي
ours	بتوعنا	بتاعِتنا	بتاعنا
yours, m.s.	بتوعك	بتاعتك	بتاعك
yours (f, s.)	بتوعك	بتاعتك	بتاعك
yours (pl.)	بتوعكم/كو	بتاعِتكم/كو	بتاعكم/كو
his	بتوعه	بتاعته	بتاعه
hers	بتوعها	بتاعِتها	بتاعها
theirs	بتوعهم	بتاعِتهم	بتاعهم

تمرين رقم ١

Answer the following questions in the affirmative, as in the example:

مثال: الطبق ده بتاعها؟ أيوه ده بتاعها.

Useful words

these دول	this (f.s.) دي	this (m.s.) دَه

١. ده الكتاب بتاعَك؟
٢. الفِنجان ده بتاعك؟
٣. الكُرسي ده بتاعَكو؟
٤. القَلَم ده بتاعه؟
٥. الأوضة دي بتاعتها؟
٦. العربيّة دي بتاعتهم؟
٧. الشُنَط دي بتوعَك؟
٨. الكُتُب دول بتوعِك؟

Note on pronunciation in مصري

In مصري some feminine nouns ending in تاء مربوطة followed by the demonstrative pronoun دي undergo a stress shift. In the word دَرَجة the stress (the emphasis) falls on the first syllable. In للدرجة دي the stress falls on the vowel of the تاء مربوطة and the phrase sounds like للدرجادي (*laddaragAAdi*).

Below are some other common examples of this type of stress pattern:

المرّة دي (المرّادي) this time

السنة دي (السنادي) this year

Another common phrase with a similar stress shift is بالنسبة لي "As for me, as far as I'm concerned".

تمرين رقم ٢

Pair Work: You have already graduated and are planning on attending an Arabic summer programme in Cairo and are being asked some questions about your previous studies. The person "interviewing" you can be your classmate or tutor who will read out the questions in مصري. You will answer in مصري using the prompts written in English:

١ عايز تدرس عربي في المدرسة دي ليه؟
I want to study in this school because I want to improve my Arabic.
٢ درست عربي فين قبل كده؟
I have studied Arabic in America.

٣ درست فين بالضبط؟
I studied at the University of Maryland for one year.
٤ درست عربي بس في الجامعة؟ ايه كان تخصصك؟
My specialization was political science and I graduated last year.
٥ وعاوز تعمل ايه في المستقبل؟
God willing, I would like to do a PhD at the American University in Cairo.
٦ الف مبروك!
Reply

تمرين رقم ٣

First match the following negative past possession phrases in مصري with their English equivalents and then use an appropriate one to answer the questions asked by your tutor or classmate (highlighted below):

I didn't have time	a	ما كانش عندي فلوس كفاية	١
I didn't have enough money	b	ما كانش عندي شقة	٢
I didn't have a good grade	c	ما كانش عندي أصحاب	٣
I didn't have a grant/scholarship	d	ما كانش عندي وقت	٤
I didn't have a flat	e	ما كانش عندي درجة كويسة	٥
I didn't have friends	f	ما كانش عندي منحة	٦

أسئلة

١. ما درستش الطب ليه؟
٢. سكنت في الفندق ليه؟
٣. ما خلصتش الدراسة ليه؟
٤. ما كنتش مبسوط في الجامعة ليه؟
٥. ما عملتش دكتوراه ليه؟
٦. ما قعدتش معاي امبارح ليه؟

خلّص/يخلّص = to finish (ECA only)

الدرس الثالِث–قراءة: جامعات عربية قديمة

من أهمّ وأقدم مراكز التعليم في العالم العربي ثلاث جامعات هي: جامعة "الأزهر" في القاهرة وجامعة "الزيتونة" في مدينة تونس عاصمة تونس وجامعة "القرويين" في مدينة فاس في المغرب. كانت كلّ مِن هذه الجامعات مدرسة في جامع، يدرس فيها الطلّاب علوم الدين الإسلامي واللغة العربية.

جامع وجامعة الزيتونة

بُنِيَ جامع الزيتونة في القرن الثامِن الميلادي، وأصبح من أهمّ مراكز التعليم في تونس.

جامع وجامعة القرويّين

تأسّس جامع القرويّين في سنة ٨٥٩ ميلاديّة (م). وكان عدد طلّابه في القرن الرابع عشر أكثر من ثمانية آلاف طالب. بعد استقِلال المغرب في سنة ١٩٥٦ تأسّست كلّيّة حُقوق وسُمِح للبَنات بالدراسة لأوّل مَرّة.

جامع وجامعة الأزهر

تأسّس الجامع الأزهر حوالي سنة ٩٧٠ م. ويُعتَبَر أهمّ مركز للدراسات العربيّة والإسلاميّة في العالم.

في الستينات من القرن العشرين تأسّست في جامعة الأزهر كلّيّة طِبّ وكلّيّة هَندَسة. وسُمح للبنات بالدراسة فيها في سنة ١٩٦٢.

كلمات جديدة

قَديم ancient

أَهَمّ most important (مُهِمّ important)

مَركَز (ج. مَراكِز) center

تَعليم instruction, teaching

عالَم world

كُلّ مِن each of

جامِع (ج. جَوامِع) mosque

عِلم (ج. علوم) science, branch of knowledge

بُنِيَ–يُبنى to be built

قَرن century

ثامِن eighth

ميلادي A.D.

تأسّس–يَتأسّس to be founded

استِقلال independence

كُلّيّة college

حَقّ (ج. حُقوق) right

سُمِح–يُسمَح to be allowed

بِنت (ج. بَنات) girl

حَوالي = تقريباً about, approximately

اعتُبِر–يُعتَبَر to be considered

طِبّ medicine

هَندَسة engineering

تعابير

الدين الإسلامي the Islamic religion

كُلّيّة حُقوق law school

لأوّل مَرّة for the first time

أسئلة

١. ماذا كان يدرس الطلّاب في الجامعات الثلاث في البداية؟

٢. كم طالباً كان يدرس في جامع القرويّين في القرن الرابع عشر؟

٣. متى تأسّست كلّيّة الطبّ في جامعة الأزهر؟

٤. مَتى سُمح للبنات بالدراسة في جامعة الأزهر وجامعة القرويّين؟

1. What did students study at the beginning in the three mosques/universities?
2. How many students studied at al-Qarawiyyiin Mosque in the 14th century?
3. When was a School of Medicine founded at al-Azhar University?
4. When were girls allowed into al-Azhar and al-Qarawiyyiin Universities?

صحّ أو خطأ؟ (companion website)

أكمل الجدول التالي.

اسم الجامع/الجامعة	الموقع	سنة التأسيس
جامع الزيتونة		
		٨٥٩ ميلادي (م.)
	القاهرة	

أكمل الجدول التالي عن جامعتك ثمّ تكلّم عنها في الصفّ.

Complete the table about your university and then tell the other students about it in the class.

خاصة/حكوميّة private/public	عدد الطُلاب (تقريبا)	سنة التأسيس	الموقع	اسم الجامعة

قواعِد

1. Passive voice in فصحى

Consider the following sentence: *The Zeituna Mosque was built in the 8th Century A.D.*
In the above text its Arabic equivalent was written as follows:

بُنِيَ جامع الزيتونة في القرن الثامِن الميلادي.

The sentence uses the "passive voice", which is used when we don't know who the subject of the verb is; we just know that the action occurred. This is done in فصحى by conjugating the verb in the past tense with a ضمّة on the first root letter and a كسرة under the second root letter.

تمرين رقم ١

Matching (companion website).

2. More on the superlative مِن أقدَم

You learned in Unit 8 that the superlative has the same form as the comparative in Arabic, with the difference lying in what comes before or after the adjective and whether the adjective is followed by مِن or a noun. Compare the following two sentences:

Cairo is bigger than Alexandria.	القاهرة أكبر من الإسكندريّة.
Cairo is the biggest city in Egypt.	القاهرة أكبر مدينة في مصر.

A common structure involving the superlative adjective usage is the following:

The al-Azhar Mosque is among the most important and most ancient centers of learning in the Arab world.	جامع الأزهر من أهمّ وأقدم مراكز التعليم في العالم العربي.

As you can see the superlative adjective precedes the noun which is definite and in plural form.

تمرين رقم ٢: ترجم إلى العربيّة

1. London is one of the biggest cities (مُدُن) in the world.
2. Alexandria is one of the most beautiful (أجمَل) cities on the Mediterranean.
3. Damascus is one of the oldest cities in the world.
4. My friend (m.) is one of the tallest students in his school.

الدرس الرابِع: مذكّرات مايا

امتِحان الثانويّة العامّة. أسئلة الثانويّة العامّة. نتائج الثانويّة العامّة. كلّ الناس يتكلّمون عن امتحان الثانويّة العامّة.

يَقول الناس في مِصر إنّ امتحان الثانويّة العامّة مُهمّ جدّاً.

الطلبة الذين يحصلون على دَرَجات عالية يدرسون الطِبّ والهندسة واللغة الإنجليزيّة والعلوم السياسية وعلوم الكمبيوتر. والطلبة الذين لا يحصلون على دَرَجات عالية يدرسون التاريخ والأدب العربي والتِجارة.

هُناك طبعاً طَلَبة يحصلون على درجات عالية ويفضّلون دِراسة هذه المَواضيع. أمّا الطلبة الذين يفشلون (لا ينجحون) في الامتحان فَلا يدخلون الجامعة، ويجب أن يأخذوا الامتِحان مَرّة أخرى.

ريم أخت سلمى الصغيرة سوفَ تأخذ امتحان التوجيهي في شهر يونيو، وهي خائفة، لأنّ الامتحان صعب جداً. سألتُها ماذا تريد أن تفعل إذا نجحت في الامتحان، فقالت لي إنّها تُريد السفر الى الخارج للدراسة في جامعة أجنبية، في أوروبا أو أمريكا. وسألتني عن الجامعات الأمريكيّة وتكاليف الدراسة وكيف تَحصُل على مِنحة. كثير من الطلبة يسألوني نفس السؤال: كيف يحصُلون على منحة للدراسة في جامعة أجنبيّة؟

كلمات جديدة

امتِحان (ج. امتِحانات) test

الذين = اللي

نَتيجة (ج. نتائِج) result

يتكلّمون = بيتكلّموا (see note in the Sociolinguistic Corner)

قال–يَقول to say

مُهِمّ important

طِبّ medicine

حَصَل-يَحصُل (عَلى) to obtain

دَرَجة (ج. دَرَجات) grade

عالي high

لُغة language

عِلم (ج. عُلوم) science, branch of knowledge

تاريخ history

تِجارة business, commerce

فَضَّل-يُفَضِّل to prefer

مَوضوع (ج. مَواضيع) subject

فَشِل-يَفشَل to fail

نجَح-يَنجَح to succeed, pass an exam

يونيو (شهر ستّة) June

فَعَل-يَفعَل = عمِل-يَعمَل to do

الخارِج = برّه abroad (outside)

أجنَبي foreign

أوروبا Europe

تَكلِفة (ج. تَكاليف) cost

نَفس same

مِنحة (ج. مِنَح) scholarship

تعابير

امتحان الثانويّة العامّة general secondary school examination

عُلوم سِياسية political science

أمّا ... فَ as for ... then

أسئلة

صحّ أو خطأ؟

تمرين رقم ١: رتّب الجمل التالية حسب ورودها في النصّ

- الطلّاب الذين لا ينجحون في امتحان الثانويّة العامّة لا يدخلون الجامعة.
- الطلّاب الذين يحصلون على علامات عالية يدرسون الطبّ والهندسة.
- امتحان الثانويّة العامّة مهمّ في مصر.
- ريم تريد الدراسة في الخارج.
- ريم خائفة.
- ريم سألت مايا كيف تحصل على منحة للدراسة.
- كثير من الطلّاب المصريّين يسألون كيف يحصلون على منحة.

قَواعِد

١. أمّا . . . ف

ف is a conjunction with a similar meaning to و "and". The main difference between the two is that ف has the additional meaning of *since, because, then,* or *so,* in a way tying the clause in which it is found to the preceding one. Consider the use of ف in the following sentence:

سألتُها ماذا تريد أن تفعل إذا نجحت في الامتحان، فقالت لي إنّها تُريد السفر الى الخارج . . .

The structure . . . ف . . . أمّا, in the sentence أمّا الطلبة الذين يفشلون في الامتحان فَلا يدخلون الجامعة, translates as: *As for the students who fail (do not succeed) in the exam, they do not enter the university.* أمّا and ف constitute one structure, so when you see أمّا look for ف, which will be prefixed to a word that follows it in the sentence.

تمرين رقم ٢

Complete the following sentences with a ف . . . أمّا clause. The first sentence is given as an example.

١. أخي يحبّ (likes) التاريخ، . . .

أخي يحبّ التاريخ، أمّا أنا فأحب العلوم.

٢. أنا أفضّل أن أدرس في الصباح، أمّا أبي . . .

٣. فدوى تريد السفر إلى أمريكا، . . .

٤. الجوّ في "سياتل" دائماً (always) ماطر، . . .

٥. في أمريكا يأكل كثير من الناس لحم الخنزير (pork)،

٦. أعجبتني بيروت كثيراً، . . .

2. إعراب of the present tense verb

You may have wondered why most of the present tense verbs in the reading selection of this lesson that refer to the plural third person (they) end in ون and in one instance end in وا:

يحصلون, يدرسون, ويفضّلون, يفشلون, ينجحون, يدخلون, but يأخذوا.

Like nouns and adjectives, present tense verbs in Arabic also have إعراب. The إعراب endings change the spelling, but not the meaning, of the word.

In the sentence ويجب أنْ يأخذوا الامتِحان مَرّة أخرى the reason why the spelling change occurs is because the verb comes after the particle أنْ:

Note that the final letter ا is silent and not pronounced.

تمرين رقم ٣: أكمل الجدولين (Complete the two tables)

أ.

Stem الصيغة المجرّدة	Translation الترجمة	Verb الفعل
تكلّم		يتكلّمون
		يَقول
حصل		يحصلون
		يدرسون
فضّل		ويفضِّلون
	they enter	يدخلون
		تأخذ
		سألتُها
		نجحَت
	she asked me	وسألتني
		يسألوني

ب.

Stem الصيغة المجرّدة	Translation الترجمة	Noun or adjective الاسم أو الصفة
عامّ	the general	العامّة
		أسئلة
نتيجة		نتائج

الطلبة		
دَرَجات		
عالية		
التاريخ		
المَواضيع		موضوع
الجامعة		
الامتحان		
للدراسة	for studying (to study)	
الجامعات		
أجنبية		

الدرس الخامس

كلمات الوحدة

أجنَبي foreign

أمّا . . . فَ as for . . . then

أهَمّ most important (مُهِمّ important)

أوروبا Europe

استِقلال independence

اعتُبِر–يُعتَبَر to be considered

الخارِج = برّه abroad (outside)

الدين الإسلامي the Islamic religion

الشرق الأوسط the Middle East

امتِحان (ج. امتِحانات) test

امتِحان الثانويّة العامّة general secondary school examination

بالنسبة ل . . . . . as for, as relates to

بتاع of, belonging to

بِنت (ج. بَنات) girl

بُنِي–يُبنى to be built

تأسّس–يَتَأسَّس to be founded

تاريخ history

تِجارة business, commerce

تَخرّج–يِتخَرَّج to graduate

تَخَصُّص specialization, major

تَعليم instruction, teaching

تَكلِفة (ج. تَكاليف) cost

ثامِن eighth

جامِع mosque

حَسَّن-يحسّن to improve

حَصَل-يَحصُل (عَلى) to obtain

حَقّ (ج. حُقوق) right

حَوالي = تقريباً about, approximately

دراسة (ج. دِراسات) study

دَرَجة (ج. دَرَجات) grade, degree, extent

سُمِح-يُسمَح to be allowed

طِبّ medicine

عالَم world

عالي high

عَلَشان (عَلى شان) for the sake of, in order to

عِلم (ج. علوم) science, branch of knowledge

عُلوم سِياسية political science

عَلى طول right away

فَشِل-يَفشَل to fail

فَضَّل-يُفَضِّل to prefer

فَعَل-يَفعَل = عمِل-يَعمَل to do

قال-يَقول to say

قَديم ancient

قَرن century

كُلّ مِن each of

كُلّيّة college

كُلّيّة حُقوق law school

لأوّل مَرّة for the first time

لُغة language

لمّا = عِندَما when

مادّة (ج. مَوادّ) subject

مَحظوظ lucky

مَركَز (ج. مَراكِز) center

مِنحة (ج. مِنَح) scholarship

مُهِمّ important

مَوضوع (ج. مَواضيع) subject

ميلادي A.D.

نَتيجة (ج. نتائِج) result

نجَح-يَنجَح to succeed, pass an exam

نَفس same

هَندَسة engineering

وَجَع دماغ headache

يتكلّمون = بيتكلّموا (see note in Sociolinguistic Corner)

يونيو (شهر ستّة) June

تمرين رقم ١–قراءة: اقرأ النصّ وأجب على الأسئلة.

Read the text and answer the questions below.

الجامعة الأمريكيّة بالقاهرة

تأسّست الجامعة الأمريكيّة بالقاهرة في سنة ١٩١٩. كان رئيسها الأوّل "تشارلز واتسون"، الذي ظلّ رئيساً لمدّة ٢٥ سنة.

في الجامعة طلّاب من أكثر من ١٠٠ دولة، وأساتذة من بلاد كثيرة ولكن أكثرهم من مصر والولايات المتّحدة.

حصلت الجامعة الأمريكيّة على المركز الأوّل في مصر والمركز الثالث في إفريقيا في سنة ٢٠١٤ حسب تصنيف "كيو إس العالمي للجامعات" (QS World University Rankings). وحصلت على المركز رقم ٣٦٠ بين جامعات العالم. وكان برنامج الماجستير في إدارة الأعمال فيها من أفضل ٢٠٠ برنامج في العالم.

في البداية كان طلّاب الجامعة من الذكور فقط، وتمّ قبول أول طالبة في سنة ١٩٢٨.

عندما تأسّست الجامعة كان موقعها في ميدان التحرير في وسط العاصمة المصريّة، وظلّ هناك إلى سنة ٢٠٠٨ عندما انتقلت إلى موقع جديد في القاهرة الجديدة.

أسئلة

صحّ أو خطأ؟ (companion website)

١. عمل تشارلز واتسون رئيساً (president) للجامعة الأمريكيّة في القاهرة حتى سنة ١٩٤٤.

٢. في الجامعة الأمريكيّة في القاهرة أساتذة من مصر وأمريكا فقط.

٣. في الجامعة الأمريكيّة في القاهرة طلّاب من مصر وأمريكا فقط.

٤. كانت الجامعة الأمريكيّة في القاهرة أحسن (أفضل) جامعة في مصر في سنة ٢٠١٤.

٥. الجامعة الأمريكيّة من أحسن ٢٠٠ جامعة في العالم.

٦. طلاب الجامعة الأمريكيّة الآن من الذكور فقط.

٧. تقع الجامعة الأمريكيّة في ميدان التحرير.

قبل ما

You learned in Unit 9 that when the particle ما comes after قبل or بعد it does not have a meaning; it simply separates these two particles from a following verb. When no verb follows بعد or قبل, the particle is not used.

تمرين رقم ٢: ترجم إلى الإنجليزيّة

١. انتِ درستِ فين قبل ما تيجي مصر؟
٢. اشتغلتِ بعد البكالوريوس، ولّا بدأت الدكتوراه بعد ما تخرّجتِ على طول؟
٣. قرّرتُ بعد ذلك أنْ لا أقول إنّ اسم أخي "مات"، ولكن ماثيو.
٤. بعد استِقلال المغرب في سنة ١٩٥٦ تأسّست كلّيّة حُقوق وسُمِح للبَنات بالدراسة لأوّل مَرّة.

Sociolinguistic Corner

Relative clauses modifying definite nouns in فصحى and in مصري

In unit 9 you learned about the word اللي, which is used in مصري for relative clauses modifying definite nouns: الموظف اللي بيشتِغل في الحكومة. This grammatical structure exists in فصحى as well. However, in فُصحى distinctions are made between masculine and feminine and between singular, dual, and plural relative pronouns. Only the three فصحى relative pronouns commonly used are introduced in this book. These are الذي, التي, and الذين.

who, that, which (masculine, singular)	الذي
who, that, which (feminine, singular)	التي
who, that, which (masculine, plural)	الذين

تمرين رقم ٣: ترجم إلى الإنجليزية.

١. بسّ أحسن من السقعة والتلج اللي عندكم . . .
٢. مش زي الفُرص اللي كانت عندي . . .
٣. احنا بنعمل اللي علينا والباقي على الله.
٤. يعني اللي بيدرس تجارة مش ذكي؟
٥. الطلبة الذين يحصلون على دَرَجات عالية . . .
٦. الطلبة الذين لا يحصلون على دَرَجات عالية . . .
٧. كان رئيسها الأوّل "تشارلز واتسون"، الذي ظلّ (remained) رئيساً لمدّة ٢٥ سنة.

More فُصحى/مصري differences in this unit

مصري	فصحى
بَقى–يِبقى	أصبح–يُصبِح
(ب) يتكلّموا	يتكلّمون
اللي	الذين
قَوي، خالِص	جِدّاً
ما بينجحوش	لا ينجحون
حَتاخُذ	سوف تأخذ
ايه	ماذا
عايزة	تريد أن
بتعمل	تفعل

تمرين رقم ٤: اختبر معلوماتك

(In Teacher's Book)

تمرين رقم ٥

Choose one of the following two topics:

1a. Create a dialogue with another student in which you discuss your reasons for choosing the school you are attending.
1b. Write about your dialogue above (about 50 words).
2a. Study the history of your university or college (or any other university you like) and prepare a short outline and present it to the class.
2b. Write a paragraph of about 50 words about the university or college you've presented in 2a.

الوحدة رقم ١٢
الأعياد والمناسبات

الدرس الأوّل

احتِفال celebrating, celebration

احتَفَل–يحتِفِل to celebrate

اِشتَرى–يِشتِري to buy

the Feast of Sacrifice (العيد الكبير = عيد الأضحى)

تلوين coloring

جَميع everyone, all

جَميل = حِلو beautiful

حَديقة (ج. حَدائق) garden, park

خَروف (ج. خِرفان) lamb

زَحمة crowdedness, congestion

شُروق sunrise

طابور line, queue

عيد (ج. أعياد) feast, festival, anniversary

عيد الفِطر Eid al-Fitr (celebration marking the end of Ramadan)

عيد ميلاد birthday

عيد الميلاد Christmas

غُروب sunset

قَديم (ج. قُدَماء) ancient

كَعكة cake

كُلّ سَنة وانتَ طيِّب! happy holidays! (lit every year and you are well)

كَلِمة word

كَنيسة (ج. كَنائس) church

مَسألة (ج. مَسائل) matter

مُفَضَّل favorite

هَديّة (ج. هَدايا) gift, present

واقِف standing

تمرين رقم ١

Read aloud the new words in Arabic:

تمرين رقم ٢: استماع وترجمة

Listen to the sentences and translate them into English on a separate piece of paper.

تمرين رقم ٣: ترجم إلى العربيّة

1. My birthday is in June (يونيو or شهر ٦)
2. Happy birthday!
3. I bought a gift from the store (دُكّان).

تمرين رقم ٤

Translate the following words into English, then identify their roots and give at least one example of a word derived from the same root. The first one is given as an example.

كلمات من نفس الجذر	الجذر	الترجمة	الكلمة
لَون color، مُلَوَّن colored	ل-و-ن	coloring	تلوين
			ثلث
			جَميع
			جَميل
			شُروق

			غُروب
			قَديم
			كَلِمة
			مَسألة
			واقِف

تمرين رقم ٥

Match each greeting with its correct response and practice saying them with a partner in class.

Response – الردّ	Greetings – التحيات
الله أكرم	كل سنة وانت طيب
وعليكم السلام	رمضان كريم
وانت طيب	عيد مبارك
الله يبارك فيك	السلام عليكم
الله يبارك فيك	مبروك

تمرين رقم ٦ (حوار قصير mini-dialogue)

Working with a partner, discuss the different holidays that you celebrate and indicate which is عيدك المفضّل.

أحتفل ب (I celebrate) (عيد ميلادي، عيد الميلاد، عيد الفطر، . . .)

عيدي المُفضَّل هو . . . .

Arabic calligraphy

Arabic calligraphy is well known for its beauty. Often the designs are too intricate for the average person to read. However, literate native speakers can recognize many of these designs because they spell commonly used expressions like: Merry Christmas (also Happy Birthday), Many Happy Returns of the Day, Happy or Blessed Eid, In the Name of Allah the Compassionate the Merciful, and God Be Praised.

تمرين رقم ٧

Part A

Connect the Arabic expressions in column أ with their English equivalents in column ب.

ب	أ
God Be Praised!	كُلّ عام وأنتُم بخير (كلّ سنة وانتو طيّبين!)
Happy Birthday (Merry Christmas)!	عيد مُبارَك!
Happy Eid!	بسم الله الرحمن الرحيم
In the name of God the Compassionate the Merciful	عيد ميلاد سعيد!
Blessed Eid!	ما شاء الله!
Many Happy Returns of the Day (Year)!	عيد سعيد!

Part B

Can you guess what the calligraphy samples below say? All the expressions are found in the table above. Write them down in your notebook once you have figured them out.

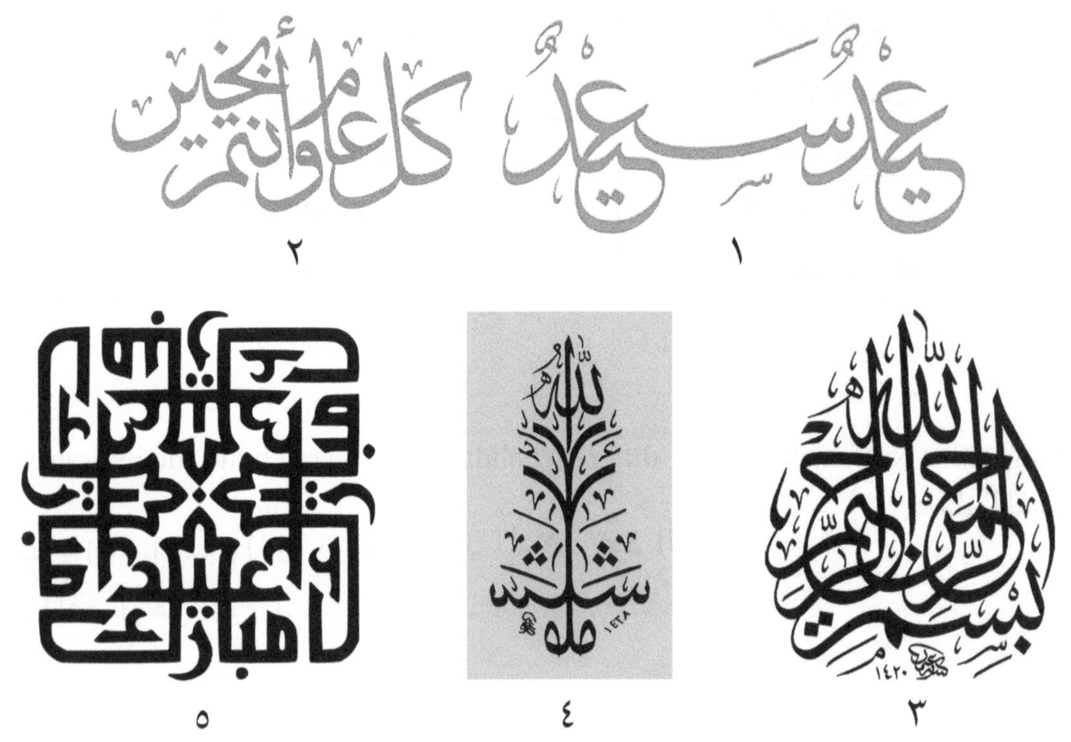

الدرس الثاني-مشاهدة: بتعرفي حاجة عن عيد الأضحى!

كلمات جديدة

عيد (ج. أعياد) feast, festival, anniversary

the Feast of Sacrifice

العيد الكبير = عيد الأضحى

كُلّ سَنة وانتم طيِّبين! many happy returns of the day! (lit. every year and you are well)

زَحمة crowdedness, congestion

اِشترى–يِشتِري to buy

لِبس clothes

هَديّة (ج. هَدايا) gift, present

خَروف (ج. خِرفان) lamb

مُعظَم most (of)

قدر–يِقدِر to be able to

وَزّع–يوَزّع to distribute

واقِف standing

طابور line, queue

فَقير (ج. فُقَراء) poor (person)

يا ريت! I wish!

أسئلة

1. What does عيد الأضحى or العيد الكبير remind Maya of?
2. Morocco (المغرب) is mentioned in the dialogue twice. Explain why it is mentioned in the two instances.
3. Why can't some Egyptians buy a lamb for عيد الأضحى?
4. What was the strange thing that Maya witnessed in downtown Cairo?
5. Why is the Qur'an mentioned?
6. Why don't people in America do the same thing that the Qur'an calls for?
7. Does Maya know where the name عيد الأضحى comes from?
8. What do Maya and أبو هاني (Salma's father) disagree about?

قَواعِد

Root types: summary

You have learned the following root types:

- Sound i.e. شرب
- Hollow i.e. نام
- Doubled i.e. حَبّ
- Assimilated i.e. وصل
- Final-weak i.e. استنى

Identifying the root letters will help you guess meanings of new words and make connections with familiar ones. It is a skill that takes time and practice, but as you learn more Arabic you will find it easier to recognize them.

One way that helps you identify roots is knowledge of related words. For example, the only letters shared between حفلة (a party) and احتفل (to celebrate) are ح – ف – ل. Recognizing this overlap in letters can help you (correctly) guess that ح – ف – ل is the root of both words.

Another way to guess the root is by recognizing what are the most common letters added to words beyond the root letters. These letters are a part of well-known patterns for deriving new words, which you will learn about in the upcoming units.

Root letters	Verb stem الصيغة المجردة	Additional letters
ع – م – ل	استعمل	-است
ق – ل – ل	استقلّ	
س – ف – ر	سافر	-ا-
ص – ب – ح	أصبح	
خ – ر – ج	تخرّج	-ت
س – م – ع	استمع	

An important step in recognizing roots is removing all grammatical suffixes and prefixes like the definite article, gender, case and plural markers, and subject and possessive pronouns. So when you see a word like بيحتفلوا, you can quickly determine that the prefixes ب and ي and the suffix وا are related to the conjugation of the verb in the present tense. This leaves four letters: ح.ت.ف.ل. How do we determine which three of these letters constitute the root? You will learn this in this and subsequent units as you learn about verb forms and noun patterns. For now, if you cannot figure out the three letters of a root try to make an intelligent guess and you will see that you will be right most, if not all, of the time.

تمرين رقم ١: أكمل الجدولين (Fill in the empty cells in the following tables.)

Part A. From this lesson

الصيغة المجرّدة	نوع الجذر Root type	الجذر	الترجمة	الفعل
		ش.ر.ي		بيشتروا
فكّر				بيفكّرني
			I attended it	حضرته
				بيشتغلوا
		و.ز.ع		بيوزّعوا
ضَحّى			he will sacrifice	حَيضحّي
				بَعث

Part B. From previous units

الصيغة المجرّدة	نوع الجذر Root type	الجذر	الترجمة	الفعل
		ع-ب-ر	It was considered	أُعتُبر
		أ – س – س		تأسّست
تكلّم				بيتكلموا
			You will find	حتلاقي
	doubled			استقلّت
سأل				وسألوني
		و – ق – ف		بتتوقّف

تمرين رقم ٢

الجزء الأوّل

Below is a list of phrases from the video. With a partner, read them out loud and try to figure out who said which sentence, Maya or Salma's father (مايا ولا أبو سلمى).

أنا كنت في وسط البلد من يومين وكان فيه زحمة قوي

انت بتعرفي حاجة عن عيد الأضحى أو العيد الكبير؟

لكن مش زيّ البلاد العربيّة الثانية

ناس كانوا واقفين في طابور

دي حاجة كويّسة قوي

يا ريت لو نعمل حاجة زيّ كده عندنا

أمريكان فقرا؟ مش معقول

الناس اللي بيقدروا، يعني اللي عندهم فلوس، بيشتروا خروف

إسماعيل، إسحاق، زيّ بعضه، ما همّ إخوات

الجزء الثاني

With your partner, come up with a small skit based on the above phrases. Put a check next to each phrase once you've used it in your skit!

الدرس الثالِث

النصّ الأوّل–استماع: انتو المصريّين بتحتفلوا بأعياد كثيرة!

كلمات جديدة

ما شاء لله God be praised
احتَفَل–يِحتِفِل to celebrate
عيد الفِطر Eid al-Fitr (celebration marking the end of Ramadan)
عيد ميلاد birthday
مِن زَمان a long time ago
اختلَف–يِختِلِف to be different
مَسألة matter
شَخصي personal

أسئلة

True or false?

1. In Egypt عيد الفطر is celebrated for three days and عيد الأضحى for four.
2. Today is Salma's birthday.
3. Maya thinks of Salma as a close friend.
4. Maya bought Salma a gift for her birthday.
5. According to Salma, not many Egyptians celebrate their birthdays.
6. According to Salma, it's hard for a family with ten children to celebrate their birthdays.

النصّ الثاني–قراءة: الاحتفال بأعياد الميلاد

مِن الفروق بين العائلات العربيّة والعائلات الغربيّة أنّ الكثير من العائلات العربيّة لا تحتفل بأعياد ميلاد أفرادها، كما في المُجتمعات الغربيّة. من أسباب ذلك أنّ العائلات العربيّة، وخصوصاً في الماضي، كانت كبيرة، فيها عشرة أشخاص أو أكثر. ومن الصعب الاحتفال بعيد ميلاد عشرة أشخاص في السنة.

ولكن عادة الاحتفال بعيد الميلاد بدأت تنتشر في المُجتَمعات العربيّة، وخصوصاً بين العائلات التي تأثّرت بالثقافة الغربيّة. تُحضِّر العائلة كعكة عيد ميلاد، وتشتري الهدايا للشخص الذي تحتفل بعيد ميلاده، ويغنّي الجميعٍ أغنية "سنة حِلوة يا جَميل"، التي لها نفس لحن أغنية Happy Birthday to you، وأحياناً يستعملون الكلمات الإنجليزية: "هابي بيرثداي تويو..."

كلمات جديدة

فَرق (ج. فُروق) difference

فَرد (ج. أفراد) individual, member

كَما as

مُجتَمَع (ج. مُجتَمَعات) society

سَبَب (ج. أسباب) reason

ذلِك (pronounced ذالِك) that

احتِفال celebrating, celebration

عادة habit, custom

انتَشَرَ–يَنتَشِر to spread

بَين between, among

الّتي = إللي that, which

تأثّر–يَتأثّر to be influenced

ثَقافة culture

حَضّر–يُحَضِّر to prepare

كَعكة cake

شَخص (ج. أشخاص) person

غَنّى–يُغَنّي to sing

جَميع everyone, all

أغنية (ج. أغاني) song

جَميل = حِلو beautiful

لَحن tune

أسئلة: صَحّ أو خطأ؟

١. كلّ العائلات العربيّة تحتفل بعيد ميلاد الأولاد والبنات فيها.

٢. كانت العائلات العربيّة في الماضي أصغر من العائلات العربيّة الآن.

٣. يحتفل عدد أكبر من العائلات العربيّة الآن بأعياد ميلاد أفرادها.

٤. الاحتفال بعيد الميلاد في العائلات العربيّة مثل الاحتفال بعيد الميلاد في العائلات الغربيّة.

٥. هناك أغنية عربيّة لها نفس لحن Happy Birthday to you!.

تمرين رقم ١–(كتابي في البيت): أكمل الجدول

	احتفل–يحتفل to celebrate	كان–يكون	استعمل–يستعمِل	اشترى–يشتري
أنا				
نحنُ	نحتفِل			

				انتَ
				انتِ
		تكونون		انتُم
				هو
	تستعمِل			هي
يشترون				هم

تمرين رقم ٢–(شفهي في الصفّ): تصريف أفعال (In Teacher's Book)

قَواعِد

2. Review of إنّ/أنّ and أنْ

You've learned that إنّ and أنّ mean "that", and are always followed by a noun (or pronoun). The difference between them is that إنّ comes after the verb قال and أنّ comes after other verbs. You also learned that أنْ comes between two verbs or between specific expressions like "it's possible that, it's difficult, it's easy", etc., and a verb with the meaning "to".

تمرين رقم ٣: ترجم إلى العربيّة

1. Salma said that today is her birthday.
2. Maya wanted (كانت تُريد) to buy Salma a present.
3. Salma said that there are many holidays in Egypt.
4. Maya thinks that birthdays are a personal matter.
5. It is hard for a family to celebrate ten birthdays!
6. The reason is that families were big in the past.

تمرين رقم ٤: الإضافة، الاسم والصفة، والجملة الكاملة

The following items include a number of إضافة phrases, noun-adjective (اسم وصفة) phrases, and one full sentence (جُملة). First translate the phrases and sentence into English, then indicate what type of structure each one is. Follow the examples.

Type	الترجمة	
اسم وصفة	many celebrations	أعياد كثيرة
إضافة	the Feast (celebration) of al-Fitr	عيد الفطر

عيد الأضحى		
مسألة شخصيّة		
العائلات العربيّة		
أعياد ميلاد أفرادها		
المجتمعات الغربيّة		
العائلات العربيّة كبيرة		
عادة الاحتفال		
الثقافة الغربيّة		
الكلمات الإنجليزيّة		

تمرين رقم ٥

Interview activity:

Below is a list of questions based on the topics and vocabulary covered in this lesson. Your أستاذ or أستاذة will assign you to either question set 1 or question set 2.

Part A

On your own, look at the questions being asked and think about what words you would like to use to ask them. What is important here is not that you perfectly translate the question word-for-word, but rather than you try to get the general meaning across with the vocabulary you already know.

Part B

Find a partner who prepared the opposite question set to you. Take turns interviewing each other. You can use the English questions below to help jog your memory about the topics.

Question set 1

1. What holidays do you celebrate? Which holiday is your favorite, and why?
2. What are the differences between birthdays in the Arab world and in Western societies?
3. How do you like to celebrate birthdays? Do you prepare a cake, sing songs, or buy presents?
4. [Write your own question here, based on the vocabulary in this unit!]

Question set 2

1. In your opinion, do you consider birthdays to be holidays or to be personal matters? Why?
2. What do you know about Eid al-Fitr and Eid al-Adha?
3. What is your favorite holiday? How have the customs of that holiday changed over time (you may want to use من زمان here)?
4. [Write your own question here, based on the vocabulary in this unit!]

الدرس الرابع: مذكّرات مايا

يا سلام، ما أجمل الجوّ في هذه الأيّام! معتدل ولطيف طول الوقت.

كان اليوم عيد شمّ النسيم. خرجتُ مع صاحباتي سلمى ورانية إلى حديقة "الفسطاط" في منطقة مصر القديمة واحتفلنا بالعيد هناك. بقينا في الحديقة من شروق الشمس حتى غروبها.

كنت أعتقد أنّ عيد شمّ النسيم هو عيد مسيحي فقط، ولكنّ رانية قالت إنّ كلّ المصريين (المسيحيين والمسلمين) يحتفلون بالعيد في هذا الوقت.

عيد شمّ النسيم من أقدم الأعياد الشعبيّة في مصر، ويرجع تاريخه الى خمسة آلاف سنة. وأصل الاسم هو الكلمة الفرعونيّة "شمو" التي تعني "عيد الخلق" أو "بداية الحياة".

وكان المصريون القدماء يعتقدون أنّ ذلك اليوم يرمز إلى بداية العالَم والحياة على الأرض. وقد تغيّر الاسم وأُضيفت إليه كلمة "النسيم" او الجو اللطيف لأنّ الناس يحتفلون بالعيد في فصل الربيع.

أكلت اليوم الفسيخ لأوّل مرّة في حياتي. والفسيخ سَمك مُملّح، وهو من الأكلات التي ياكلها المصريّون في عيد شمّ النسيم. قُلت كانت هذه أوّل مرّة أكلت فيها الفسيخ، وستكون آخر مرّة، لأنّني ما أحبَبته أبداً، وخصوصاً رائحته.

من تقاليد عيد شمّ النسيم عادة تلوين البيض التي بدأت في زمن المصريّين القدماء قبل آلاف السنين. ونفس العادة موجودة الآن في عيد الفصح (Easter) في كثير من بلاد العالم.

كلمات جديدة

ما أجمَل how beautiful

حَديقة (ج. حَدائق) garden, park

بَقي–يَبقى to stay

شُروق sunrise

غُروب sunset

اِعتَقَد–يَعتَقِد to believe

مَسيحي Christian

شَعبي popular

أصل origin

فَرعوني Pharaonic

عَنى–يَعني to mean

عيد الخَلق Creation Festival

حَياة life

قَديم (ج. قُدَماء) ancient

رَمَز–يَرمُز to symbolize

قَد (see grammar note below)

تغيّر–يتغيَّر to change

أُضيف–يُضاف to be added

نَسيم breeze

لَطيف nice, pleasant

فَسيخ salted fish

مُمَلّح salted

سَـ = سَوفَ = حَ will

آخِر last

أبَداً = خالِص at all

رائحة smell

تَقليد (ج. تقاليد) tradition

تلوين coloring

بَيض eggs

زَمَن time

بِلاد country, land

أسئلة

١. إلى أين ذهبَت مايا؟ مع مَن؟ ماذا فعلت هناك؟

٢. مَن يحتفل بعيد "شمّ النسيم" حسب رانية؟

٣. مَتى يحتفل المصريّون بعيد شمّ النسيم؟

٤. إلى مَتى يرجع تاريخ عيد شمّ النسيم؟

٥. ما هو أصل عبارة "شمّ النسيم"؟

٦. ماذا تعني كلمة "شمو" الفرعونيّة القديمة؟

٧. هل أحبّت مايا "الفسيخ"؟ كيف عرفت ذلك؟

٨. مَتى بدأت عادة نقش البيض؟

٩. لِماذا ذُكر عيد الفصح في النصّ؟

1. Where did Maya go? With whom? What did she do there?
2. Who celebrates شمّ النسيم, according to Ranya?
3. When do Egyptians celebrate شمّ النسيم?
4. To what period does the history of شمّ النسيم go back?
5. What is the origin of the phrase شمّ النسيم?
6. What does the ancient Egyptian word شمو mean?
7. Did Maya like الفسيخ? How do you know that?
8. When did the tradition of egg decoration start?
9. Why is Easter mentioned in the text?

قَواعِد

قَد

When the particle قَد, which is found only in فصحى, is followed by a verb in the past tense, it simply affirms that the verb has taken place. So, in the phrase وقد تغيّر الاسم is simply translated as "the name changed".

The forms of the Arabic verb

You have learned that the overwhelming majority of Arabic words are derived from roots. Roots can be defined as the basic elements of meaning, and words derived from them represent extensions or modifications of the basic meaning. For example, the root ك – ت – ب has the basic meaning of *writing*. Among words derived from that root are:

he wrote	كَتَب
he corresponded with	كاتَب
writer	كاتب
something written	مَكتوب
writing	كتابة
book	كِتاب
office	مَكتَب
library, bookshop	مَكتَبة

There are specific patterns for deriving words from roots. You have already learned some of these patterns for nouns, such as the active participle (فاكر، كاتِب) and the comparative (أجمل، أصغر).

This system of roots and patterns, found in other Semitic languages such as Hebrew, Aramaic, and Ethiopic, is particularly helpful in acquiring new vocabulary. If you know the root and the pattern of a given word, you can likely guess its general meaning.

In addition to noun patterns, Arabic has a robust system of verb patterns. You will learn the most common and productive nine patterns in this book.

In describing patterns, the letters ف – ع – ل are used to refer to the three letters of the root. You can think of ف – ع – ل as placeholders, similar to the way that x and y are variables used to represent numbers in math equations.

Third root letter ل	Second root letter ع	First root letter ف

Note that while it is theoretically possible to pair any three-letter root with all nine patterns, in reality not all root-pattern combinations are actually used.

Form I: فعل–يفعل

The most common verb pattern in Arabic is Form I. It contains only the three root letters, as in the verbs درس، كتب، شرب، بدأ، كان, etc.

Form I gives the basic meaning of a verb.

(examples) أمثلة	Present	Past	Form
دَرَس–يدرُس شرِب–يشرَب وصَل–يصِل	يفعَل، يفعُل، يفعِل (varies)	فعَل	I

Form VIII: اِفتَعَل–يَفتَعِل

Form VIII verbs have an additional ا and ت in the past tense, and an additional ت in the present tense.

(examples) أمثلة	Present	Past	Form
احتَفَل–يَحتَفِل اشتَرى – يَشتَري اِستَمَع – يَستَمِع	يَفتَعِل	افتَعَل	VIII

Historically, Form VIII verbs had a reflexive meaning. So, in the Qur'an, for example, there are pairs of verbs, one in Form I and another in Form VIII, that are based on the same root, with the Form VIII verb expressing the meaning "for oneself".

شَرى–يَشري to sell (Form I)

اشترى–يشتري to buy (sell to oneself) (Form VIII)

In contemporary usage, Form VIII verbs usually contain a related but more abstract meaning than their Form I counterparts, such as the difference between "to hear" (I) and "to listen" (VIII).

to hear (Form I) سمِع–يسمع

to listen (Form VIII) استَمع–يستَمِع

تمرين رقم ١

For the following verbs, all taken from Maya's diary of Lesson 4,

a. give a full English translation (of the verb and all suffixes and prefixes),
b. identify the root,
c. identify the stem,
d. write down the form of the verb, using both فعل and the form number.

الوزن ورقمه Verb form and number	الصيغة المجرّدة Stem	الجذر Root	الترجمة	الفعل Verb
فعل، I	خرج	خ-ر-ج	I went out	خرجت
افتعل، VIII	احتفل	ح-ف-ل	And we celebrated	واحتفلنا
				بقينا
		ك-و-ن		كُنت
				أعتقد
				قالت
				يحتفلون
				ويرجع
				وكان
				يعتقدون
				يرمز
				قُلت
				وستكون
				بدأت

الدرس الخامس

كلمات الوحدة

آخِر last

أَبَداً = خالِص at all

احتِفال celebrating, celebration

احتَفَل–يِحتِفِل to celebrate

اختلَف–يِختِلِف to be different

اشتَرى–يِشتِري to buy

أُضيف–يُضاف to be added

اعتَقَد–يَعتَقِد to believe

أغنية (ج. أغاني) song

الّتي = إللي that, which

العيد الكبير the Feast of Sacrifice

انتَشَر–يَنتَشِر to spread

بَقي–يَبقى to stay

بِلاد country, land

بَيْض eggs

بَين between, among

تأثّر–يَتأثَّر to be influenced

تغيّر–يتغيَّر to change

تَقليد (ج. تقاليد) tradition

تَقويم calendar

تلوين coloring

ثَقافة culture

جَميع everyone, all

جَميل = حِلو beautiful

حَديقة (ج. حَدائق) garden, park

حَضّر–يُحَضِّر to prepare

حَياة life

خَروف (ج. خِرفان) lamb

ذلِك (ذالِك (pronounced

رائحة smell

رَمَز–يَرمُز to symbolize

زَحمة crowdedness, congestion

زَمَن time

سَـ = سَوفَ = حَ will

سَبَب (ج. أسباب) reason

شَخص (ج. أشخاص) person

شَخصي personal

شُروق sunrise

شَعبي popular

طابور line, queue

عادة habit, custom

عِبارة phrase

عَنى–يَعني to mean

عيد (ج. أعياد) feast, festival, anniversary

عيد الخَلق Creation Festival

عيد الفِطر Eid al-Fitr (celebration marking) the end of Ramadan

عيد ميلاد birthday

غُروب sunset

غَنّى–يُغنّي to sing

فَرد (ج. أفراد) individual, member

فَرعوني Pharaonic

فَرق (ج. فُروق) difference

فَسيخ salted fish

فَقير (ج. فُقَراء) poor (person)

قدِر–يِقدِر to be able to

قَديم (ج. قُدَماء) ancient

كان–يَكون to be

كَعكة cake

كُلّ سَنة وانتم طيِّبين! many happy returns (lit. every year and you are well)

كِلمة word

كَما as

كَنيسة (ج. كَنائس) church

لِبس clothes

لَحن tune

لم أكن أعرِف I did not know, I was not aware

ما أجمَل how beautiful

ما شاء الله God be praised

مُجتَمَع (ج. مُجتَمَعات) society

مَسألة (ج. مَسائل) matter

مَسيحي Christian

مُعظَم most (of)

مُمَلّح salted

مِن زَمان a long time ago

مُناسَبة (ج. مُناسَبات) occasion

نَسيم breeze

هَديّة (ج. هَدايا) gift, present

واقِف standing

وَزّع–يِوَزّع to distribute

يا ريت! I wish!

تمرين رقم ١: املأ الفراغات

تعني، حديقة، سنة، العالم، عيد، غروبها، فقط، كلمة، مصر، الناس، الوقت

الجوّ في هذه الأيّام مُعتَدِل ولطيف طول الوَقت. كان اليوم .... شمّ النسيم. خرجتُ مع صاحباتي سلمى ورانية إلى .... "الفسطاط" في منطقة مصر القديمة واحتفلنا بالعيد هناك. بقينا في الحديقة من شروق الشمس حتى .... كنت أعتقد أنّ عيد شمّ النسيم هو عيد مسيحي ....

.... ، ولكنّ رانية قالت إنّ كلّ المصريين يحتفلون بالعيد في هذا
....

عيد شمّ النسيم من أقدم الأعياد الشعبيّة في.................. ، ويرجع تاريخه
الى خمسة آلاف................. وأصل الاسم هو الكلمة الفرعونيّة "شمو"
التي .... "عيد الخلق" أو "بداية الحياة".

وكان المصريون القدماء يعتقدون أن ذلك اليوم يرمز إلى بداية............
والحياة على الأرض. وقد تغيّر الاسم، وأُضيفت إليه................ "النسيم"
او الجو اللطيف لأنّ............. يحتفلون بالعيد في فصل الربيع.

تمرين رقم ٢

Give the meaning and the root of each of the following words and list at least one more word derived from the same root and its meaning. Follow the example.

كلمات من نفس الجذر	الجذر	الكلمة ومعناها
east شَرق	ش–ر–ق	sunrise شُروق
		غُروب
		احتفال
		مُجتَمَع
		مَسألة
		قَديم
challenge		
		ميلاد

Sociolinguistic Corner

١. بدأت تنتشر

You learned in Unit 6 that the particle أن comes in between two verbs in فصحى (but not مصري). There are a few verbs in فصحى that do not require this particle when they occur in the first position. One of these verbs is "started to . . . ". You saw this in the phrase بدأت تنتشر ("it started to spread"). With that in mind, complete the following table:

تمرين رقم ٣–أكمل الجدول التالي:

مصري		فصحى		
عايز يسافِر	بدا يدرُس	يريد أن يسافِر	بدأ يدرُس	
				أنا
عايزين نسافِر		نريد أن نسافر		نحنُ/إحنا
				انتَ
	بديتِ . . .		بدأتِ تدرسين	انتِ
				انتُم/انتو
				هو
				هي
	بدوا يدرسوا		بدأوا يدرسون	هم

2. Relative pronouns

You learned in Unit 11 that the equivalent of the English relative pronouns *which, that, whose,* and *whom* in مصري is اللي and in فصحى the three words الذي (m.s.), التي (f.s.), and الذين (m.pl). You have seen several examples of الذين and الذي, as in الطلبة الذين يحصلون على دَرَجات عالية . . . "the students who obtain high grades . . ." and كان رئيسها الأوّل "تشارلز واتسون" الذي ظلّ رئيساً لمدّة ٢٥ سنة "its first president was Charles Watson, who remained president for 25 years. You will see examples of التي in the next exercise.

تمرين رقم ٤: ترجم إلى الإنجليزيّة

١. ده عَشان القرآن بيقول اللي بيقدر يذبح خروف لازم يدّي ثلثه للفقراء.

٢. عَشان الناس اللي بيقدروا، يعني اللي عندهم فلوس، بيشتروا خروف وبيذبحوه وبياكلوا منّه، وبيوزّعوا على الفقراء.

٣. أصل الاسم هو الكلمة الفرعونيّة "شمو" التي تعني "عيد الخلق" أو "بداية الحياة".

٤. من تقاليد عيد شمّ النسيم عادة نَقش البيض التي بدأت في زمن المصريّين القدماء قبل آلاف السنين.

٥. الفسيخ سَمك مُملّح، وهو من الأكلات التي ياكلها المصريّون في عيد شمّ النسيم.

تمرين رقم ٥: مناقشة وكتابة (discussion and writing)

Discuss with a classmate and then write up in about 50–75 words:

1. your favorite holiday,
2. your last birthday,
3. a comparison of holidays in your country with Arab holidays.

الوحدة رقم ١٣
التسوّق

الدرس الأول

بَلَدي local

تَخفيض discount, lowering, reducing

تَسَوُّق shopping

تَقليدي traditional

رِجّالي for men

سِتّاتي for women

سوق market

شَتَوي for the winter

صوف wool

صيفي for the summer

فاتِح (light color)

فِكرة idea

قُطن cotton

قِماش cloth

كَلَف-يُكلّف to cost

كُم sleeve

لِبس-يِلبِس to wear

لَذيذ delicious

مَبلَغ (ج. مَبالغ) sum, amount

مَحَلّ (دُكّان) shop, store

مَقاس size

نوع (ج. أنواع) kind, type

وَجبة (ج. وَجبات) meal

(Feminine)	(Masculine)
بيضاء	أبيض
سوداء	أسود
حمراء	أحمر
خضراء	أخضر
زرقاء	أزرق
صفراء	أصفَر
بُنّيّة	بُنّي
بُرتُقاليّة	بُرتُقالي
رماديّة	رمادي

تمرين رقم ١

Matching (companion website).

تمرين رقم ٣: حوارات قصيرة (short dialogues) (في الصفّ)

Study the following pictures of fruits and vegetables. Can you relate some of their names to words you already know (in Arabic or other languages)?

Your teacher will ask you to create short dialogues using these words.

(More suggestions in Teacher's Book)

تمرين رقم ٤

Assign the following words to the correct category.

بنطلون – طماطم – موز – جاكيتة – عصير ليمون – فستان – جلابيّة – تفاح – بطاطس – بطيخ – حليب – صوف – صيفي – برتقال – خُبز

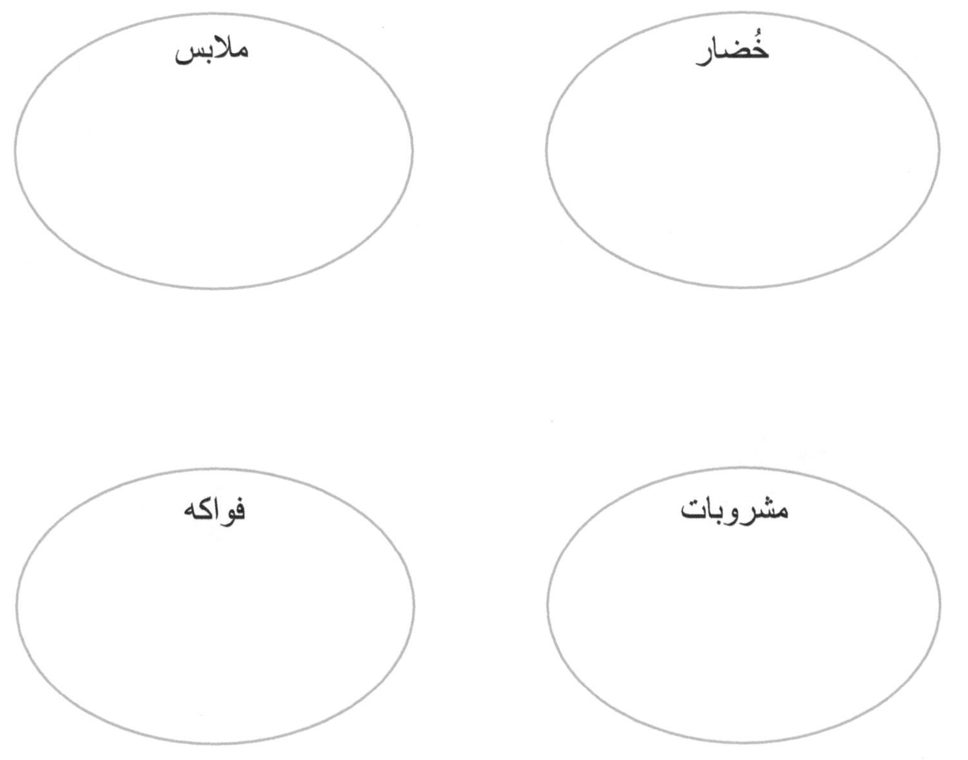

تمرين رقم ٥

Match each of the following phrases with the appropriate picture below. Then, translate the phrases into English in your notebook.

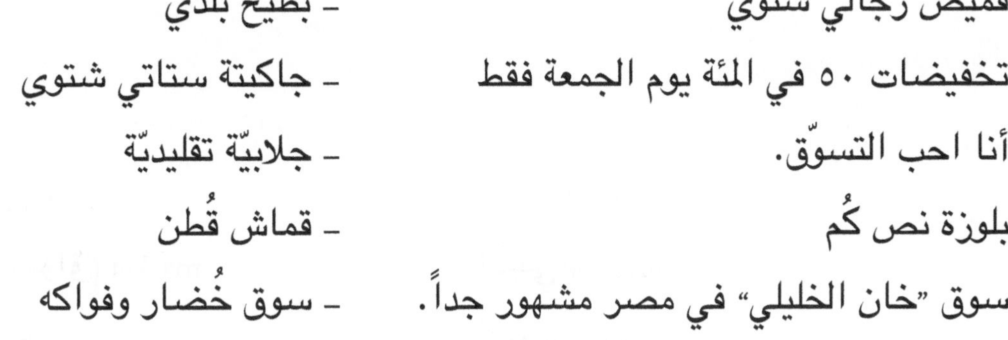

- قميص رجالي شتوي
- بطيخ بلدي
- تخفيضات ٥٠ في المئة يوم الجمعة فقط
- جاكيتة ستاتي شتوي
- أنا احب التسوّق.
- جلابيّة تقليديّة
- بلوزة نص كُم
- قماش قُطن
- سوق "خان الخليلي" في مصر مشهور جداً.
- سوق خُضار وفواكه

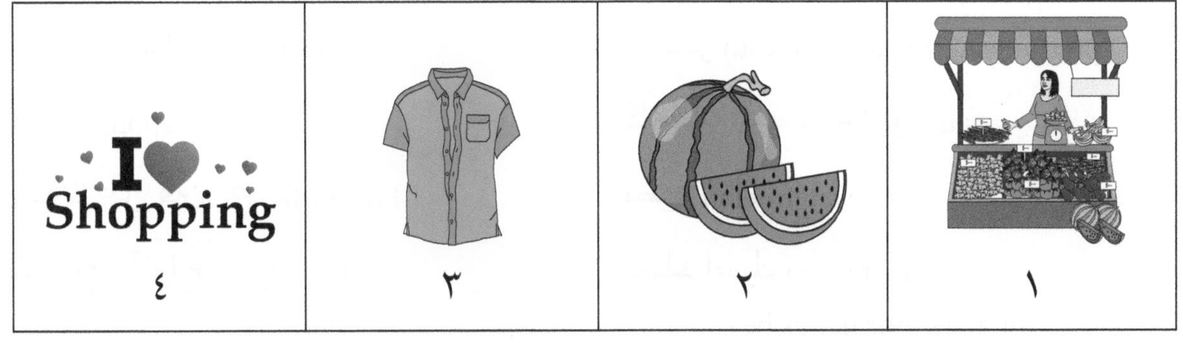

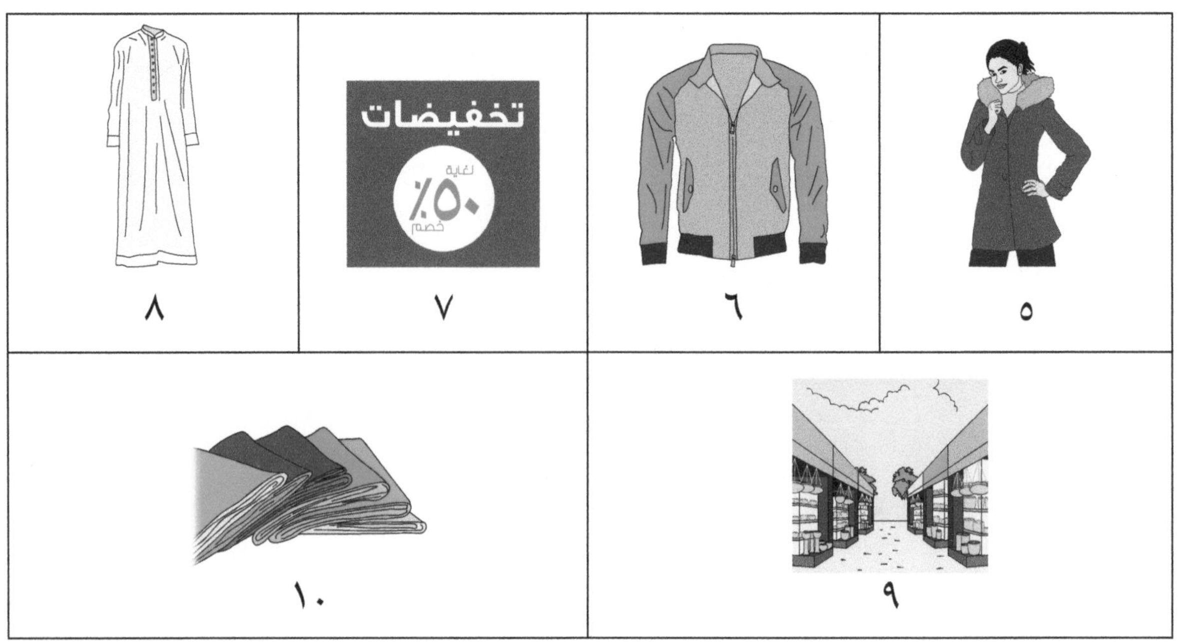

تمرين رقم ٦

Matching (companion website)

الدرس الثاني–مُشاهدة: في سوق التوفيقية في وسط البلد

كلمات جديدة

تَسَوّق shopping

سوق (ج. أسواق) market

موز bananas

بَلَدي local

يا سِتّي my dear madam

تُفّاح applies

مِنين؟=مِن فين؟ From where?

نوع (ج. أنواع) kind, type

أحلى sweeter

ادّيني give me

كيلو kilogram

طماطِم tomatoes

حاضِر presently, ready (to serve you)

كُلّه عَلى بَعضه all together

بَطّيخ watermelon

تِسلم اِيديك thank you (lit. may your hands be sound)

أسئلة

1. What types of bananas does the fruit and vegetable seller have?
2. How much would the seller sell a kilogram of each type to Maya?
3. How many types of apples are there? What are they?
4. What did Maya end up buying? How much did she pay?
5. How did the seller describe the watermelon?

قَواعِد

اثنين كيلو، أربعة دولار

You have learned that Arabic has dual numbers. So the equivalent of the English "two houses" is بيتين. You have also learned that with the numbers 3–10 the plural form of the noun is used: ثلاث بيوت.

In certain situations, such as ordering food and drinks, weights and measures, and currencies, the number generally precedes the counted noun and does not agree with it, as in the following examples:

one tea	واحد شاي
three coffees	ثلاثة قهوة
two *koshari's* (Egyptian dish)	اثنين كشري
one oven-baked pasta	واحد مكرونة في الفرن
three orange juices	ثلاثة عصير (بُرتُقان=بُرتُقال)
two (dishes of) *fuul* (fava beans)	اثنين فول
four kilos of apples	أربعة كيلو تُفّاح
five kilos of cheese	خمسة كيلو جبنة
seven kilometers	سبعة كيلومتر
eight dollars	ثمانية دولار
ten pounds	عشرة جنيه

تمرين رقم ١: ترجم إلى العربيّة (مَصري)

Translate the following phrases into Egyptian Arabic.

1. Give me one kilo of apples, please.
2. I would like two coffees and one tea.
3. I would like one *koshari* and one *falafel* please.
4. Give me two kilos of oranges.

5. I would like one mango (مانجا) juice and three lemon juices please.
6. I would like one oven-baked pasta and she would like one *fuul.*

The *taa marbuuTa* as an individualizer

You have already seen how the *taa marbuuTa* acts as a feminine marker in words such as:

teacher (f.)	مُدَرِّسة
Egyptian (f.)	مَصريّة
student (f.)	طالبة
lecturer (f.)	أستاذة

The *taa marbuuTa* often acts as an "individualizer" for collective items such as apples and oranges as can be seen below:

تفّاح apples	تُفّاحة an apple
برتقان oranges	برتقانة an orange

تمرين رقم ٢: ترجم إلى الإنجليزيّة

تفّاحة

تفّاحتين

٢٠ تفّاحة

ثلاثة كيلو تفّاح

تُفّاح

تمرين رقم ٣: ترجم إلى العربيّة

One banana ______________________________

Two bananas ______________________________

One kilogram of bananas ______________________________

Bananas ______________________________

تمرين رقم ٤: تكلّم مع زميلك وكون جُمل او حوارات قصيرة

Working with a partner use the phrases/expressions below. You will make a skit in which one of you is the buyer and one is the seller. Be creative!

- مش عارف/عارفة:
- انا خايف/خايفة من:
- انا فاهم/فاهمة إنّه
- هو دكتور في مستشفى؟ لا قصدي هو........................
- الكتاب معاك أو معاه؟
- اللي عايز/عايزة..................لازم........................

الدرس الثالِث–استماع: قميص قُطن ولّا جلّابيّة؟

النصّ الأوّل

كلمات جديدة

خَبَر (ج. أخبار) news

نَهار day

دوَّر–يِدَوَّر = بحث–يبحث to look for

زي بعضه it is all the same

أصل...... because, since, as a matter of fact

جاي next

بَعَث–يِبعَث to send

لِبس–يِلبِس to wear

قَرا–يِقرا to read

لِعِب–يِلعَب to play

قَرَّر–يِقرَّر to decide

في الأوّل first

قَميص shirt

قُطن cotton

جَلابيّة (ج. جَلاليب) *gallabiyya*

تَقليدي traditional

فِكرة idea

هايل awesome

طَب = طيّب ok, so

قِدِر–يِقدِر to be able to

دول those

حِتّة part, area

مَشهور famous

رِجّالي for men

سِتّاتي for women

أسئلة

1. What did Maya spend all day long doing?
2. What gift ideas does Salma give Maya?
3. What places does Maya suggest for getting a present?
4. What joke does Maya make?
5. What is Khan el-Khalili famous for?
6. How is Maya going to going to get there?

النصّ الثاني

كلمات جديدة

مَحَلّ store
طَلَب request
كُمّ sleeve
نُصّ كُم short sleeve (lit. half sleeve)
مَقاس size
قَدّ the same size as
أزرَق blue
فاتِح light (color)
أصفَر yellow
نَوعيّة quality
أهوه here it is
تَخفيض discount
شِتوي for the winter
صوف wool
صيفي for the summer
قِماش cloth
رَمادي gray
كُحلي navy blue
غامِق dark
بُصّ! Look!
زِيادة extra, more
عشان خاطرِك for you
مَبروك! congratulations, may you enjoy it!
خُذي! take!

أسئلة

1. What did Maya tell the shopkeeper she is looking for?
2. What kind of shirt does Maya want?
3. What size does Maya's brother wear?
4. What color shirts are in the shop?
5. How much did the shopkeeper ask for a shirt initially?
6. How much would he sell the three shirts for?

7. How many types of *gallabiyyas* (جلاليب) are there in the shop? How does the shop-keeper describe them?
8. What color *gallabiyya* did Maya buy?
9. How much did Maya pay for the whole thing in the end?

تمرين رقم ١: شفهي في الصفّ (تصريف أفعال في الماضي والمضارع)

(In Teacher's Book)

قواعد

The imperative

This lesson contains several examples of the imperative (giving commands):

خليني أشوف Let me see!
شوفي القماش See the fabric!
بُصّ يا سيدي Now look here sir!

The imperative is formed from the present tense verb الفعل المضارع, as follows:

	بَصّ	راح
Step 1: start with the present tense verb	تبُصّ - تبُصّي- تبُصّوا	تروح - تروحي - تروحوا
Step 2: remove the present conjugation prefix	بُصّ! بُصّي! بُصّوا! Look	روح! روحي! روحوا! Go!

If the verb is derived from a sound root, there is one additional step needed: a helper *alif* ا must be put in front of the verb. This *alif* makes it easier to pronounce the imperative. The vowel that goes with this *alif* is either ضمّة or كسرة, depending on the middle short vowel of the verb itself. If this middle vowel is a ضمّة then the vowel that goes with the *alif* is ضمّة; if it is فتحة or كسرة, the vowel is كسرة.

If the middle vowel is a كسرة or فتحة, the helper *alif* takes a كسرة.	If the middle vowel is a ضمّة, the helper *alif* takes a ضمّة.
he listens – يسمَع	he leaves – يخرُج
listen! – اِسمَع!	Get out! – أُخرُج!

Below are more examples for deriving imperative commands from sound verbs.

	دَخَل	شِرِب
Step 1: start with the present tense verb	تدخُل، تدخُلي، تدخُلوا	تشرَب، تِشرَبي، تشرَبوا
Step 2: remove the initial prefix for conjugation	دخُل، دخُلي، دخُلوا	شرَب، شرَبي، شرَبوا
Step 3: add ا with كسرة or ضمّة	اُدخُل، اُدخُلي، اُدخُلوا Enter!	اِشرَب، اِشرَبي، اِشرَبوا Drink!

Sound verbs that already have an initial *alif* أ as their first root letter don't need this extra *alif* added.

تأكُل - تأكُلي - تأكُلوا	تأخذ - تأخذي - تأخذوا
كُل! - كُلي! - كُلوا!	خُذ! - خُذي! - خُذوا!

The negative imperative (e.g. "don't eat!") is basically the second person of the present tense of any verb, with the "mish sandwich", as in the following examples:

Don't drink!	ما تِشرَبش!
Don't speak!	ما تتكلِّمش!
Don't go!	ما تروحش!
Don't buy!	ما تشتريش!

تمرين رقم ٢: شفهي في الصفّ: الأمر (the imperative)

(In Teacher's Book)

Object pronouns are attached to imperative verbs regularly, as in ساعِدني "help me", إدّيني "give me", etc.

تمرين رقم ٣: ترجم إلى الإنجليزيّة

(In Teacher's Book)

تمرين رقم ٤

Make up ten commands in مصري using the following verbs and vary the person you are addressing (m.s., f.s., pl.). Give at least two negative imperatives. Then translate your commands into English.

خرَج-يخرُج، ترَك-يترُك، خلّى-يخلّي، نام-ينام، طَلَب-يطلُب، سأل-يسأل، قال-يقول

الدرس الرابِع: مذكّرات مايا

اليوم ذهبت الى سوق الخضار واشتريت بَعض الفَواكِه والخُضار والحليب والعصير والخبز.

أسعار الخضار والفواكه في السوق وأسعار الأكل في المطاعم أرخص من أمريكا بكثير. كيلو الطماطم مثلاً بأقلّ من عشرة جنيه مصري، يعني حوالي نصف دولار. رخيص جدّاً، ولَذيذ جدّاً أيضاً. الفواكه والخضار هنا ألذّ بكثير من الفواكه والخضار في أمريكا.

يُسمّي المصريّون الخبز "عيش". تَفاجأتُ عندما سمعت الكلمة لأوّل مرّة. كنت أفكّر أنّ كلّ العرب يسمّونه "خبز".

ولكن مُنذُ وُصولي إلى مصر سمعت كلمة "عيش" عدّة مرّات، ولم أفكّر في البداية أنّ هناك عَلاقة بين هذه الكلمة والفِعل عاش-يعيش حتّى أخبرَتني سلمى بِذلِك. وأضافت أنّ للخبز أو "العيش" مَكانة خاصّة في الطعام العربي، فالعرب يأكلونه في أكثر الوَجبات.

عندما قلت لسلمى إنّ الخبز أو العيش رخيص جدّاً وهذا شيء جيّد، قالت صحيح أنّ الخبز رخيص ولكن هو السبَب في مَشاكل كثيرة في مصر. فهو رخيص لأنّ الحكومة تَدعَمه، وهذا يُكلّف الدولة مَبالغ كبيرة ويُضعف الاقتِصاد المصري. وكلّما حاوَلت الحكومة إنهاء الدعم قامَت مُظاهَرات وطالَب الناس بتَخفيض الأسعار مرّة أخرى.

كلمات جديدة

بَعض some	سَمّى-يُسمّي to call
فَواكِه fruit	تفاجأ-يَتَفاجأ to be surprised
خُضار vegetables	مُنذُ since
لَذيذ delicious	مَرّة (ج. مَرّات) time
ألذّ more delicious	عَلاقة relationship

فِعل verb

حَتّى until

أخبَر-يُخبِر to tell, inform

أضاف-يُضيف to add

مَكانة status

طَعام food

وَجبة (ج. وَجبات) meal

هذا = this

مُشكِلة (ج. مَشاكِل) problem

دعَم-يَدعَم to support

كَلّف يُكَلِّف to cost

مَبلَغ (ج. مَبالغ) sum, amount

أضعَف-يُضعِف to weaken

اقتِصاد economy

كلّما whenever

حاوَل-يُحاوِل to try

إنهاء ending

دَعم support

قام-يَقوم to erupt, take place

مُظاهرة (ج. مُظاهَرات) demonstration

طالَب-يُطالِب to demand

تَخفيض lowering, reducing

أسئلة

صحّ أو خطأ؟ (companion website)

يمكن استعمال كلّ من العبارات التالية كعنوان لواحدة من فقرات النصّ. اربط بين الفقرة والعنوان الذي يناسبها.

The following three phrases can be used as headings for the three paragraphs of the text. Indicate which title goes with which paragraph.

١. الخبز يعني الحياة في مصر
٢. الفواكه والخضار في مصر رخيصة ولذيذة
٣. رُخص الخبز مشكلة

رتّب الجمل التالية حسب ورودها في النصّ.

- الخبز مهمّ جدّاً في مصر.
- الخضار رخيصة في مصر.
- الخضار غالية في أمريكا.
- الفواكه في مصر ألذّ من الفواكه في أمريكا.

- تفاجأت مايا عندما سمعت كلمة "عيش".
- تقوم مظاهرات في مصر عندما تحاول الحكومة أن تُنهي الدعم للخبز.
- دعم الخبز ليس جيّداً (= مش كويّس) للاقتصاد المصري.
- دور (role) الخبز في الغذاء العربي أهمّ من دوره في الغذاء الأمريكي.

قَواعِد

Past tense negation with لم

You learned earlier on that the past tense, in both فصحى and مصري, is negated with the particle ما. A slightly more formal way to express negation of the past tense in فصحى is with the particle لم. Look at the phrases and their translations below. How would you describe the way لم is used?

لم أفكّر في البداية أنّ هناك عَلاقة بين هذه الكلمة والفِعل عاش-يعيش.
I didn't think at the beginning that there was a relationship between this word and the verb عاش-يعيش.

لم أفكّر is the negative counterpart of the past tense verb فكّرت "I thought".

You may have noticed that the change from فكّرت to لم أفكّر is similar to that from "I thought" to "I did not think" in English, where the verb is changed from "thought" to "think".

Verb forms

In the previous unit two verb patterns were introduced: Form I (فعل-يَفعَل) and Form VIII (افتعل-يفتعل). In this unit two more forms will be introduced: Forms II and IV.

Form II: فَعَّل- يُفَعِّل

This form has two distinguishing features:

a. the doubling of the root's middle letter through the شدّة,

b. a ضمّة on the present tense prefix.

Form II usually has a causative or transitive meaning. A good example of a verb that shows its causative meaning is درّس-يدرِّس, which means "to teach or to make someone learn". Compare it with the basic meaning found in the Form I verb دَرَس-يدرُس "to study".

Form IV: أَفعَل–يُفعِل

The distinguishing features of this form are:

a. the أ prefix in the past tense,

b. the ضمّة on the present tense prefix.

Form IV often has a causative meaning as well. A good example of this form is أضعَف–يُضعِف "to weaken, to make someone or something weak". Compare with ضعُف–يضعَف "to become weak".

(examples) أمثلة	Present	Past	Form
فكّر–يُفكّر	يُفَعِّل	فَعَّل	II
أَعلَن–يُعلِن	يُفعِل	أَفعَل	IV

تمرين رقم ٢

For the following verbs, all taken from the texts of this unit,

a. give a full English translation (of the verb and all suffixes and prefixes),
b. identify the root (remember that الف or ى do not exist at the root level; they derive from ي or و),
c. identify the stem,
d. write down the form of the verb (I, II, IV, or VIII) using both فعل and the form number. Some cells have been filled in to help you.

الوزن ورقمه	الصيغة المجرّدة	الجذر	الترجمة	الفعل
فعل، I	قال	ق-و-ل	we said	قُلنا
				يلبسها
		ق–ر–ر	you, f.s. decide	تُقرّري
				حاركِب
	اشترى			واشتريت
		س–م–ي		يُسَمّي
				كُنت
				أفكّر

أخبرتني				
وأضافَت		ض–ي–ف		أفعل،
قُلت				
قالَت				
تَدعمه				
يُكلِّف				
ويُضعِف				
قامَت		ق–و–م		

الدرس الخامس

كلمات الوحدة

أضعَف–يُضعِف to weaken

اقتِصاد economy

ألذّ more delicious

إنهاء ending

أهوه here it is

بُصّ! Look!

بَطّيخ watermelon

أبيَض white

أحلى sweeter

أخبَر–يُخبِر to tell, inform

ادّيني give me

أزرَق blue

أصفَر yellow

أصل . . . . . . because, since, as a matter of fact

بَعَث–يِبعَث to send

سِتّاتي for women

سَمّى–يُسمّي to call

سوق (ج. أسواق) market

شَتَوي for the winter

صوف wool

صيفي for the summer

طالَب–يُطالِب to demand

طَب = طيّب ok, so

طَلَب request

طماطِم tomatoes

عشان خاطرِك for you

عَلاقة relationship

غامِق dark (color)

طَعام food

فاتِح light (color)

فِعل verb

فِكرة idea

فَواكِه fruit

في الأوّل first

قام–يَقوم to erupt, take place

قَدّ the same size as

قِدِر–يِقدِر to be able to

قَرا–يِقرا to read

قَرَّر–يقرّر to decide

قُطن cotton

أضاف–يُضيف to add

بَعض some

بَلَدي local

تَخفيض discount, lowering, reducing

تِسلم اِيديك thank you (lit. may your hands be sound)

تَسَوّق shopping

تفاجأ–يَتَفاجأ to be surprised

تُفّاح applies

تَقليدي traditional

جاي next

جَلابيّة (ج. جَلاليب) *gallabiyya*

حاضِر presently, ready (to serve you)

حاوَل–يُحاوِل to try

حِتّة part, area, piece

حَتّى until

خَبَر (ج. أخبار) news

خُذي! take!

خُضار vegetables

دعَم–يَدعَم to support

دَعم support

دوَّر–يِدَوَّر = بحث–يبحث to look for

دول those

رِجّالي for men

رَمادي gray

زي بعضه it is all the same

قِماش cloth

مُشكِلة (ج. مَشكلات) problem

مُظاهرة (ج. مُظاهَرات) demonstration

مَقاس size

مَكانة status

مُنذُ since
مِنين = مِن فين؟ from where?
موز bananas
نُصّ كُم short sleeve (lit. half sleeve)
نَهار day
نوع (ج. أنواع) kind, type
نَوعيّة quality
هايل awesome
وَجبة (ج. وَجبات) meal
يا سِتّي my dear madam
زِيادة extra, more
قَميص shirt
كُحلي navy blue

كلّف–يُكلّف to cost
كلّما whenever
كُلّه عَلى بَعضه all together
كُمّ sleeve
كيلو kilogram
لا زال is still
لبِس–يِلبِس to wear
لَذيذ delicious
لِعِب–يِلعَب to play
مَبروك! congratulations, may you enjoy it!
مَبلَغ (ج. مَبالغ) sum, amount
مَحَلّ store
مَرّة (ج. مَرّات) time

تمرين رقم ١: املأ الفراغات

بكثير، جيّد، الخبز، العرب، للخبز، مَشاكل، المصري، والعشاء، وخبز

ذهبت مايا الى سوق الخضار واشترت فواكه وخضار وحليب.........
كانت أسعار الخضار والفواكه أرخص من أمريكا ....

تفاجأت مايا عندما عرفت أنّ المصريّين يسمّون................"عيش"، والعيش يعني الحياة. وقالت لها سلمى إنّ...................أو العيش مَكانة خاصّة في الطعام العربي لأنّ............يأكلونه في الفطور والغداء
....

عندما قالت مايا لسلمى إنّ الخبز رخيص جدّاً وهذا شيء.........، قالت سلمى صحيح أنّ الخبز رخيص ولكن هو السبَب في..................كثيرة في مصر، ويُضعف الاقتصاد...................

تمرين رقم ٢ (استماع) بكم رغيف العيش لو سمحت؟

أسئلة

In the dialogue between Maya and the bread seller,

1. What two things does the bread seller find unusual about Maya's requests?
2. What does Maya find unusual about the seller's dealing with her?

تمرين رقم ٣

Write the meaning of each of the following words and give at least one example of a word derived from the same root and give its meaning. The first one is given as an example.

green أخضَر	The vegetables	الخضار
		الكلمة
		أفكّر
		وُصولي
		الطعام
		وطالَب

تمرين رقم ٤: كلمات متقاطعة

١٠	٩	٨	٧	٦	٥	٤	٣	٢	١	
										١
										٢
										٣
										٤
										٥
										٦
										٧
										٨
										٩
										١٠

عمودي	أفقي
١. جمع "جلّابيّة"؛ جذر" جميل"	١ .كُلّ؛ للرجال وليس للبنات والنساء
٣. أوّل شهر في السنة؛ عكس "فاتح"	٣. جمع "أغنية"؛ ممكن
٥. سادس شهر في السنة	٤. جذر "مواصلات"
٦. جذر "مخصوص"	٥. كان المصريّون القدماء يلوّنونه والآن يلوّنه الناس في عيد الفصح
٧. حلو	٦. عكس "شِتوي"
٨. في مصر أكثر من أيّ دولة في العالم	٨. جمع "جبل"؛ جمع "خروف"
٩. عكس "شويّة" أو "قليل"	١٠. نلبسه وله كُمّ؛ جذر "فاتح"
١٠. يفكّر أو يعتقد عكس "يفشل"	

Sociolinguistic Corner

1. This and that

Early on in this book, you learned the مصري words ده and دي:

This is no good!	ده مش كويس خالص!
This is Salma, Maya's friend	دي سلمى، صاحبة مايا

These pronouns exist in فصحى as well. In fact, you have seen them all before!

هذا شيء جيد	هذا	this (m.s.)
الطقس ممتاز في هذه الأيام	هذه	this (f.s.)
من أسباب ذلك أنّ العائلات العربيّة كانت كبيرة	ذلك	that (m.s.)
تَفاجأتُ عندما سمعت تلك الكلمة لأوّل مرّة	تلك	that (f.s.)

2. على راسي

You may have noticed that both the fruit and vegetable and clothing store salespeople used words and expressions that you don't generally hear in similar places in the West, like على شانك/عَشانِك, تسلم ايديك, and على راسي. Arabs use these expressions and many more in their daily interactions. If translated literally into English they might sound funny, but in the Arab context they are not different from "thank you", "will be happy to", "my pleasure", etc.

Here are four such expressions used in the dialogues of this unit with their literal and idiomatic meanings.

Idiomatic meaning	Literal meaning	Expression
For you (I am giving you a good deal)	For your sake	عَشانِك/عَلى شانِك
Thank you	May your hands be sound!	تِسلم إيديك
Very willingly (Italian *volentieri!*)	On my head!	عَلى راسي
May you enjoy it!	Congratulations!	مَبروك

تمرين رقم ٥: احكي واكتب (٥٠–٧٥ كلمة)

1. Create a dialogue with your classmate in which one of you is a salesperson and the other customer in an Arab shop (سوق-fruit and vegetable market, clothing store, etc.) Ask about and negotiate prices, pay or receive payment. Make it funny and interesting.
2. Plan a trip to go shopping with your roommate. Discuss transportation to and from where you will be shopping, what time, what you will be buying, etc.
3. Describe an interesting or strange shopping experience that happened to you or to someone you know.

الوحدة رقم ١٤
الأكل والصحّة

الدرس الأوّل

إيد hand, arm

بِسكُر with sugar

بسيطة not serious

بَصَل onions

بَطْن stomach

بقلاوة *baklawa* (a dessert)

ثوم garlic

جار neighbor

جَعان (=جوعان) hungry

حالاً immediately

حَساسيّة allergy

دَواء medicine

راس head

رَجُل (ج. رِجال) man

رِجل foot

سلامتِك! I hope you are ok (lit. your safety)

صَلصة sauce

ضَغط دَم blood pressure

طانت aunt, auntie

فَتّة *fatta* (name of a dish)

فِنجان cup

قرفة cinnamon

كتّر خيرك = شُكراً (lit. may your goodness be plentiful!)

كُشَري، طَعمِيّة، بابا غنّوج names of dishes

لَبَن = حليب milk

مُخيف frightening, scary

مَرِض-يَمرَض to become sick

مَريض = عَيّان sick

مَسكين unlucky, poor, unfortunate

مَشى-يَمشي to go

وَجع pain

تمرين رقم ١

A good number of words in the above list belong to four categories: health (صِحّة), people (ناس), food (أكل), and parts of the body (جِسم). Make four lists in which you include all the words in each category. Follow the examples.

جِسم	ناس	أكل	صِحّة
إيد	جار	سُكّر	دَواء

تمرين رقم ٢

Label the pictures.

دَواء، رَجُل، بَقلاوة، ثوم، سُخن، مُستشفى، صَلصة، بَصَل، فِنجان، قرفة، ضَغط دَم، لَبَن، مَريض، مَشى

______

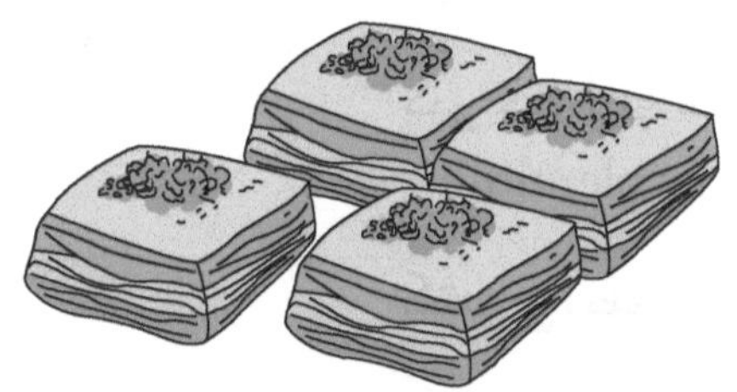
______

______

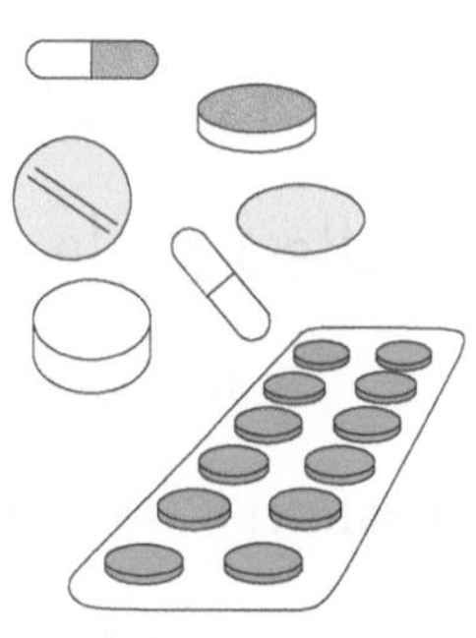
______

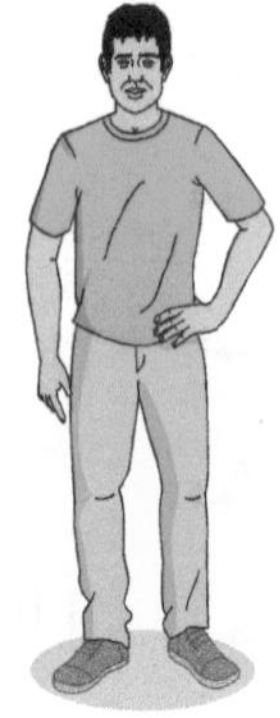
______

______

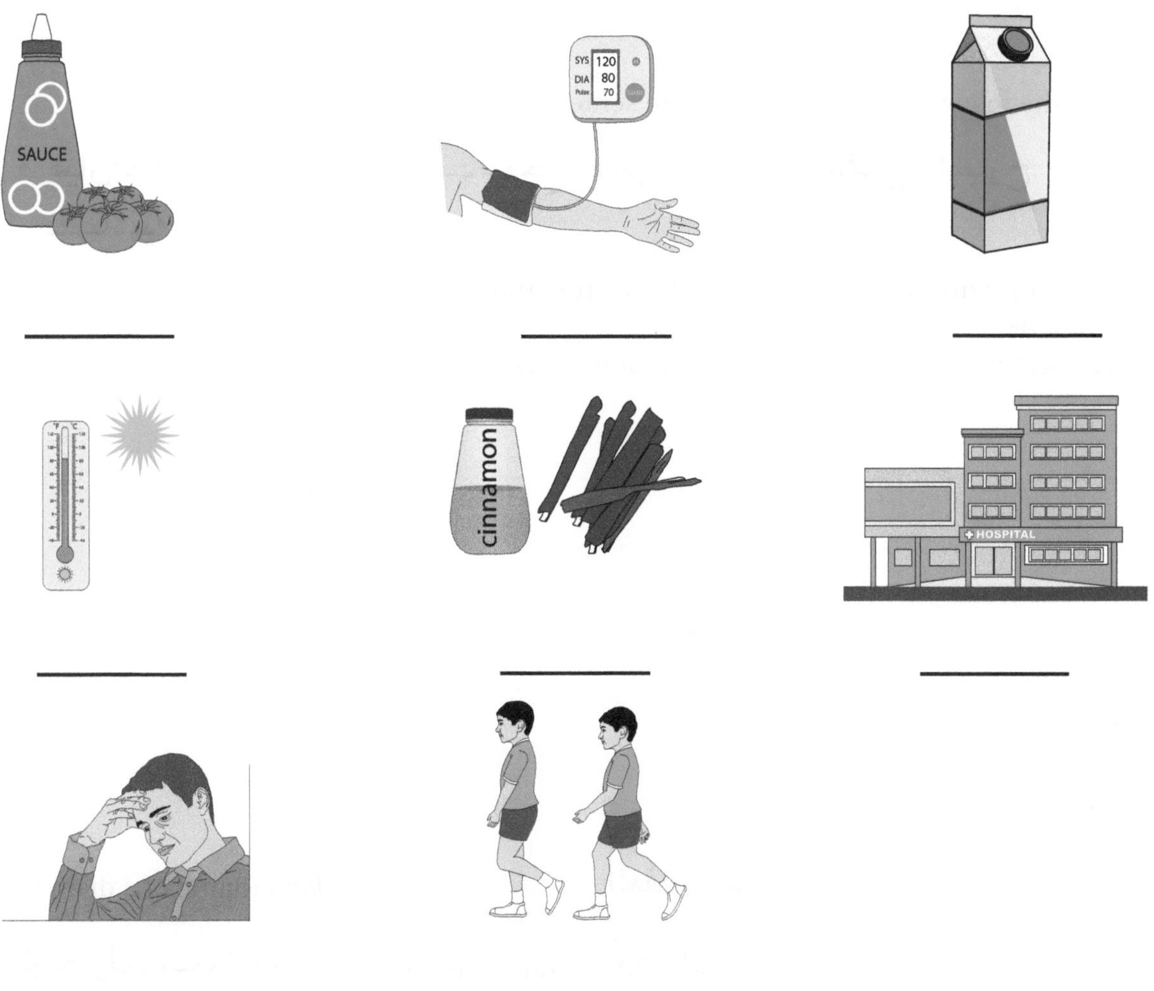

تمرين رقم ٣

You will hear five sentences. Each of them contains one or more words from the list below. For each sentence, write down on a separate piece of paper the word that you hear from the list and write its meaning in English.

بطن، حساسيّة، راس، سُكّر، شاي، فنجان، قهوة، لبن، مريض، مسكينة، وجع

(In Teacher's Book)

تمرين رقم ٤

Match each phrase with its appropriate response and practice it with your partner.

١. اتفضّل شاي بسُكر.		سلامتِك.
٢. انا مريضة اليوم.		ليه؟ ان شاء الله كُله تمام. انتَ مريض؟
٣. لازم اروح للمُستشفى حالاً.		لحمة ورُز وثوم وبصل وشويّة قرفة.
٤. عندك حساسيّة؟		شكراً. كثر خيرك!
٥. فيه ايه في "الفتّة"؟		لا، الحمد لله.

تمرين رقم ٥: حوارات قصيرة

1. Use the following words in complete sentences

   عيان/عيانة - النهار ده - سلامتك - وجع - بطن - رحت - مستشفى - امبارح - حساسيّة

2. Working with a classmate, use the words and expressions above to create a mini dialogue.
3. Perform your mini dialogue in front of the class.

الدرس الثاني - مشاهدة: الفتة لذيذة قوي!

النصّ الأوّل

كلمات جديدة

فَتّة *fatta* (name of a dish)

كتّر خيرِك = شُكراً (lit. may your goodness be plentiful!)

طانت aunt, auntie

تَمام perfect, fine

العفو = عَفواً

ثوم garlic

بَصَل onions

قِرفة cinnamon

كُشَري، طَعمِيّة، بابا غنّوج names of dishes

أسئلة

True or false?

1. This is the second time that Maya has eaten *fatta* (فتّة) in Egypt.
2. أمّ هاني lists five ingredients in the فتّة.
3. Maya ate بابا غنّوج in downtown Cairo.
4. Maya did not like the بابا غنّوج at Filfila.
5. Samira thinks that restaurant food is not very good.

النصّ الثاني

كلمات جديدة

شارِب having drunk

عَصير juice

فِنجان cup

بسُكّر with sugar

لَبَن = حليب milk

جاب–يِجيب to bring

قِدِر–يِقدِر to be able to

ضَغط دَم blood pressure

طالِع high, has gone up

أهيه (feminine equivalent of أهوه) here it is

أسئلة

True or false?

1. Maya had tea and juice before drinking the coffee.
2. Maya wanted sugar in her coffee.
3. Maya had her coffee with milk.
4. أمّ هاني does not drink coffee in the afternoon.

قَواعِد

شاربة

Remember that in مصري the active participle is often translated with the present tense as in:

مش عارِف I don't know

أنا ساكِن I live

عايِز I want

If you use the active particle with لسّه (still), it gives the meaning of having just done something. Therefore, the sentence لكن أنا لسه شاربةَ شاي translates as "but I just drank tea!"

تمرين رقم ١: ترجم إلى الإنجليزيّة

١. انتِ لسه ما شربتيش القهوة عندنا.

٢. فنجان قهوة لو سمحت. بس مش عايزة أتعبك!

٣. تشربي القهوة بسكّر ولا مِن غير (without) سُكّر؟

٤. أنا ما أقدرش أشرب قهوة بعد الظهر عَشان ضغط الدم عندي طالع.

تمرين رقم ٢

You are at "Groppi Ginayna" in downtown Cairo (وسط البلد) and are ordering a few drinks for you and three friends. Below is the type of dialogue you have had with the waiter before but the order of the lines has been jumbled up. Working with a classmate, try to "unjumble" the dialogue by placing the correct number in the right-hand column as to indicate the correct order. The first one has been entered already:

حاضر.	جرسون	
عاوزين قهوة وشاي بس ولّا عاوزين حاجة حلوة (something sweet) كمان؟	جرسون	
عندكو ايه النهار ده؟	انت	
عندنا أم علي كمان.	جرسون	
أهلا وسهلاً - اتفضّل - حضرتكو عاوزين تشربوا ايه؟	جرسون	١
بس فيها سكر كثير. عندكو حاجة ثانية؟	انت	
عاوز واحد قهوة بلبن وثلاثة شاي من فضلك.	انت	
طيب - تقدر تجيب لنا اثنين بقلاوة وواحد أم علي* لو سمحت.	انت	
عندنا بقلاوة لذيذة قوي!	جرسون	

*Egyptian milk pudding (Umm 'Ali) = أم علي

الدرس الثالِث-استماع : كلّنا أكلنا الفتة وما تعبناش!

النصّ الأوّل

كلمات جديدة

سلامتِك! I hope you are ok (lit. your safety)

راس head

عَيّان sick, unwell

كَمان also

وَجع pain

جار neighbor

أسئلة

1. Why did Maya need a taxi?
2. Where does Maya have pain?
3. Who is أحمد أباظة?

النصّ الثاني

كلمات جديدة

مَسكين unlucky, poor, unfortunate

صَلصة sauce

فِعلاً truly

حَطّ–يِحُطّ to put

سَمنة fat

خلّينا let us

حَساسيّة allergy

حالاً immediately

أسئلة

True or false?

1. Salma's mother, Samira, thinks that Maya may have got sick from the food.
2. This is the first time that Maya had فتّة.
3. أمّ هاني agrees with Salma that it may have been the food.
4. أمّ هاني knows some people who are allergic to fat (سمنة).
5. Samira thinks that Maya could be sick from studying.

النصّ الثالث

كلمات جديدة

بسيطة not serious, simple

استريّح – يستريّح to rest

بقلاوة *baklawa* (a dessert)

ربّنا يِخلّيك = شُكراً thank you (lit. May God keep you)

واضِح clear

جَعان hungry

دَواء medicine

سُخن = حامي hot

نام–يَنام to sleep

أسئلة

1. What was the cause of Maya's sickness according to the doctor?
2. What did the doctor give Maya?
3. What will happen in four or five hours?
4. What did Salma's mother, Samira, offer the doctor?

ممكن + المضارع (present tense)

You learned in Unit 12 that Arabic does not have an infinitive in the English sense, i.e. a form of the verb that is not conjugated for person or time. So the literal translation of the English sentence *I have to* (or *must*) *go to the hospital right away* is *I have to* (or *must*) *I go to the hospital right away*. The following exercise provides more examples.

تمرين رقم ١: ترجم إلى الإنجليزيّة.

١. مُمكن تقولي لها "طانت".

٢. ممكن تطلبي لي تاكسي؟

٣. لكن عايزة تروحي المستشفى ليه؟

٤. ممكن أكلّمه.

٥. مش أحسن أروح المستشفى؟

٦. خلينا نستنّى شويّة.

٧. إديت لها دواء عَشان تنام وتستريّح.

٨. خلّيني أجيب لَك صحن فتّة.

قَواعِد

عيّانة، تعبانة

In the dialogue of Lesson 3, Salma asks Maya if she is sick using the word عيّانة. Maya replies by saying that she is تعبانة شويّة.

Both عيّانة and تعبانة belong to a limited group of adjectives with the ending ان that express "temporary states". So whereas the adjective بارِد means "cold", the adjective بَردان means "feeling cold now". Other commonly used adjectives in this groups are جَعان (or جوعان) "hungry", عَطشان "thirsty", and زَعلان "upset".

تمرين رقم ٢

You are studying in Cairo and have a friend, who doesn't speak Arabic, visiting from Canada. You are both invited to a friend's house in Heliopolis (مصر الجديدة). Your friend has some health issues which you need to explain to your host as he offers you things to eat and drink. Act as an interpreter between the host and your friend.

Facts about your friend:
You studied in Toronto with him last year. He can't drink coffee with milk because he has an allergy. He can't eat a lot of sugar. He can't drink orange juice because he has a stomach ache! He has high blood pressure and will see a doctor in downtown Cairo.

١. صاحبك منين؟

٢. صاحبك عاوز يشرب قهوة بلبن؟

٣. طيب، حاجيب له فنجان قهوة من غير لبن. اجيب له بقلاوة؟

٤. لا، لا، البقلاوة دي من البيت وما فيهاش سكر كثير.

٥. صاحبك عاوز عصير برتقان؟

٦. مسكين، جاري دكتور ممكن ييجي يشوفه.

الدرس الرابِع–قراءة: مذكّرات مايا

أكتب مذكّراتي الآن في بيت سلمى. ركبنا الاوتوبيس إلى الإسكندريّة بعد ظُهر أمس. كانت رحلة الأوتوبيس مُخيفة: كان السائق يتكلّم مع رجل جالس في المقدّمة. أحياناً كان يرفع يده عن عجلة القيادة، وأحياناً أخرى كان يتكلّم على الموبايل . . . والاوتوبيس كان يمشي بسرعة كبيرة.

أخذنا تاكسي من محطّة الاوتوبيسات إلى بيت سلمى. وصلنا البيت الساعة الثانية بعد الظهر. ومنذ وصولي وحتى مرضت (أنا الآن مريضة في السرير) وأنا آكل وأشرب: عصير، شاي، قهوة، فواكه، فتّة، شاي مرّة ثانية . . .

كان الغداء اليوم "فتّة". كانت الفتّة لذيذة جدّاً، مُمكن أحسن أكلة أكلتها في حياتي. بعد الغداء شربنا الشاي والعصير والقهوة وأكلنا الفواكه.

حوالي الساعة الرابعة بعد الظهر شعرت بوجع في رأسي وبطني، وكنت أريد أن أذهب الى المستشفى، ولكن سلمى قالت لي إنّ جارهم أحمد أباظة طبيب.

جاء الدكتور أحمد وسألني بعض الأسئلة، وقال إنّ السبب في مرضي هو أنّني أكلت وشربت كثيراً في بيت سلمى، وقال يجب أن أستريّح ولا آكل أو أشرب شيئاً حتى تستريّح معدتي.

كلمات جديدة

مُخيف frightening, scary

رَجُل (ج. رِجال) man

مُقدّمة front

رَفَع-يَرفَع to raise

عَجَلة قِيادة steering wheel

أخرى other

موبايل mobile or cell phone

مَشى-يَمشي to go

مَرِض-يَمرَض to become sick

مَريض = عَيّان sick

يجب أن = لازِم must

أسئلة

صحّ أو خطأ؟ (companion website)

تمرين رقم ١

The following five phrases can be used as headings for the five paragraphs of the text. Indicate which title goes with which paragraph.

١. أكل وشرب كثير

٢. ألذّ أكلة أكلتها

٣. رحلتي إلى الإسكندريّة

٤. سبب مَرَضي

٥. مَرَضي

تمرين رقم ٢

رتّب الجمل التالية حسب ورودها في النصّ.

- أخذت مايا وسلمى تاكسي من محطّة الأوتوبيس إلى البيت.
- أستريّحت مايا.
- أكلت مايا وشربت كثيراً في بيت سلمى.

- سافرت مايا من القاهرة إلى الإسكندريّة بالأوتوبيس.
- سأل الطبيب مايا بعض (some) الأسئلة.
- كانت سواقة السائق خطيرة (dangerous).
- كانت مايا تريد أن تذهب إلى المستشفى.
- مايا مرضت من الأكل والشرب.

قَواعِد

The Past Progressive Tense in Arabic

In previous units, you saw examples of the simple past tense like in the following sentences:

- كانت رحلة الأوتوبيس مُخيفة (the bus trip was scary)
- أكلنا الفواكه (we ate fruit)

In this lesson, you have seen a new way of expressing past tense:

كان السائق يتكلّم مع رجل جالس في المقدّمة The driver was speaking with a man sitting in the front
الاوتوبيس كان يمشي بسرعة كبيرة The bus was moving at high speed

This tense is known as the past progressive. It describes past tense actions that were continuous or ongoing. It can be translated in slightly different ways in English depending on the context.

The past progressive is formed by conjugating كان in the past tense followed by a conjugated present tense verb. See the examples below:

عندما كنت صغيرة كنت أريد أن أصبح طبيبة When I was little, I wanted to become a doctor.
أيام المدرسة الثانوية كانوا يأكلون البيتزا كل يوم في الغداء. In high school they used to eat pizza every day at lunch.

Form V (تفعّل)

This form is related to Form II. In terms of its form it has the same shape as II plus the prefix ت. In terms of meaning, it is often the passive or reflexive of Form II.

So عَلّم (Form II) has the meaning of "he taught" and تعلّم (Form V) means "he has been taught, he learned".

Form X (استفعل)

Verbs in Form X are distinguished by the prefix ست found before the root letters.

(examples) أمثلة	Present	Past	Form
to specialize تَخصَّص-يتَخَصَّص-تَخَصُّص	يَتَفَعَّل	تَفَعَّل	V
to use استعمَل-يَستَعمِل-استِعمال	يَستَفعِل	اِستَفعَل	X

تمرين رقم ٣: أكمل الجدول التالي. (Complete the following table.)

الوزن ورقمه	الصيغة المجرّدة	الجذر	الترجمة	الفعل
فعل، I	قال	ق-و-ل	you (f.) say	تقولي
				بتاكلي
			and you (f.) will see	وحتشوفي
				تشربي
	جاب			أجيب
				(ما) أقدرش
				تطلبي
			I speak to him	أكلّمه
		ك-و-ن		وحيكون
				تروحي
				(ما) أكلتش
		ح-ط-ط	They do not put	(ما) بيحطّوش
				بنعمل
	خلّى	خ-ل-ي		خلينا
				وحَنعرف
		ن-و-م		تنام
		ر-ي-ح		وتستريح
				أكتب

				يتكلّم
				يَرفع
				مَرضت
				شَعرت
	استريّح			أستريّح

الدرس الخامس

كلمات الوحدة

أخرى other (f.)

استريّح – يستريّح to rest

أهوه here it is (feminine equivalent of) أهيه

بابا غنّوج *baba ghannouj* (name of a dish)

بِسُكَّر with sugar

بسيطة not serious

بَصَل onions

بقلاوة *baklawa* (a dessert)

تَمام perfect, fine

ثوم garlic

جاب–يِجيب to bring

جار neighbor

جَعان (= جوعان) hungry

حالاً immediately

حَساسيّة allergy

حَطّ–يِحُطّ to put

خلّينا let us

دَواء medicine

راس head

شُكراً = ربّنا يِخليك (lit. may God keep you)

رَجُل (ج. رِجال) man

رَفَع–يَرفَع to raise

حامي = سُخن hot

سلامتك! I hope you are ok (lit. your safety)

سَمنة fat

شارِب having drunk

صَلصة sauce

ضَغط دَم blood pressure

طالِع high, has gone up

طانت aunt, auntie

طَعمِيّة *falafel* in Egypt

عَجَلة قِيادة steering wheel

عَصير juice

عَفواً = العفو you're welcome

عَيّان sick, unwell

فَتّة *fatta* (name of a dish)

فِعلاً truly

فِنجان cup

قِدِر-يِقدِر to be able to

قِرفة cinnamon

كتّر خيرك = شكراً thank you
(lit. may your goodness be plentiful!)

كُشَري name of an Egyptian dish

كَمان also

لَبَن = حليب milk

مُخيف frightening, scary

مَرِض-يَمرَض to become sick

مَريض = عَيّان sick

مَسكين unlucky, poor, unfortunate

مَشى-يَمشي to go

مُقدّمة front

موبايل mobile or cell phone

نام-يَنام to sleep

واضِح clear

وَجع pain

يجب أن = لازِم must

تمرين رقم ١: املأ الفراغات

إلى، أنْ، أنْ، إنّ، أنّني، بَعد، حتّى، عَن، في، مع، مِن، وحتّى

أكتب مذكّراتي الآن في بيت سلمى. ركبنا الاوتوبيس .... الإسكندريّة بعد ظُهر أمس. كانت رحلة الأوتوبيس مُخيفة: كان السائق يتكلّم .... رجل جالس في المقدّمة. أحياناً كان يرفع يده .... عجلة القيادة، وأحياناً أخرى كان يتكلّم على الموبايل، والاوتوبيس كان يمشي بسرعة كبيرة.

أخذنا تاكسي .... محطّة الاوتوبيسات إلى بيت سلمى. وصلنا البيت الساعة الثانية بعد الظهر. ومنذ وصولي .... مرضت (أنا الآن مريضة في السرير) وأنا آكل وأشرب: عصير، شاي، قهوة، فواكه، فتّة، شاي مرّة ثانية.

كان الغداء اليوم "فتّة". كانت الفتّة لذيذة جدّاً، مُمكن أحسن أكلة أكلتها .... حياتي. بعد الغداء شربنا الشاي والعصير والقهوة وأكلنا الفواكه.

حوالي الساعة الرابعة .... الظهر شعرت بوجع في رأسي وبطني، وكنت أريد .... أذهب الى المستشفى، ولكن سلمى قالت لي .... جارهم أحمد أباظة طبيب.

جاء الدكتور أحمد وسألني بعض الأسئلة، وقال إنّ السبب في مرضي هو .... أكلت وشربت كثيراً في بيت سلمى، وقال يجب .... أستريّح ولا آكل أو أشرب شيئاً .... تستريّح معدتي.

قَواعِد

The use of كان to express past and future actions and states

In Unit 11 you learned about expressing possession in the past tense using كان as in كان مَعايَ ثلاث شنط and كان عندي شقّة في الإسكندريّة.

This use of كان and its past tense conjugations is not restricted to possession. It is often used to refer to past actions and states or to "move" the time of an event or a situation to the past, as shown in the following examples:

يريد محمود أن يُصبح أولاده وبناته أطبّاء ومهندسين. Mahmoud wants his sons and daughters to become doctors and engineers.	كان محمود يُريد أن يُصبح أولاده وبناته أطبّاء ومهندسين. Mahmoud wanted his sons and daughters to become doctors and engineers.
I have عندي	I had كان عندي

تمرين رقم ٢: ترجم الجُمَل التالية (the following sentences) إلى الإنجليزيّة:

مصري

١. كُنت بافكّر انّه كلّ العرب بيسمّوه "خُبز".

٢. كانوا بيشتروا لبس العيد.

٣. كانوا واقفين في طابور.

٤. كان لازم تقولي لي مِن زمان.

فُصحى

١. وكان المصريون القدماء يعتقدون أن ذلك اليوم يرمز إلى بداية العالَم والحياة على الأرض.

٢. كانت رحلة الأوتوبيس مُخيفة.

٣. كان السائق يتكلّم مع رجل جالس في المقدّمة.

٤. أحياناً كان يرفع يده عن عجلة القيادة، وأحياناً أخرى كان يتكلّم على الموبايل.

٥. الاوتوبيس كان يمشي (drive, go) بسرعة كبيرة.

٦. كان الغداء اليوم "فتّة" . كانت الفتّة لذيذة جدّاً.

٧. كنت أريد أن أذهب الى المستشفى.

تمرين رقم ٣ (قِراءة): كلمات أجنبيّة دخلت العربيّة

في الوحدة السادسة قرأت كثيراً من الكلمات غير العربيّة مثل سندويشة، برجر، مايونيز، كاتشب، كراميل، كولا، سفن أب، بيبسي، فريش، نسكافيه، وكابوشينو. هذه كلمات أجنبيّة دخلت اللغة العربيّة قبل وقت قصير، ولذلك من السهل معرفة أصلها الأجنبي. وقبل هذه الكلمات دخلت أسماء أنواع كثيرة من الطعام إلى اللغة العربيّة من اللغات الهنديّة والفارسيّة واليونانيّة والإيطاليّة، مثل بهارات، باذنجان، نارنج، فاصوليا، بازيلّا، شاي، سُكّر، رُزّ، قهوة، بطاطس (بَطاطا في بلاد الشام)، وطماطم (بندورة في بلاد الشام).

وقد دخلت أسماء بعض المأكولات والمشروبات العربيّة إلى اللغات الأوروبيّة. بعض هذه الأسماء لم تكُن عربيّة في الأصل كالسكّر والقهوة والنارنج، وبعضها عربيّ الأصل مثل الحمّص والفلافل والتبّولة.

أسئلة

1. The above passage includes different types of foreign words that have been borrowed into Arabic. Some of these words are almost identical to their English counterparts like برجر، سندويشة, and كاراميل. Others are quite different. Make a bilingual Arabic–English list of all these borrowings.

2. It is easy to see the relationship between سُكّر and *sugar*, between حمّص and *humus*, الكحول and *alcohol*, but it is not easy to relate the following three English words to their Arabic origin, a word you already know: *sorbet*, *syrup*, and *sherbet*. What do you think is their Arabic origin?

تمرين رقم ٤: حضّر، ناقش، ثمّ اكتب

Prepare, discuss in class, and then write up a composition of about 50–75 words about one of the following topics:

1. You ate something and got sick. How did you get sick, how did you feel, what did you do to feel better . . .? Make sure you use the words introduced in this unit.
2. Describe and comment on Maya's experience as a guest in Salma's house.

الوحدة رقم ١٥
الرياضة والهوايات

الدرس الأوّل

تَبادُل exchanging

تَعَرُّف getting to know

رِياضة (ج. رياضات) sport

صورة (ج. صُوَر) picture

طَبخ cooking

غَلَب-يَغلِب to win over, to beat (someone)

فاز-يَفوز to win

فَريق (ج. فِرَق) team

قِراءة reading

كتابة writing

لاعِب player

لَعِب playing

لعِب-يلعَب to play

لُعبة game, sport

ماهِر skilled

مُباراة match

مِن أشهَر among the most famous

هواية (ج. هِوايات) hobby

الجَري	تنس طاوِلة	تِنِس أرضي	كرة السلّة	الكُرة الطائرة	كُرة القَدَم

تمرين رقم ١

With reference to the above list and images, label each item as رياضة or هِواية.

١. كُرة القدم
٢. قراءة الكُتُب
٣. التعرُّف على ناس
٤. تبادُل الصور على الانترنت
٥. الكرة الطائرة
٦. السفر إلى أماكن جديدة
٧. الكتابة
٨. التنس الأرضي
٩. الطبخ
١٠. مُشاهدة الأفلام في السينما
١١. لعبة "سكرابل" مع الأصدقاء (=الأصحاب)

تمرين رقم ٢: جذور وكلمات

List all the words you know that are derived from each of the following roots and give their English meanings.

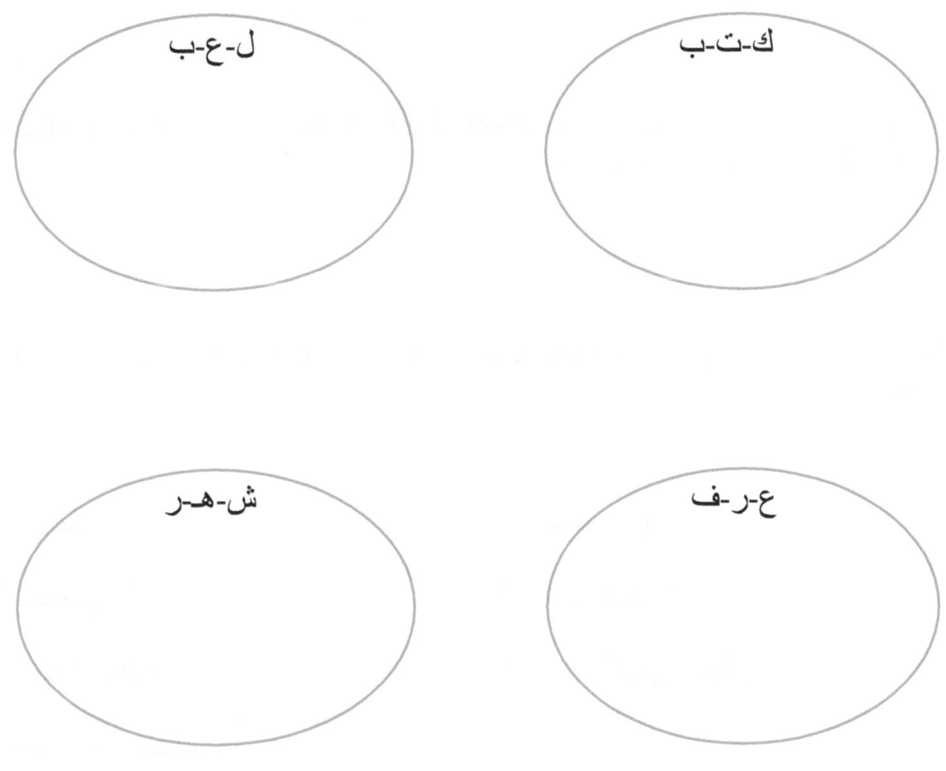

تمرين رقم ٣: ما هي الكلمة الغريبة (Identify the odd word)

١. كُرة القدم تنس الطاولة كُرة السلّة الطبخ

٢. قراءة مشاهدة التلفزيون كُتب كتابة

٣. مباراة رياضة فريق هواية

٤. ماهِر مُمرّض مُحاسب موظّف

٥. فاز درّس غَلب لُعب

تمرين رقم ٤

الجزء الأوّل

At home (في البيت): Complete the following sentences.

١. رياضتي المُفضلة هي ....

٢. فريقي المُفضل هو ....

٣. لاعبي/لاعبتي المُفضل/المُفضلة هو/هي ....

٤. هوايتي المُفضلة هي ....

٥. في رأيي اللاعب .... أفضل من اللاعب ....

الجزء الثاني

In class (في البيت): Ask your classmate about their favorite sports, athlete, etc. and compare their responses to your answers above.

تمرين رقم ٥

Look up the following people and write a sentence or two about each one on a separate piece of paper.

١. سارة عطار

٢. رانيا علواني

٣. هداية ملاك وهبة

٤. علاء الدين أبو القاسم

٥. مانوت بول

٦. محمد صلاح

٧. زين الدين زيدان

الدرس الثاني-مشاهدة: ايه رياضتك المفضّلة؟

كلمات جديدة

رِياضة sports

هواية (ج. هِوايات) hobby

كُرة قَدَم football, soccer

لعِب-يِلعَب to play

فَريق team

تفرّج-يِتفَرَّج to watch

تِنِس أرضي tennis (lit. ground tennis)

مُختلِف different

ضَعيف weak

مُنتَشِر widespread

مَحبوب loved, liked

أسئلة

1. What is Salma's favorite sport?
2. Does she play it now?
3. What sports can Salma play?
4. What sport or sports does Maya play?
5. What sports does Egyptian TV show?
6. Why doesn't Salma watch American football on the internet?
7. Which sports are most popular in America?

تمرين رقم ١

In your notebook, translate the following negative sentences into English. Then rewrite the Arabic into positive sentences by removing the negation.

١. لا، أنا ما بالعبش كرة قدم دلوقتِ.

٢. ما بتلعبيش رياضة خالِص (at all)

٣. لكن أنا مش كويّسة قوي.

٤. لأ أبداً (أنا) ما شفتَهاش.

٥. لكن مش ممكن تشوفي كرة القدم الأمريكيّة.

٦. وما شفتيهاش حتّى على الانترنت؟

٧. علشان الكمبيوتر بتاعي ما بيشتغلش كويس والإنترنت ضعيف.

٨. والله، مش عارفة يا مايا.

تمرين رقم ٢

Interview activity:

Below is a list of questions based on the topics and vocabulary covered in this lesson. Your أستاذ or أستاذة will assign you to either question set 1 or question set 2.

Part A

On your own, look at the questions being asked and think about what words you would like to use to ask them. What is important here is not that you perfectly translate the question word-for-word, but rather you try to get the general meaning across with the vocabulary you already know.

Part B

Find a partner who prepared the opposite question set to you. Take turns interviewing each other. You can use the English questions below to help jog your memory about the topics.

Question set 1

1. What sport is your favorite? Are you good at it?
2. Did you play sports when you were young? Which sports?
3. Are there big differences between American football and regular football (soccer)? What are they?
4. [Write your own question here, based on the vocabulary in this unit!]

Question set 2

1. What sports do you play now? Are you good at it?
2. Do you like watching sports on TV? Which sports?
3. In your opinion, which is the most widespread and best-loved sport in the world?
4. [Write your own question here, based on the vocabulary in this unit!]

النصّ الأوّل-قراءة: التعرّف على شباب وشابّات

الاسم: محمد أبو الفول **الجنس:** ذكر **العمر:** ٢٨ سنة **الجنسيّة:** مصري **المهنة:** محاسب **الهوايات:** القراءة، السفر، مشاهدة الأخبار، لعب كرة القدم. **يريد:** التعرّف على فتاة عمرها ١٨-٢٥ سنة، بهدف الصداقة أو الزواج في المستقبل.	**الاسم:** س.م. **الجنس:** أنثى **العمر:** ٢٢ سنة **الجنسيّة:** كويتيّة **المهنة:** طالبة **الهوايات:** القراءة، مشاهدة الأفلام المصريّة، السفر. **تريد:** التعرّف على شباب، عُمر ٢٥-٣٥ سنة، بهدف الصداقة والمراسلة.
الاسم: رشا ت **الجنس:** أنثى **العمر:** ٢٨ سنة **الجنسيّة:** سعوديّة **المهنة:** مساعدة مدير في بنك **الهوايات:** السفر، لعب تنس الطاولة **تريد:** التعرّف على شباب وشابّات، كلّ الأعمار، بهَدَف الصداقة والزواج في المستقبل.	**الاسم:** صالح محمد صالح **الجنس:** ذكر **العمر:** ٣٥ **الجنسيّة:** فلسطيني **المهنة:** سائق سيّارة نقل **الهوايات:** لعب كرة السلّة، مشاهدة الأخبار على قناة الجزيرة. **يريد:** التعرّف على فتاة مسلمة عمرها ٢٠-٣٠ بهدف الزواج.
الاسم: منى ريحاوي **الجنس:** أنثى **العمر:** ١٩ **الجنسيّة:** لبنانيّة **المهنة:** طالبة **الهوايات:** القراءة، مشاهدة الأخبار، الطبخ. **تريد:** التعرّف على شابّ بهدف الصداقة والزواج في المستقبل.	**الاسم:** شادي غليون **الجنس:** ذكر **العمر:** ٢٤ **الجنسيّة:** سوري **المهنة:** مهندس **الهوايات:** السفر، الكتابة، لعب كرة القدم **يريد:** التعرّف على شباب وشابّات من دول عربيّة مختلفة بهدف المراسلة وتبادل الأخبار والصور عن البلاد العربيّة.

كلمات جديدة

sex, gender جِنس

male ذَكَر

reading قِراءة

travel سَفَر

playing لَعِب

getting to know تَعَرُّف

فَتاة = بِنت

goal هَدَف

with the goal of, for the purpose of بِهَدَف

friendship صَداقة

marriage زَواج

future مُستَقبَل

female أنثى

young man شابّ (ج. شَباب)

young woman شابّة (ج. شابّات)

channel قَناة

Muslim مُسلم

cooking طَبخ

exchanging تَبادُل

picture صورة (ج. صُوَر)

اسئلة

١. ما هي جنسيّة صالح محمد صالح؟ ماهي مهنته؟

٢. ما هو جنس س.م؟

٣. ما هي هوايات محمد ابو الفول؟ كم عمره؟

٤. لماذا يريد شادي غليون التعرُف على شباب وشابات؟

٥. من يحبّ لعب كرة القدم؟ مشاهدة الأفلام الأمريكيّة؟ السفر؟

٦. في رأيك، هل يجب على صالح محمد صالح التعرّف على منى ريحاوي؟ على شادي غليون؟ لماذا/لماذا لا؟

1. What is the nationality of صالح محمّد صالح? What is his occupation?
2. What is the gender of س.م.?
3. What are the hobbies of محمّد أبو الفول? How old is he?
4. Why does شادي غليون want to get to know other young men and women?
5. Who likes to play soccer? Watching Egyptian movies?
6. In your opinion, should صالح محمّد صالح get to know شادي غليون؟ مُنى ريحاوي? Why or why not?

تمرين رقم ١: كتابة

اكمل الجدول التالي عن نفسك او عن شخص آخر.

Fill out the following table about yourself or someone you know.

الاسم: ....

الجنس: ....

العُمر: ....

الجنسيّة: ....

المهنة: ....

الهوايات: ....

أريد/يُريد التعرّف على .... بهدف ....

تمرين رقم ٢: سؤال وجواب

Work with a partner in the class asking and answering the following questions.

- بتعلب تنس كل يوم؟
- شُفت الكرة امبارح في التلفزيون؟
- شربت شاي امبارح؟
- لعبت باسكت (كرة سلّة) الأسبوع اللي فات؟
- أكلت كشري امبارح؟
- عندك عربية جديدة؟
- تفرّجت على البرنامج امبارح؟
- فيه لاعبين مشهورين في الفريق ده؟
- بتحب تلعب رياضة؟
- بتعرف تستعمل كمبيوتر؟

Conversation Activity

You and your classmates all filled out your own profiles in تمرين رقم ١. Your task is to now go around the room and learn what you have in common with your classmates – who are you the most similar to? Interview as many people as possible.

النصّ الثاني-قراءة: زين الدين زيدان

لاعب كُرة القدم الفرنسي "زين الدين زيدان" واحد من أشهر نُجوم كُرة القدم في العالم. وُلد لعائلة جزائريّة تعيش في مدينة "مرسيليا" في جنوب فرنسا في سنة ١٩٧٢، ولعب مع عدد من الفِرَق في الولايات المتّحدة وفرنسا قبل أن ينضمّ إلى المنتخب الفرنسي عام ١٩٩٤. لعب مع المنتخب الفرنسي ٦٥ مباراة وسجّل ١٨ هدفاً. وفي عام ٢٠١١ انضمّ إلى فريق "ريال مدريد" الإسباني.

حَصَل زين الدين زيدان على لَقَب أفضل لاعب أوروبي ثلاث مرّات في السنوات ١٩٩٨ و ٢٠٠٠ و ٢٠٠٣، وفاز بجائزة أفضل لاعب كُرة قدم في العالم في سنة ٢٠٠٠. كما حصل المنتخب الفرنسي بقيادته على "كأس العالم" عام ١٩٩٨، و "كأس أوروبا" عام ٢٠٠٠. وفاز مع "ريال مدريد" بلقب "الدوري الإسباني" و "دوري أبطال أوروبا" و "كأس السوبر" الأوروبية و "كأس العالم للأندية".

كلمات جديدة

لاعِب player

أشـهَر most famous

مِن أشـهَر among the most famous

وُلِد-يولَد to be born

عَدَد number

فَريق (ج. فِرَق) team

الوِلايات المُتّحدة the United States

انضَمّ-يَنضمّ to join

مُنتَخَب = فَريق (lit. selected)

مُباراة match

سَجّل-يُسَجِّل to score

حَصَل (على) to obtain

لَقَب title

أفضَل = أحسَن best

أوروبي European

فاز-يَفوز to win

جائِزة prize, award

كَما also, as, as well

قِيادة leadership

بقيادته under his leadership

دَوري (sports) league

بَطَل (ج. أبطال) champion

كَأس cup

نادي (ج. أندِية) club

أسئلة

اكتب صحّ أو خطأ.

١. زين الدين زيدان لاعب مشهور.

٢. زين الدين زيدان جزائري فرنسي.

٣. وُلد زين الدين زيدان في الجزائر.

٤. لعب زين الدين زيدان مع المنتخب الفرنسي ومع فريق إسباني.

٥. سجّل زين الدين زيدان ١٨ هدفاً في سنة ١٩٩٤.

٦. كان زين الدين زيدان أفضل لاعب أوروبي في سنة ٢٠٠٣.

٧. فاز زين الدين زيدان بجائزة أفضل لاعب كرة قدم في العالم.

٨. حصل الفريق الفرنسي على كأس العالم في سنة ١٩٩٨.

٩. فاز فريق ريال مدريد بكأس أوروبا.

تمرين رقم ٣: ترجم العبارات التالية (Translate the following phrases)

١. لاعب كرة القدم الفرنسي

٢. فريق ريال مدريد الإسباني

٣. أفضل لاعب أوروبي

٤. فاز بلقب الدوري الإسباني

٥. كأس العالم للأندية

قَواعِد

The verbal noun (المصدر)

Many of the hobbies and activities listed above are related to verbs that you have already learned.

Hobby/activity (nouns)	Verbs
قِراءة الكُتُب	قرأ-يقرأ
السَفر	سافر-يُسافِر
مُشاهَدة الأخبار	شاهد-يُشاهد
لَعِب كرة القدم	لعب-يلعب

The nouns in orange above are known as "verbal nouns" (مَصادِر, pl. of مَصدَر), because they are derived from verbs.

المصدر is used to talk about verbs in a general or abstract sense. Look at the examples below:

لعب الرياضة كل يوم عادة مهمة للصحة. Playing sports every day is an important habit for good health.
أحب طبخ المأكولات من ثقافات مختلفة. I like cooking food from different cultures.
... بهدف المراسلة وتبادل الأخبار والصور. ... for the purpose of corresponding (correspondence) and exchanging news and pictures.

The verbal noun, general concepts, and definiteness

In Arabic, general concepts and ideas are considered definite, such as الأدب العربي (Arabic Literature) and الصيف (summertime). The same is true for المصدر – since it is a noun describing a general action, it is normally definite. If it is in an إضافة construct such as مُشاهدة الأفلام, normal rules of definiteness apply.

تمرين رقم ٤

The following nouns are taken from the first reading text of this lesson. For each noun, indicate whether you think it is or is not a مصدر. Refer to the text if you are unsure.

القِراءة، السَفر، مُشاهَدة ، لَعِب، التعرّف، الصَداقة، المُراسلة، مُسلِمة، الطَبخ، الجِنسيّة، المِهنة، مُهندِس، مُختلِفة، تبادُل، الأخبار، البِلاد، مُساعِدة

Verbal nouns and verb forms

Verbal nouns derived from Form I verbs follow different patterns, as in the following examples:

Pattern الوزن	المصدر	Verb الفعل
فِعالة	قِراءة	قرأ
فِعالة	كِتابة	كَتَب
فَعْل	طَبْخ	طَبَخ

فَعْل	لَعْب	لَعِب
فُعول	حُصول	حَصَل

Verbal nouns derived from the other forms (II–X) generally follow one specific pattern each.

So far, you have been introduced to Forms II, IV, V, VIII, and X. Here are their verbal noun patterns with examples that you have seen in this book. Do you remember their meanings?

Meanings of the examples معاني الأمثلة	Examples أمثلة	المصدَر	Form
reduction تخفيض ؛exercising, exercise تمرين	تمرين، تخفيض	تَفعيل	فَعَّل II
	إعلان	إفعال	أفعَل IV
	تسوُّق، تعرُّف	تَفَعُّل	تَفَعَّل V
	احتِفال، امتِحان	افتِعال	افتعل VIII
	استِقلال	استِفعال	استفعَل X

The remaining three verb forms (III, VI, VII) will be introduced along with their verbal nouns.

الدرس الرابِع–قراءة: مُذكّرات مايا

قبل أسبوعين ذهبت أنا وسلمى ورانية الى سوق "بِستي ستارز" واشترينا طاولة تِنِس. ووضعناها في غرفة الجلوس، مكان الأوراق والكتب والأطباق وكاسات الشاي.

دفعتُ أنا نصف ثمن الطاولة ودفعت سلمى ورانية النصف الثاني. كانت طاولة مُستعمَلة، ولَم تَكُن غالية كثيراً. كانت فكرة شراء الطاولة فكرتي، فقد شعرتُ أنّني بحاجة للرياضة والتمرين لأنّ وزني بدأ يزيد. فكما ذكرت، الطعام المصري لذيذ جدّاً ورخيص، لذلك كنت آكُل كثيراً.

مُفاجأة كبيرة! قبل أن نشتري الطاولة قالت رانية إنّها لَم تلعَب تنس الطاولة في حياتها، فهي لا تحبّ الرياضة، حتّى في التلفزيون.

لعبتُ مع سلمى، وكانت رانية تتفرّج. ثمّ قالت إنّها تريد أن تتعلّم كيف تلعب. علّمتها قوانين اللعبة وكيف تلعبها. بعد أسبوع فقط بدأت تَغلبني وتَغلب سَلمى؛ أصبحت لاعبة ماهرة.

أمس زارتنا مُنى، أخت سلمى الممرّضة، ولعبتُ معها. كانت لاعبة ممتازة، وقالت إنّها لعبت في فريق المدرسة عندما كانت في المدرسة الثانويّة. لعبت معها أكثر من ساعة أو ساعتين، وتعلّمت منها أشياء كثيرة. أعتقد أنّني سأغلب رانية عندما نلعب المرّة القادمة!

كلمات جديدة

طاوِلة (ج. طاوِلات) table

وَرَقة (ج. أوراق) paper, piece of paper

طَبَق (ج. أطباق) dish

نِصف half

مُستعمَل used

لَم تَكُن it was not

فَقَد (ف + قَد) see grammar note

شَعَر-يَشعُر to feel

حاجة need

بِحاجة لِ، إلى in need of

تَمرين exercise

وَزن weight

ذَكَر-يَذكُر to mention

طَعام food

مُفاجَأة surprise

حَتّى even (Do you remember other meanings of this word?)

عَلّم-يُعَلِّم to teach

قانون (ج. قَوانين) rule

لُعبة game, sport

غَلَب-يَغلِب to win over, to beat (someone)

ماهِر skilled

أمس = مبارِح yesterday

زار-يَزور to visit

شَيء (ج. أشياء) = حاجة (ج. حاجات) thing

أسئلة

١. لماذا ذهبت مايا وفدوى ورانية الى سوق "ستي ستارز"؟
٢. مَن دفع ثمن الطاولة؟
٣. لماذا لم تكُن الطاولة غالية؟
٤. لماذا قرّرت مايا شراء الطاولة؟
٥. ماذا كانت المُفاجأة؟
٦. لماذا لم تلعب رانية تنس الطاولة في حياتها؟
٧. ماذا علّمت مايا رانية؟
٨. هل تعلّمت رانية لعبة تنس الطاولة؟
٩. مَن هي مُنى؟ لماذا هي ماهرة في لعبة تنس الطاولة؟
١٠. لماذا تعتقد مايا انها ستغلب رانية المرّة القادمة؟

تمرين رقم ١: أكمل كلّ واحدة من العبارات في العمود أ بما يناسبها في عمود ب، كما في المثال

Create complete sentences by joining each phrase in column أ with the correct phrase from column ب. Follow the example.

	أ	ب
١	اشترت مايا وسلمى ورانية	لاعبة ممتازة
٢	بدأت رانية	قوانين لعبة تنس الطاولة
٣	تعلّمت مايا	في غرفة الجلوس
٤	علّمت مايا رانية	أن يزيد وزنها
٥	قالت رانية	تغلب مايا وسلمى
٦	كانت مُنى	إنها لا تحبّ الرياضة
٧	دفعت مايا نصف الثمن	طاولة تنس

٨	لا تريد مايا	ودفعت سلمى ورانية النصف الثاني
٩	وضعت مايا وفدوى طاولة التنس	أشياء كثيرة من مُنى

١. اشترت مايا وسلمى ورانية طاولة تنس.

تمرين رقم ٢: أكمل الجدول التالي

الفعل	الترجمة	الجذر	الصيغة المجرّدة	الوزن ورقمه
ذهبت				
واشترينا		ش-ر-ي		
ووضعناها	and we put it (her)			فعل، I
تكُن	she is		كان	
نَشتَري				
تُحبّ		ح-ب-ب		IV،
تَتفرّج				
يزيد			أراد	
تَتعلّم	she learns			
علّمتها				
تَغلبني				
زارتنا				
وتعلّمت				
أعتَقِد				
سأغلب				
نَلعب				

الدرس الخامس

كلمات الوحدة

أشهَر most famous
أفضَل = أحسَن best
الوِلايات المُتّحدة the United States
أمس = مبارِح yesterday
أنثى female
انضَمّ-يَنضَمّ to join
أوروبي European
بِحاجة لِ، إلى in need of
بَطَل (ج. أبطال) champion
بقيادته under his leadership
بِهَدَف with the goal of
تَبادُل exchanging
ذَكَر male
رِياضة sports
زار-يَزور to visit
زَواج marriage
سَجّل-يُسَجِّل to score
سَفَر travel
شابّ (ج. شَباب) young man
شابّة (ج. شابّات) young woman
شَعَر-يَشعُر to feel
تَعَرّف getting to know
تفرّج-يِتفَرَّج to watch
تَمرين exercise
تِنِس أرضي tennis (lit. ground tennis)
جائِزة prize, award
جِنس sex, gender
حاجة need
حَتّى even (Do you remember other meanings of this word ?)
حَصَل (على) to obtain
دَوري (sports) league
ذَكَر-يَذكُر to mention
فَريق (ج. فِرَق) team
فَوز winning
قانون (ج. قَوانين) rule
قِراءة reading
قَناة channel
قِيادة leadership
كَأس cup
كُرة قَدَم football, soccer
كَما also, as, as well

شَيء (ج. أشياء) = حاجة (ج. حاجات) thing

صَداقة friendship

صورة (ج. صُوَر) picture

ضَعيف weak

طاوِلة (ج. طاوِلات) table

طَبخ cooking

طَبَق (ج. أطباق) dish

طَعام food

عَدَد number

عَلّم-يُعَلِّم to teach

غَلَب-يَغلِب to win over, to beat (someone)

ف and, and so, as

فاز-يَفوز to win

فَتاة = بِنت

مُنتَخَب = فَريق team

مُنتَشِر widespread

نادي (ج. أندِية) club

نِصف half

هَدَف goal

لاعِب player

لَعِب playing

لعِب-يلعَب to play

لُعبة game, sport

لَقَب title

ماهِر skilled

مُباراة match

مَحبوب beloved, liked

مُختلِف different

مُستعمَل used

مُستَقبَل future

مُسلم Muslim

مُفاجَأة surprise

مِن أشهَر among the most famous

هواية (ج. هِوايات) hobby

وَرَقة (ج. أوراق) paper, piece of paper

وَزن weight

وُلِد-يولَد to be born

تمرين رقم ١: املأ الفراغات

تلعب، تلعب، تلعبها، سأغلب، لاعبة، لاعبة، لعبَتْ، لعبتُ، وتغلب، ولعبتُ، نلعب

مُفاجأة كبيرة! قبل ما اشترينا الطاولة قالت رانية إنّها لم .... تنس الطاولة في حياتها، فهي لا تحبّ الرياضة، حتّى في التلفزيون.

.... مع سلمى، وكانت رانية تتفرّج. ثمّ قالت إنّها تريد أن تتعلّم كيف .... علّمتها قوانين اللعبة وكيف .... بعد أسبوع فقط بدأت تغلبني .... سَلمى؛ أصبحت .... ماهرة.

أمس زارتنا مُنى، أخت سلمى المرّضة، .... معها. كانت .... ممتازة، وقالت إنّها .... في فريق المدرسة عندما كانت في المدرسة الثانويّة. لعبتُ معها أكثر من ساعة أو ساعتين، وتعلّمت منها أشياء كثيرة. أعتقد أنّني .... رانية عندما .... المرّة القادمة!

قَواعِد

The conjunction ف

The particle ف is a conjunction generally similar to و "and" in meaning, but often with some "color" added to it, like "as", "and so", "since", "as a result of that", etc., depending on the context.

You first learned this particle as a part of the phrase أما... ف...(as for... so...). In the following two-sentence sequence ف occurs twice with two slightly different meanings. Study the Arabic sentences and compare them with their English translation below. (Remember that قد simply affirms a past tense action and does not have a meaning of its own.)

The idea of buying the table was my idea, as I felt that I was in need of sports and exercise because my weight began to increase. And as I mentioned, Egyptian food is very delicious and inexpensive, so I was eating a lot.	كانت فكرة شراء الطاولة فكرتي، فقد شعرتُ أنّني بحاجة للرياضة والتمرين لأنّ وزني بدأ يزيد. فكما ذكرت، الطعام المصري لذيذ جدّاً ورخيص، لذلك كنت آكُل كثيراً.

Now translate the following sentence:

قبل أنْ نشتري الطاولة قالت رانية إنّها لَم تلعَب تنس الطاولة في حياتها، فهي لا تحبّ الرياضة، حتّى في التلفزيون.

Looking up words in the dictionary

As was pointed out earlier, the overwhelming majority of words in Arabic are derived from three-letter roots. There are three main exceptions to this generalization: four-letter roots; "function" words (prepositions, conjunctions, pronouns, demonstratives, and many adverbials); and foreign borrowings. Four-letter roots constitute a small minority. Two of the most common such roots that you have already seen are هـ–ن–د–س (هَندسة، مُهندس) and ت–ر–ج–م (تَرجم، تَرجمة، مُترجم).

Function words and foreign borrowings are generally arranged alphabetically: الذي، هذا ، ده، دلوقت، كمبيوتر، أمريكا ، معكرونة، etc. Words derived from three- and four-letter roots are arranged alphabetically by root. So the words معروف، يعرف، and التعرّف are listed under the root ع-ر-ف. The words هندسة and مهندس would be listed under the root هـ-ن-د-س.

The different verb and noun stems derived from that root are listed under it. While the root is the three- or four-letter combination associated with a specific meaning, the stems represent the actual words derived from that root without the affixes representing grammatical functions such as tense, number, gender, definiteness, and case. You may recall that for verbs the stem is the form equivalent to English *he-past tense*. So the stem of ينجحون "they succeed" is نجح "he succeeded". For nouns and adjectives, the stem is the singular, indefinite, masculine form: المرّضة → مُمرِّض. In nouns where التاء المربوطة is not a mark of feminineness, as in جامعة, التاء المربوطة is part of the stem.

In the following paragraphs the focus will be on deriving words from three-letter roots since they constitute the majority.

Two words taken from Unit 16 will be used here to illustrate the process of looking up words in the dictionary: حتشتغلي and المخابَرات.

حتشتغلي

Even if you don't know the meaning of this word in مصري you know by now what elements in it are likely to be added affixes: ح is the future marker, ت-ي is the present tense affix. After removing these elements we will have the four-letter sequence شتغل. Assuming that the word is derived from a three-letter root, which is true of the overwhelming majority of cases, which of these four letters is likely to be an affix?

Knowledge of the verb forms will help you identify the root. You may remember that the distinguishing feature of Form VIII is the insertion of ت between the first and second letter of the root. Also helpful is knowledge of words sharing the same letters. In this case the words مشغول and شُغل may come to mind.

Based on all of this, you can conclude that the root is most likely ش-غ-ل. Under that root you will see the verb اشتغل-يشتغل "to work".

المُخابرات

The first step in identifying the root and stem of this word is to remove the definite article and the plural marking. You know by now that in most instances plural ات is attached to nouns that end in التاء المربوطة, so the stem of the word is most likely مُخابَرة. It could also be مُخابَر because you don't know at this stage whether التاء المربوطة is part of the stem or is a feminine marker. If the stem is مُخابَر or مُخابَرة, then what is the root?

You have seen many examples of an initial م that is added to create a stem from the three-letter root: مُشاهدة, مُساعِد, مَدرسة, مُدرّس, etc. Another candidate for removal in words with four or more letters are vowel letters since vowels are frequently added to the letters of the root to create new noun (and verb) patterns. Consequently, the three letters خ-ب-ر are most likely the root letters. As in the case of حتشتغلي above, knowledge of other words derived from the same root such as خِبرة, أخبر, خبر, etc. helps identify the root letters of المخابرات.

As was pointed out in the discussion of the different types of roots, recognizing roots of words is a skill that takes time and practice. You have already learned most affixes added to roots to create different types of words.

You will notice that weak roots, i.e. *assimilated, hollow, final-weak,* and *doubled* are harder to recognize than sound roots. But the more Arabic you know, the easier it will be to recognize relationships among families of words and the root of each family.

You may find the following tips helpful in root identification:

1. The consonants of a root generally stay stable from one form to another in the same family. If you look at the words طارت, طيارة, طيران, you will notice that the consonants ط and ر stay the same. This is an indication that they are part of the root. The alternation between ي and ا is typical of hollow roots.
2. Remember that ا and ى cannot be part of a root. At the root level, the ا and ى appear as either و or ي. After taking out all suffixes and prefixes and arriving at the form طار, you need to figure out whether the root form of ا is ي or و. You can tell for the most part whether a verb derives from و or ي by looking at the other members of the family: for example, طيارة and يطير are derived from the same root as طار, and both include ي. It is therefore likely that the root of طار is طير, not طور.
3. Certain consonants cannot be part of an affix and hence have to be a part of the root. These consonants include غ, ع, ظ, ط, ص, ز, ر, ذ, د, خ, ح, ج, ث, and ق. Some consonants, like ل, ف, ب, occur as prefixes but not as suffixes; the consonant هـ occurs as a suffix only.

فصحى and مصري dictionaries

One additional challenge that students of Arabic face is that not all words are found in one dictionary. As was mentioned in the Introduction, the great majority of words are shared by فصحى and مصري. But there are a minority that are found in one, but not in the other. As examples one can cite the word اللي "that, which, who", which is found in مصري but not فصحى and the words الذين, التي, الذي, which have the same meaning and which are found in فصحى but not in مصري. Thus, we recommend that you should use two dictionaries, one to cover فصحى and another to cover مصري. While most of the words introduced in the book are found in both types of dictionaries, all of the material in the reading selections will be found in a فصحى dictionary and all the material found in the مشاهدة and استماع texts will be found in a مصري dictionary. A good modern فصحى dictionary is *The Hans Wehr Dictionary of Modern Written Arabic* and a good مصري dictionary is *A Dictionary of Egyptian Arabic* by Martin Hinds and El-Said Badawi.

One difference between these two dictionaries is that the Hans Wehr lists the verb form number, not the verb itself, except for Form I verbs where the verb rather than its form number is listed, while Hinds and Badawi lists the actual verb. So for the verb اشتغل- يشتغل, Hans Wehr lists the Roman numeral VIII while Hinds and Badawi lists اشتغل- يشتغل, with no number.

تمرين رقم ٢

1. Following is the list of words of this unit found above rearranged according to word roots, with a few exceptions. Based on the above discussion, explain why the exceptions are not arranged according to their roots.
2. In your opinion, which way of looking up words in Arabic is better: the one below or the one at the beginning of this lesson?

yesterday	أمس = امبارِح	أ-م-س
female	أنثى	أ-ن-ث
European		أوروبي
exchanging	تَبادُل	ب-د-ل
match	مُباراة	ب-ر-ي
champion	بَطَل (ج. أبطال)	ب-ط-ل
tennis (lit. ground tennis)		تِنِس أرضي
sex, gender	جِنس	ج-ن-س
prize, award	جائِزة	ج-ي-ز
beloved, liked	مَحبوب	ح-ب-ب
to obtain	حَصَل-يحصُل (على)	ح-ص-ل

need	حاجة	ح-و-ج
in need of	بِحاجة لِ، إلى	
even		حَتّى
different	مُختلِف	خ-ل-ف
(sports) league	دَوري	د-و-ر
male	ذَكَر	ذ-ك-ر
to mention	ذَكَر-يذكُر	
sports	رِياضة	ر-و-ض
marriage	زَواج	ز-و-ج
to visit	زار-يَزور	ز-و-ر
to score	II (سَجَّل-يُسَجِّل)	س-ج-ل
travel	سَفَر	س-ف-ر
Muslim	مُسلم	س-ل-م
young man	شابّ (ج. شَباب)	ش-ب-ب
young woman	شابّة (ج. شابّات)	
to feel	شَعَر-يَشعُر	ش-ع-ر
most famous	أشهَر	ش-هـ-ر
among the most famous	مِن أشهَر	
thing	شَيء (ج. أشياء) = حاجة (ج. حاجات)	ش-ي-ء
friendship	صَداقة	ص-د-ق
picture	صورة (ج. صُوَر)	ص-و-ر
weak	ضَعيف	ض-ع-ف
to join	VII (انضمّ-ينضَمّ) (Form VII will be introduced in Unit 18.)	ض-م-م

cooking	طَبخ	ط-ب-خ
dish	طَبَق (ج. أطباق)	ط-ب-ق
food	طَعام	ط-ع-م
table		طاوِلة (ج. طاوِلات)
number	عَدَد	ع-د-د
getting to know	تَعَرّف	ع-ر-ف
to teach	(علَم-يعلّم) II	ع-ل-م
used	مُستعمَل	ع-م-ل
to win over, to beat (someone)	غَلَب-يَغلِب	غ-ل-ب
and, and so, as		ف
girl بنت =	فَتاة	ف-ت-و
surprise	مُفاجَأة	ف-ج-أ
to watch	(تفرّج-يتفرّج) V	ف-ر-ج
team	فَريق (ج. فِرَق)	ف-ر-ق
best	أفضَل = أحسَن	ف-ض-ل
to win	فاز-يَفوز	ف-و-ز
winning	فَوز	
future	مُستَقبَل	ق-ب-ل
reading	قِراءة	ق-ر-أ
channel	قَناة	ق-ن-و
leadership	قِيادة	ق-و-د
under his leadership	بقيادته	
rule		قانون (ج. قَوانين)
cup	كَأس	ك-أ-س

football, soccer	كُرة قَدَم	ك-و-ر
also, as, as well		كَما
player	لاعِب	ل-ع-ب
playing	لَعِب	
to play	لعِب-يلعَب	
game, sport	لُعبة	
title	لَقَب	ل-ق-ب
exercise	تَمرين	م-ر-ن
skilled	ماهِر	م-هـ-ر
team مُنتَخَب	فَريق	ن-خ-ب
club	نادي (ج. أندِية)	ن-د-ي
widespread	مُنتَشِر	ن-ش-ر
half	نِصف	ن-ص-ف
goal	هَدَف	هـ-د-ف
with the goal of	بِهَدَف	
hobby	هواية (ج. هِوايات)	هـ-و-ي
paper, piece of paper	وَرَقة (ج. أوراق)	و-ر-ق
weight	وَزن	و-ز-ن
to be born	وُلِد-يولَد	و-ل-د
the United States	الوِلايات المُتّحدة	و-ل-ي

Please note that from now on the lists of words that appear in Lesson 5 of the remaining units will be arranged according to word roots. This is also how words are organized in the Arabic-English glossary in the back of the book.

تمرين رقم ٣: كلمات متقاطعة

	١	٢	٣	٤	٥	٦	٧	٨	٩	١٠
١										
٢										
٣										
٤										
٥										
٦										
٧										
٨										
٩										
١٠										

أفقي

١. ننام فيه عندما نسافر؛ عكس "ليل"

٣. نحتاجه عندما نسافر إلى دولة أخرى

٤. أحسن

٥. نحصل عليها بعد العمل أو بعد مباراة رياضيّة

٦. يحبّه الناس كثيراً

٧. حَرف جرّ (preposition)

٨. صيغة المقارنة (comparison, comparative) من "مشهور"؛ من الألوان وليس على وزن "أفعل"

١٠. من الألوان وليس على وزن "أفعل"؛ بنت

عمودي

١. نشرب فيه القهوة؛ ممتاز في عمله

٣. جمع "دولاب"؛ ضمير (pronoun) المتكلّم المُفرد

٥. "نُصّ" بالفصحى

٧. مايا لم تُحبّ (ما حبّت) .... الفسيخ

٨. فتاة

٩. عاصمة المملكة العربيّة السعوديّة بدون أل التعريف (the definite article)

١٠. "إن شاء الله .... يا دكتور أحمد"

تمرين رقم ٤: حضّر، ناقش في الصفّ، ثمّ اكتب

١. لاعبك المُفضل (اسم الرياضة والفريق، عمره/ها، رقم القميص، هل كان مع فريق آخر من قبل، من اي جامعة، ....)

٢. رياضتك المفضّلة. منذ (since) متى تلعبها، أين، مع من، لماذا تحبّها، الخ؟

الوحدة رقم ١٦
أسئلة غريبة

الدرس الأوّل

أسرة = عائلة (عيلة) family
أُغنِية (ج. أغاني) song
جَواب answer
حكومة government
دُكّان = مَحَلّ shop, store
دين religion
راتِب salary
سَبَب (ج. أسباب) reason

غَريب strange
مُخابرات intelligence services
مَخطوب engaged
مُغَنّي singer
مَقهى café, coffee house
موسيقى music
وَزارة الخارجيّة Ministry of Foreign Affairs, State Department

Question words in Arabic أدوات الاستفهام

مَصري	فُصحى	
إزّاي	كيف	how
أَيّ	أَيّ	which
مين	مَن	who

إيه	ماذا	what
ليه	لِماذا	why
فين	أَينَ	where
مِنين، مِن فين	مِن أينَ	from where
كَم (كام)	كَم	how much, how many
بِكَم (بِكام)	بِكَم	for how much
إمتى	مَتى	when
مِن إمتى	مُنذُ مَتى	since when
---	هَل	for yes/no questions

تمرين رقم ١

Fill in the blanks using some of the فُصحى question words in the above table and translate the questions into English.

هل ـ أيّ ـ ماذا ـ أين ـ مُنذ متى

١. .... تَسكن؟

٢. .... تعمل مع المُخابرات؟

٣. .... مدينة سوف تزور؟

٤. .... انتِ مخطوبة؟

٥. .... تدرس في الجامعة؟

تمرين رقم ٢

Write down each of the following words under its appropriate category.

كم ـ جامع ـ أب ـ أخ ـ مُخابرات ـ مَسيحي ـ مُحاسِب ـ لِماذا ـ شُرطي ـ مُهندس ـ مُسلِم ـ مُغنّي ـ أمّ ـ زوج/زوجة ـ أغنية ـ أُخت ـ كَنيسة ـ مَتى ـ إسلام ـ وَزارة الخارجيّة ـ راتِب ـ هل ـ مُعلِّم ـ قانون ـ كيف

حكومة	وظيفة	دين
موسيقى	سؤال	أسرة /عائلة

تمرين رقم ٣

Someone you just met on the plane asks you the questions below. Determine whether each question is سؤال عادي (a typical, usual question) or سؤال غريب (a strange question).

١. كم أخ واخت عندك؟

٢. انتِ متجوّزة؟

٣. كم مُرتّبَك (salary) في الشهر؟

٤. دينك إيه؟

٥. مِن إمتى بتدرسي عربي؟

٦. في رأيك، أيّ أحسن الحياة في أمريكا ولّا الحياة في مصر؟

٧. رأيك إيه بالرئيس الأمريكي؟

تمرين رقم ٤

Use each of the following key words to form meaningful questions then ask a partner in the class who answers accordingly. The first one is given as an example below.

١. ليه/عربي : ....

٢. إزّاي/قَهوة : ....

٣. مخطوبة : ....

٤. فين/دُكان : ....

٥. بِكام/موبايل : ....

٦. مين/مُغَنّي : ....

٧. أيّ/موسيقى : ....

٨. مِن فين (منين)/أسرة : ....

٩. إيه/أغنية : ....

مثال

ليه بتدرس عربي؟

عَشان أشتغل مع الحكومة.

تمرين رقم ٥

Below is a list of answers. On a separate piece of paper, write an appropriate question for each one.

١. بادرس عربي لأسباب كثيرة.

٢. انا مش متجوّزة وماعنديش "بويفرند".

٣. اسرتي ساكنة في لندن.

٤. انا بخير، شكراً.

٥. في عائلتي خمسة: أنا ووالدي ووالدتي وأخوي وأُختي.

تمرين رقم ٦

In your notebook, write five questions of your own you'd like to ask your classmates.

تمرين رقم ٧

Listen to the song below and fill in the missing question words found in the main chorus. Now translate the song into English and compare your translation to a classmate's.

كنت ....؟ وانا ....؟ جيت لي ....؟

والأيام دي كانت غايبة عني ....؟

كنت .... ؟ وانا .... ؟ جيت لي .... ؟

والأيام دي كانت غايبة عني .... ؟

الدرس الثاني–مشاهدة: انتِ مخطوبة ولّا لسّه؟

كلمات جديدة

engaged مَخطوب

to be, to have been بقى–يِبقى ل

how much (see grammar note below) قدّ إيه

How much (how long) has been for you? بقى لك قدّ إيه؟

family أسرة = عائلة

remaining, rest باقي

forgive me سامحيني

fine, ok عادي

marriage جَواز

for example مثلاً

thus, this way كِده

stop it please, enough خَلاص بَقى

seriously بجَدّ (بِجاد)

to look بَصّ–يِبُصّ

auntie (French *tante*) طانط

frankly بِصراحة

all the time على طول

presently, whatever you say حاضر

whatever you say (lit. your requests are orders) طَلباتك أوامر

أسئلة

1. What "strange" questions does the woman (أمّ محمود) ask Maya?
2. Why doesn't Maya have a boyfriend?

قَواعِد

بقى لك قدّ ايه؟

A common way of asking "for how long?" in مصري is the question:

بَقى (لك) قَدّ ايه؟

This literally translates as "how long has it been (for you)?" Note that there is a similar shift in where the stress, or emphasis, is placed on the word similar to the phrase للدرجة ده. Thus, you would pronounce the question as *ba'AAlik 'addi eeh?*

تمرين رقم ١

الجزء الأوّل

Listen to the online recordings to hear how this question is pronounced for all the pronouns.

مِثال

بقى لك كم شهر بتدرس عربي؟

بقى لي . . .

الجزء الثاني

Answer the questions below about yourself on a separate piece of paper.

١. بقى لك قد ايه بتدرس عربي؟

٢. انتِ مخطوبة/انتَ خاطِب؟ ليه لأ؟

٣. عندك وقت كتير الفصل ده؟

٤. أسرتك ساكنة فين؟

٥. انتِ عندِك "بويفريند"؟ انتَ عندَك "جيرل فريند"؟

٦. انت عندك كم سنة؟ امتى عيد ميلادك؟

٧. مين أكبر وأصغر واحد في عائلتك؟

الجزء الثالث

Ask your partner the questions above and report their answers to the class.

الدرس الثالِث–استماع: بتدرسي عربي عشان بتحبي المحشي؟

النصّ الأوّل

كلمات جديدة

مَعَلِشّ no matter

برّه outside, abroad

طلع to turn out to be

أصلي original, from the country

خالِص completely, at all

شَكل appearance, the way one looks

تعابير

بَقى لي it's been for me

زَيّ الفُلّ great, wonderful, wonderfully (lit. like jasmine)

أمّ الدنيا mother of the world

أسئلة

1. What did the driver think about Maya's nationality? Why?
2. How does the driver describe Egypt?

النصّ الثاني

كلمات جديدة

سَبَب (ج. أسباب) reason

ثقافة culture

موسيقى music

أُغنِية (ج. أغاني) song

حَديث modern

مُغَنّي = مُطرِب singer

طَرَب rapture (in music)

حَس-يحِسّ to feel

تَعابير

فُرصة سعيدة pleased to meet you

عَشان = على شان for, for the sake of

مات-يموت في to love to an extreme (lit. to die in)

النصّ الثالث

كلمات جديدة

درّس-يدرّس to teach

خلّص-يِخلّص to finish, complete

حُكومة government

مُخابرات intelligence services

شخصيا personally

تدريس = تعليم teaching, instruction

عيب shame, shameful

بَلاش no need, let's not

كَنيسة church

تعبير

وَزارة الخارجيّة Ministry of Foreign Affairs, State Department

أسئلة

1. Where has Maya studied Arabic?
2. What is she planning to do after graduation?
3. The state of Michigan is mentioned twice. Why is it mentioned?
4. Are there more Muslims or more Arabs in the United States according to Maya?
5. How does the US differ from Egypt in religious matters?
6. Does the driver agree with Maya on the issue of religious discussions?

قَواعِد

شَكله مصري، شكلها مصريّة

The word شكل "form, shape" is used to refer to how people look. And as a noun, possessive pronouns are attached to it to indicate its reference. So شكلُه means "he looks, شكلها "she looks, etc.". The word also has the meaning of "appear to be" like شكلك تعبان "You look tired, you appear to be tired".

تمرين رقم ١ (تكوين جمل وحوارات قصيرة)

الجزء الأوّل

Make a table that includes شكل inflected for all persons (أنا ، انتَ، انتِ، الخ).

الجزء الثاني

Create and share with the rest of the class eight sentences using the word شكل with the eight different pronouns, such as the following:

شكلك فرنسي. انتَ من فرنسا؟

شكلهم عيّانين النهارده.

الجزء الثالث

Use some of the following words and expressions to form short dialogues:

١. حضرتك من فين:

٢. كمان:

٣. يا سلام!:

٤. أكيد:

٥. اول حاجة:

٦. أكيد سمعت عن ....

٧. الأغاني الحديثة .... بس الأغاني القديمة ....

٨. بتروح/بتروحي لـ .... ؟

٩. انت .... طبعاً؟

١٠. ايه دينك؟

الدرس الرابع–قراءة: مذكّرات مايا

أسئلة كثيرة ومتوقّعة، سائق التاكسي يَسأل، الطلبة يسألون، صاحِب الدُكّان يسأل، عامِل المَقهى يسأل. كلّهم يسألون. يسألون من أين أنا وأين درست العربيّة ومتى وصلت إلى مصر وكم سأبقى فيها وأيّ المدن زُرت وأيّ المدُن سأزور. كما قُلت، هذه أسئلة عاديّة ومتوقّعة.

ولكن هناك أسئلة غريبة وغير متوقّعة أيضاً. لم أتوقّع أن يسألني أحد عن ديني وعُمري وهل عندي "بويفرند" وهل أنا مخطوبة ومتى سأتزوّج وهل أختي متزوّجة وكم راتب أبي الشهري.

ولكن أغرب سؤال سمعته حتى الآن كان في سيّارة التاكسي الذي ركبته اليوم. في البداية سألني السائق أسئلة عاديّة: منذ متى أدرس العربيّة، ولماذا أدرسها. عندما قلت له إنّني أحبّ الأكل العربي والموسيقى العربيّة والثقافة العربيّة شعرتُ أنّه لم يصدّقني. ثمّ سألني إذا كنتُ سأشتغل مع المخابرات الأمريكيّة، ال CIA. سؤال غريب! قُلت له: "لا، إنّني لا أريد العمل مع الحكومة الأمريكيّة." ولكنّي شَعرت أنّه لن يصدّقني مَهما كان جوابي.

كلمات جديدة

متوقّع expected	عامِل worker
عادي ordinary	مَقهى café, coffee house
دُكّان = مَحَلّ shop, store	بَقي–يَبقى to remain, stay

غَريب strange

هَل (see grammar note below)

راتِب salary

لِماذا why

صَدّق–يُصَدّق to believe

مَهما whatever, regardless of

جَواب answer

أسئلة

١. ما هي الأسئلة المتوقّعة التي سألها الناس؟
٢. ما هي الأسئلة الغريبة أو غير المتوقّعة؟
٣. ما هو أغرب سؤال سأله الناس؟
٤. هل فكّرت مايا أنّ سائق التاكسي صدّق جوابها؟

رتّب الجمل التالية حسب ورودها في النّص.

- بعض الناس سألوا مايا عن دينها.
- لا تعرف مايا إذا صدّق سائق التاكسي جوابها.
- بعض الناس سألوا مايا عن راتب أبيها الشهري.
- بعض الناس في مصر يسألون أسئلة غريبة.
- كثير من الناس في مصر يسألون أسئلة عاديّة.
- سأل سائق التاكسي مايا إذا كانت ستشتغل مع المخابرات الأمريكيّة.
- قالت مايا لسائق التاكسي إنّها تحبّ الأكل العربي.
- قالت مايا لسائق التاكسي إنّها تحبّ الموسيقى العربيّة.

قَواعِد

1. هل

هل is a **فصحى** particle that initiates questions which require a yes/no answer. The equivalent in **مصري** has no such particle but uses a rising intonation. In indirect speech, **هل** is translated as "whether".

الترجمة	مَصري	فُصحى
Are you engaged?	انتِ مخطوبة؟	هل انتِ مخطوبة؟
The taxi driver asked me if/ whether I am engaged.	سألني سوّاق العربيّة اذا أنا مخطوبة.	سألني سائق السيّارة هل أنا مخطوبة.

2. More on verb negation in فُصحى

You learned that verbs in مصري are negated with the ما-ش "sandwich". In فُصحى verb negation is more complex and depends on the tense of the verb.

1. Past tense verbs are negated in two ways:
   a. ما + the verb in the past tense

I did not travel ما سافرت

they did not ask ما سألوا

we did not eat ما أكلنا

   b. لم + the verb in the present tense (more formal than negation with ما + past tense):

I did not travel لم أسافر

they did not ask لم يسألوا

we did not eat لم نأكل

2. Present tense verbs are negated with لا:

he does not travel لا يسافر

they do not ask لا يسألون

we do not eat لا نأكل

3. Future-reference verbs (i.e. present tense verbs used to refer to future time) are negated with لن:

سَيُسافر ← he will not travel لَن يُسافِر

سَوفَ نَأكل ← we will not eat لَن نأكل

سيسألوا ← they will not ask لَن لَن يسألوا

تمرين رقم ١: ترجم إلى الإنجليزيّة

١. الطلبة الذين لا يحصلون على دَرَجات عالية يدرسون التاريخ والأدب العربي والتِجارة.

٢. أمّا الطلبة الذين لا ينجحون في الامتحان فَلا يدخلون الجامعة، ويجب أن يأخذوا الامتِحان مَرّة أخرى.

٣. لم أفكّر في البداية أنّ هناك عَلاقة بين هذه الكلمة والفِعل عاش–يعيش.

٤. قُلت كانت هذه أوّل مرّة أكلت فيها الفسيخ، وستكون آخر مرّة، لأنّني ما أحبَبته أبداً، وخصوصاً رائحته.

٥. لم أتوقّع أن يسألني أحد عن ديني وعُمري وهل عندي "بويفرند" وهل أنا مخطوبة ومتى سأتزوّج وهل أختي متزوّجة وكم راتب أبي الشهري.

٦. شعرتُ أنّه لم يصدّقني.

٧. ثمّ سألني إذا كنتُ سأشتغل مع المخابرات الأمريكيّة، ال CIA. سؤال غريب! قُلت له: "لا، إنّني لا أريد العمل مع الحكومة الأمريكيّة."

٨. ولكنّي شَعرت أنّه لن يصدّقني مَهما كان جوابي.

الدرس الخامس

كلمات الوحدة

أ-س-ر	أسرة = عائلة	family
أ-ص-ل	أصلي	original, from the country
غ-ن-ي	أُغنِية (ج. أغاني)	song
أمّ الدنيا		mother of the world
ب-ق-ي	باقي	remaining, rest
ج-د-د	بِجَدّ	seriously
ب-ر-ر	برّه	outside, abroad
ب-ص-ص	بَصّ-يبُصّ	to look
ص-ر-ح	بِصراحة	frankly
ب-ق-ي	بقى لك قدّ إيه؟	how much (how long) has it been for you?

it's been for me	بَقى لي	
to be, to have been	بقى-يِبقى ل	
to remain, stay	بَقي-يَبقى	
no need, let's not		بَلاش
teaching, instruction	تدريس = تعليم	د-ر-س
culture	ثقافة	ث-ق-ف
answer	جَواب	ج-و-ب
marriage	جَواز	ج-و-ز
presently, whatever you say	حاضر	ح-ض-ر
modern	حَديث	ح-د-ث
to feel	حَسّ-يحِسّ	ح-س-س
government	حُكومة	ح-ك-م
to finish, complete	(خلّص-يخلّص) II	خ-ل-ص
completely, at all	خالِص	
stop it please, enough	خَلاص بَقى	
to teach	(درّس-يدرّس) II	د-ر-س
shop, store	دُكّان = مَحَلّ	د-ك-ك
who, which	= اللي	الّذي
salary	راتِب	ر-ت-ب
wonderfully (lit. like jasmine)		زَيّ الفُلّ
forgive me!	سامحيني	س-م-ح
reason	سَبَب (ج. أسباب)	س-ب-ب

personally	شخصيّاً	ش-خ-ص
appearance, the way one looks	شَكل	ش-ك-ل
to believe	صَدّق-يُصَدّق	ص-د-ق
auntie (French *tante*)		طانط
rapture (in music)	طَرَب	ط-ر-ب
whatever you say (lit. your requests are orders)	طَلباتِك أوامر	ط-ل-ب
to turn out to be	طلع	ط-ل-ع
ordinary, fine, ok	عادي	ع-د-ي
worker	عامِل	ع-م-ل
for, for the sake of		على شان (عَشان)
all the time		على طول
shame, shameful	عيب	ع-ي-ب
strange	غَريب	غ-ر-ب
pleased to meet you	فُرصة سعيدة	ف-ر-ص
how much		قدّ إيه
thus, this way		كِده
church	كَنيسة	ك-ن-س
why		لِماذا
to love to an extreme (lit. to die in)	مات-يموت في	م-و-ت
expected	مُتَوَقّع	و-ق-ع
for example	مثلاً	م-ث-ل
intelligence services	مُخابرات	خ-ب-ر
engaged	مَخطوب	خ-ط-ب

no matter		مَعَلِشّ
singer	مُغَنّي = مُطرِب	غ-ن-ي
café, coffee house	مَقهى	ق-ه-و
whatever, regardless of		مَهما
music		موسيقى
yes/no question word		هَل
Ministry of Foreign Affairs, State Department	وَزارة الخارجيّة	و-ز-ر

تمرين رقم ١: املأ الفراغات

هل، مُنذُ، مَع، مَع، مَتى، لَهُ، لَهُ، لماذا،

لكنّي، كَم، كَم، في، عَن، حتّى، أين، أيّ، أنّه، أن، الّذي، إذا

أسئلة كثيرة ومُتَوَقّعة، سائق التاكسي يَسأل، الطلبة يسألون، صاحِب الدُكّان يسأل، عامِل المَقهى يسأل. كلّهم يسألون. يسألون من أين أنا و .... درست العربيّة ومَتى وصلت إلى مصر و .... سأبقى فيها وأيّ المدن زُرت و .... المدُن سأزور. كما قُلت، هذه أسئلة عاديّة ومُتوَقّعة.

ولكن هناك أسئلة غريبة وغير متوقّعة أيضاً. لم أتوقّع .... يسألني أحد .... ديني وعُمري وهل عندي "بويفرند" و .... أنا مَخطوبة و .. .. سأتزوّج وهَل أختي متزوّجة و .... راتب أبي الشهري.

ولكن أغرب سؤال سمعته .... الآن كان في سيّارة التاكسي .... ركبته اليوم .... البداية سألني السائق أسئلة عاديّة: .... متى أدرس العربيّة، و .... أدرسها. عندما قلت .... إنّني أحبّ الأكل العربي والموسيقى العربيّة والثقافة العربيّة شعرتُ .... لم يصدّقني. ثمّ سألني ....

كنتُ سأشتغل............ المخابرات الأمريكيّة، ال CIA. سؤال غريب! قُلت............ : "لا، إنّني لا أريد العمل............ الحكومة الأمريكيّة." و............ شعرت أنّه لن يصدّقني مهما كان جوابي.

تمرين رقم ٢: أكمل الجدول التالي

الفعل	الترجمة	الجذر	الصيغة المجرّدة	الوزن ورقمه
بافكّرش				
بُصّي		ب.ص.ص		فعل، I
طلعتِ				
باحبّ		ح.ب.ب	حبّ	
تخلّصي				فعّل، II
حتعملي	you will do			
بنحبّش				
يسألون				
زُرت				
أتوقّع				
يسألني				
سأتزوّج				تفعّل، V
سمعته				
قُلت		ق.و.ل		
أحِبّ		ح.ب.ب	أَحَبّ	
يُصدّقني				
سأشتغل				

Sociolinguistic Corner: حبّ–يحبّ، أحَبّ–يُحِبّ

In Exercise 2 above there were two verbs with the same meaning derived from the root ح.ب.ب (باحِبّ and أحِبّ). If you did the exercise correctly, you should have assigned باحبّ to Form I and أحبّ to Form IV. Such a difference is indicative of certain differences between the spoken Arabic dialects on the one hand, such as مصري, and فصحى on the other. Form IV verbs in فصحى often have their equivalents in مصري in Form I or II. Here are a few examples:

	مصري	فُصحى
to inform	خَبّر II	أخبر IV
to return something	رجّع II	أرجع IV
to feel	حَسّ I	أحَسّ IV

تمرين رقم ٣: أكمل الجدول التالي

كلمات من نفس الجذر	الجذر	المعنى	
Morocco المغرِب ،west غرب	غ-ر-ب	Strange, stranger	غَريب
			تدريس
			صَدّق
			عامِل

تمرين رقم ٤: حضّر، ناقش في الصفّ، ثمّ اكتب (حوالي ١٠٠ كلمة)

1. Create a dialogue with another student in which you ask and/or answer questions about topics that are considered too private.
2. Describe Maya's experience in Salma's house, particularly the conversation she had with أمّ محمود.

الوحدة رقم ١٧
زيارة مناطق أخرى

الدرس الأوّل

ارتِفاع height

أسّسَ-يُؤسِّس to found

اشتَهر-يَشتَهِر to be famous

اعتُبِر-يُعتُبَر to be considered

أعجَب-يُعجِب to please

الإسكندر الكبير Alexander the Great

البحر الأبيض المتوسّط the Mediterranean Sea

البحر الأحمر the Red Sea

أهَمّيّة importance

زار-يزور to visit

زيارة a visit

سياحة tourism

سياحي touristic

شَعبي popular, working class

فَضّل-يُفَضّل to prefer

قَلعة castle, citadel

لطيف nice

مَتحَف (ج. مَتاحِف) museum

مُحاضَرة (ج. مُحاضَرات) lecture

مَركَزي central

مَسرَح (ج. مَسارِح) theater

مَعروف known, well-known

مَعلَم (ج. مَعالِم) landmark

مَكتبة library

مُمتِع enjoyable

مَملوء filled

مَنارة lighthouse

مِنطَقة (ج. مَناطق) region, area

ميناء (ج. مَوانئ) port

هادِئ quiet

هَرَم (ج. أهرام) pyramid

تعابير

I wish, desire to visit نفسي أزور

I want to visit عايز/عايزة أزور

I will miss you (f.) حتوحشيني/(m.) حتوحشني

together مع بعض

تمرين رقم ١

With reference to the above list, label the following pictures in Arabic.

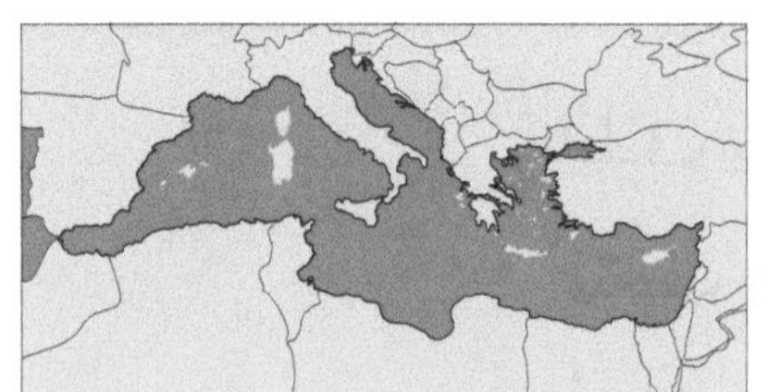

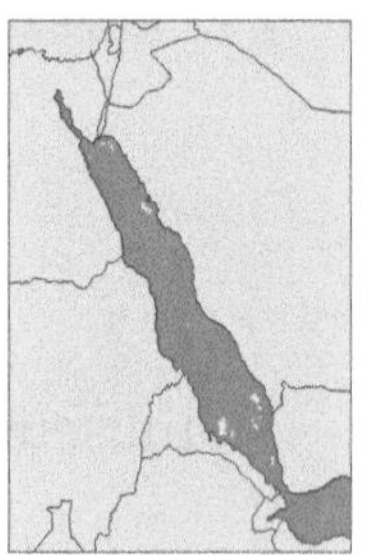

______________ ______________ ______________

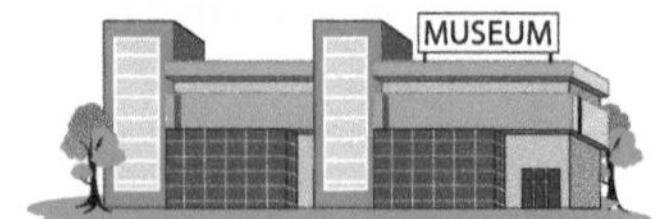

______________ ______________ ______________

______________ ______________

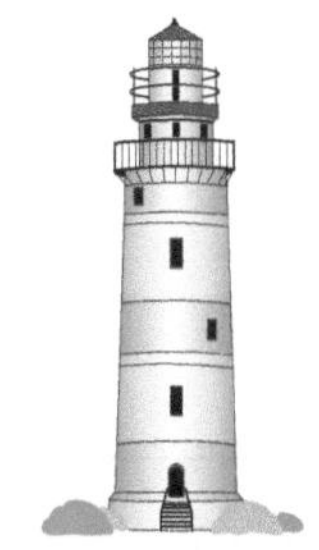

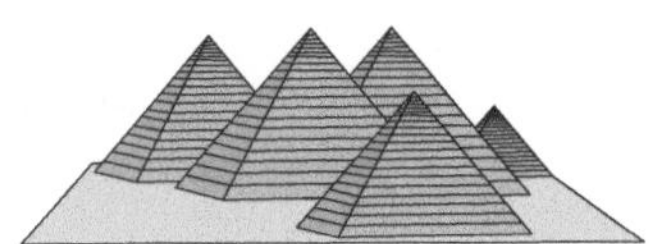

___________ ___________ ___________

تمرين رقم ٢: ما هي الكلمة الغريبة؟

آثار مركزي سياحة متحف

مَملوء مدينة منطقة ميناء

اشتهر اعتبر شعبي أعجب

مَسرَح مُمتِع مَتحف مَعلَم

هادئ مَعروف لطيف ارتِفاع

تمرين رقم ٣

Translate the following words into English, then identify their roots and give at least one example of a word derived from the same root. The first one is given as an example.

الكلمة	الترجمة	الجذر	كلمات من نفس الجذر
أهمّيّة	importance	هـ-م-م	مُهِمّ important، هامّ important، أهَمّ more important
يوّسّس			
اشتَهر			
زيارة			
يُفضِّل			
معروف			
مكتبة			
مَعلَم			

تمرين رقم ٤

Fill in the blanks using the words in the word bank.

مَعروف - مُمتعة - منطقة - مَتحف - أسّس

١. يجب أن أزور . . . . .البحر الأحمر.

٣. "اللوفر" . . . . .في باريس.

٤. . . . . .الإسكندر الكبير مدينة الإسكندريّة.

٥. كانت رِحلتي الى السودان . . . . .جدّاً.

تمرين رقم ٥

(Oral in class) Discuss a journey you have taken, or wish to take, with a partner in class. Start the conversation with one of the following expressions:

١. نفسي أزور . . . .

٢. عايز/عايزة أزور. . . . .

٣. حتوحشني/حتوحشيني يا . . . .

٤. مع بعض . . . .

الدرس الثاني-مشاهدة: المعادي والزمالك زيّ أمريكا وأوروبا، ولاّ لأ؟

كلمات جديدة

حتّة part

أثَر (ج. آثار) ruins, antiquities

فرعوني Pharaonic

ألطَف nicer (think of لطيف)

عام-يعوم = سبح-يسبَح to swim

خواجة (ج. خواجات) = أجنبي (ج. أجانِب) foreigner

مَجنون crazy, mad

صَحّ = صحيح correct

سياحي touristic

مَكتبة library

القلعة the Citadel (in Cairo)

مُحاضَرة (ج. مُحاضَرات) lecture

اتّفق-يتّفِق to agree

تعابير

حتوشحيني I will miss you (see grammar note)

من غير ما = بدون without

مِن زمان for a long time

نِفسي=عايز I want, would like

جَبل موسى Mt. Sinai

البحر الأحمر the Red Sea

المسرح الروماني Roman Amphitheater

مع بعض together

أسئلة

1. Why has Maya wanted to visit Palestine for a long time?
2. What parts of Egypt outside of Cairo does Maya want to visit?
3. Why would it be hard to visit Luxor and Aswan?
4. What does Maya want to do when she travels to the Sinai?
5. Which part of Egypt does Salma recommend visiting?
6. What touristic places can Maya visit in Alexandria?
7. What does Maya want to do on the beach?
8. When are they traveling to Alexandria?

قَواعِد

حتوحشيني

Note that in the verb حتوحشيني "I will miss you" the first person pronoun is the object and the second person pronoun is the subject. So, grammatically, the verb translates as "you will make me lonesome" or "you will make me miss you". (Think of French *Tu me manques* or Italian *mi manchi*.)

تمرين رقم ٢: أكمل الجدول التالي

الفعل	الترجمة	الجذر	الصيغة المجرّدة	الوزن ورقمه
خلّصت			خلّص	
حتوحشيني			وحش	
تشوفي				
درِّسني				
بيتكلم				
تزوريها		ز-و-ر		

				حيكون
				وأطلع
				بنروح

تمرين رقم ٣ (حوار)

Match the following Egyptian expressions with their English equivalents and then translate the accompanying sentences orally into مَصري.

معقول	على طول	خواجات	حَرّ موت	بَرّه	طبعاً	نفسي	من زمان	تقريباً	لسّه

foreigners	boiling hot	I feel like	straight away	roughly	ages ago	outside	reasonable	not yet/ still	of course

I haven't been to Lebanon *in ages* but *I feel like* going next summer.

There are some lovely places you can visit *outside* Cairo.

Are you going to Jerusalem *straight away* or will you visit Amman first?

It was *boiling hot* in Sharm el Sheikh but the hotel was *reasonable.*

I still have not yet seen the area near the Citadel.

Aswan is *roughly* two hours from Luxor by train.

Of course there are a lot of *foreigners* in Marrakesh in the summer.

تمرين رقم ٤ (حوار)

You are staying at the Crillon Hotel in Alexandria and you ask the receptionist (موظف الاستقبال) to recommend a few places to see. Working with a classmate, use the English prompts to create your questions in مَصري and your classmate can read the answers in مَصري before you swap roles.

You	Good morning. I haven't been to Alexandria in ages. Is there a good museum near here?		
		أيوه – المتحف الروماني مش بعيد من هنا أبداً	موظف
You	The Graeco Roman museum? I will go there tomorrow as today I feel like sitting by the sea.		

You		طيب في الحالة دي مُمكِن تزور مكتبة اسكندرية عشان هي قريبة من البحر	موظف
You	The Library of Alexandria? I don't really feel like sitting in a library today. I would rather sit outside.		
		بتحب الآيس كريم؟	موظف
You	I don't really feel like ice-cream. Do you know a good fish restaurant close to the sea?		
		أيوه ـ فيه حتة فيها مطاعم سمك كويسة مش بعيدة من هنا	موظف
You	Are the restaurants expensive or cheap? I don't have a lot of money.		
		مش غالية ولا رخيصة ـ معقول يعني	موظف
You	Great, I will go there then. Thanks a lot.		

الدرس الثالِث

قراءة: الإسكندريّة

تقع الإسكندريّة في شمال مصر على البَحر الأبيَض المُتَوسّط على بُعد حوالي ١١٥ ميلاً (١٨٠ كيلومتراً) شمال غرب القاهرة.

الإسكندريّة من أهمّ مُدُن البحر الأبيض المتوسّط في القَديم والحديث. كانت مركزاً هامّاً للتجارة والعِلم والثقافة اليونانيّة وعاصمة مصر مُنذُ أسّسّها الإسكندر الكبير في سنة ٣٣٢ قبل الميلاد (ق.م).

دخل العرب المسلمون مصر في سنة ٦٤٢ ميلاديّة (م.) ونقلوا عاصمة البلاد إلى المنطقة المَعروفة الآن بالقاهرة. ولكن بقيت الإسكندريّة مركزاً تجاريّاً وصِناعيّاً وثقافيّاً هامّاً، وبقي ميناؤها من أهمّ مَوانئ البحر الأبيض المتوسّط.

تُعتبر الإسكندريّة الآن ثاني مدينة في الأهمّيّة في مصر بعد العاصمة، القاهرة. ويزيد عدد سكّانها على أربعة ملايين نسمة.

أكثر سُكّان الإسكندريّة الآن، مثل باقي مصر، عَرَب مسلمون سُنّة، وهناك أقلّيّة من المسيحيّين الأقباط.

كانت هناك جالِيات من اليونان والإيطاليّين والسوريّين واليَهود. وكانت الفرنسيّة اللُغة العامّة لهذه الجاليات التي كانت تشكّل ١٠٪ من السكّان في سنة ١٩٤٧. ولكنّها اختَفت بشكل كامل تقريباً نَتيجة سياسات التأميم في زَمَن الرَئيس جمال عبد الناصر.

اشتَهرت الإسكندريّة في الماضي بمَكتبتها التي كانت تحتوي على أكثر من ٧٠٠ ألف كتاب، والمنارة التي كان يزيد ارتِفاعها عَلى ١٢٠ متراً.

ومِن مَعالِم الإسكندريّة الآن قلعة "قايتباي" والمَسرَح الروماني ومكتبة الإسكندريّة الجديدة ومَتحف الإسكندريّة القَومي والمتحف اليوناني الروماني.

كلمات جديدة

البَحر الأبيَض المُتوسّط the Mediterranean Sea

بُعد distance

يوناني Greek

مَدينة (ج. مُدُن) city

أسّس–يُؤسِّس to found

الإسكندر الكَبير Alexander the Great

نَقل–يَنقُل to move, transfer

مَعروف known, well-known

صِناعي industrial

ميناء (ج. مَوانئ) port

أُعتُبِر–يُعتَبَر to be considered

أهَمّيّة importance

جالِية (ج. جالِيات) community (especially foreign)

يَهود Jews

اِختَفى–يَختَفي to disappear

نَتيجة result

نَتيجة لِ as a result of

تَأميم nationalization

زَمَن time

رَئيس president

أَقَلّيّة (ج. أقلّيّات) minority

قِبطي (ج. أقباط) Coptic

اِشتَهَر–يَشتَهِر to be famous

اِحتَوى–يَحتَوي (على) to contain

مَنارة lighthouse

اِرتِفاع height

زاد–يَزيد (عَلى) to exceed

مَعلَم (ج. مَعالِم) landmark

مَسرَح (ج. مَسارِح) theater

مَتحَف (ج. مَتاحِف) museum

قَومي national

أسئلة

١. أين تقع الإسكندريّة؟
٢. مَتى تأسّست؟
٣. مَتى دخلها العرب المسلمون؟
٤. لِماذا فقدت الإسكندريّة بعض أهمّيتها بعد دخول العرب المسلمين؟
٥. ما هو عدد سكّان الإسكندريّة الآن؟
٦. ما هي الجاليات غير المصريّة التي كانت تعيش في الإسكندريّة في نهاية الأربعينات من القرن العشرين؟
٧. ما هو دين وإثنيّة (ethnicity) سكّان الإسكندريّة الآن؟
٨. ما هي بعض مَعالم الإسكندريّة الهامّة في الماضي والحاضر؟

صحّ أو خطأ؟ (companion website)

رتّب الجمل التالية حسب ورودها في النصّ.

- أسّس الإسكندر الكبير الإسكندريّة في القرن الرابع قبل الميلاد.
- القاهرة أهمّ من الإسكندريّة.
- أمّم جمال عبد الناصر كثيراً من الشركات والمحلّات التي كانت تملكها الجاليات غير العربيّة.
- دخل العرب المسلمون الإسكندريّة في القرن السابع.
- فقدت الإسكندريّة بعض أهمّيتها لأنّ القاهرة أصبحت عاصمة مصر.
- في الإسكندريّة أقلّيّة قبطيّة كبيرة.
- في الإسكندريّة قلعة مشهورة ومسرح ومكتبة كبيرة وعدد من المتاحف.
- كانت هناك جالية يونانيّة كبيرة في الإسكندريّة.

تمرين رقم ١: أكمل الجدول التالي

الفعل	الترجمة	الجذر	الصيغة المجرّدة	الوزن ورقمه
تقع	it (she) is located			
أسّسها				فعّل، II
دخلها				
فقدت		ف-ق-د		
نقلوا				
بقيت				
تُعتبر				
ويزيد				
اختَفت		خ-ف-ي		افتعل، . . .
اشتَهرت				
تحتوي			احتَوى	

تمرين رقم ٢

The following three words, taken from the reading passage on Alexandria, are مصادر (pl. of مصدر, verbal noun). With reference to the discussion of verbal nouns in Unit 15, Lesson 5, can you tell which verb forms these words based off of مصادر are derived from?

تَقريباً، التأميم، ارتِفاعها

الدرس الرابِع–قراءة: مذكّرات مايا

هَرَبت من مكدونالدز وستاربكس وكنتاكي فرايد تشكن في الولايات المتّحدة، ولكنّي وجدتها هنا في الزمالك! أُفَضِّل سوق التوفيقية القديم في "وسط البلد" في القاهرة لأنّه مملوء بالمقاهي والمطاعم الشَعبيّة. تَعتَقد صاحباتي المصريات أنّني مجنونة لأنّني أُفَضِّل مناطق القاهرة القديمة على المناطق الحديثة. (أرجو أن لا تَظنّ بعض تِلك الصاحبات أنّ هذه مؤامَرة من مؤامَرات المُخابرات المَركزِيّة الأمريكيّة!)

في التاكسي الذي ركبته الى "السقّارة" اليوم، سألني السائق لماذا جئتُ الى مصر وماذا أعجبني فيها. عندما قُلت له إنّني أحبّ منطقة وسط البلد والمناطق القديمة في القاهرة ولا أحبّ الزمالك والمعادي أعجبه ذلك كثيراً، وقال إنّه لا يحبّ المعادي أبداً، فَقَد كانت تلك المناطق حدائق ومناطق مَفتوحة، وكانت جميلة جدّاً ونَظيفة وهادِئة. أمّا الآن فهي مملوءة بالسيّارات والبنايات العالية، وكلّ شيء فيها أغلى من وسط البلد بكثير.

كانت رِحلتي الى السقّارة مُمتِعة جدّاً. رأيت الآثار المصرية القديمة ومَشيت أكثر من أربع ساعات حَول مِنطقة الهَرَم. كان الطقس جميلاً جدّاً، دافئاً ومُشمساً. هذا شيء جميل جدّاً في مصر في هذه الأيّام، طقس دافئ ومُشمس كلّ يوم تقريباً. يقولون إنّ الطقس سَوفَ يتغيّر بعد شهر أو شهرين ويصبح حارّاً جدّاً. هذا ليس مُهِمّاً بالنسبة لي، لأنّني سأكون في ريف نيويورك في ذلك الوقت، ولَن يكون الطقس حارّاً هناك.

كلمات جديدة

هَرَب–يَهرُب to run away

فَضّل–يُفَضّل to prefer

مَملوء filled

شَعبي popular, working class

رَجا–يَرجو (أن) to hope for

ظَنّ–يَظنّ = فكّر–يُفكّر = اعتقد–يعتَقِد to think, believe

تِلك that (f.)

مُؤامَرة (ج. مُؤامَرات) conspiracy

مَركَزي central

أعجَب–يُعجِب to please

مَفتوح open

نَظيف clean

هادِئ quiet

أمّا . . . فَ as for . . ., but

مُمتِع enjoyable

حَول around

هَرَم (ج. أهرام) pyramid

تَغَيَّر–يَتَغيّر to change

لَن will not

أسئلة

أ.

١. مِن ماذا هربت مايا؟

٢. ماذا تفضّل؟ لِماذا؟

٣. لماذا تفكّر بعض صاحبات مايا أنّها مجنونة؟

٤. لماذا لا يحبّ سائق السيّارة منطقة المعادي؟

٥. ماذا رأت مايا في رحلتها إلى السقّارة؟

٦. ما هو الشيء الجميل في مصر في هذه الأيّام حسَب مايا؟ لماذا؟

٧. ما هو الشيء الذي ليس مهمّاً لمايا؟ لماذا؟

ب. رتّب الجمل التالية من ١ ـ ٨ حسب ما جاءت في النصّ.

______ استمتعت مايا بزيارة السقّارة.

______ تغيّر الطقس ليس مهمّاً بالنسبة لمايا.

______ تكلّمت مايا مع سائق التاكسي.

______ مايا لا تحبّ مناطق القاهرة الحديثة.

______ سائق التاكسي لا يحبّ المعادي.

______ سافرت مايا إلى السقّارة بالتاكسي.

______ في مناطق القاهرة الحديثة مطاعم ومقاهي أمريكيّة.

______ كانت المعادي منطقة جميلة.

قَواعِد

١. أعجَبَني

In the grammar note about the verb حتوحشيني "I will miss you", it was mentioned that the first person pronoun is the grammatical object and the second person pronoun is the subject. أعجبني "I liked" has a similar structure. It translates literally as: "it pleased me".

تمرين رقم ١: ترجم إلى العربيّة

1. I liked the book *Plato's Republic*.
2. She liked Beirut. (Remember that the names of cities are feminine.)
3. I liked the students in this school. (Remember that when a verb precedes its subject it remains singular.)
4. We liked the new name.
5. We did not like the new location.

تمرين رقم ٢: أكمل الجدول التالي

الفعل	الترجمة	الجذر	الصيغة المجرّدة	الوزن ورقمه
هَربت				
أَفَضّل				
تَعتقد				
يَظنّ		ظ-ن-ن		فعل، I
رَكبته				
جِئت		ج-ي-ء	جاء	
أعجَبني				
أحِبّ			أحَبّ	
يقولون				
يتَغيّر				
سأكون				

٢. اسم الفاعل (the active participle)

In Units 3 and 5 you learned about active participles like عايز، ساكن، فاكِر. These participles, which follow the pattern فاعِل are derived from Form I verbs.

You also learned in Unit 15 that the verbal nouns (المصادر) of the different verb forms follow specific patterns, تفعيل (Form II), إفعال (Form IV), تفَعُّل (Form V), افتِعال (Form VIII), and استفعال (Form X).

All the Arabic verb forms follow specific patterns in deriving active participles. The Arabic name for the active participle (اسم الفاعِل) is taken from the active participle pattern of Form I verbs.

Some active participle patterns are more common than others. The following table shows the most common of these patterns.

Form number	Form الوزن	اسم الفاعل Active Participle	أمثِلة
I	فعَل–يفعل	فاعِل	resident ساكِن

teacher مُدَرِّس	مُفَعِّل	فَعَّل–يُفَعِّل	II
enjoyable, fun مُمتِع	مُفعِل	أَفعَل–يُفعِل	IV
middle مُتَوَسِّط	مُتَفَعِّل	تَفَعَّل–يَتَفَعَّل	V
widespread مُنتَشِر	مُفتَعِل	افتَعَل–يَفتَعِل	VIII

تمرين رقم ٣

With reference to the above table, complete the following table. Follow the examples.

Method of derivation	الصيغة المجرّدة	الجذر	الترجمة	الكلمة
Active participle of Form IV	مُسلِم	س-ل-م	The Muslims	المسلمون
				وهادِئة
				مُمتِعة
				ومُشمِساً
				دافئ
Challenge				
				المُتّحدة

الدرس الخامس

كلمات الوحدة

ruins, antiquities	أَثَر (ج. آثار)	أ-ث-ر
to found	(أسّس-يُؤَسِّس) II	أ-س-س
conspiracy	مُؤامَرة (ج. مُؤامَرات)	أ-م-ر
nationalization	تَأميم	أ-م-م

Alexander the Great		الإسكندر الكَبير
as for. . ., (but)		أمّا . . . فَ
distance	بُعد	ب-ع-د
the Mediterranean Sea		البَحر الأبيَض المُتَوسّط
the Red Sea		البحر الأحمر
museum	مَتحَف (ج. مَتاحِف)	ت-ح-ف
that (feminine)		تِلك
community (especially foreign)	جالِية (ج. جالِيات)	ج-ل-ي
crazy, mad	مَجنون	ج-ن-ن
Mt. Sinai		جَبل موسى
part	حِتّة	ح-ت-ت
lecture	مُحاضَرة (ج. مُحاضَرات)	ح-ض-ر
around	حَول	ح-و-ل
to contain	VIII (اِحتَوى-يَحتَوي (على))	ح-و-ي
to disappear	VIII (اختَفى-يَختَفي)	خ-ف-ي
foreigner	أجنَبي (ج. أجانِب) =	خواجة (ج. خواجات)
city	مَدينة (ج. مُدُن)	د-ي-ن
to hope for	رَجا-يَرجو (أن)	ر-ج-و
height	ارتِفاع	ر-ف-ع
central	مَركَزي	ر-ك-ز
president	رَئيس	رأ-س
time	زَمَن	ز-م-ن
to exceed	زاد-يَزيد (عَلى)	ز-ي-د

theater	مَسرَح (ج. مَسارِح)	س-ر-ح
Roman Amphitheater	المسرح الروماني	
touristic	سياحي	س-ي-ح
popular, working class	شَعبي	ش-ع-ب
to be famous	(اشتَهَر-يَشتَهِر) VIII	ش-هـ-ر
correct	صَحّ = صحيح	ص-ح-ح
industrial	صِناعي	ص-ن-ع
to فكّر–يُفكِّر = اعتقد–يعتَقِد = think, believe	ظَنّ–يَظنّ	ظ-ن-ن
to be considered	(اعتُبِر–يُعتَبَر) VIII	ع-ب-ر
to please	(أعجَب–يُعجِب) IV	ع-ج-ب
known, well-known	مَعروف	ع-ر-ف
landmark	مَعلَم (ج. مَعالِم)	ع-ل-م
to swim	عام–يعوم = سَبَح–يسبَح	ع-و-م
to change	(تغيّر–يتغيَّر) V	غ-ي-ر
open	مَفتوح	ف-ت-ح
to prefer	(فَضَّل–يُفضِّل) II	ف-ض-ل
Pharaonic		فرعوني
minority	أقلّيّة (ج. أقلّيّات)	ق-ل-ل
national	قَومي	ق-و-م
Coptic		قِبطي (ج. أقباط)
the Citadel (in Cairo)		القلعة
library	مَكتبة	ك-ت-ب
nice	لطيف	ل-ط-ف

will not		لَن
enjoyable	مُمتِع	م-ت-ع
city	مَدينة (ج. مُدُن)	م-د-ن
filled	مَملوء	م-ل-أ
port	ميناء (ج. مَوانئ)	م-و-ن
together		مع بعض
for a long time		مِن زمان
without بدون =		من غير ما
result	نَتيجة	ن-ت-ج
as a result of	نَتيجة لِ	
clean	نَظيف	ن-ظ-ف
I want, would like	نِفسي = عايِز	ن-ف-س
to move, transfer	نَقل–يَنقُل	ن-ق-ل
lighthouse	مَنارة	ن-و-ر
quiet	هادِئ	هـ-د-أ
to run away	هَرَب–يَهرُب	هـ-ر-ب
pyramid	هَرَم (ج. أهرام)	هـ-ر-م
importance	أهَمّيّة	هـ-م-م
I will miss you	حتوشحيني	و-ح-ش
to agree (to, on)	VIII (اتّفق–يتّفِق (عَلى)	و-ف-ق
Jews		يَهودي (ج. يَهود)
Greek		يوناني

تمرين رقم ١: املأ الفراغات

تقريباً، التي، التي، التي، على، على، في، في، مِن، مِن، مِن، مُنذُ، لكن، هناك

تقع الإسكندريّة في شمال مصر على البَحر الأبيَض المُتَوسّط . . . . بُعد حوالي ١١٥ ميلاً (١٨٠ كيلومتراً) شمال غرب القاهرة.

الإسكندريّة . . . . أهمّ مُدُن البحر الأبيض المتوسّط في القَديم والحديث. كانت مركزاً هامّاً للتجارة والعِلم والثقافة اليونانيّة وعاصمة مصر . . . . أسّسها الإسكندر الكبير في سنة ٣٣٢ قبل الميلاد (ق.م).

دخل العرب المسلمون مصر . . . . سنة ٦٤٢ ميلاديّة (م.) ونقلوا عاصمة البلاد إلى المنطقة المَعروفة الآن بالقاهرة. و . . . . بقيت الإسكندريّة مركزاً تجاريّاً وصِناعيّاً وثقافيّاً هامّاً، وبقي ميناؤها . . . . أهمّ مَوانئ البحر الأبيض المتوسّط.

تُعتبر الإسكندريّة الآن ثاني مدينة في الأهمّيّة . . . . مصر بعد العاصمة، القاهرة. ويزيد عدد سكّانها . . . . أربعة ملايين نسمة.

أكثر سكّان الإسكندريّة الآن، مثل باقي مصر، عَرَب مسلمون سنّة، و . . . . أقلّيّة من المسيحيّين الأقباط.

كانت هناك جالِيات من اليونان والإيطاليّين والسوريّين واليَهود. وكانت الفرنسيّة اللغة العامّة لهذه الجاليات . . . . كانت تشكّل ١٠٪ من السكّان في سنة ١٩٤٧. ولكنّها اختَفت بشكل كامل . . . . نَتيجة سياسات التأميم في زَمَن الرَئيس جمال عبد الناصر.

اشتَهرت الإسكندريّة في الماضي بمَكتبتها . . . . كانت تحتوي على أكثر من ٧٠٠ ألف كتاب، والمنارة . . . . كان يَزيد ارتِفاعها عَلى ١٢٠ متراً.

و . . . . مَعالِم الإسكندريّة الآن قلعة "قايتباي" والمَسرَح الروماني ومكتبة الإسكندريّة الجديدة ومَتحف الإسكندريّة القَومي والمتحف اليوناني الروماني.

Sociolinguistic Corner

Negation in فصحى and مصري

As you have learned, Arabic uses different types of negation depending on the type of word or structure negated. Furthermore, there are some differences between negation in فصحى and in مصري.

تمرين رقم ٢

الجزء الأوّل

Match the following *negative* phrases in مصري in the right-hand column with their فصحى equivalents in the left-hand column.

١	ما باشتغلش في المدرسة دي	أ	لا يفهم صديقي العربية
٢	مايا ما عندهاش عربية في مصر	ب	الطلّاب الذين لا ينجحون لا يدرسون في الجامعة
٣	سلمى ما زارتش أمريكا من قبل	ت	لن تسافر سلمى إلى بريطانيا هذه السنة
٤	ما فيش شغل النهار ده	ث	لم تشاهد مايا لعبة كرة القدم من قبل
٥	الطلاب اللي ما بينجحوش ما بيدرسوش في الجامعة	ج	لا أعمل في هذه المدرسة
٦	سلمى مش حَتسافر بريطانيا السنة دي	ح	لا أحب أن العب كرة القدم
٧	صاحبي ما بيفهمش عربي	خ	لم تزر سلمى أمريكا من قبل
٨	ما لعبناش باسكت امبارح	د	ليس عند مايا سيارة في مصر
٩	أنا ما باحبش العب كُرة	ذ	ليس هناك عمل اليوم
١٠	أخويَ ما عندوش هوايات كثير	ر	لم نلعب كرة السلة أمس
١١	مايا ما شافتش ماتش (لُعبة) كرة قبل كده	ز	أخي ليس عنده هوايات كثيرة

الجزء الثاني

Using the example sentences above, fill in the chart with the appropriate negation words used for each case.

	فصحى	مصري
Past tense verbs		
Present tense verbs		
Future tense verbs		
Nouns and adjectives		

تمرين رقم ٣: كلمات متقاطعة

١٠	٩	٨	٧	٦	٥	٤	٣	٢	١	
										١
										٢
										٣
										٤
										٥
										٦
										٧
										٨
										٩
										١٠

عَمودي (down)	أفُقي (across)
١. مِن مَعالِم الإسكندريّة	١. عَكس (opposite) "غربي"
٣. مدينة مصريّة كبيرة في جنوب مصر؛ جَذر (root) "مفتوح"	٣. مدينة مصريّة على ساحل البحر الأبيض المتوسّط

٥. "كان عايز" بالفُصحى؛ مَن بجانب بيتك (next to)	مُفرد "أنواع"
٦. عَدد سكّان الإسكندريّة أكثر من خمسة ملايين . . .	٦. مصري غير مسلم
٨. مصري قديم	٧. جذرها "ج-ن-ن"
٩. زَمَن	٨. أجنبي
١٠. عكس "بارِد"؛ أنا عايز	١٠. جَمع "كُرسي"

تمرين رقم ٤: حضّر، ناقش، ثمّ اكتب (حوالي ١٠٠ كلمة)

١. مدينة أو دولة عربيّة زُرتها أو تحبّ أن تزورها.

٢. ما رأيك في تاريخ الإسكندريّة، كيف كانت في الأربعينات من القرن العشرين وكيف هي الآن؟

الوحدة رقم ١٨
زيارة فلسطين

الدرس الأوّل

أصل origin

أصلاً originally

بِشَكل خاصّ in particular

بِشَكل عامّ in general

جِسر bridge

حائِط المَبكى the Wailing (Western) Wall

حَيّ (ج. أحياء) neighborhood, quarter

شُعور feeling

عمِل-يعمَل to do, make

في نَظَر in the eyes of, in the point of view of

قبُّة الصَخرة the Dome of the Rock

قدّم-يُقدِّم to offer

كَنيسة القِيامة Church of the Holy Sepulchre

لاجِئ (ج. لاجِئين) refugee

مُخَيَّم (refugee) camp

مَسؤول responsible

المَسجِد الأقصى al-Aqsa Mosque

مُسَخَّن *musakhkhan* (a well-known Palestinian dish)

مُقدّس holy, sacred

مَكان (ج. أماكن) place

مَملكة kingdom

من الحامض للحلو all kinds (lit. from the sour to the sweet)

مَولِد place of birth

نبي prophet

وُجود presence, existence

تمرين رقم ١

Translate each of the following words, identify its root (الجذر), and give at least two words derived from the same root. You can use a dictionary if you need to. The first one is given as an example.

كلمات من نفس الجذر	الجذر	المعنى	الكلمة
to own مَلِك king، ملك-يملِك	م-ل-ك	kingdom	مملكة
			يعمَل
			يُقَدِّم
			وُجود
			شُعور
	س-أ-ل		مَسؤول
			مُقَدَّس

تمرين رقم ٢

Copy each word or phrase next to its English meaning. Use the list above if needed.

أصْل فلسطيني - المملكة العربيّة السعوديّة - بشكل خاص - مكان عامّ - مَسجد - مَولد النبي مُحمد - كنيسة - حائط - في نظري - مُخيّم لاجئين

1. in particular	
2. wall	
3. in my view	
4. public place	
5. church	
6. refugee camp	
7. Palestinian origin	
8. mosque	
9. Prophet Muhammad's birthplace	
10. The Kingdom of Saudi Arabia	

تمرين رقم ٣

Match the questions in column أ with their answers in column ب and then practice saying them with a classmate.

أ	ب
١. حضرتك من الأردن؟	اكيد، من الحامض للحلو.
٢. فيه فنادق قريبة من وسط البلد؟	اعتقد الكلمة من أصل كنعانيّ وتعني "مدينة السلام".
٣. ايه اشهر أكلة فلسطينيّة؟	فيه خدمات لكنها فقيرة مثل الأحياء في الدول الفقيرة.
٤. ايه يعني اسم "القُدس"؟	أيوا، لكن اصلي من مدينة "بيت لحم" في فلسطين.
٥. ازّاي الحياة في مخيمات اللاجئين؟	المسخّن من أشهر الأكلات الفلسطينيّة.

تمرين رقم ٤

The video on the companion website has a recipe for the well-known Palestinian dish مُسخّن. Watch the video and write down the in your notebook five main ingredients in Arabic.

الدرس الثاني–مشاهدة: أصلي من مدينة يافا

النصّ الأوّل

كلمات جديدة

أصلاً originally

مُخَيّم (refugee) camp

هَلأّ = دِلوَقتِ now

مَساحة area

أسئلة

1. Where is the taxi driver from originally?
2. Where did his grandfather and his father live?

3. What is there in the بلاطة refugee camp besides places to live?
4. How are the services at the بلاطة refugee camp compared to the services in نابلس?

النصّ الثاني

كلمات جديدة

كنافة kinafi (a well-known Palestinian dessert)

عِمِل–يِعمَل to make

عزومة invitation

بَلا تَعب بَلا بَطّيخ nonsense (lit. no "tired" no watermelon)

ضيف (ج. ضُيوف) guest

من الحامض للحلو all kinds (lit. from the sour to the sweet)

أسئلة

1. What did the taxi driver say about الكنافة النابلسيّة?
2. What did he say about المسخّن?
3. Where is Maya going to eat مسخّن? With whom?
4. What type of hotel does Maya want?

تمرين رقم ١: أكمل الجدول التالي

الفعل	الترجمة	الجذر	الصيغة المجرّدة	الوزن ورقمه
هربوا				
وسكنوا				
سمعِت				
بيعملوه	they make it			
اتفضّلوا				تفعّل، ...
بتاكلوا				

				قلتِ
		أ-خ-ذ		باخذكم
				تنزلوا
			we will look for	حَندوّر
		و-ص-ل		نوصل
				بتعرف

تمرين رقم ٢

الجزء الأوّل

Below is a list of some of the phrases from the video. With a partner, read them out loud and try to figure out who said which phrase, مايا ولا سَوّاق التاكسي?

حضرتك من نابلس أصلاً؟

مساحته صغيرة، ممكن نصّ كيلومتر مربّع بسّ.

أيوه ، أنا لسه ساكن في المخيّم.

فيه مدارس ومستشفيات ومطاعم وحاجات زيّ كده ؟

مش زي الخَدَمات اللي في مدينة نابلس.

طبعاً، لكن ما فيه أحسن من الأكل النابلسي.

شكراً على العَزومة، لكن مش عاوزين نتعبك.

بلا تعب بلا بطّيخ! اتفضّلوا لبيتنا.

حييجي نابلس بكره إن شاء الله.

والله لسّه مش عارفة.

فنادق كثيرة، من الحامض للحلو.

الجزء الثاني

With your partner, come up with a small skit based on the phrases above. You will need to add your own lines to make sure it makes sense!

الدرس الثالِث

قراءة: القدس

مُقدِّمة

القُدس مدينة مُقَدّسة في نظر اليهود والمسيحيين والمسلمين. من أهمّ الأماكن المقدّسة فيها حائِط المَبكى، وكَنيسة القيامة، والمَسجِد الأقصى، ومسجد قُبّة الصَخرة.

القدس مُقدّسة في نظر اليهود لأنّها القِبلة التي يَتَوجّهون اليها في صَلاتِهم. وتَحتوي على بَقايا "جَبل الهَيكَل" الذي كان النبي إبراهيم سَيضحّي بابنه إسحاق عليه.

وبالنسبة للمسيحيين، تَرجع أهمّيّة القدس إلى أنّها مكان صَلب السيّد المسيح. ويعتبر المسيحيّون القدس بِشَكل خاصّ وفلسطين بشكل عامّ مَولِد دينهم.

أمّا بالنسبة للمسلمين، فإنّ أهمّيّة القدس ترجع بشكل رئيسي إلى وُجود الحَرَم الشريف فيها، وهو، حسب اعتِقاد المسلمين، مَكان عُروج النبي مُحمّد الى السماء في ليلة الإسراء.

تاريخ القدس

القُدس من أقدم المُدُن في العالم. يَعتقد المُؤرّخون أنّ أصل اسمها هو "أوروسَليما"، أي "مدينة السلام" باللغة الكنعانيّة. ورغم ذلك الاسم، فإنّ تاريخ القُدس بعيد عن السلام: فقد دُمّرت ثلاث مرّات على الأقلّ، وحوصِرت أكثر من ٢٠ مرّة، وهوجِمت أكثر من ٥٠ مرّة، واحتُلّت أكثر من ٤٠ مرّة.

يرجع تاريخ القُدس إلى حوالي سنة ٣٠٠٠ قبل الميلاد (ق.م.) وفي حوالي سنة ١٠٠٠ ق.م. احتلّها المَلك داوود، وصارت عاصمة مَملكة اسرائيل. وفي سنة ٥٨٦ ق.م. دمّرها نَبوخذ نَصّر البابلي. ثمّ أرجعها الملك سايروس، مَلك بِلاد فارِس، لليهود في سنة ٥٣٨ ق.م.

احتلّ الرومان القدس سنة ٦٣ ق.م. وثار اليهود على الحكم الروماني في سنة ٦٦ م، فَحاصر الجيش الروماني بقيادة "تيتوس" المدينة ودمّرها في سنة ٧٠ م.

وفي سنة ٦١٤ احتلّ الفُرس القدس، وبقيت تحت حكمهم حتّى دخلها العرب المسلمون سنة ٦٣٧م.، وَبنوا فيها مسجد قبّة الصخرة حوالي سنة ٦٩٠ ميلاديّة.

وفي سنة ١٠٩٩ م. احتلّ الصليبيّون القدس وأقاموا فيها مملكة مَسيحيّة، ولكنّها رجعت الى حكم المسلمين في سنة ١١٨٧ بعد معركة "حطين" بين المسلمين والصليبيّين. بقيت القُدس تحت حكم المسلمين إلى نهاية الحَرب العالميّة الأولى عندما احتلّتها بريطانيا.

كلمات جديدة

مُقَدِّمة introduction

مُقَدّس holy, sacred

في نَظَر in the eyes of

حائِط المَبكى the Wailing (Western) Wall

كَنيسة القِيامة Church of the Holy Sepulchre

المَسجِد الأقصى al-Aqsa Mosque

قُبّة الصَخرة the Dome of the Rock

قِبلة direction of prayer

توجّه-يَتَوجّه to face, to direct oneself towards

صَلاة prayer

بَقيّة (ج. بَقايا) remnant

جَبل الهَيكَل Temple Mount

نَبي prophet

إبراهيم Abraham

ضَحّى-يُضَحّي to sacrifice

اِبن son

إسحاق Isaac

رَجَع-يَرجِع to go back, refer

صَلب crucifixion

السَيّد المَسيح Jesus Christ (lit. the Master the Messiah)

بِشَكل خاصّ in particular

بِشَكل عامّ in general

اِعتَبَر-يَعتَبِر to consider

مَولِد place of birth

وُجود presence, existence

الحَرَم الشريف the Noble Sanctuary

اعتِقاد belief

عُروج ascending

سَماء sky, heaven

ليلة الإسراء the Night of *al-Israa'* (ascension)

مُؤرِّخ (ج. مُؤرِّخون) historian

سَلام peace

كَنعاني Canaanite

رَغم despite, in spite of

إنّ truly, in reality (used only in specific contexts)

دَمّر-يُدَمِّر to destroy (see note about the passive below)

عَلى الأقلّ at least

حاصَر-يُحاصِر to besiege (see note about the passive below)

هاجَم-يُهاجِم to attack (see note about the passive below)

احتَلّ-يَحتَلّ to occupy (see note about the passive below)

المَلك داوود King David

نَبوخَذ نَصّر Nebuchadnezzar

بابلي Babylonian

أرجَع-يُرجِع to return (something)

بِلاد فارِس Persia

ثار-يثور (عَلى) to rebel (against)

الصليبيّون the Crusaders

أقام-يُقيم to set up, establish

الحَرب العالميّة الأولى World War I

أسئلة

١. تاريخ وحدَث (date and event). أكمل الجدول التالي:

١٠٠٠ ق.م.	احتلّ الملك داوود القدس وصارت عاصمة مملكة إسرائيل.
٥٨٦ ق.م.	
٦٣ ق.م.	
٦٦ م.	
٧٠ م.	
٦١٤ م.	
٦٣٧ م.	
١٠٩٩ م.	
١١٨٧ م.	
١٩١٨ م.	

٢. إجابات قصيرة

١. ما هي بعض الأماكن المقدّسة في القُدس؟

٢. لماذا القدس مقدّسة عند اليهود والمسيحيّين والمسلمين؟

٣. ما هو أصل كلمة "القدس"؟

٤. كم مرّة دُمّرت القدس؟ كم مرّة حوصِرت؟ كم مرّة هوجِمت؟ كم مرّة احتُلّت؟

٣. صحّ أو خطأ؟ (companion website)

٤. رتّب الجمل التالية حسب ورودها في النصّ.

١. احتلّ الفرس القدس في نفس القرن الذي دخلها فيه العرب المسلمون.

٢. أقام الصليبيّون مملكة مسيحيّة في القدس.

٣. القدس مهمّة في اليهوديّة والمسيحيّة والإسلام.

٤. بقايا "جبل الهَيكَل" موجودة في القدس.

٥. تاريخ القدس ليس سلميّاً.

٦. يرجع اسم مدينة القدس إلى اللغة الكنعانيّة.

٧. يعتقد المسلمون أنّ النبي محمّد عرج إلى السماء من القدس.

٨. يعتقد المسيحيّون أنّ السيّد المسيح صُلب في القدس.

قَواعِد

1. Verb forms: Form III

One of the first verbs you have learned is a Form III verb. It is the verb سافر-يُسافر. The distinguishing feature of this form is the ا that is inserted between the first and second consonants of the root. Other examples of this verb form are شاهَد-يُشاهِد "to watch", ساعَد-يُساعِد "to help", and هاجَم-يُهاجِم "to attack". Form III verbs often contain an associative meaning, an action occurring between two or more people.

The مصدر of Form III verbs follows the pattern مُفاعَلة. You've already seen a few examples of this pattern: مُشاهَدة "watching", مُساعَدة "helping, help", and مُراسَلة "corresponding, correspondence".

2. More on the passive voice

You learned in Unit 11 that in فُصحى a Form I past tense verb is changed from active to passive voice by using ضمّة on the first letter of the root and كسرة under the second letter.

بَنى ← بُني

سَمَح ← سُمِح

In Form III verbs, which have ا between the first and second consonants of the root, the ا is changed into و in the passive of the past tense verb.

هاجَم ← هوجِم

تمرين رقم ١

The following four verbs found in the reading passage about Jerusalem are in the passive voice. For each of them,

1. give a full translation,
2. identify the root,
3. identify the stem (الصيغة المجرّدة); remember that الصيغة المجرّدة for verbs is the form that is equivalent to English he + past tense in the active voice,
4. identify the form using فعل and the Roman numeral.

Some cells have been filled in.

الوزن ورقمه	الصيغة المجرّدة	الجذر	الترجمة	الفعل
فاعل، III	هاجَم	هـ-ج-م	and she was attacked	وهوجِمت
				دُمّرت
				وحوصِرت
	احتلّ	ح-ل-ل	it was occupied	واحتُلّت

الدرس الرابِع

قراءة: مذكّرات مايا

شُعور غَريب. أوّل مرّة في حياتي أدخُل مخيّم لاجئين. رأيت مُخيّمات اللاجئين في الأردن، ولكنّي كُنتُ أخاف أن أدخلها. كُنت أفكّر أنّ الفلسطينيّين في المخيّم سوف يَكرهونني لأنّني أمريكية ولأنّ أمريكا تُساعِد إسرائيل. وفي نَظَرهم، إسرائيل هي المَسؤولة عن وضعهم. ولكنّ المخيّم لا يختلف كثيراً عن الأحياء الفقيرة في كثير من مُدُن العالم الثالث، في الهند ونيجيريا والمكسيك.

كما قلت، كنت أفكّر أنّ أهل المخيّم سيكرهونني لأنّني أمريكية، ولكن عائلة محمود أبو الرزّ، سائق التاكسي الذي ركبت معه من الجِسر، كانت لطيفة جدّاً. المشكلة لم تكُن أمريكا أو إسرائيل أو اللاجئين، ولكن كثرة الأكل والشرب. عندما وصلت الى بيت محمود مع صاحبي دان قدّموا لنا عصير برتقال. كان الطقس حارّاً وكنت عَطشانة جدّاً. بعد العصير جاء الشاي، ثمّ الغداء: مُسخّن دَجاج. أوّل مرّة في حياتي أكلت مسخّن دجاج. ولا أكذِب إذا قلت انّ المسخّن أطيب أكلة أكلتها في حياتي. أكلت حتّى شبعت، ولكن قالوا "لا، لازم تاكلوا كمان". وأكلت حتى شعرت أنّ معدتي سَتَنفجِر. ولكن، والحمد لله، لم تنفجر معدتي. ثمّ شربنا قهوة وبيبسي ورجعنا مع محمود الى الفندق. عند الفندق حاولت أن أدفَع لمحمود أجرة التاكسي، ولكنّه رَفَض، لأنّنا ضيوف، حَسَب قَوله.

كلمات جديدة

شُعور feeling

وَضع situation

لاجِئ (ج. لاجِئين) refugee

حَيّ (ج. أحياء) neighborhood, quarter

كَرِه-يَكرَه to hate

جِسر bridge

مَسؤول responsible

قدّم-يُقَدِّم to offer

عَطشان thirsty

مُسَخّن Palestinian dish made of chicken, bread, onions, and spices

دَجاج chicken

كَذَب-يَكذِب to lie

شَبِع-يَشبَع to be full

اِنفَجَر-يَنفَجِر to explode

رَفَض-يَرفُض to refuse

قَول saying

أسئلة

١. لماذا كانت مايا تخاف أن تدخل مخيّمات اللاجئين؟

٢. لماذا ذُكرت الهند في النصّ؟

٣. مَن هو محمود أبو الرزّ؟ كيف عاملت (treated) عائلته مايا؟

٤. ماذا كانت المشكلة؟

٥. ما هو المُسخّن؟ ماذا تَقول مايا عنه؟

٦. هل أخذ محمود أجرة التاكسي من مايا؟ لماذا؟

رتّب الجمل التالية من ١–٩، حسب ما جاءت في نصّ القراءة.

_٢_ أمريكا تساعد إسرائيل.

___ المخيّمات مثل الأحياء الفقيرة في الهند.

___ حاولت مايا أن تدفع أجرة التاكسي.

___ رفض محمود أن يأخذ الأجرة من مايا.

___ شربت مايا الشاي.

___ شربت مايا العصير.

___ شربت مايا القهوة.

___ كانت مايا تخاف أن تدخل المخيّمات.

___ كانت المشكلة الأكل والشرب.

قَواعِد

1. Past tense negation with لَم and hollow root verbs

You learned earlier that the past tense in فصحى can be negated more formally by using لَم with a *present* tense verb. Although لم is used with a present tense verb, it gives the meaning of the negative *past* tense.

When لم is used with hollow root verbs, a small spelling change occurs. Look at the examples below, and see if you can guess the rule:

Negating with لم (past tense)	Present tense
لم أنَم	أنا أنام
لم تقُل	أنتَ تقول
لم يخَف	هو يخاف

As you can see, when using لم with past tense hollow verbs, the middle long vowel changes into a short vowel. This shows up in Maya's diary with the sentence:

المشكلة لم تكُن أمريكا أو إسرائيل أو اللاجئين.

This spelling change only occurs for pronouns that *don't* have suffixes in their present tense conjugations (أنا – نحن – أنتَ – هو – هي). For pronouns that require suffixes as a part of their conjugation (أنتِ – أنتم – هم), the suffix acts as a "barrier" to prevent the middle long vowel from getting shortened.

2. Form VII

So far, seven verb forms have been introduced, as shown in the following table.

مصدَر	Active participle		Form
Many patterns	فاعِل	فعل-يفعَل، يفعِل، يفعُل	I
تفعيل	مُفَعِّل	فعّل-يُفعِّل	II
مُفاعَلة	مُفاعِل	فاعَل-يُفاعِل	III
إفعال	مُفعِل	أفعَل-يُفعِل	IV
تفعُّل	مُتفَعِّل	تَفَعَّل-يتَفَعَّل	V

VIII	افتَعَل-يفتَعِل	مُفتَعِل	افتِعال
X	استَفعَل-يَستَفعِل	x	استِفعال

The distinguishing feature of Form VII is the prefix اِن attached to the root letters in the past tense conjugation. In the present tense conjugation the initial ا is deleted and replaced by the subject person prefix.

Form	Past	Present	مصدَر	مِثال (examples)
VII	اِنفَعَل	يَنفَعِل	اِنفِعال	اِنفَجَر، يَنفَجِر، اِنفِجار to be exploded

Form VII often has a passive meaning:

كَسَر–يَكسِر "to break (something)" اِنكَسَر–يَنكَسِر "to be broken"

تمرين رقم ١: أكمل الجدول التالي

الفعل	الترجمة	الجذر	الصيغة المجرّدة	الوزن ورقمه
أدخُل	I enter			
كُنت				
أدخلها				
أفكّر				
يكرهونني				
تُساعد				
يَختلف				
قدّموا				
شَبعت				
سَتنفجِر				
حاولت				

				أدفع
				رفَض

الدرس الخامس

كلمات الوحدة الجديدة

Abraham		إبراهيم
son		إبن
historian	مُؤرِّخ (ج. مُؤرِّخون)	أ-ر-خ
Isaac		إسحاق
truly, in reality (used in specific contexts)		إنّ
originally	أصلاً	أ-ص-ل
remnant	بَقيّة (ج. بَقايا)	ب-ق-ي
Persia	بِلاد فارِس	ب-ل-د
Babylonian		بابلي
nonsense (lit. no "tired" no watermelon)		بَلا تَعب بَلا بَطّيخ
to rebel (against)	ثار-يثور (عَلى)	ث-و-ر
Temple Mount	جَبل الهَيكَل	ج-ب-ل
bridge	جِسر	ج-س-ر
World War I	الحَرب العالميّة الأولى	ح-ر-ب
the Noble Sanctuary	الحَرَم الشريف	ح-ر-م
to besiege	III (حاصَر-يُحاصِر)	ح-ص-ر
to occupy	VIII (احتَلّ-يَحتَلّ)	ح-ل-ل

all kinds (lit. from the sour to the sweet)	من الحامض للحلو	ح-م-ض
the Wailing (Western) Wall	حائِط المَبكى	ح-و-ط
neighborhood, quarter	حَيّ (ج. أحياء)	ح-ي-و
(refugee) camp	مُخَيّم	خ-ي-م
chicken	دَجاج	د-ج-ج
invitation	دَعوة	د-ع-و
to destroy	II (دَمّر-يُدَمِّر)	د-م-ر
to return (something)	IV (أرجع-يُرجِع)	ر-ج-ع
to go back, refer	رَجَع-يَرجِع	ر-ج-ع
despite, in spite of	رَغم	ر-غ-م
to refuse	رَفَض-يَرفُض	ر-ف-ض
responsible	مَسؤول	س-أ-ل
al-Aqsa Mosque	المَسجِد الأقصى	س-ج-د
well-known Palestinian dish	مُسَخّن	س-خ-ن
		ع-د
peace	سَلام	س-ل-م
sky, heaven	سَماء	س-م-و
Jesus Christ (lit. the Master the Messiah)		السَيّد المَسيح
to be full	شَبِع-يَشبَع	ش-ب-ع
feeling	شُعور	ش-ع-ر
in particular	بِشَكل خاصّ	ش-ك-ل
in general	بِشَكل عامّ	ش-ك-ل
the Crusaders	الصليبيّون	ص-ل-ب
crucifixion	صَلب	

prayer	صَلاة	ص-ل-و
to sacrifice	II (ضَحّى-يُضَحّي)	ض-ح-ي
guest	ضيف (ج. ضُيوف)	ض-ي-ف
to consider	VIII (اِعتَبَر-يَعتَبِر)	ع-ب-ر
ascending	عُروج	ع-ر-ج
thirsty	عَطشان	ع-ط-ش
belief	اعتِقاد	ع-ق-د
to make	عِمِل-يِعمَل	ع-م-ل
at least		عَلى الأقلّ
to explode	VII (اِنفَجَر-يَنفَجِر)	ف-ج-ر
direction of prayer	قِبلة	ق-ب-ل
holy, sacred	مُقَدّس	ق-د-س
to offer	II (قَدَّم-يُقَدِّم)	ق-د-م
introduction	مُقَدِّمة	
saying	قَول	ق-و-ل
to set up, establish	IV (أقام-يُقيم)	ق-و-م
the Dome of the Rock		قُبّة الصَخرة
to lie	كَذَب-يَكذِب	ك-ذ-ب
to hate	كِرِه-يَكرَه	ك-ر-ه
Church of the Holy Sepulchre	كَنيسة القِيامة	ك-ن-س
place	مَكان (ج. أماكن)	ك-و-ن
kinafi (a dessert)		كِنافة
Canaanite		كنعاني
refugee	لاجِئ (ج. لاجِئين)	ل-ج-أ

the Night of *al-Israa'* (ascension)	ليلة الإسراء	ل-ي-ل
area	مَساحة	م-س-ح
King David	الملك داوود	م-ل-ك
kingdom	مَملكة	
prophet	نَبي	ن-ب-ي
in the eyes of	في نَظَر	ن-ظ-ر
Nebuchadnezzar		نَبوخَذ نَصّر
to attack	III (هاجَم-يُهاجِم)	ه-ج-م
now	دِلوَقتِ = الآن	هَلّأ
presence, existence	وُجود	و-ج-د
to face, to direct oneself towards	V (توجّه-يَتَوجّه)	و-ج-ه
situation	وَضع	و-ض-ع
place of birth	مَولِد	و-ل-د

تمرين رقم ١

Matching (companion website)

تمرين رقم ٢

The words marked with an asterisk all start with the letter م, except for the word الأماكِن, the plural of مَكان.

The م in this position can be part of the root of the word, it can indicate a place, or it can indicate an active participle.

Make a list of these words and for each of them:

1. give an English translation,
2. identify the stem (الصيغة المجرّدة),
3. identify the root,
4. indicate which of the four functions listed above the initial م serves.

Follow the examples.

أمثلة

Function of the ميم	الجذر	الصيغة المجرّدة	الترجمة	الكلمة
part of the root	م–س–ح	مسيحي	and the Christians	والمسيحيين
active participle of Form IV	س–ل–م	مُسلِم	and the Muslims	والمُسلِمين
place	ب–ك–ي	مبكى	the place of wailing	المَبكى

القُدس مَدينة* مُقَدَّسة في نظر اليهود والمسيحيين* والمُسلمين*. مِن أهمّ الأماكن* المُقدّسة فيها حائِط المَبكى* وكَنيسة القيامة والمَسجِد* الأقصى ومَسجد قبُة الصَخرة.

القدس مُقدَّسة في نظر اليهود لأنّها القِبلة التي يَتوجّهون اليها في صَلاتِهم. وتَحتوي على بَقايا "جَبل الهَيكَل" الذي كان النبي إبراهيم سَيضحّي بابنه إسحاق عليه.

وبالنسبة للمَسيحيين، تَرجع أهمّيّة القدس إلى أنّها مَكان* صَلب السيّد المَسيح*، وللقدس بِشَكل خاصّ وفلسطين بشكل عامّ مَكانة* خاصّة في نظر المَسيحيّين الذين يَعتَبرونها مَولِد* دينهم.

أمّا بالنسبة للمُسلمين، فإنّ أهمّيّة القدس ترجع بشكل رئيسي إلى وُجود الحَرَم الشريف فيها، وهو، حسب اعتِقاد المسلمين، مَكان عُروج النبي مُحمّد الى السماء في ليلة الإسراء.

القُدس من أقدم المُدُن* في العالم. يَعتقد المُؤرّخون* أنّ أصل اسم المدينة هو "أوروسَليما"، أي "مَدينة السلام" باللغة الكنعانيّة. ورغم ذلك الاسم، فإنّ تاريخ القُدس بعيد عن السلام: فقد دُمّرت ثلاث مَرّات* على الأقلّ، وحوصِرت أكثر من عشرين مَرّة، وهوجِمت أكثر من ٥٠ مَرّة، واحتُلّت أكثر من أربعين مَرّة.

يرجع تاريخ القُدس إلى حوالي سنة ٣٠٠٠ ق.م. وفي حوالي سنة ١٠٠٠ ق.م. احتَلّها المَلك* داوود، وصارت عاصمة مَملكة* اسرائيل.

. . .

وفي سنة ١٠٩٩ م. احتلّ الصليبيّون القُدس وأقاموا فيها مَملكة مسيحيّة، ولكنّها رجعت الى حكم المُسلمين في سنة ١١٨٧ بعد مَعركة* "حطّين" بين المُسلمين والصليبيّين.

تمرين رقم ٣: أكمل الجدول التالي

الفعل	الترجمة	الجذر	الصيغة المجرّدة	الوزن ورقمه
يَتَوجّهون	they face	و-ج-ه	توجّه	تفعّل، V
وتَحتوي				
تَرجع				
يَعتَبرونها				
يَعتقد				
دمّرها				
وثار		ث-و-ر		
فَحاصر				
ودمّرها				
وبقيت				
دخلها				
وَبنوا				
وأقاموا		ق-و-م	أقام	
رجعت				
احتلّتها				

تمرين رقم ٤

With reference to the verb form table in Lesson 4 of this unit, complete the following table. Some cells have been filled in.

Method of derivation	الصيغة المجرّدة	الجذر	الترجمة	الاسم أو الصفة
				اعتِقاد
				الإسراء
	مُؤرِّخ	أ-ر-خ		المُؤرّخون
Form VIII ،مصدر				احتِلالها
				المسلمون
Form I ،اسم فاعل	لاجئ			لاجئين
				المُشكلة

تمرين رقم ٥: حضّر، ناقش، ثم اكتب (حوالي ١٠٠ كلمة)

١. مُعامَلة (treatment) سائق التاكسي محمود أبو الرّز لمايا.

٢. ماذا تعرف عن مشكلة فلسطين؟

٣. أهمّيّة القدس لليهود والمسيحيّين والمسلمين.

٤. الأكل الفلسطيني.

Sociolinguistic Corner

Reading: "What's in a name? Monuments and sacred places in Jerusalem"

الوحدة رقم ١٩
انطِباعات مايا

الدرس الأوّل

آمَن–يُؤمِن to believe, have faith in
اختلاف (ج. اختلافات) difference
أزعَج–يُزعِج to bother, disturb
استَطاع–يَستَطيع = قدِر–يقدِر (أن) (to be able (to
اِستَغرَب–يَستَغرِب to find (something) strange
أقلّيّة minority
أمام in front of
اِنتَهى–يَنتَهي to end
انطِباع (ج. انطِباعات) impression
بِداية beginning
تحَسّن–يَتَحَسّن to improve
جاوَب–يُجاوِب to answer
جنّة heaven, paradise
دَور role
سَهل easy
صُعوبة (ج. صُعوبات) difficulty
عَلاقة relationship
غريب strange
كَرَم hospitality
كَلّم–يُكَلِّم to speak to
مُتَدَيّن religious
مُجتمع society
مُزعِج disturbing
مَشروع project
مَطبوخ cooked
نار hell, fire
واجَه–يُواجِه to face

تمرين رقم ١: اكتب عكس كلّ من الكلمات التالية

سأل، صعب، بدأ، جَنّة، أكثريّة، سُهولة، نِهاية

تمرين رقم ٢: أكمل الجدول التالي

الكلمة	المعنى	الجذر	كلمات من نفس الجذر ومَعانيها
انطِباع	impression	ط-ب-ع	طَبعاً of course
استغرَب			
مَشروع			
صُعوبة			
كَلَّم			
مَطبوخ			
مُجتَمَع			
واجَه			

تمرين رقم ٣: املأ الفراغات

Fill in the blanks using the correct word from the word bank.

اختلافات، الجنّة، تتحسّن، متديّنون، دور، صعوبات، العلاقات، الغريب، المجتمع، مُزعجة

١. أريد أن . . . . لغتي العربيّة ولذلك سوف اسافر إلى دولة عربيّة في الصيف.

٢. هناك . . . . ثقافيّة واجتماعية كثيرة بين . . . . العربي والمجتمع الأمريكي.

٣. من الأشياء التي لم أعرفها قبل دراسة اللُغة العربيّة . . . . الدين في المجتمع العربي.

٤. أكثر الناس . . . . ، يؤمنون بالله و . . . . والنار.

٥. الشيء . . . . كان الأسئلة الكثيرة التي يسألها الناس عن العُمر والدين والزواج، أسئلة أعتبرها . . . .

٦. أرجو أن تتحسّن . . . . الأمريكيّة العربيّة أكثر وأكثر.

٧. كانت هناك . . . . كثيرة في بداية السنة، أمّا الآن فليس هناك مشاكل كثيرة.

تمرين رقم ٤: استعمل كلّاً من الكلمات التالية في جملة، كما في المثال،

آمَن–يُؤمِن، أزعَج–يُزعِج، استَطاع–يَستَطيع، أمام، دَور، كَرَم

مِثال: آمَن–يُؤمِن

أكثر العرب يؤمنون بالله والجنّة والنار.

الدرس الثاني

انطِباعات مايا: الجُزء الأوّل

أربعة شهور. أربعة شهور عِشت في العالم العربي وتعلّمت الكثير: عن الشعب العربي، عن الثقافة العربيّة، الكرَم العربي، والأكل العربي، كما تحسّنت لغتي العربيّة كثيراً.

في البداية كانت هناك صعوبات كثيرة، فرغم أنّني كنت أتكلّم العربيّة، في التاكسي وفي المطعم وفي الفندق وفي المكاتب الحكوميّة، فقد كانت هناك اختلافات ثقافيّة وأشياء كثيرة لا يتعلّمها الطالب في الصفّ.

كنت قد تعلّمت العامّيّة والفصحى قبل وصولي إلى مصر – العامّيّة للحديث اليومي، والفصحى في القراءة والكتابة وفي فهم الأخبار – ولذلك كان سهلاً أن أتحدّث مع الناس. وقد واجه الطلبة الذين درسوا الفصحى فقط صعوبات أكثر منّي ولم يستطيعوا التحدّث مع الناس في البداية لأنّ العرب لا يستعملون الفصحى في الحديث.

أكبر مشكلة واجهتها في البداية هي أنّ الكثير من المصريين وخصوصاً الشباب يحبّون التكلّم بالإنجليزيّة. ولكن كلّما كلّموني بالإنجليزيّة جاوبت بالعربيّة حتى تعوّدوا أن يكلّموني بالعربيّة طول الوقت.

من الأشياء التي لم أعرفها قبل وصولي إلى مصر دور الدين في المجتمع العربي. كنت قد درست أنّ أكثر العرب مسلمون وأنّ هناك أقلّيّات مسيحيّة، ولكن لم أدرس أنّ أكثر الناس متديّنون، يؤمنون بالله والجنّة والنار، ويصومون في شهر رمضان ويصلّون، وخصوصاً يوم الجمعة.

كلمات جديدة

انطِباع (ج. انطِباعات) impression

كَرَم hospitality

تحَسّن–يَتَحَسّن to improve

صُعوبة (ج. صُعوبات) difficulty

سَهل easy

واجَه–يُواجِه to face

استَطاع–يَستَطيع = قدر–يقدِر (أن) (to be able to)

جاوَب–يُجاوِب to answer

تَعَوّد–يَتَعَوَّد to get used to

كَلّم–يُكلِّم to speak to

دَور role

مُتَدَيّن religious

آمَن–يُؤمِن to believe, have faith in

جَنّة heaven, paradise

نار hell, fire

صام–يَصوم to fast

رَمَضان Ramadan (the fasting month)

صَلّى–يُصَلّي to pray

أسئلة

١. ماذا تعلّمت مايا خلال الأربعة شهور؟

٢. لماذا واجه الطلاب الذين درسوا العربيّة في جامعات أخرى صعوبات أكثر في نظر مايا؟

٣. متى تُستعمل الفصحى؟

٤. لماذا كان التحدث مع الناس سهلاً بالنسبة لمايا؟

٥. ما هي المشاكل التي واجهتها مايا في الأيّام الأولى؟

٦. كيف حَلّت (solved) مايا المشكلة؟

٧. ماهي الاشياء الجديدة التي تعلمتها مايا عن دور الدين في العالم العربي؟

تمرين رقم ١: أكمل كلّ واحدة من العبارات في عمود أ بما يناسبها في عمود ب

أ	ب
تعلّمت الكثير عن	مَشاكِل كثيرة
تعلّمت في الجامعة	في المجتمع الأمريكي
كنت أتكلم العربيّة	في التاكسي والمطعم والفندق
هل هناك دور كبير للدين	خصوصاً يوم الجمعة
هناك اختلافات ثقافيّة كثيرة	بين العالم العربي والعالم الغربي
واجه الطلاب	الشعب العربي والثقافة العربيّة
يحبّ الشباب المصريّون	التحدّث باللغة الإنجليزية
يصلّي أكثر الناس	أنّ أكثر العرب مسلمون

قَواعِد

١. كُنت قَد + فعل

You have learned that when the particle قَد is followed by a verb in the past tense it does not have a meaning of its own; it simply affirms that the action has taken place.

تاريخ القُدس بعيد عن السلام: فقد دُمّرت ثلاث مرّات على الأقلّ.	The history of Jerusalem is far from peaceful: it was destroyed three times at least.

When it follows the verb كان (in any of its conjugations) the two elements and the following verb have a meaning similar to that of the English past perfect tense, the tense with had + the past participle.

كنت قد تعلّمت العاميّة والفصحى قبل وصولي إلى مصر.	I had learned the colloquial and فُصحى before my arrival in Egypt.

تمرين رقم ٢: ترجم إلى الإنجليزيّة

كنت قد درست أنّ أكثر العرب مسلمون وأنّ هناك أقلّيّات مسيحيّة.

٢. لم يستطيعوا

You have learned that using لم for a formal past tense negation causes a spelling change in hollow verbs: the long middle vowel changes into a short vowel: قال–يقول–لم يَقُل.

You also learned that لم does not affect verbs conjugated for أنتِ – أنتم – هم. This is because these pronouns require suffixes as a part of their present tense conjugation. The effect of لم is shown on the suffix not on the middle long vowel: final ن is dropped and in the case of the plural pronouns أنتم and هُم it is replaced by a silent ا.

The suffix acts as a "barrier" to prevent the middle long vowel from getting shortened.

Negated past tense with لم	Present tense	
لم أرِد	أُريد	أنا
لم نرِد	نُريد	نحن
لم ترِد	تُريد	أنتَ
لم تريدي	تُريدين	أنتِ
لم تريدوا	تُريدون	أنتم
لم يرِد	يُريد	هو
لَم تُرِد	تُريد	هي
لَم يريدوا	يُريدون	هم

تمرين رقم ٣

Maya wrote in her diary:

. . . ولم يستطيعوا التحدّث مع الناس في البداية لأنّ العرب لا يستعملون الفصحى في الحديث

In your own words, rewrite the rules for لم above. Then, use your version to explain the difference in both meaning and spelling of "لم يستطيعوا" and "لا يستعملون".

تمرين رقم ٤: أكمل الجدولين التاليين.

أ.

الفعل	الترجمة	الصيغة المجرّدة	الجذر	الوزن ورقمه
عِشت				
تحسّنت				
يتعلّمها				
أتحدّث				
يَستطيعوا			ط-و-ع	
يَستَعملون				
واجهتها				
جاوَبت				
تَعوّدوا				
كَلّموني				
يُؤمنون				
ويَصومون				
ويُصلّون				

ب.

الاسم أو الصفة	الترجمة	الجذر	الصيغة المجرّدة	Method of derivation
انطِباعات			انطِباع	مصدر of Form VII
اختِلافات		خ-ل-ف		
مُتديّنون	religious (pl.)			

الدرس الثالِث

انطِباعات مايا: الجُزء الثاني

تَفاجأت كثيراً في أوّل ليلة نمتها في القاهرة فقد صَحوتُ مُبَكّراً على صَوت المُؤذّن. لم أعرف في البداية ماذا كان الصوت، وخِفت كثيراً، ولم أنَم جيّداً، ولكن بعد مدّة قصيرة تَعوّدت على صوت المؤذّن ولم يُزعِجني أبداً.

ولكن المُزعِج كان الأسئلة الكثيرة التي يَسألها الناس عَن الدين. سَألوني مثلاً: هل أنا مَسيحيّة أو يَهوديّة، وما رأيي في الدين الإسلامي. كانوا يَستغربون عندما قُلت لهم انّني لستُ مُتديّنة ولا أفكّر في الدين كثيراً. هُم يُفكّرون بالدين ويَتَحدّثون عنه كثيراً.

ربُما كانت أصعَب مُشكلة هي مُشكلة الأكل. فالأكل المِصري لَذيذ جدّاً، وخصوصاً الفتّة والمحشي والكُشَري والفول والطَعميّة، (الّطعميّة هي الاسم المصري لِلفلافِل.) تَحتوي هذه المأكولات على دُهن أو سُكّر كَثير. وهي مَوجودة في البيوت والمَطاعِم ومَحلاّت الحَلويّات، وهي رَخيصة أيضاً. كل أنواع الطعام، المطبوخ وغير المطبوخ، أرخص من أمريكا بكثير. لذلك زاد وزني كثيراً (لن أقول كم أصبح وزني الآن!)

عِندما دَعاني أصحابي الى بُيوتهم كان يَجب عَليّ أن آكل وأشرب الكَثير. وقد مَرضتُ مَرّة أو مَرّتين من كثرة الأكل، وخُصوصاً في بِداية إقامتي في مِصر.

اشتريت أنا وسلمى ورانية طاولة تنس ولعبنا في الشقّة، وكان ذلك مُمتِعاً، وقد تَحَسّن لَعِبي كثيراً، ولكن اكتشفت أنّ رِياضة تنس الطاولة لا تَكفي لِتَخفيف الوزن.

كلمات جديدة

صَحا–يَصحو to wake up

مُبَكّر early

صَوت sound, voice

مُؤَذّن muezzin, the man calling for prayer

أزعَج–يُزعِج to bother, disturb

مُزعِج disturbing

اِستَغرَب–يَستَغرِب to find (something) strange

مَطبوخ cooked
دَعا–يَدعو to invite
زاد–يَزيد to go up
تَخفيف making lighter, reducing
وَزن weight

أسئلة

١. لماذا تفاجأت مايا في أوّل ليلة نامتها في عمّان؟

٢. ماذا أزعج مايا أكثر من المؤذّن؟

٣. ما هي مشكلة الأكل التي تتكلّم عنها مايا؟

٤. كيف كان الطعام الرخيص مشكلة؟

٥. لماذا مرضت مايا أكثر من مرة عندما دعاها أصحابها الى بيوتهم؟

٦. مَن اشترى طاولة تنس؟ لماذا؟

تمرين رقم ١: رتّب الجمل من ١ –١٠ حسب ما جاءت في النصّ

__ مايا لا تفكّر في الدين أبداً.

__ اشترت مايا وفدوى ورانية طاولة تنس.

__ الأسئلة التي سألها الناس عن الدين أزعجت مايا كثيراً.

__ الأكل في مصر أرخص من الأكل في أمريكا.

__ الأكل مشكلة كبيرة.

__ العرب يفكّرون بالدين كثيراً.

__ تعوّدت مايا على صوت المؤذّن.

__ خافت مايا كثيراً.

__ صحَت مايا على صوت المؤذّن.

__ مرضت مايا من كثرة الأكل.

تمرين رقم ٢

Matching (companion website)

Form VI

The distinguishing feature of this form is the ا between first and second root letters and the prefix ت before the first root letter.

مِثال	مصدَر	Present	Past	Form
تَفاجأ–يَتَفاجأ to be surprised	تَفاعُل	يَتَفاعَل	تَفاعَل	VI

Like Form III, Form VI often carries an associative meaning of an action occurring between two or more people.

تمرين رقم ٣: أكمل الجدولين التاليين

أ.

الوزن ورقمه	الصيغة المجرّدة	الجذر	الترجمة	الفعل
				صحوت
				أعرف
				وخِفت
				أنَم
				تعوّدت
				يُزعجني
				يسألها
				سألوني
				يستغربون

قُلت				
يفكّرون				
ويتحدّثون				
تحتوي				
دعاني				
يجب				
اشتريت				
تحسّن				
اكتَشَفت				
تكفي				

ب.

الاسم أو الصفة	الترجمة	الجذر	الصيغة المجرّدة	Method of derivation
المُؤذّن		أ-ذ-ن		Active participle of Form II
المُزعج				
الإسلامي			إسلام	
مُتديّنة				
والمَحشي		ح-ش-و		
مُمتعاً				Active participle of Form IV
لتَخفيف				

الدرس الرابِع

انطِباعات مايا: الجُزء الثالث والأخير

كلمة أخيرة

قبل سفري الى البلاد العربيّة، كُنت قَد قرأت وسمعت أن المصريّين، ورُبّما العَرَب والمُسلمين بشكل عامّ، يَكرهون أمريكا. لذلك كنت أفكّر أنّهم سيكرهونني. ولكنّي وَجدت أنّهم لايكرهون الشعب الأمريكي أبداً، ولايكرهون أمريكا أبداً. عَلى العَكس، الكثير منهم، وخصوصاً الشباب، يَحلُمون بالهِجرة أو السفر الى أمريكا والدراسة في جامعاتها والعيش في مُدُنها مثل نيويورك وشيكاغو وبوستن وواشنطن.

لكنّهم يكرهون سِياسة الحكومة الأمريكيّة لأنّها تَدعَم الحكومة الإسرائيليّة وسياساتها وتدعم الحكومات العربيّة الدكتاتوريّة. أرجو أن تتغيّر تلك السياسة وأن تبدأ الحكومة الأمريكيّة بدعم الشعوب بَدَل الحكومات، وتُساعد في نَشر الديمقراطيّة والدِفاع عن حُقوق الإنسان. ليس عِندي شكّ أنّ ذلك سَيُحسّن العلاقات الأمريكيّة العربيّة.

سأرجع إن شاء الله، وأعيش في بلد عربي لِمدّة سنة أو أكثر. رغم أنّني عِشت لمدّة أربعة شهور في مِصر، وزرت فلسطين والأردن، وأشعر أنّني أفهم لغة الشرق العربي جيّداً، فقد سمعت الكثير عن بلاد المغرب وشعوبها. أريد أن أزور ليبيا وتونس والجزائر والمغرب.

بعد سنتين سأفكّر في هذا المَشروع، وأقرّر أين سأسافر، ولكن الآن لا أرى أمامي الا الدِراسة والامتِحانات والواجِبات التي لا تنتهي.

كلمات جديدة

كُنت قَد قرأت I had read	حلِم–يَحلُم (ب) to dream (of)
رُبّما perhaps, maybe	هِجرة immigration
عَلى العَكس on the contrary	سِياسة (ج. سِياسات) policy

دَعَم–يَدعَم to support
شَكّ doubt
دِكتاتوري dictatorial
حَسَّن–يُحسِّن to improve
بَدَل instead of
مَشروع project
نَشر spreading
أمام in front of
دِفاع defending
واجِب (ج. واجِبات) homework
حُقوق الإنسان human rights
اِنتَهى–يَنتَهي to end

أسئلة

١. ماذا سمعت وقرأت مايا في الصحف الكبيرة وقنوات التلفزيون الرئيسيّة؟
٢. ماذا تعلّمت خلال رحلتها في الأردن عن ذلك؟
٣. ماذا يكره العرب حسب مايا؟
٤. كيف تغيّر الوضع؟
٥. أين ستعيش مايا عندما ترجع الى العالم العربي؟
٦. لماذا لا يمكنها السفر والعيش هناك الآن؟

تمرين رقم ١: أين الجملة غير الصحيحة؟

According to the reading passage, eight of the following ten statements are correct and two are not, one incorrect and one is not mentioned. Identify these two.

١. الحكومة الأمريكيّة ساعدت الحكومات الدكتاتورية العربيّة.
٢. الشباب العرب يكرهون أمريكا.
٣. العرب لا يكرهون الشعب الأمريكي.
٤. مايا تريد زيارة ليبيا.
٥. مايا تفهم لغة المغرب العربي جيّداً.
٦. سوف ترجع مايا إلى العالم العربي.
٧. عند مايا عمل كثير.
٨. كثير من العرب يحبّون السفر الى أمريكا.
٩. يحبّ كثير من العرب الدراسة في الجامعات الأمريكية.
١٠. يكره العرب سياسة الحكومة الأمريكية.

تمرين رقم ٢: ابحث عن الكلمات المعرّفة في النصّ وأكمل الكلمات المُتقاطعة.

١. بدأت في تونس وانتقلت (moved) إلى مصر ثمّ ليبيا ثمّ سوريا
٢. ليس مع
٣. لا يحبّ
٤. يساعد
٥. ليس ديمقراطيّاً
٦. يسكن
٧. عكس "نهاية"
٨. بعد الشتاء وقبل الصيف
٩. عكس "مشرِق"
١٠. تتصوّر أو تفكّر وهي نائمة
١١. دولة في شمال إفريقيا تُريد مايا زيارتها
١٢. جمع شعب

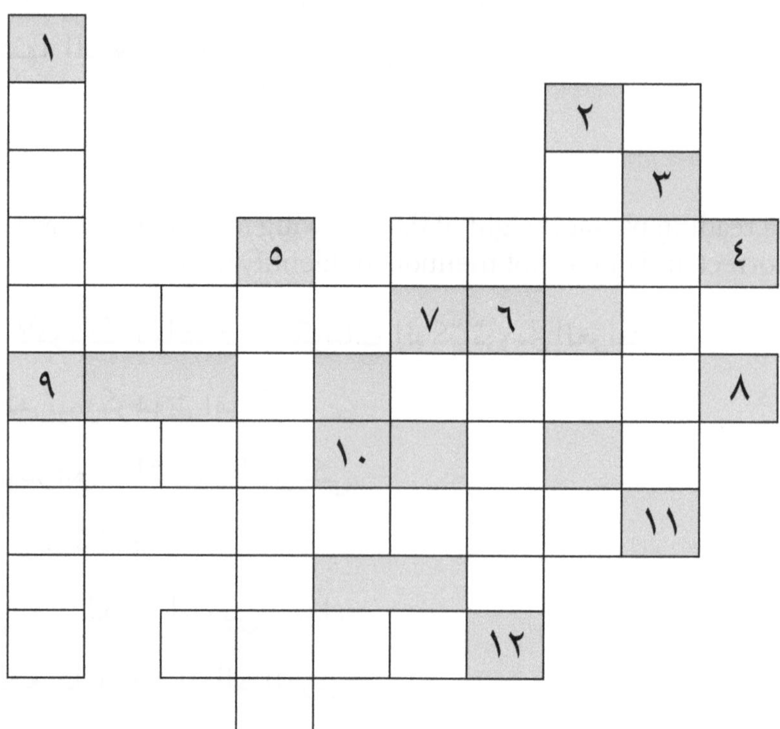

Verb form summary

The following table provides a summary of the nine verb forms that have been introduced in this book. Form IX has not been introduced since it is quite limited; it is restricted to colors and defects and will be introduced in the second volume of *'Arabiyyat al-Naas*.

Verb forms and their derivatives

مصدَر	Active participle		Form
Many patterns	فاعِل	فعل–يفعَل، يفعِل، يفعُل	I
تفعيل	مُفَعِّل	فعّل–يُفعِّل	II
مُفاعَلة	مُفاعِل	فاعَل–يُفاعِل	III
إفعال	مُفعِل	أفعَل–يُفعِل	IV
تفعُّل	مُتفَعِّل	تَفَعّل–يَتَفَعَّل	V
تَفاعُل	مُتَفاعِل	تَفاعَل–يَتفاعَل	VI
انفِعال	مُنفَعِل	اِنفَعَل–يَنفَعِل	VII
افتِعال	مُفتَعِل	افتَعَل–يفتَعِل	VIII
استِفعال	مُستَفعِل	استَفعَل–يَستَفعِل	X

Examples

	مصدَر	Active participle		Form
to know	Many patterns	عارِف	عرِف–يعرِف	I
to employ	تَوظيف	مُوَظِّف	وَظّف–يُوَظِّف	II
to help	مُساعَدة	مُساعِد	ساعَد–يساعِد	III
to inform	إخبار	مُخبِر	أَخبَر–يُخبِر	IV
to specialize	تَخَصُّص	مُتَخَصَّص	تَخَصَّص–يَتَخَصَّص	V
to reach an understanding	تَفاهُم	مُتَفاهِم	تَفاهَم–يَتفاهَم	VI
to explode	اِنفِجار	مُنفَجِر	اِنفَجَر–يَنفَجِر	VII
to celebrate	اِحتِفال	مُحتَفِل	اِحتَفَل–يَحتَفِل	VIII
to use	اِستِعمال	مُستَعمِل	اِستَعمَل–يَستَعمِل	X

تمرين رقم ٣: أكمل الجدول التالي.

أ.

الفعل	الترجمة	الجذر	الصيغة المجرّدة	الوزن ورقمه
يَكرهون				
أفكّر				
سيكرهونني				
يَحلُمون				
تَدعَم				
تتغيّر				
أرجو				
وتُساعد				
سَيُحسّن				
سأرجع				
وأشعر				
أفهم				
أريد				
وأقرّر				
سأسافر				
تنتهي		Think of نهاية		

الدرس الخامس

كلمات الوحدة

muezzin, the man calling for prayer	مُؤذّن	أ-ذ-ن
in front of	أمام	أ-م-م
to believe, have faith in	IV (آمَنَ–يُؤمِن)	أ-م-ن
instead of	بَدَل	ب-د-ل
early	مُبَكّر	ب-ك-ر
to answer	III (جاوَب–يُجاوِب)	ج-و-ب
heaven, paradise		جَنّة
to improve (something)	II (حَسَّن–يُحَسِّن)	ح-س-ن
to improve, to become improved	V (تَحَسَّن-يَتَحَسَّن)	ح-س-ن
human rights	حُقوق الإنسان	ح-ق-ق
to dream (of)	حلِم–يَحلُم (ب)	ح-ل-م
making lighter, reducing	تَخفيف	خ-ف-ف
to support	دَعَم–يَدعَم	د-ع-م
to invite	دَعا–يَدعو	د-ع-و
defending	دِفاع	د-ف-ع
role	دَور	د-و-ر
religious	مُتَدَيّن	د-ي-ن
dictatorial		دِكتاتوري
perhaps, maybe		رُبّما

Ramadan (the fasting month)		رَمَضان
to bother, disturb	IV (أزعَج–يُزعِج)	ز-ع-ج
disturbing	مُزعِج	
to go up	زاد–يَزيد	ز-ي-د
easy	سَهل	س-هـ-ل
policy	سِياسة (ج. سِياسات)	س-و-س
project	مَشروع	ش-ر-ع
doubt	شَكّ	ش-ك-ك
to wake up	صَحا–يَصحو	ص-ح-و
difficulty	صُعوبة (ج. صُعوبات)	ص-ع-ب
to pray	II (صَلّى–يُصَلّي)	ص-ل-و
sound, voice	صَوت	ص-و-ت
to fast	صام–يَصوم	ص-و-م
cooked	مَطبوخ	ط-ب-خ
impression	انطِباع (ج. انطِباعات)	ط-ب-ع
to be able (to)	X (اِستَطاع–يَستَطيع)	ط-و-ع
on the contrary	عَلى العَكس	ع-ك-س
to get used to	V (تَعوّد–يَتَعَوَّد)	ع-و-د
to fine (something) strange	X (اِستَغرَب–يستغرِب)	غ-ر-ب
hospitality	كَرَم	ك-ر-م
to speak to	II (كَلَّم–يُكلِّم)	ك-ل-م
I had . . .		كُنت قَد . . .

ن-ش-ر	نَشر	spreading
ن-هـ-ي	VIII (اِنتَهى–يَنتَهي)	to end
ن-و-ر	نار	hell, fire
هـ-ج-ر	هِجرة	immigration
و-ج-ب	واجِب (ج. واجِبات)	homework
و-ج-هـ	III (واجَه–يُواجِه)	to face
و-ز-ن	وَزن	weight

عزيزي الطالب، عزيزتي الطالبة،

ألف مبروك! لقد وصلتم مع نهاية هذه الوحدة إلى نهاية الكتاب. يُمكنكم الآن فهم الكثير من النصوص والمُحادثات باللغة العربيّة. كَما يُمكنكم قراءة نصوص عَربيّة كثيرة، بعضها تقدرون أن تقرأوها وتفهموها بدون مُعجم (قاموس) وبعضها تحتاجون إلى مُعجم. ولكن الحروف العربيّة، التي كانت تظهر لكم قبل شهور قليلة فقط رُموزاً غَريبة لا تَعرفون الفرق بينها وبين حُروف لغة أجنبيّة أخرى كالصينيّة واليابانيّة والفارسيّة واليونانيّة، تقدرون الآن أن تقرأوها وتفهموا الكثير من معانيها.

ويُمكنكم التكلّم والكتابة عن أمور كثيرة مثل المعلومات الشخصيّة والعائلة والدراسة والعمل والأكل والشرب والسفر والطقس وغير ذلك. وإذا سافرتُم الآن إلى بلد عربي يمكنكم التفاهم مع الناس بالعربيّة في كثير من أمور الحَياة اليوميّة: في المطار، في التاكسي، في الفندق، في المطعم وغيرها من الأماكن.

وتعلّمتم أيضاً شيئاً عن تاريخ مصر وثقافتها والحياة فيها. ومصر، كما تعرفون، هي أكبر ومن أهمّ الدول العربية.

ورغم أنّكم تعلّمتم اللهجة المصريّة للتكلّم (والفصحى للقراءة والكتابة طبعاً) فإنّ ذلك لا يعني أنّكم لا تقدرون على التحدّث مع العرب الذين يتكلّمون لهجات أخرى، فأكثر العرب يفهمون اللهجة المصريّة. كذلك عندما يتحدّث العرب الذين يتكلّمون لهجات مختلفة مع بعضهم البعض، كالعراقيّين والمصريّين مثلاً، فإنّهم يغيّرون في طريقة حديثهم ويستعملون الكثير من كلمات الفصحى حتى يتمكّنوا من التفاهُم.

تمرين رقم ١: قد

ترجم إلى الإنجليزيّة

١. تَفاجأت كثيراً في أوّل ليلة نمتها في القاهرة فقد صَحوتُ مُبَكّراً على صَوت المُؤذّن.

٢. وقد مَرضتُ مَرّة أو مَرّتين من كثرة الأكل، وخُصوصاً في بِداية إقامتي في مِصر.

٣. وقد تَحَسّن لَعِبي كثيراً.

٤. قبل سفري الى البلاد العربيّة، كُنت قَد قرأت وسمعت أن العَرَب يَكرهون أمريكا.

تمرين رقم ٢: اختبر معلوماتك

(In Teacher's Book)

تمرين رقم ٣: حضّر، ناقِش، ثمّ اكتب (حوالي ١٠٠ كلمة)

أ. خطّط لزيارة دولة عربيّة: لماذا تريد أن تزور هذه الدولة، مدّة الزيارة، ماذا تريد أن ترى، الخ.

Plan a visit to an Arab country. Explain why you want to visit it, for how long, what you want to see, etc.

ب. لماذا تتعلّم العربيّة؟ (Why are you learning Arabic?)

ت. المرحلة التالية في تعلّمك للغة العربيّة (The next stage in your study of Arabic)

ث. أكتب فقرة تبدأ بواحدة من العبارات التالية
(Write a paragraph starting with one of the following phrases/sentences):

- أربعة شهور عشت في العالم العربي وتعلّمت الكثير: عن الشعب العربي، عن . . .
- تفاجأت كثيراً في أوّل ليلة . . .
- ربّما كانت أصعب مشكلة هي مشكلة . . .
- قبل سفري الى البلاد العربيّة، كنت قد قرأت وسمعت . . .
- بعد سنتين سوف . . .

Glossaries

Following are two comprehensive glossaries of the words introduced in the book.

In the Arabic–English glossary, words are arranged by root, except in the following cases, which are listed alphabetically:

1. words which are not clearly derived from three- or four- letter roots,
2. proper names, like أبو ظبي، أغسطس,
3. expressions, like إن شاء الله، أهلاً وسهلاً

In the English–Arabic glossary, words are arranged alphabetically, except in the case of the definite article "the" and "to" of the infinitive, which are not considered in the alphabetical arrangement.

In both glossaries,

1. the icon "◆" appears next to words that are found in فصحى, but not in مصري, and a "*" appears next to words that are found in مصري but not in فصحى,
2. مصري words with a systematic correspondence to فصحى words, such as دَوا/دواء, or where there is a slight difference in pronunciation that does not affect the shape of the word like يَدرُس/يدرِس, are listed in the glossaries in their فصحى forms. The correspondences are explained in the grammar notes and "sociolinguistic corner" in the different units of the book,
3. verbs are listed in their basic form, i.e. the third person masculine singular in the past and present tenses. Form I verbs are not marked by a Roman numeral indicating the form number. The derived Forms II through X are marked with the number followed by the verb in parentheses. The English is presented in the infinitive,
4. the following abbreviations are used:
   a. ج. (for جمع) = "plural"
   b. f. = feminine
   c. m. = masculine
   d. pl. = plural
   e. adj. = adjective
   f. n. = noun
   g. lit. = literally
   h. adj. = adjective
   i. n. = noun

Arabic–English glossary

أ

أَب		father
أ - ب - د	أبَداً = خالِص*	at all
إبراهيم		Abraham
إبن		son
أَبوظبي		Abu Dhabi
أ - ث - ر	أثَر (ج. آثار)	ruins, antiquities
	V (تأثّر - يَتَأَثَّر)	to be influenced
أ - ج - ر	للإيجار	for rent
أَخ		brother
أُخت		sister
أ - خ - ذ	أخذ - ياخُذ	to take
أ - خ - ر	آخِر	last
	أُخرى•	another, f.
	أخير	last
أ - د - ب	أدَب إنجليزي	English literature
أ - د - ي	II (أدّى-يِدّي)*	= أعطى - يعطي to give
ادّيني*		give me

if		إذا
muezzin, the man calling for prayer	مُؤَذّن	أ - ذ - ن
date, history	تاريخ (ج. تَواريخ)	أ - ر - خ
date of birth	تاريخ ميلاد	
historian	مُؤَرِّخ (ج. مُؤَرِّخين)	
Jordan		الأُردُن
how		إزّاي*
elevator, lift		اسانسير
teacher, professor		أُستاذ
Isaac		إسحاق
= عائلة، عيلة* family	أُسرة	أ - س - ر
to found	II (أسّس - يؤسّس)	أ - س - س
to be founded	V (تأسّس - يَتَأسَّس)	
sorry	آسِف	أ - س - ف
Alexander the Great		الإسكَندر الكَبير
name		اِسم
your name (polite)		اِسم حَضرِتك
Asian	أسيَوي	آسيا
entry visa	تَأشيرة دُخول	أ - ش - ر
because, since, as a matter of fact . . .	أَصْل . . . *	أ - ص - ل
originally	أصْلاً	
original, from the country	أصْلي	
August		أغُسطُس
certainly	أكيد	أ - ك - د

foods, dishes	مَأكولات	أ ـ ك ـ ل
except, to (as in “a quarter to four”)		إلّا
= دِلوَقتِ* now		الآن◆
= اِللي* that, which		الّتي◆
= اللي* who, which		الّذي◆
God (Allah)		الله
God knows!		الله أعلم!
may God have mercy on him!		الله يرحمه!
that, which		اِللي*
to		إلى
mother		أُمّ
Mother of the World (Cairo)		أُمّ الدُنيا
Umm ʻAli (name of a dessert)		أُمّ عَلي
as for. . . (then, but. . .)		أمّا . . . فَ
= أمْس◆ yesterday		امبارح*
the United Arab Emirates	الإمارات العَرَبيّة المُتَّحدة	أ ـ م ـ ر
conspiracy	مُؤامَرة (ج. مُؤامَرات)	
America		أَمريكا
= امبارِح* yesterday	أمْس◆	أ ـ م ـ س
in front of	أمام	أ ـ م ـ م
nationalization	تَأميم	
to believe, have faith in	IV (آمَن ـ يُؤمِن)	ا ـ م ـ ن
truly, in reality		إنّ
to		أنْ
that		أنّ

اِن شاء الله		God willing
أنا		I
انتِ		you (f.)
انتَ		you (m.)
إنّني◆، إنّي*		that I
إنّها		that she
أ - ن - ث	أُنثى	female
أ - ن - ي	X (استنّى - يِستَنّى) *	to wait
أهلا بيك*		welcome to you
أهلاً وسهلاً		welcome
أهلاً وسهلاً بيكِ*		welcome to you (response to أهلاً وسهلا)
أهوه*		here it is (m.)
أهيه*		here it is (f.)
أو		or
أوتوبيس (ج. أوتوبيسات)		bus
أوروبا		Europe
أوروبي		European
أ - و - ل	أوّل	first
	أولى	first
	في الأوّل	first
	لأوّل مَرّة	for the first time
أين◆		where *فين =
إيه*		what
أيوه*		yes

ب

baba ghannouj (name of a dish)		بابا غنّوج
Babylonian		بابلي
of, belonging to		بتاع*
to look for	بَحَث - يبحَث (عَن) ◆	ب - ح - ث
sea	بَحر (ج. بُحور)	ب - ح - ر
the Mediterranean Sea	البَحر الأبيَض المُتَوسّط	
the Red Sea	البحر الأحمر	
from the sea	بَحري	
to start	بدأ - يَبدأ	ب - د - أ
beginning	بِداية	
instead of	بَدَل	ب - د - ل
exchanging	تَبادُل	
orange		بُرتُقالي
it seems	يَبدو	ب - د - و
tower	بُرج	ب - ر - ج
cold	بارِد	ب - ر - د
outside, abroad	برّه*	ب - ر - ر
congratulations, may you enjoy it!	مَبروك!	ب - ر - ك
match	مُباراة	ب - ر - ي
Britain		بريطانيا
not serious	بسيطة	ب - س - ط
direct	مُباشِر	ب - ش - ر
to look	بَصّ - يبُصّ*	ب - ص - ص

English	Arabic	Root
look!	بُصّ! *	
onions	بَصَل	ب - ص - ل
potatoes		بَطاطِس
watermelon	بَطّيخ	ب - ط - خ
nonsense (lit. no "..." no water-melon)	بَلا ... بَلا بَطّيخ*	
champion	بَطَل (ج. أبطال)	ب - ط - ل
to send	بَعَث - يِبعَث	ب - ع - ث
distance	بُعد	ب - ع - د
afternoon	بَعد الظُهر	
then, and then	بَعدين*	
far	بَعيد	
God forbid! (lit. may bad things be far!)	بعيد الشرّ!	
some	بَعض	ب - ع - ض
Baghdad		بَغداد
baklawa (a dessert)		بَقلاوة
remaining, rest	باقي	ب - ق - ي
how much (how long) has it been for you?	بَقى لك قدّ إيه؟*	
to become, to remain, to stay	بَقى - يِبقى*	
it's been ... for me	بَقى لي ... *	
remnant	بَقيّة (ج. بَقايا)	
tomorrow	بُكرة*	ب - ك - ر
early	مُبَكّر	
no need, let's not		بَلاش*

country, land	بِلاد	ب - ل - د
Persia	بِلاد فارِس	
local	بَلَدي	
sum, amount	مَبلَغ (ج. مَبالغ)	ب - ل - غ
balcony		بَلكونة (ج. بَلكونات)
girl	بِنت (ج. بَنات)	ب - ن - ت
bank		بَنك (بُنوك)
brown	بُنّي	ب - ن - ن
to be built	بُنِي - يُبنى◆	ب - ن - ي
cooker		بوتاجاز
house	بيت (ج. بُيوت)	ب - ي - ت
dormitory, student hostel	بيت طَلَبة	
Beirut		بيروت
white	أبيَض	ب - ي - ض
eggs	بيض	
between, among	بَين	ب - ي - ن

ت

taxi		تاكسي
name of a dish, typically Lebanese		تَبّولة
business, commerce	تِجارة	ت - ج - ر
museum	مَتحَف (ج. مَتاحِف)	ت - ح - ف
table		تَرابيزة (ج. تَرابيزات) *
to leave	تَرَك - يترُك	ت - ر - ك
tired	تَعبان	ت - ع - ب

ت - ف - ح	تُفّاح	apples
تِلك◆		that (f.)
ت - م - م	تَمام	perfect, fine
تِنِس أرضي		tennis (lit. ground tennis)
تونِس		Tunis, Tunisia

ث

ث - ق - ف	ثَقافة	culture
ث - ل - ث	ثالِث	third
	الثَلاثاء	Tuesday
	ثُلث◆، تِلت*	one-third
ث - ل - ج	ثَلج (ج. ثُلوج)	snow
	ثَلّاجة (ج. ثَلّاجات)	refrigerator
ث - م - ن	ثامِن	eighth
	ثَمَن	price
ث - ن - ي	الإثنين	Monday
	ثاني	second, other
ث - و - ر	ثار - يثور (عَلى)	to rebel (against)
ث - و - م	ثوم	garlic
ثُمّ◆		= بَعدين* then, and then

ج

جاي*		= قادِم◆ coming, next
ج - ب - ل	جَبَل (ج. جِبال)	mountain
	جَبل الهَيكَل	Temple Mount

Mt. Sinai	جَبل موسى	
mountainous	جَبَلي	
seriously	(بِجَدّ = بجاد)*	ج - د - د
grandfather	جَدّ	
very	جِدّاً	
grandmother	جَدّة (ج. جَدّات)	
new	جَديد	
to try	II (جَرَّب - يُجَرِّب)	ج - ر - ب
Algeria, Algiers		الجَزائِر
bridge	جِسر (ج. جُسور)	ج - س - ر
dry	جافّ	ج - ف - ف
dryness, drought	جَفاف	
gallabiyya	جَلابيّة (ج. جَلاليب)	ج - ل - ب
he sat	جَلَس♦	ج - ل - س
community (especially foreign)	جالية (ج. جالِيات)	ج - ل - ي
Friday	الجُمعة	ج - م - ع
mosque	جامِع (ج. جَوامِع)	
university	جامِعة (ج. جامِعات)	
everyone, all	جَميع	
society	مُجتَمَع (ج. مُجتَمَعات)	
beautiful	جَميل = حِلو	ج - م - ل
Arab Republic of Egypt	جُمهورية مصر العَربيّة	ج - م - هـ - ر
foreign, foreigner	أجنَبي (ج. أجانِب)	ج - ن - ب
south	جَنوب	

ج - ن - س	جِنس	sex, gender
	جِنسِيّة (ج. جِنسِيّات)	nationality, citizenship
ج - ن - ن	جَنّة	paradise, heaven
	مَجنون (ج. مَجانين)	crazy, mad
جِنيه مَصري		Egyptian pound
ج - هـ - ز	جاهِز	ready
ج - و - ب	III (جاوب - يُجاوِب)	to answer
	جَواب (ج. أجوبة)	answer
ج - و - د/ ج - ي - د	جَيِّد◆	= كويّس* good
ج - و - ز	جَواز*	= زَواج◆ marriage
	جَواز (ج. جَوازات) سَفَر	passport
ج - و - ع	جوعان، جَعان*	hungry
ج - و - و	جَوّ	weather
ج - ي - ء	جاي*	= قادِم coming, next
	جِه - ييجي*	to come
	جيت*	I came
ج - ي - ب	جاب - يِجيب	to bring
ج - ي - ر	جار (ج. جيران)	neighbor
ج - ي - ز	جائِزة (ج. جَوائز)	prize, award

ح

حالاً		immediately
حَتّى		until, even
ح - ب - ب	حَبّ - يِحِبّ*، أحبّ - يُحِبّ◆	to like, to love

beloved, liked	مَحبوب	
part, area	حِتّة (ج. حِتَت)*	ح - ت - ت
to reserve, to book	حَجَز-يحجِز	ح - ج - ز
one, someone (with negation, anyone)		حَد
accident	حادِث (ج. حَوادِث)	ح - د - ث
to happen	حَدث - يحدُث♦	
modern	حَديث	
garden, park	حَديقة (ج. حَدائق)	ح - د - ق
World War I	الحَرب العالميّة الأولى	ح - ر - ب
hot	حارّ	ح - ر - ر
the Noble Sanctuary	الحَرَم الشريف	ح - ر - م
it depends, according to	حَسَب	ح - س - ب
accountant	مُحاسِب (ج. مُحاسِبين)	
to feel	حَسّ - يحِسّ	ح - س - س
allergy, sensitivity	حَساسيّة	
to improve (something)	II (حَسَّن - يحسّن)	ح - س - ن
to improve (onself)	V (تحَسَّن - يَتَحسّن)	
stuffed (food)	مَحشي	ح - ش - ي
to besiege	III (حاصَر - يُحاصِر)	ح - ص - ر
to obtain	حَصَل - يَحصُل (عَلى)	ح - ص - ل
presently, whatever you say	حاضر	ح - ض - ر
to prepare	II (حَضّر - يُحَضِّر)	
you (lit. your presence)	حَضرتِك	
lecture	مُحاضَرة (ج. مُحاضَرات)	
to put	حَطّ - يِحُطّ*	ح - ط - ط

station, terminal	مَحَطّة (ج. مَحطّات)	
lucky	مَحظوظ	ح - ظ - ظ
celebrating, celebration	احتِفال (ج. احتفالات)	ح - ف - ل
to celebrate	VIII (احتَفَل - يحتِفِل)	
suitcase شَنطة =	حقيبة (ج. حقائب) ◆	ح - ق - ب
right	حَقّ (ج. حُقوق)	ح - ق - ق
human rights	حُقوق الإنسان	
government	حُكومة (ج. حُكومات)	ح - ك - م
governmental	حُكومي	
to occupy	VIII (احتَلّ - يَحتَلّ)	ح - ل - ل
store, shop دُكّان (ج. دَكاكين) =	مَحَلّ (ج. مَحلّات)	
to dream (of)	حلِم - يَحلُم (ب)	ح - ل - م
better, the best (lit. sweeter, sweetest)	أحلى	ح - ل - و
beautiful (lit. sweet)	حِلو	
thank God!	الحمدُ لِلّه!	ح - م - د
red	أحمَر	ح - م - ر
all kinds (lit. from the sour to the sweet)	من الحامِض للحِلو	ح - م - ض
carrying	حَمل	ح - م - ل
bathroom	حَمّام (ج. حمّامات)	ح - م - م
thing, need	حاجة	ح - و - ج
in need of	بِحاجة لِ، إلى	
the Wailing Wall	حائِط المَبكى	ح - و - ط
to try	III (حاوَل - يُحاوِل)	ح - و - ل
about, approximately تقريباً =	حَوالي	

	حَول◆	around
ح-و-ي	VIII (احتَوى-يَحتَوي (على)) ◆	to contain
ح-ي-ن	أحياناً	sometimes
ح-ي-و/ح-ي-ي	حَياة	life
	حَيّ (ج. أحياء)	neighborhood, quarter
	أحياء	biology

خ

خ-ب-ر	IV (أخبَر-يُخبِر)	to tell, inform
	خَبَر (ج. أخبار)	news
	مُخابَرات	intelligence services
خ-د-م	أيّ خِدمة؟	can I help you? (lit. any service?)
	خِدمة (ج. خَدَمات)	service
خ-ر-ج	خرَج-يخرُج	to come out, go out
	IV (أخرَج-يُخرِج) ◆	to take out
	خارِج◆	abroad, outside = برّه*
	V (تَخرّج-يتخَرّج)	to graduate
الخَرطوم		Khartoum (the capital of Sudan)
خ-ر-ف	الخُريف	fall, autumn
	خَروف (ج. خِرفان)	lamb
خ-ص-ص	تَخَصُّص (ج. تخصُّصات)	specialization, major
	خاصّ	private
	خُصوصاً	especially
	مَخصوص	special
خ-ض-ر	أخضَر	green

vegetables	خُضار	
engaged	مَخطوب	خ-ط-ب
line	خَطّ	خ-ط-ط
discount, lowering, reducing	تَخفيض	خ-ف-ض
making lighter, reducing	تَخفيف	خ-ف-ف
to disappear	VIII (اختَفى - يَختَفي)	خ-ف-ي
the Gulf	الخليج	خ-ل-ج
at all, completely	خالِص	خ-ل-ص
done, finished	خَلاص*	
stop it please! enough!	خَلاص بَقى! *	
to finish, complete	II (خلّص - يخلّص) *	
to be different	VIII (اختلَف - يِختلِف)	خ-ل-ف
different	مُختلِف	
to leave, let	II (خَلّى - يخلّي) *	خ-ل-ي
let us	خلّينا*	
let me	خلّيني*	
Thursday	الخَميس	خ-م-س
to be afraid	خاف - يخاف	خ-و-ف
foreigner (ج. أجانِب) = أجنبي		خواجة (ج. خواجات)
afraid	خايف*، خائف♦	خ-و-ف
frightening, scary	مُخيف	
(refugee) camp	مُخَيّم (ج. مُخيّمات)	خ-ي-م

د

chicken	دَجاج♦	د-ج-ج
to enter	دَخَل - يدخُل	د-خ-ل

	مَدخَل (ج. مَداخِل)	entrance
د - خ - ن	تَدخين	smoking
	II (دَخّن - يُدخّن)	to smoke
د - ر - ج	دَرَجة (ج. دَرَجات)	grade, degree, class, extent
د - ر - س	تدريس	= تعليم teaching, instruction
	دِراسة (ج. دِراسات)	study
	دَرس (ج. دُروس)	lesson
	دَرَس - يدرِس	to study
	مُدَرّس (ج. مُدرّسين)	= أستاذ (ج. أساتذة) teacher
	مَدرَسة (ج. مَدارِس)	school
	مَدرَسة ثانَويّة	secondary school, high school
	II (درّس - يدرّس)	to teach
د - ع - م	دعَم - يَدعَم	to support
	دَعم	support
د - ع - و	دَعا - يَدعو◆، دَعا - يدعي*	to invite
	دَعوة (ج. دَعوات)	invitation
د - ف - ء	دافِئ	warm
د - ف - ع	دِفاع	defending
	دَفَع - يدفَع	to pay
د - ق - ق	دَقيقة (ج. دقائق)	minute
دِكتاتوري		dictatorial
دُكتور (ج. دَكاترة)		= طبيب physician, doctor
د - ك - ك	دُكّان (ج. دَكاكين)	= مَحَلّ (ج. مَحلّات) shop, store
الدِلتا		the Delta
دِلوقتِ*		now

to destroy	II (دَمّر - يُدَمِّر)	د - م - ر
Damascus		دِمشق
this (m.)		دَه*
Doha (the capital of Qatar)		الدوحة
role	دَور (ج. أدوار)	د - و - ر
to look for ◆بحث - يبحث=	II (دوَّر - يِدَوَّر) *	
(sports) league	دَوري	
those		دول*
country	دَولة (ج. دُوَل)	د - و - ل
international	دَولي	
cupboard	دولاب (ج. دَواليب)	د - و - ل - ب
always	دايماً*، دائماً◆	د - و - م
medicine	دَواء	د - و - ي
this (f.)		دي
manager	مُدير (ج. مُدراء)	د - ي - ر
the Islamic religion	الدين الإسلامي	د - ي - ن
religious	مُتَدَيّن	

ذ

ticket	تَذكَرة (ج. تذاكِر)	ذ - ك - ر
to mention	ذَكَر - يَذكُر	
to study at home, to do homework	III (ذاكِر - يِذاكِر) *	
male	ذَكَر (ج. ذُكور)	
diary (memoirs)	مُذكّرات	
smart	ذَكي	ذ - ك - ي

that (m.)		ذلك◆
to go	ذَهَب - يَذهَب◆	ذ - هـ - ب
		ر
head	راس (ج. رُؤوس)	ر - أ - س
president	رَئيس	
main	رَئيسي	
to see *= شاف - يشوف	رأى - يَرى◆	ر - أ - ي
in your opinion	في رأيَك	
God be with you, good luck!	ربّنا معاك	ر - ب - ب
(lit. May God keep you) = شُكراً	ربّنا يِخلّيك*	
homemaker = سِتّ بيت	ربّة بيت	
Rabat (the capital of Morocco)	الرَباط	ر - ب - ط
Wednesday	الأربعاء	ر - ب - ع
spring	الربيع	
fourth	رابِع	
quarter, one-fourth	رُبع	
perhaps, maybe		رُبّما◆
salary	راتِب (ج. رَواتِب)	ر - ت - ب
to go back, refer	رَجَع - يَرجِع	ر - ج - ع
to return (something)	IV (أرجَع - يُرجِع)◆	
for men	رِجّالي	ر - ج - ل
man	رَجُل (ج. رِجال) ◆	
to hope for	رَجا - يَرجو (أن)	ر - ج - و
hello, hi	مَرحبا	ر - ح - ب

ر - ح - ل	رِحلة (ج. رِحلات)	trip
ر - ح - م	الله يرحمه!	may God have mercy on him!
ر - خ - ص	أرخَص	cheaper
	رَخيص	cheap
رُزّ		rice
رُز بلبن		rice pudding (lit. rice with milk)
ر - ط - ب	رَطب	humid
ر - غ - م	رَغم	despite, in spite of
ر - ف - ض	رَفَض - يَرفُض	to refuse
ر - ف - ع	ارتِفاع	height
	رَفَع - يَرفَع	to raise
ر - ق - م	رَقم (ج. أرقام)	number
ر - ك - ب	رِكِب - يِركَب	to ride
ر - ك - ز	مَركَز (ج. مَراكِز)	center
	مَركَزي	central
ر - م - د	رَمادي	gray
ر - م - ز	رَمَز - يَرمُز	to symbolize
رَمَضان		Ramadan (the fasting month)
ر - و - ح	راح - يروح*	to go
ر - ي - ح	X (استريّح – يستريّح)	to rest, to relax
	رائحة	smell
ر - ي - د	IV (أراد - يُريد) ◆	to want
ر - و - ض/ر - ي - ض	الرياض	Riyadh (the capital of Saudi Arabia)
	رِياضة	sports
	رِياضيّات	math, maths, mathematics

ز

ز - ح - م	زَحمة	crowdedness, congestion
ز - ر - ق	أزرَق	blue
ز - ع - ج	IV (أزعَج - يُزعِج)	to bother, disturb
	مُزعِج	disturbing
ز - م - ن	زَمَن	time
	مِن زَمان	it has been a long time, for a long time
ز - و - ج	زَواج♦	= جَواز* marriage
ز - و - ر	زار - يزور	to visit
ز - و - ل	لا زال♦	(is, are) still
زَيّ*		like
زَيّ الفُلّ*		wonderful, wonderfully (lit. like jasmine)
زَيّ بعضه*		it is all the same
ز - ي - د	زاد - يَزيد	to increase, go up
	زاد - يَزيد (عَلى)	to exceed
	زِيادة	extra, more

س

سَـ♦		= سَوفَ♦ = حَ* will
س - أ - ل	سَأَل - يسأل	to ask
	سؤال (ج. أسئِلة)	question
	مَسألة (ج. مَسائل)	matter, issue
	مَسؤول (ج. مَسؤولين)	responsible
س - ب - ب	سَبَب (ج. أسباب)	reason

English	Arabic	Root
Saturday	السبت	س - ب - ت
week	أُسبوع (ج. أسابيع)	س - ب - ع
for women	سِتّاتي	س - ت - ت
my dear madam	يا سِتّي*	
al-Aqsa Mosque	المَسجِد الأقصى	س - ج - د
to score	II (سَجّل–يسجِّل)	س - ج - ل
coastal	ساحِل	س - ح - ل
= حارّ hot	سُخن	س - خ - ن
well-known Palestinian dish	مُسَخّن	
theater	مَسرَح (ج. مَسارِح)	س - ر - ح
bed	سَرير	س - ر - ر
Roman Amphitheater	المَسرح الروماني	
faster	أسرَع	س - ر - ع
fast	سَريع	
to help	III (ساعَد - يُساعِد)	س - ع - د
assistant	مُساعِد (ج. مُساعِدين)	
Saudi Arabia	السعودية	
= ثَمَن price	سِعر (ج. أسعار)	س - ع - ر
to travel	III (سافر- يسافِر)	س - ف - ر
travel	سَفَر	
Muscat (the capital of Oman)	مَسقَط	س - ق - ط
= بَرد cold	سَقعة*	س - ق - ع
with sugar	بِسُكَّر	س - ك - ر
secretary		سِكرتير
living	ساكِن	س - ك - ن

inhabitants	سُكّان	
to live	سَكَن - يِسكُن	
for living, residing	للسكن	
unlucky, poor, unfortunate	مَسكين	
climbing	تَسَلّق	س - ل - ق
thank you (lit. may your hand be safe or sound)	تِسلم ايدَك*	س - ل - م
peace	سَلام	
wow!	يا سَلام	
I hope you are ok (lit. your safety)	سلامتِك!	
Muslim	مُسلم (ج. مُسلِمين)	
to be allowed	سُمِح - يُسمَح♦	س - م - ح
to hear	سَمِع - يَسمَع	س - م - ع
fish	سَمَك (ج. أسماك)	س - م - ك
fat	سَمنة	س - م - ن
sky, heaven	سَماء	س - م - و
to call	II (سَمّى - يُسمّي)	س - م - ي
sandwich		سَندويشة (ج. سندويشات)
year	سنة (ج. سِنين، سَنَوات)	س - ن - و
easy	سَهل	س - هـ - ل
black	أسوَد	س - و - د
Sudan	السودان	
Syria		سوريا
policy	سِياسة (ج. سِياسات)	س - و - س
hour, clock, watch	ساعة (ج. ساعات)	س - و - ع

سَوفَ◆		will *حَ =
س-و-ق	تَسَوّق	shopping
	سائق (ج. سائقين) ◆	driver * (ج. سَوّاقين) =سَوّاق
	سوق (ج. أسواق)	market
س-ي-ح	سِياحي	touristic
السَيّد المَسيح		Jesus Christ (lit. the Master the Messiah)
س-ي-ر	سَيّارة (ج. سَيّارات)	car*(ج. عَرَبيّات) =عربيّة

ش

ش-ب-ب	شابّ (ج. شَباب)	young man
	شابّة (ج. شابّات)	young woman
ش-ب-ع	شَبِع-يَشبَع	to be full
ش-ت-و	الشتاء	winter
	شتوي	for the winter
ش-خ-ص	شَخص (ج. أشخاص)	person
	شَخصي	personal
	شَخصياً	personally
ش-ر-ب	شارِب	having drunk
ش-ر-ع	شارِع (ج. شَوارِع)	street
	مَشروع (ج. مَشاريع)	project
ش-ر-ق	شَرق	east
	الشَرق الأوسَط	the Middle East
	شُروق	sunrise
ش-ر-ك	شَرِكة (ج. شَرِكات)	company
	شَركة طَيَران	airline (company)

to buy	VIII (اِشتَرى - يَشتَري)	ش - ر - ي
coast	شَطّ	ش - ط - ط
popular, working class	شَعبي	ش - ع - ب
to feel	شَعَر - يَشعُر	ش - ع - ر
feeling	شُعور	
to work	VIII (اشتغَل - يِشتِغِل)	ش - غ - ل
work	شُغل	
hospital	مُستَشفى (ج. مُستَشفَيات)	ش - ف - ي
apartment	شَقّة (ج. شُقَق)	ش - ق - ق
hotel apartment	شَقّة فندقيّة	
to thank	شَكَر - يَشكُر	ش - ك - ر
thank you	شُكراً	
thanks a lot	شُكراً جَزيلاً	ش - ك - ر
doubt	شَكّ	ش - ك - ك
appearance, the way one looks	شَكل	ش - ك - ل
in particular	بِشَكل خاصّ	
in general	بِشَكل عامّ	
problem	مُشكِلة (ج. مَشكلات)	
sun	شَمس	ش - م - س
=يسار left	شِمال	ش - م - ل
north	شَمال	
=حَقيبة♦ suitcase	شَنطة	ش - ن - ط
viewing, watching	مُشاهَدة	ش - هـ - د
more, most famous	أشهَر	ش - هـ - ر
month	شهر (ج. شُهور)	

	شَهريّاً	monthly
	مَشهور	famous
	مِن أشهَر	among the most famous
	VIII (اشتهر - يشتهِر)	to be famous
	شاف - يِشوف*	to see
ش - و - ي	مَشوي	baked, grilled
ش - ي - ء	شَيء (ج. أشياء)	= حاجة (ج. حاجات) * thing

ص

ص - ب - ح	صَباح الخير	good morning
	صَباح النور	good morning (answer)
	صَباحاً	in the morning
ص - ح - ب	صاحِب (ج. أصحاب)	friend; owner
ص - ح - ح	صَحّ	= صحيح correct
ص - ح - ر	صَحراوي	desert-like
ص - ح - و	صَحا - يَصحو•	to wake up
ص - د - ر	صُدور	issue, issuing
ص - د - ق	صَداقة	friendship
	II (صَدَّق - يُصَدِّق)	to believe (that someone is telling the truth)
	صَديق (ج. أصدِقاء)	= صاحِب (ج. أصحاب) friend
ص - ر - ح	بِصَراحة	frankly
ص - ع - ب	صَعب	difficult
	صُعوبة (ج. صُعوبات)	difficulty
ص - غ - ر	صَغير•، صُغَيَّر*	small
	أصغَر	smaller, younger

low (temperature)	صُغرى◆	
yellow	أصفَر	ص ـ ف ـ ر
crucifixion	صَلب	ص ـ ل ـ ب
the Crusaders	الصَليبيّين	
sauce		صَلصة
to pray	II (صلّى ـ يُصَلّي)	ص ـ ل ـ و
prayer	صَلاة	
lost and found box		صندوق المفقودات
industrial	صِناعي	ص ـ ن ـ ع
Sana'a (the capital of Yemen)	صَنعاء	
sound, voice	صَوت (ج. أصوات)	ص ـ و ـ ت
picture	صورة (ج. صُوَر)	ص ـ و ـ ر
wool	صوف	ص ـ و ـ ف
to fast	صام ـ يَصوم	ص ـ و ـ م
to shout	صاح ـ يَصيح	ص ـ ي ـ ح
summer	الصيف	ص ـ ي ـ ف
for the summer	صَيفي	
Chinese		صيني

ض

exactly	بالضَبط	ض ـ ب ـ ط
to sacrifice	II (ضَحّى ـ يُضَحّي)	ض ـ ح ـ ي
to weaken	IV (أضعَف ـ يُضعِف)	ض ـ ع ـ ف
weak	ضَعيف	
blood pressure	ضَغط دَم	ض ـ غ ـ ط

ض - م - م	VII (انضَمّ - يَنضَمّ)	to join
ض - ي - ع	ضاع - يَضيع	to be lost
	II (ضَيّع - يضيّع)	to lose
ض - ي - ف	IV (أضاف - يُضيف)	to add
	ضيف (ج. ضُيوف)	guest

ط

طابور		line, queue
طانت		aunt, auntie
طاوِلة (ج. طاوِلات)		table * =تَرابيزة (ج. تَرابيزات)
ط - ب - ب	طِبّ	medicine
	طَبيب (ج. أطِبّاء)	physician =دُكتور (ج. دكاترة)
ط - ب - خ	طَبخ	cooking
	مَطبَخ (ج. مطابِخ)	kitchen
	مَطبوخ	cooked
ط - ب - ع	انطِباع (ج. انطِباعات)	impression
	طَبعاً	of course
ط - ب - ق	طَبَق (ج. أطباق)	dish
ط - ر - ب	طَرَب	rapture (in music), enjoyment
طَرابلس		Tripoli
ط - ر - ق	طَريق (ج. طُرُق)	road
ط - ع - م	طَعام	food
	طَعمِيّة	*falafel* (in Egypt)
	مَطعَم (ج. مَطاعِم)	restaurant
ط - ق - س	طَقس	weather =جَوّ

ط - ل - ب	طَلَب - يطلُب	to ask for, order
	III (طالَب - يُطالِب)	to demand
	طَلب	request
	طالِب (ج. طُلّاب)	student
	طَلباتِك أوامر	whatever you say (lit. your requests are orders)
ط - ل - ع	طلع*	to turn out to be
	طالِع*	high, has gone up
طماطِم		tomatoes
ط - و - ع	X (استَطاع - يَستَطيع) ♦	= قدِر - يقدِر (أن) to be able to
ط - و - ل	طول الوَقت	the whole time
	طَويل	long
	طيّب، طَب*	ok, so
ط - ي - ر	طار - يطير	to fly/take off
	طَيّارة (ج. طَيّارات)	= طائرة (ج. طائرات) airplane
	مَطار (ج. مَطارات)	airport

ظ

ظ - ن - ن	ظَنّ - يَظنّ	= فكّر - يُفكِّر = اعتقد - يعتَقِد to think, believe
ظ - ه - ر	مُظاهرة (ج. مُظاهَرات)	demonstration

ع

ع - ب - ر	VIII (اعتَبَر - يَعتَبِر)	to consider
	عِبارة	phrase
ع - ج - ب	IV (أعجَب - يعجِب)	to please

ع - ج - ل	عَجَلة قِيادة	steering wheel
ع - د - د	عَدّاد (ج. عَدّادات)	counter, meter
	عَدَد	number
ع - د - ل	مُعتَدِل	moderate
ع - د - ي	عادي	ordinary, fine, ok
العِراق		Iraq
ع - ر - ب	عَرَبي	Arab, Arabic
	عَرَبيّة (ج. عَرَبيّات)*	= سيّارة (ج. سيّارات) car
ع - ر - ج	عُروج	ascending
ع - ر - ف	تَعَرّف	getting to know
	V (تعرّف - يتعرّف)	to get to know
	عارِف	aware, knowing
	عرف - يَعرِف	to know
	مَعروف	known, well-known
	مش عارف*	not knowing
عَشان*		because (of), for the purpose of, for the sake of
عَشان خاطرِك*		for you
ع - ص - ر	عَصير	juice
ع - ص - م	عاصِمة (ج. عَواصِم)	capital
ع - ط - ش	عَطشان (ج. عَطشانين)	thirsty
ع - ط - ي	IV (أعطى - يعطي)	= أدّى-يِدّي* to give
ع - ظ - م	مُعظَم	most (of)
ع - ف - و	العفو	= عَفواً (you're) welcome
ع - ق - د	VIII (اعتقَد - يعتَقِد)	to believe

belief	اعتِقاد	ع - ق - د
sensible, possible, reasonable	مَعقول	ع - ق - ل
on the contrary	عَلى العَكس	ع - ك - س
relationship	عَلاقة (ج. عَلاقات)	ع - ل - ق
to learn	V (تعَلّم - يتعلّم)	ع - ل - م
instruction, teaching	تَعليم	
world	عالَم	
science, branch of knowledge	عِلم (ج. علوم)	
to teach	II (عَلّم - يُعَلِّم)	
political science	عُلوم سِياسية	
for information	للاستِعلام	
landmark	مَعلَم (ج. مَعالِم)	
ad, announcement	إعلان (ج. إعلانات)	ع - ل - ن
high	عالي	ع - ل - و/ع - ل - ي
on	عَلى	
for the sake of, in order to = عَلَشان، عَشان	عَلى شان*	
at least	عَلى الأقلّ	
on the side	على الجَنب	
straight, straight away, all the way	على طول	
to where	عَلى فين*	
Amman		عَمّان
Oman		عُمان
age	عُمر (ج. أعمار)	ع - م - ر
to do, make, work	عمِل - يِعمَل	ع - م - ل

to use	X (استعمَل - يستَعمِل)	
worker	عامِل (عُمّال)	
work	عَمَل (ج. أعمال)	
used	مُستعمَل	
at, have		عِند
when		عِندَما
you (pl.) have, with you (pl.)		عِندكم، عندُكو*
address, title	عُنوان (ج. عَناوين)	ع - ن - و - ن
to mean	عَنى - يَعني	ع - ن - ي
it means, in other words	يَعني	
habit, custom	عادة (ج. عادات)	ع - و - د
usually	عادةً	
ordinary, usual	عادي	
to get used to	V (تَعَوّد - يَتَعَوَّد)	
= سَبَح - يسبَح to swim	عام - يعوم*	ع - و - م
shame, shameful	عيب	ع - ي - ب
feast, festival, anniversary	عيد (ج. أعياد)	ع - ي - د
Creation Festival	عيد الخَلق	
the Festival of *shamm al-nasiim*	عيد شَمّ النَسيم	
Easter	عيد الفِصح	
Eid al-Fitr (celebration marking the end of Ramadan)	عيد الفِطر	
the Feast of Sacrifice	العيد الكبير	
birthday	عيد ميلاد	
to live	عاش - يَعيش	ع - ي - ش

ع - ي - ل	عائِلة (ج. عائلات)	= أسرة (ج. أُسَر)، عيلة (ج. عيلات)* family
ع - ي - ن	عَيّان*	= مريض sick, unwell
	مِن عينيّ	will be happy to (lit. from my eyes)

غ

غَد		= بُكرة tomorrow
غ - د - ر	مُغادَرة	departure
غ - ر - ب	X (استغرب - يستَغرِب)	to find (something) strange
	المَغرِب	Morocco
	غَرب	west
	غُروب	sunset
	غَريب	strange, stranger
غ - ر - ف	غُرفة (ج. غُرَف)	= أوضة (ج. أوَض)* room
	غُرفة نوم	= أوضة نوم* bedroom
غ - ل - ب	غَلَب - يَغلِب	to win over, to beat (someone)
غ - ل - و	غالي	expensive
غ - م - ق	غامِق	dark (color)
غ - ن - ي	أُغنِية (ج. أغاني)	song
	II (غَنّى - يُغنّي)	to sing
	مُغَنّي	= مُطرِب singer
غ - ي - ر	II (غيّر - يغيّر)	to change (something)
	V (تغيَّر - يِتغَيّر)	to change (oneself)
	غير	not, other than
	مِن غير*	without

ف

English		Arabic	Root
and, and so, as			ف
fatta (name of a dish)		فَتّة	ف - ت - ت
light (color)		فاتِح	ف - ت - ح
open		مَفتوح	
	= بِنت girl	فَتاة♦	ف - ت - ي
to be surprised		VI (تفاجأ - يَتَفاجأ)	ف - ج - أ
surprise		مُفاجَأة (ج. مُفاجَآت)	
to explode		VII (انفجر - ينفجِر)	ف - ج - ر
luxurious		فَخم	ف - خ - م
to watch		V (تفرّج - يِتفَرَّج)	ف - ر - ج
to become happy		فَرِح - يفرَح	ف - ر - ح
chicken		فِراخ* = دَجاج♦	ف - ر - خ
individual, member		فَرد (ج. أفراد)	ف - ر - د
furnished		مَفروش	ف - ر - ش
opportunity		فُرصة (ج. فُرَص)	ف - ر - ص
pleased to meet you		فُرصة سعيدة	
Pharaonic			فَرعوني
difference		فَرق (ج. فُروق)	ف - ر - ق
France			فَرَنسا
team		فَريق (ج. فِرَق)	
salted fish		فَسيخ	ف - س - خ
to fail		فَشِل - يَفشَل	ف - ش - ل
season		فَصل (ج. فُصول)	ف - ص - ل
	= أحسَن best	أفضَل	ف - ض - ل

English	Arabic	Root
please, go ahead, take	اتفضّل	
to prefer	II (فَضَّل - يُفَضِّل)	
favorite	مُفَضّل	
empty, unfurnished	فاضي*	ف - ض - ي
breakfast	فُطور	ف - ط - ر
verb	فِعل	ف - ع - ل
= عمِل - يَعمَل to do	فَعَل - يَفعَل◆	
truly	فِعلاً	
to lose	فَقَد - يفقِد◆	ف - ق - د
poor (person)	فَقير (ج. فُقَراء)	ف - ق - ر
= بَسّ * only		فَقَط◆
= فكّر - يِفَكَّر to think	VIII (افتَكَر - يِفتِكِر) *	ف - ك - ر
to think	II (فكّر - يِفَكَّر)	
idea	فِكرة	
remembering	فاكِر*	
fruit	فَواكِه	ف - ك - هـ
Palestine		فِلِسطين
Florida		فلوريدا
cup		فِنجان (ج. فَناجين)
hotel		فندُق
understanding	فاهِم	ف - هـ - م
to win	فاز - يَفوز	ف - و - ز
winning	فَوز	
in		في
physics		فيزياء

where		فين*
there is, there are		فيه*
in it, it has		فيها

ق

reception hall, lounge		قاعة استِقبال
Cairo		القاهرة
the Dome of the Rock		قبّة الصَخرة
Coptic		قِبطي (ج. أقباط)
before	قَبل	ق - ب - ل
= قبل before	قبل ما	
two months before my trip (lit. before my trips by two months)	قَبل رِحلتي بشهرين	
direction of prayer	قِبلة	
future	مُستَقبَل	
acceptable	مَقبول	
the same size as		قَدّ*
how much		قَد ايه*
to be able to	قدِر - يقدر	ق - د - ر
Jerusalem	القُدس	ق - د - س
holy, sacred	مُقَدّس	
coming, next	قادِم	ق - د - م
ancient	قَديم (ج. قُدَماء)	
front, introduction	مُقدّمة (ج. مُقدِّمات)	
to offer	II (قدّم - يقدّم)	
to read	قرأ - يَقرأ	ق - ر - أ

reading	قِراءة	
closer	أقرب	ق-ر-ب
about, approximately حوالي =	تَقريباً	
close, near	قريب	
to decide	II (قرّر - يُقرّر)	ق-ر-ر
cinnamon	قِرفة	ق-ر-ف
century	قَرن (ج. قُرون)	ق-ر-ن
economy, economics	اقتِصاد	ق-ص-د
intention, meaning	قَصد	
I mean, my intention	قَصدي	
story	قِصّة (ج. قِصَص)	ق-ص-ص
train	قطار (ج. قطارات) = قَطْر (ج. قُطُرات)*	ق-ط-ر
Qatar	قَطَر	
cotton	قُطن	ق-ط-ن
to jump	قَفَز - يَقفِز	ق-ف-ز
tradition	تَقليد (ج. تقاليد)	ق-ل-د
traditional	تَقليدي	
the Citadel (in Cairo)	القلعة	ق-ل-ع
independence	استِقلال	ق-ل-ل
minority	أقلّيّة (ج. أقلّيّات)	
a little شويّة* =	قليلاً◆	
cloth	قِماش	ق-م-ش
shirt	قَميص (ج. قُمصان)	ق-م-ص
rule	قانون (ج. قَوانين)	ق-ن-ن

ق - ن - و	قَناة	channel
ق - هـ - و	قَهوة	coffee
	مَقهى (ج. مَقاهي)	café, coffee house
ق - و - د	قِيادة	leadership
	بقيادة	under the leadership of
ق - و - ل	قال - يَقول	to say
	قَول	saying
ق - و - م	قام - يَقوم	to erupt, take place
	IV (أقام - يُقيم) ◆	to set up, establish
	تَقويم	calendar
	قَومي	national
ق - و - ي	قَوي*	a lot, very
ق - ي - س	مَقاس	size

ك

كارت (ج. كُروت)		card
كَأس		cup
كافين		caffeine
ك - ب - ر	أكبر	bigger, older
	كَبير	big, old, older
ك - ت - ب	كِتاب (ج. كُتُب)	book
	مكتَب (ج. مَكاتِب)	office
	مَكتبة (ج. مَكتَبات)	library, bookshop
	مَكتوب	written
ك - ث - ر	أكثر	more than, most

at most	بالكثير	
(lit. may you have a lot!) شُكراً =	كثّر خيرِك! *	
many, much	كثير (ج. كثار)	
navy blue	كُحلي	ك - ح - ل
thus, this way		كِده
to lie	كَذَب - يَكذِب	ك - ذ - ب
chair		كُرسي (ج. كَراسي)
hospitality	كَرَم	ك - ر - م
to hate	كَرِه - يَكرَه	ك - ر - هـ
football, soccer	كُرة قَدَم	ك - ر - و
broken	مَكسور	ك - س - ر
name of an Egyptian dish		كُشَري
cake		كَعكة
enough	كِفاية	ك - ف - ي
to cost	II (كلّف - يُكلّف)	ك - ل - ف
cost	تَكلِفة (ج. تَكاليف)	
every, each, all	كُلّ	ك - لـ - ل
all together	كُلّه عَلى بَعضه*	
many happy returns of the day! (lit. every year and you are well)	كُلّ سَنة وانتم طيِّبين!	
whenever	كلّما	
college	كُلّيّة (ج. كُلّيّات)	
law school	كُلّيّة حُقوق	
to speak (to)	II (كلّم - يُكلِّم)	ك - ل - م
to speak	V (تكلّم - يِتكَلّم)	

English		Arabic	Root
word		كلمة (ج. كلمات)	
how much, how many			كَم
sleeve			كُمّ
also, as, as well			كَما◆
also			كَمان*
in full, complete		بالكامِل	ك-م-ل
kunafa/kinafi (a dessert)			كنافة
I had. . .			كُنت قد◆ . . .
Canada			كَندا
church		كَنيسة (ج. كَنائس)	ك-ن-س
Church of the Holy Sepulchre		كَنيسة القِيامة	
Canaanite			كنعاني
electricity		كَهرَباء	ك-هـ-ر-ب
drinking glass			كوب (ج. أكواب) ◆
to be		كان - يَكون	ك-و-ن
place		مَكان (ج. أماكن)	
status		مَكانة	
Kuwait			الكُويت
air-conditioning		تكييف	ك-ي-ف
	how *اِزّاي =	كَيف◆	
air-conditioned		مُكَيّف	
kilogram, kilometer			كيلو
chemistry			كيمياء

ل

to wear, put on	لبِس - يلبِس	ل - ب - س
clothes	لِبس، مَلابِس	
= حليب milk	لَبَن	ل - ب - ن
refugee	لاجِئ (ج. لاجِئين)	ل - ج - أ
meat	لَحمة	ل - ح - م
tune	لَحن (ج. ألحان)	ل - ح - ن
more delicious	ألذّ	ل - ذ - ذ
delicious	لَذيذ	
= يجب أن◆ must, necessary	لازم*	ل - ز - م
nice	لطيف	ل - ط - ف
player	لاعِب (ج. لاعبين)	ل - ع - ب
playing	لَعِب	
to play	لعِب - يلعَب	
game, sport	لُعبة	
language	لُغة (ج. لُغات)	ل - غ - و
sign	لافِتة (ج. لافِتات)	ل - ف - ت
title	لَقَب (ج. ألقاب)	ل - ق - ب
to find	III (لاقى - يِلاقي) *	ل - ق - ي
to meet	VIII (التقى - يَلتَقي)	
coloring	تلوين	ل - و - ن
color	لون (ج. ألوان)	
night	ليل (ج. لَيالي)	ل - ي - ل
the Night of *al-Israa'* (ascension)	ليلة الإسراء	
no		لأ

because		لأنّ
Lebanon		لُبنان
but		لكِن
did not		لم◆
= عِندَما◆ when		لمّا
= ليه* why		لِماذا◆
will not		لَن◆
= من فضلِك if you please		لو سمحتِ
if you want		لَو عايز*
Libya		ليبيا
= مِش* not		لَيْسَ◆
to you		ليكِ*

م

did not		ما
how beautiful!		ما أجمَل!
I don't know		ما عرفش*
= ايه* what		ماذا◆
God be praised		ما شاء الله
there isn't, there aren't		ما فيش*
meter		مِتر
subway, underground		مِترو
enjoyable	مُمتِع	م - ت - ع
for example	مثلاً	م - ث - ل

for free, no charge	مَجّاني	م - ج - ن
test	امتِحان (ج. امتِحانات)	م - ح - ن
general secondary school examination	امتِحان الثانويّة العامّة	
subject	مادّة (ج. مَوادّ)	م - د - د
period of time	مُدّة	
city	مَدينة (ج. مُدُن)	م - د - ن
time	مَرّة (ج. مَرّات)	م - ر - ر
sinckness, illness	مَرَض	م - ر - ض
to become sick, to become ill	مرِض - يَمرَض	
sick *عَيّان =	مَريض	م - ر - ض
exercise	تَمرين (ج. تَمارين)	م - ر - ن
area	مَساحة (ج. مَساحات)	م - س - ح
in the evening	مَساءً	م - س - ي
Christian		مَسيحي (ج. مَسيحيّين)
not ♦لَيسَ =		مِش*
ok	ماشي*	م - ش - ي
to go, walk	مَشى - يمَشي، مِشي - يِمشي*	م - ش - ي
Egypt		مَصر
Heliopolis (lit. New Egypt)		مصر الجَديدة
last, past	ماضي♦	م - ض - ي
rain	مَطَر	م - ط - ر
with		مَع
together		مَع بَعض
Don't worry!		مَعَلش!*

م - ك - ن	مُمكِن، يمكن	(it is) possible
م - ل - أ	مَملوء♦	filled
م - ل - ح	مُمَلّح	salted
م - ل - ك	مَلَك - يَملِك	to own
	مَملكة (ج. مَمالِك)	kingdom
	المَلك داوود	King David
مِن		from
مِن زمان		for a long time
من فضلِك		= لو سَمَحت if you please
م - ن - ح	مِنحة (ج. مِنَح)	scholarship
مُنذُ♦		since
م - ن - ع	مَمنوع	prohibited, forbidden
مِنين*		= مِن فين؟ from where?
م - هـ - ر	ماهِر	skilled
مَهما		whatever, regardless of
موبايل		mobile (phone), cell phone
م - و - ت	مات - يَموت	to die
	مات - يموت في	to love to an extreme (lit. to die in)
موز		bananas
موسيقى		music
م - و - ن/م - ي - ن	ميناء (ج. مَوانئ)	(sea) port
م - ي - ز	مُمتاز	excellent
	مُمَيَّز	distinguished
مَيّة*		water
مَيّة ساقعة*		cold water

ن

ناس		people
نَبوخَذ نَصّر		Nebuchadnezzar
ن - ب - ي	نَبي (ج. أنبِياء)	prophet
ن - ت - ج	نَتيجة (ج. نتائِج)	result
	نَتيجة لِ	as a result of
ن - ج - ح	نجَح - يَنجَح	to succeed, pass an exam
ن - ج - م	نجمة (ج. نُجوم)	star
ن - خ - ب	مُنتَخَب (ج. مُنتَخَبات)	= فَريق (ج. فِرَق) team
ن - د - ي	نادي (ج. أندِية، نَوادي)	club
ن - س - ب	بالنسبة ل . . .	as for, in relation to. . .
	مُناسَبة (ج. مُناسَبات)	occasion
ن - س - م	نَسيم	breeze
ن - ش - ر	VIII (انتَشَر - يَنتَشِر)	to spread
	مُنتَشِر	widespread
	نَشر	spreading
ن - ص - ص	نُصّ*	half
	نُصّ كُم*	short sleeve (lit. half sleeve)
ن - ص - ف	نِصف◆	half
ن - ط - ق	مَنطَقة (ج. مَناطِق)	area, region
ن - ظ - ر	في نَظَر	in the eyes of
ن - ظ - ف	II (نَظّف - يُنَظِّف)	to clean
	نَظيف	clean
ن - ف - س	نَفس	same

English	Arabic	Root
the same thing	نَفس الشيء	
I want, would like *عايِز =	نِفسي*	
to move, transfer	نَقل - يَنقُل	ن - ق - ل
day, daytime	نَهار	ن - هـ - ر
today	النهار دَه*	
ending	إنهاء	ن - هـ - ي
end	نِهاية (ج. نِهايات)	
to end	VIII (اِنتَهى - يَنتَهي)	
lighthouse	مَنارة	ن - و - ر
hell, fire	نار	
kind, type	نوع (ج. أنواع)	ن - و - ع
quality	نَوعيّة	
to sleep	نام - يَنام	ن - و - م
the Nile	النيل	ن - ي - ل

هـ

English	Arabic	Root
to attack	III (هاجَم - يُهاجم)	هـ - ج - م
quiet	هادِئ	هـ - د - أ
goal, aim	هَدَف (ج. أهداف)	هـ - د - ف
with the goal of, with the aim of	بِهَدَف	
gift, present	هَديّة (ج. هَدايا)	هـ - د - ي
this (f.), these *دي =		هذه•
to run away	هَرَب - يَهرُب	هـ - ر - ب
pyramid	هَرَم (ج. أهرام)	هـ - ر - م

Root	Word	English
هكَذا◆		thus, this way = كِده*
هَل◆		yes/no question word
هَلّأ (شامي)		now = دِلوَقتِ* = الآن◆
هـ - م - م	أَهَمّ	more, most important
	أَهَمّيّة	importance
	مُهِمّ	important
هِنا*، هُنا◆		here
هِناك*، هُناك◆		there, there is, there are
هـ - ن - د - س	مُهندس (ج. مُهَندِسين)	engineer
	مُهندس كُمبيوتر	computer engineer
	هَندَسة	engineering
هِندي		Indian
هُوّ*، هُوَ◆		he
هـ - و - ي	هَواء	air
	هواية (ج. هِوايات)	hobby
هِيّ*، هِيَ◆		she
هـ - ي - ل	هايل*	awesome, amazing, wonderful
هـ - ج - ر	هِجرة	immigration

و

Root	Word	English
واحة		oasis
والله...		by God, the truth is . . .
و - ج - ب	واجِب (ج. واجِبات)	homework
	وَجبة (ج. وَجبات)	meal
	يجب (أن) ◆	must = لازِم*

present, found	مَوجود	و - ج - د
to find	وَجد - يَجِد◆	
presence, existence	وُجود	
pain	وَجع	و - ج - ع
headache	وَجَع دماغ	
to face	III (واجَه - يُواجِه)	و - ج - هـ
to face, to direct oneself towards	V (توجّه - يَتَوَجّه)	
Sunday	الأحد	و - ح - د
one, someone (with negation, anyone)	حَد*	
by oneself	لَوَحد . . .	
to miss	وحَش - يوحَش*	و - ح - ش
flowers	وَرْد	و - ر - د
paper, piece of paper	وَرَقة (ج. أوراق)	و - ر - ق
Ministry of Foreign Affairs, State Department	وَزارة الخارجيّة	و - ز - ر
to distribute	II (وَزّع - يِوَزّع)	و - ز - ع
weight	وَزن	و - ز - ن
to reach, arrive at	وَصَل - يصِل◆، وصِل - يوصَل*	و - ص - ل
to contact, get in touch with	VIII (اتّصَل - يِتّصِل)	
delivering, transporting	تَوصيل	
for contacting, calling	للاتّصال	
public transportation, public transport	مُواصَلات عامّة	
arrival	وُصول	
clear	واضِح	و - ض - ح

و - ض - ع	مَوضوع (ج. مَواضيع)	subject
	وَضع (ج. أوضاع)	situation
	وَضَع - يَضَع	to put
و - ظ - ف	مُوظّف (ج. موظفين)	employee
و - ع - د	مَوعد (ج. مَواعيد)	time, appointed time
و - ف - ق	VIII (اتّفق - يتّفِق (عَلى))	to agree (to, on)
و - ق - ع	مُتَوَقّع	expected
	مَوقِع (ج. مَواقِع)	location
	وَقع - يَقَع◆	to be located
و - ق - ف	V (تَوَقف - يتوقَّف)	to stop
	واقِف	standing
	II (وَقّف - يِوَقِّف)	to stop (someone)
وَلّا		or
و - ل - د	اتولِد - يِتولِد*	to be born
	للأولاد	for (the) boys
	مَولِد	place of birth
	ميلادي	A.D.
	وِلادة	= ميلاد birth
	وُلِد - يولَد	to be born
و - ل - ي	وِلاية (ج. وِلايات)	state
	الوِلايات المُتّحدة	the United States

ي

ي - م - ن	اليَمَن	Yemen
	يَمين	right

يا ريت! *		I wish!
ياه		wow! O, Oh, what's the matter?
يجب أن◆		Look up under و- ج – ب
يَد		hand
يَنايِر		January
يَهودي (ج. يَهود)		Jew
يوناني		Greek
يونيو		June
ي – و – م	يوم (ج. أيّام)	day

English–Arabic glossary

A

A.D.	ميلادي
about, approximately	حَوالي، تَقريباً
Abraham	إبراهيم
abroad, outside	خارِج، بَرّه*
Abu Dhabi	أَبو ظبي
acceptable	مَقبول
accident	حادِث (ج. حَوادِث)
accountant	مُحاسِب (ج. مُحاسِبين)
advertisement, announcement,	إعلان (ج. إعلانات)
to add	IV (أضاف - يُضيف)
address, title	عُنوان (ج. عَناوين)
afraid (active participle)	خائف
afternoon	بَعد الظُهر
age	عُمر (ج. أعمار)
to agree (on)	VIII (اتّفق - يتّفِق (عَلى))
air	هَواء
air-conditioned	مُكَيّف
air-conditioning	تكييف
airline (company)	شَركة (ج. شرِكات) طَيَران
airplane	طَيّارة (ج. طَيّارات)
airport	مَطار (ج. مَطارات)
the al-Aqsa Mosque	المَسجِد الأقصى
Alexander the Great	الإسكَندر الكَبير
Algeria, Algiers	الجزائر
all kinds (lit. from the sour to the sweet)	من الحامِض للحِلو
allergy, sensitivity	حَساسيّة
also	كَمان*، بَرضُه*، أيضاً♦
also, as, as well	كَما♦
always	دائماً
America	أَمريكا
Amman	عَمّان

among the most famous	مِن أشهَر
ancient	قَديم (ج. قُدَماء)
and, and so	و
annoying, disturbing	مُزعِج
another, other (m./f.)	اخر/أُخرى◆، ثاني/ثانية*
to answer	III (جاوب - يُجاوِب)
answer	جَواب (ج. أجوِبة)
apartment, flat	شَقّة (ج. شُقَق)
appearance, the way one looks	شَكل (ج. أشكال)
apples	تُفّاح
Arab, Arabic	عَرَبي
the Arab Republic of Egypt	جُمهورية مصر العَربيّة
area (as in the area in km²)	مَساحة (ج. مَساحات)
area, region	مَنطَقة (ج. مَناطِق)
around	حَول
arrival	وُصول
as a result of	نَتيجة لِ
as for... (then, but...)	أمّا ... فَ
as for, in relation to...	بالنسبة ل ...
ascending	عُروج
Asian	أسيَوي
to ask (a question)	سَأَل - يسأَل
to ask for, order, request	طَلَب - يطلُب
assistant, helper	مُساعِد (ج. مُساعِدين)
at all, never	أبداً، خالِص*
at least	عَلى الأقلّ
at most	بالكثير
at, to have	عِند
to attack	III (هاجَم - يُهاجِم)
August	أغُسطُس
aunt, auntie	طانت
aware, knowing	عارِف
awesome, amazing	هايل*

B

baba ghannouj (name of a dish)	بابا غنّوج
Babylonian	بابلي
Baghdad	بَغداد
baked, grilled	مَشوي
baklawa (a dessert)	بَقلاوة
balcony	بَلكونة (ج. بَلكونات)
bananas	موز
bank	بَنك (ج. بنوك)
bathroom	حَمّام (ج. حَمّامات)
to be	كان - يَكون

to be able to	X (استَطاع - يَستَطيع)
	◆، قدِر - يقدر
to be afraid (of)	خاف - يخاف (من)
to be allowed	سمِح - يُسمَح
beautiful	جَميل = حِلو
because	عَشان (عَلى شان)*
because, since, actually	أَصْل . . . *
to become, to remain, to stay	بَقى - يِبقى*
to remain, to stay	بَقِي-يَبقى◆
bed	سَرير (ج. سَرايِر)
bedroom	غُرفة (ج. غُرَف) نوم،
	أوضة (ج. أُوَض) نوم*
been (have been doing something since. . .)	بَقى لي . . . *
before (+ noun)	قَبل
before (+ verb)	قبل ما
beginning	بِداية
Beirut	بيروت
belief	اعتِقاد
to believe, think	VIII (اعتقَد - يعتَقِد)
to believe (that someone is telling the truth)	II (صَدَّق - يُصَدِّق)
to believe (in), have faith (in)	IV (آمَن - يُؤمِن)
beloved, liked	مَحبوب

to besiege	III (حاصَر - يُحاصِر)
best	أفضَل
better, the best (lit. sweeter, sweetest)	أحلى
between, among	بَين
big, old, older	كَبير
biology	أحياء
birth	وِلادة
birthday	عيد ميلاد
black	أسوَد
blood pressure	ضَغط دَم
blue	أزرَق
book	كِتاب (ج. كُتُب)
to book, reserve	حَجَز-يحجِز
to be born	وُلِد - يولَد◆
to be born	اتوِلِد - يِتوِلِد*
to bother, disturb	IV (أزعَج - يُزعِج)
breakfast	فُطور
breeze	نَسيم
bridge	جِسر (ج. جُسور)
to bring	جاب - يِجيب*
Britain	بريطانيا
broken	مَكسور
brother	أخ (ج. إخوات، إخوان)
brown	بُنّي

to be built	بُني - يُبنى
bus	أوتوبيس (ج. أوتوبيسات)
business, commerce	تِجارة
but	لكِن
to buy	VIII (اِشترى - يَشترِي)
by oneself	لَوَحد . . .

C

café, coffee house	مَقهى (ج. مَقاهي)
caffeine	كافين
Cairo	القاهرة
cake	كَعكة
calendar	تَقويم
to call (give a name to someone)	II (سَمّى - يُسمّي)
I came	جيت*
can I help you? don't mention it (lit. any service?)	أيّ خِدمة؟
Canaanite	كنعاني
Canada	كَندا
capital	عاصِمة (ج. عَواصِم)
car	سَيّارة (ج. سَيّارات)، عربيّة (ج. عَرَبيّات)*
card	كارت (ج. كُروت)
carrying	حَمل
to celebrate	VIII (احتَفَل - يحتِفِل)
celebrating, celebration	احتِفال (ج. احتِفالات)
center	مَركَز (ج. مَراكِز)
central	مَركَزي
century	قَرن (ج. قُرون)
certainly	أكيد
chair	كُرسي (ج. كَراسي)
champion	بَطَل (ج. أبطال)
to change (something)	II (غيّر - يغيّر)
to change (oneself)	V (تغيَّر - يِتغَيّر)
channel	قَناة
cheap	رَخيص
chemistry	كيمياء
chicken	دَجاج♦، فِراخ*
Chinese	صيني
Christian	مَسيحي (ج. مَسيحيّين)
church	كَنيسة (ج. كَنائس)
Church of the Holy Sepulchre	كَنيسة القِيامة
cinnamon	قِرفة
the Citadel (in Cairo)	القلعة
city	مَدينة (ج. مُدُن)
clean	نَظيف

to clean	II (نَظَّف - يُنَظِّف)
clear	واضِح
climbing	تَسَلّق
close, near	قريب
cloth	قِماش
clothes	لِبس، مَلابِس
club	نادي (ج. أندِية)
coast	شَطّ
coastal	ساحِلي
coffee	قَهوة
cold (adj.)	بارِد
cold (n.)	بَرد، سَقعة*
college	كُلّيّة (ج. كُلّيّات)
color	لون (ج. ألوان)
coloring	تلوين
come	جِه - ييجي*
come out, go out	خرَج - يخرُج
coming, next	قادم♦، جاي*
community (especially foreign)	جالِية (ج. جالِيات)
company	شَرِكة (ج. شَرِكات)
computer engineer	مُهندس (ج. مُهندِسين) كُمبيوتر
congratulations, may you enjoy it!	مَبروك!
to consider	VIII (اعتَبَر - يَعتَبِر)
conspiracy	مُؤامَرة (ج. مُؤامَرات)
to contact, get in touch with	VIII (اتّصَل - يتّصِل)
(for) contacting, calling	للاتّصال
to contain	VIII (اِحتَوى - يَحتَوي (على))
cooked	مَطبوخ
cooker	بوتاجاز
cooking	طَبخ
Copt	قِبطي (ج. أقباط)
correct	صَحّ
correct	صحيح
to cost	II (كلّف - يُكلّف)
cost	تَكلِفة (ج. تَكاليف)
cotton	قُطن
counter, meter	عَدّاد (ج. عَدّادات)
country, nation-state	دَولة (ج. دُوَل)
country, land	بِلاد
crazy, mad	مَجنون
Creation Festival	عيد الخَلق
crowdedness, congestion	زَحمة
crucifixion	صَلب
the Crusaders	الصَليبيّين
culture	ثَقافة

cup	فِنجان (ج. فَناجين)، كَأس (ج. كُؤوس)
cupboard	دولاب (ج. دَواليب)

D

Damascus	دِمشق
dark (color)	غامِق
date of birth	تاريخ ميلاد
date, history	تاريخ (ج. تَواريخ)
day	يوم (ج. أيّام)
day, daytime	نَهار
to decide	II (قرّر - يُقرّر)
defending	دِفاع
delicious	لَذيذ
more delicious	ألذّ
delivering, transporting	تَوصيل
the Delta	الدِلتا
demand	III (طالَب - يُطالِب)
demonstration	مُظاهرة (ج. مُظاهَرات)
departure	مُغادَرة
depends, according to	حَسَب
desert-like	صَحراوي
despite, in spite of	رَغم
to destroy	II (دَمّر - يُدَمِّر)
diary (memoirs)	مُذكّرات
dictatorial	دِكتاتوري
did not	لَم◆
to die	مات - يَموت
to differ, be different	VIII (اختلَف - يختلِف)
difference	فَرق (ج. فُروق)
different	مُختلِف
difficult	صَعب
difficulty	صُعوبة (ج. صُعوبات)
direct	مُباشِر
direction of prayer	قِبلة
to disappear	VIII (اختَفى - يَختَفي)
discount, lowering, reducing	تَخفيض
dish	طَبَق (ج. أطباق)
distance	بُعد
distinguished	مُمَيَّز
to distribute	II (وَزّع - يِوَزّع)
to do	فَعَل - يَفعَل◆
to do, make	عَمِل - يعمَل
does not*, did not	ما
doctor, physician	طَبيب (ج. أطِبّاء)
doctor, physician	دكتور (ج. دكاترة)
Doha (the capital of Qatar)	الدوحة

the Dome of the Rock	قبّة الصَخرة
don't worry	مَعَلش!*
done, finished	خَلاص*
doubt	شَكّ (ج. شُكوك)
to dream (of)	حلِم - يَحلُم (ب)
drinking glass	كوب (ج. أكواب)
driver	سائق (ج. سائقين)♦، سَوّاق (ج. سَوّاقين)*
dry	جافّ
dryness, drought	جَفاف

E

early	مُبَكّر♦، بدري*
east	شَرق
Easter	عيد الفِصح
easy	سَهل
economy, economics	اقتِصاد
eggs	بيض
Egypt	مَصر
Egyptian pound	جِنيه مَصري
Eid al-Fitr (celebration marking the end of Ramadan)	عيد الفِطر
eighth	ثامِن
electricity	كَهرَباء
elevator, lift	اسانسير (ج. أسانسيرات)
employee	مُوظّف (ج. موظفين)
empty, available, vacant	فاضي*
end	نِهاية (ج. نِهايات)
to end, to be finished	VIII (اِنتَهى - يَنتَهي)
ending	إنهاء
engaged	مَخطوب
engineer	مُهندس (ج. مُهَندِسين)
engineering	هَندَسة
English literature	أدَب إنجليزي
enjoyable	مُمتِع
enough	كِفاية
to enter	دَخَل - يدخُل
entrance	مَدخَل (ج. مَداخِل)
entry visa	تَأشيرة (ج. تأشيرات) دُخول
especially	خُصوصاً
Europe	أوروبا
European	أوروبي
(in the) evening	مَساءً♦
every, each, all	كُلّ
everyone, all	جَميع

exactly	بالضَبط
to exceed	زاد - يَزيد (عَلى)
excellent	مُمتاز
except, to (as in "a quarter to four")	إلّا
exchanging	تَبادُل
exercise	تَمرين (ج. تَمارين)
expected	مُتَوَقّع
expensive	غالي
to explode	VII (انفجر - ينفجِر)
extra, more	زِيادة
(in the) eyes (of)	في نَظَر

F

to face (someone)	III (واجَه - يُواجِه)
to face, to direct oneself towards	V (توجّه - يَتَوجّه)
to fail	فَشِل - يَفشَل
falafel (in Egypt)	طَعمِيّة
fall, autumn	الخُريف
family	عيلة (ج. عيلات) *، عائِلة (ج. عائلات) ♦ أُسرة (ج. أُسَر) ♦
famous	مَشهور
famous (to be)	VIII (اشتهر - يشتهِر)
far	بَعيد
fast, quick	سَريع
to fast	صام - يَصوم
fat (n.)	سَمنة
father	أَب
fatta (name of a dish)	فَتّة
favorite	مُفَضّل
feast, festival, anniversary	عيد (ج. أعياد)
the Feast of Sacrifice	العيد الكبير
to feel	شَعَر - يَشعُر، حَسّ - يحِسّ*
feeling	شُعور
female	أُنثى
festival of *shamm an-nasiim*	عيد شَمّ النَسيم
filled, full	مَملوء♦، مَليان*
to find	III (لاقى - يِلاقي) *، وَجد - يَجد♦
to find (something strange)	X (استغرب - يستَغرِب)
to finish, complete	II (خلّص - يخلّص) *
fire, hell	نار
first (m.)	أوّل
first (at first)	في الأوّل
first (f.)	أولى
fish	سَمَك (ج. أسماك)
flowers, roses	وَرْد

fly, take off	طار - يطير
food	طَعام
foods, dishes	مَأكولات
football, soccer	كُرة قَدَم
for a long time, it has been a long time	مِن زمان
for boys, for children	للأولاد
for example	مثلاً
for free, no charge	مَجّاني
for information	للاستِعلام
for living, residing	للسكن
for the first time	لأوّل مَرّة
for the sake of, in order to	عَشان (عَلى شان) *
for the summer	صَيفي
for the winter	شَتَوي
for women	سِتّاتي
for you/for your sake	عَشان خاطرِك*
foreign, foreigner	أجنَبي (ج. أجانِب)
to found, establish, set up	II (أسّس - يؤسّس)
to be founded	V (تأسّس - يَتَأسَّس)
fourth	رابِع
France	فرنسا
frankly	بِصَراحة
Friday	الجُمعة
friend	صَديق (أصدِقاء)
friend; owner	صاحِب (ج. أصحاب)
friendship	صَداقة
frightening, scary	مُخيف
from	مِن
from the sea	بَحري
from where	من أين♦؟ مِنين*؟ مِن فين*؟
front, introduction	مُقدّمة (ج. مُقدِّمات)
fruit	فَواكِه
to become full, satisfied	شَبِع - يَشبَع
furnished	مَفروش
future	مُستَقبَل

G

gallabiyya (type of Egyptian clothing)	جَلابيّة (ج. جَلاليب)
game, sport	لُعبة (ج. لُعَب)
garden, park	حَديقة (ج. حَدائق)
garlic	ثوم
general secondary school examination	امتِحان الثانويّة العامّة
to get to know	V (تعرّف - يتعرّف)
to get up	قام - يَقوم
to get used to	V (تَعَوّد - يَتَعَوَّد)
getting to know	تَعَرّف

gift, present	هَديّة (ج. هَدايا)
girl	بِنت (ج. بَنات)، فَتاة◆
to give	II (أدّى-يِدّي)*، IV (أعطى-يعطي) ◆
give me	ادّيني*
to go	راح - يروح*، ذَهَب - يَذهَب◆
to go back, return	رَجَع - يَرجِع
to go, walk	مَشى - يَمشي
goal, aim	هَدَف (ج. اهداف)
)with the (goal (aim) of. . .	بِهَدَف
God (Allah)	الله
God be praised!	ما شاء الله!
God be with you, good luck!	ربّنا معاك!
God forbid! (lit. may bad things be far)	بعيد الشرّ!
God knows!	الله أعلم!
God willing!	إن شاء الله!
(by) God, the truth is. . .	والله . . .
good	جَيّد◆، كويّس*
good morning	صَباح الخير
good morning (answer to صَباح الخير)	صَباح النور
government	حُكومة (ج. حُكومات)
governmental	حُكومي
grade, degree, class, extent	دَرَجة (ج. دَرَجات)
to graduate	V (تَخرّج - يِتخَرَّج)
grandfather	جَدّ (ج. جُدود)
grandmother	جَدّة (ج. جَدّات)
gray, grey	رَمادي
Greek	يوناني
green	أخضَر
guest	ضيف (ج. ضُيوف)
the Gulf	الخليج

H

habit, custom	عادة (ج. عادات)
half	نُصّ*، نِصف◆
hand	يَد
to happen	حَدث - يحدُث◆
to become happy	فَرِح - يفرَح
to hate	كَرِه - يَكرَه
having drunk something already	شارِب
he, he is	هُوّ، هُوَ
head	راس (ج. رُؤوس)
headache	وَجَع دماغ
to hear, listen	سَمِع - يَسمَع
height	ارتِفاع

Heliopolis (lit. New Egypt)	مصر الجَديدة
hell, fire	نار
hello, hi	أهلاً
to help, assist	III (ساعَد - يُساعِد)
here, over here	هنا
here it is (f.)	أهيه*
here it is (m.)	أهوه*
high	عالي
high, has gone up	طالِع
historian	مُؤرِّخ (ج. مُؤرِّخين)
hobby	هواية (ج. هِوايات)
holy, sacred	مُقَدّس
homemaker, housewife	ربّة بيت
homework	واجِب (ج. واجِبات)
to hope for	رَجا - يَرجو
hospital	مُستَشفى (ج. مُستَشفَيات)
hospitality, generosity	كَرَم
hot (weather)	حارّ
hot (to touch)	سُخن
hotel	فندُق (ج. فَنادِق)
hotel apartment	شَقّة (ج. شُقَق) فندقيّة
hour, clock, watch	ساعة (ج. ساعات)
house	بيت (ج. بُيوت)
how	إزاي*، كَيف♦
how beautiful!	ما أجمَل!
how much (extent) ECA	قَد ايه*
how long have you been?	بَقى لك قدّ إيه؟*
how many	كم
how much	بكم
human rights	حُقوق الإنسان
humid	رَطب
hungry	جوعان، جَعان*

I

I	أنا
I had. . .	كُنت قَد . . .♦
I hope you are ok (lit. your safety)	سلامتك!
I mean, my intention	قَصدي
idea	فِكرة (ج. أفكار)
if	إذا
if you want	لَو عايز*
immediately	حالاً
immigration	هِجرة
importance	أهَمّيّة
important	مُهِمّ
impression	انطِباع (ج. انطِباعات)

to improve (oneself)	V (تحَسَّنَ - يَتَحسّن)
to improve (something)	II (حَسَّنَ - يحسّن)
in	في
in front of	أمام
in full, complete	بالكامِل
in general	بِشَكل عامّ
in it, it has	فيها
in particular	بِشَكل خاصّ
in your opinion	في رأيَك
to increase, go up	زاد - يَزيد
independence	استِقلال
Indian	هِندي
individual, member	فَرد (ج. أفراد)
industrial	صِناعي
to be influenced	V (تأثّر - يَتَأثّر)
inhabitants	سُكّان
instead of	بَدَل
instruction, teaching	تَعليم
intelligence services	مُخابَرات
intention, meaning	قَصد
international	دَولي
invitation	دَعوة (ج. دَعوات)، عَزومة*
to invite	دَعا - يَدعو♦، عزم/ يعزم*
Iraq	العراق
Isaac	إسحاق
the Islamic religion	الدين الإسلامي
issue, issuing	صُدور
it has been a long time, for a long time	مِن زَمان
it is all the same	زَيّ بعضه*

J

January	يَنايِر
Jerusalem	القُدس
Jesus Christ (lit. the Master the Messiah)	السَيّد المَسيح
Jew, Jewish	يَهودي (ج. يَهود)
to join	VII (انضَمّ - يَنضَمّ)
Jordan	الأُردُن
juice	عَصير
to jump	قَفَز - يَقفِز♦
June	يونيو

K

Khartoum (the capital of Sudan)	الخَرطوم
kilogram, kilometer	كيلو
kind, type	نوع (ج. أنواع)
King David	المَلك داوود

kingdom	مَملكة (ج. مَمالِك)
kitchen	مَطبَخ
to know	عرف - يَعرِف
I don't know	ما اعرفش*
known, well-known	مَعروف
koshari (an Egyptian dish of lentils and pasta)	كُشَري
kunafa/kinafi (a dessert)	كِنافة
Kuwait	الكُويت

L

lamb	خَروف (ج. خِرفان)
landmark	مَعلَم (ج. مَعالِم)
language	لُغة (ج. لُغات)
last, final	آخِر، أخير
last, past	اِللي فات*، ماضي♦
law school	كُلّيّة حُقوق
leadership	قِيادة
to learn	V (تعلّم - يتعلّم)
to leave, leave behind	تَرَك - يترُك، ساب - يسيب*
to leave, let, allow	II (خَلّى - يخلّي) *
Lebanon	لبنان
lecture	مُحاضَرة (ج. مُحاضَرات)
left	شِمال*، يسار♦
lesson	دَرس (ج. دُروس)
let me	خلّيني*
library	مَكتبة
Libya	ليبيا
to lie	كَذَب - يكذِب
life	حَياة
light (color)	فاتِح
lighthouse	مَنارة
to like, love	أحبّ - يُحِبّ♦، حَبّ - يِحِبّ*
like, similar to	مِثل♦، زَيّ*
line, handwriting	خَطّ
line, queue	طابور
a little	قليلاً♦، شويّة*
to live, reside	سَكَن - يسكُن
to live, be alive	عاش - يَعيش
living	ساكِن
local	بَلَدي
to be located	وَقع - يَقَع♦
location	مَوقِع
long	طَويل
to look	بَصّ - يبُصّ*
to look for	II (دوَّر - يِدَوَّر+على) *، بحث - يبحث+عن♦

must	يجب أن◆، لازم*
to lose	II (ضَيّع - يضيّع)، فَقَد - يفقِد◆
to be lost	ضاع - يَضيع
lost and found box, lost property	صندوق المفقودات
a lot, very	جداً◆، قَوي*
to love to an extreme, crazy about (lit. to die in)	مات - يموت في
low (temperature)	صُغرى◆
lucky	مَحظوظ
luxurious	فَخم

M

main	رَئيسي
making lighter, reducing	تَخفيف
male	ذَكَر (ج. ذُكور)
man	رَجُل (ج. رِجال) ◆، راجل (ج. رِجّالة) *
manager	مُدير (ج. مُدَراء)
many happy returns of the day! (lit. every year and you are well)	كُلّ سَنة وانتم طيِّبين!
many, much	كثير (ج. كثار)
market	سوق (ج. أسواق)
marriage	زَواج◆، جواز*
match	مُباراة (ج. مُبارَيات)
math	رِياضيّات
matter, issue	مَسألة (ج. مَسائل)
may God have mercy on him!	الله يرحمه!
may God keep you!	ربّنا يِخلّيك!
meal	وَجبة (ج. وَجبات)
to mean	عَنى - يَعني
means, in other words	يَعني
meat	لَحمة
medicine	دَواء
medicine (discipline)	طِبّ
the Mediterranean Sea	البَحر الأبيَض المُتوسّط
to meet	VIII (التقى - يَلتَقي)
(for) men	رِجّالي
to mention	II (ذَكَر - يَذكُر)
meter	متر (ج. أمتار)
the Middle East	الشَرق الأوسَط
milk	لَبَن*، حليب
Ministry of Foreign Affairs, State Department	وَزارة الخارجيّة
minority	أقلّيّة (ج. أقلّيّات)
minute	دَقيقة (ج. دَقائق)
to miss	وحَش - يوحَش*
mobile (phone), cell phone	موبايل (ج. موبايلات)

moderate مُعتَدِل
modern حَديث
Monday الإثنين
month شهر (ج. شُهور)
monthly شَهريّاً
more than, most أكثر
more, most famous أشهَر
more, most important أَهَمّ
morning صَباحاً
Morocco المَغرِب
mosque جامِع (ج. جَوامِع)، مَسجِد (ج. مَساجِد)
most (of) مُعظَم
mother أُمّ
Mother of the World (Cairo) أُمّ الدُنيا
mountain جَبَل (ج. جِبال)
mountainous جَبَلي
to move, transfer نَقل - يَنقُل
Mt. Sinai جَبَل (موسى)
muezzin, the man calling for prayer مُؤَذِّن
musakhkhan (well-known Palestinian dish) مُسَخّن
Muscat (the capital of Oman) مَسقَط
museum مَتحَف (ج. مَتاحِف)
music موسيقى
Muslim مُسلم (ج. مُسلِمين)
must يجب (أن) ♦، لازِم*
my dear madam يا سِتّي*

N

name اِسم (ج. أسماء، أسامي)
name (polite) اِسم حَضرِتك
national قَومي
national team (lit. chosen, selected) مُنتَخَب (ج. مُنتَخَبات)
nationality, citizenship جِنسِيّة (ج. جِنسِيّات)
nationalization تَأميم
navy blue كُحلي
Nebuchadnezzar نبوخذ نصّر
need حاجة (ج. حاجات)
(in) need of بِحاجة لِ، إلى
neighbor جار (ج. جيران)
neighborhood, quarter حَيّ (ج. أحياء)
new جَديد
news خَبَر (ج. أخبار)
nice لطيف
night ليل (ج. لَيالي)

the Night of *al-Israa'* (ascension)	ليلة الإسراء
the Nile	النيل
no	لأ
no need, let's not	بَلاش
the Nobel Sanctuary (in Jerusalem)	الحَرَم الشريف
nonsense (lit. no "..." no watermelon)	بَلا ... بَلا بَطّيخ*
north	شَمال
not	مش*، لَيسَ◆
not knowing, I don't know	مش عارف*
not serious, simple	بسيطة
not, other than	غير
now	الآن◆، دِلوَقتِ*
now (Levantine)	هَلّأ
number	رَقَم (ج. أرقام)
number	عَدَد (ج. أعداد)

O

oasis	واحة (ج. واحات)
obtain, get hold of	حَصَل - يَحصُل (عَلى)
occasion	مُناسَبة (ج. مُناسَبات)
to occupy	VIII (احتَلّ - يَحتَلّ)
of course	طَبعاً
of, belonging to	بتاع*
to offer, present	II (قدّم - يقدّم)
office	مكتَب (ج. مَكاتِب)
ok, fine	ماشي*
ok, so, right then	طيّب، طَب*
Oman	عُمان
on	عَلى
on the contrary	عَلى العَكس
on the side	على الجَنب
one, someone (with negation, anyone)	أحد◆، حَد*
one-third	ثلث
onions	بَصَل
only	فقط◆، بس*
open	مَفتوح
opportunity	فُرصة (ج. فُرَص)
or	أو، وَلّا*
orange (color)	بُرتُقالي
ordinary, fine, ok	عادي
original, from the country	أَصْلي
originally	أَصْلاً
outside, abroad	خارج◆، برّه*
to own	ملَك - يَملِك

P

pain	وَجع
Palestine	فِلسطين
paper, piece of paper	وَرَقة (ج. أوراق)
paradise, heaven	جَنّة
part, area	حِتّة (ج. حِتَت)*
passport	جَواز (ج. جَوازات) سَفَر
to pay	دَفَع - يدفَع
peace	سَلام
people	ناس
perfect, fine	تَمام
perhaps, maybe	رُبّما
period of time	مُدّة
Persia	بِلاد فارِس
person	شَخص (ج. أشخاص)
personal	شَخصي
personally	شَخصياً
Pharaonic	فرعوني
phrase	عِبارة (ج. عِبارات)
physician, doctor	دُكتور (ج. دَكاترة)، طبيب (ج. أطِبّاء)
physics	فيزياء
picture	صورة (ج. صُوَر)
place	مَكان (ج. أماكن)
place of birth	مَولِد، مَكان الوِلادة
to play	لِعِب - يِلعَب
player	لاعِب (ج. لاعِبين)
playing	لَعِب
to please	IV (أعجَب - يعجِب)
please, if you please	من فضلك! لو سمحت!
please, go ahead, take	اتفضّل
pleased to meet you	فُرصة سعيدة
policy	سِياسة (ج. سِياسات)
political science	عُلوم سِياسية
poor (person)	فَقير (ج. فُقَراء)
popular, working class	شَعبي
port	ميناء (ج. مَوانِئ)
(it is) possible	مُمكن
potatoes	بَطاطِس
to pray	II (صَلّى - يُصَلّي)
prayer	صَلاة
to prefer	II (فَضّل - يُفَضِّل)
to prepare	II (حَضّر - يُحَضِّر)
presence, existence	وُجود
present, found, located	مَوجود
presently, whatever you say	حاضر

president	رَئيس (ج. رُؤساء)
price	ثَمَن، سِعر (ج. أسعار)
private	خاصّ
prize, award	جائِزة (ج. جوائز)
problem	مُشكِلة (ج. مَشكلات)
prohibited, forbidden	مَمنوع
project	مَشروع (ج. مَشاريع)
prophet	نَبي (ج. انبِياء)
public transportation	مُواصَلات عامّة
to put	وَضَع - يَضَع◆، حَطّ - يحُطّ*
pyramid	هَرَم (ج. أهرام، أهرامات) ◆

Q

Qatar	قَطَر
quality	نَوعيّة
a quarter, one-fourth	رُبع
question	سؤال (ج. أسئِلة)
quiet, calm	هادِئ

R

Rabat (the capital of Morocco)	الرَباط
rain	مَطَر
to raise	رَفَع - يَرفَع
Ramadan (the fasting month)	رَمَضان
rapture (in music), enjoyment	طَرَب
reach, arrive at	وَصَل - يصِل◆، وصِل - يوصَل*
to read	قرأ - يَقرَأ
reading	قِراءة
ready	جاهِز
reason	سَبَب (ج. أسباب)
to rebel (against)	ثار - يثور (عَلى)
reception hall, lounge	قاعة (ج. قاعات) استِقبال
red	أحمَر
the Red Sea	البحر الأحمر
refrigerator	ثَلّاجة (ج. ثلّاجات)
refugee	لاجِئ (ج. لاجِئين)
refugee camp	مُخَيّم (ج. مُخيّمات)
to refuse	رَفَض - يَرفُض
relationship	عَلاقة (ج. عَلاقات)
religious	مُتَدَيّن
remainder, left-over	بَقيّة (ج. بَقايا)
remaining, rest	باقي
remembering, remember	فاكِر*
rent	للإيجار

request	طَلب
responsible	مَسؤول
rest	استريّح – يستريّح
restaurant	مَطعَم (ج. مَطاعِم)
result	نَتيجة (ج. نتائِج)
to return (something)	IV (أرجَع - يُرجِع) ◆
rice	رُزّ
rice pudding (lit. rice with milk)	رُزّ بلبن
ride	رِكِب - يِركَب
right (legal)	حَقّ (ج. حُقوق)
right (direction)	يَمين
Riyadh (the capital of Saudi Arabia)	الرياض
road	طَريق (ج. طُرُق)
role	دَور
Roman Amphitheater	المَسرح الروماني
room	غُرفة (ج. غُرَف)، أوضة (ج. أوَض) *
ruins, antiquities	أثَر (ج. آثار)
rule	قانون (ج. قَوانين)
to run away, flee	هَرَب - يَهرُب

S

to sacrifice	II (ضَحّى - يُضَحّي)
salary	راتِب
salted	مُمَلّح
salted fish	فَسيخ
same	نَفس
the same size as	قَدّ*
the same thing	نَفس الشيء
Sana'a (the capital of Yemen)	صَنعاء
sandwich	سَندويشة (ج. سندويشات)
Saturday	السبت
sauce	صَلصة
Saudi Arabia	السعودية
to say	قال - يَقول
saying	قَول (ج. أقوال)
scholarship	مِنحة (ج. مِنَح)
school	مَدرَسة (ج. مَدارِس)
science, branch of knowledge	عِلم (ج. علوم)
to score	سَجّل - يُسَجِّل
sea	بَحر (ج. بُحور)
season	فَصل (ج. فُصول)
second, other	ثاني
secondary school, high school	مَدرَسة (مَدارِس) ثانَويّة
secretary	سِكرتير
to see	شاف - يِشوف*، رأى - يَرى◆

it seems	يَبدو
to send	بَعَث - يبعَث
sensible, possible, reasonable	مَعقول
seriously	بِجَدّ
service	خِدمة (ج. خَدَمات)
to set up, establish	IV (أقام - يُقيم)
sex, gender	جِنس
shame, shameful	عيب
she	هِيَ
shirt	قَميص (ج. قُمصان)
shop, store	دُكّان (ج. دَكاكين)
shop, store	مَحَلّ (ج. مَحلّات)
shopping	تَسَوّق
short sleeve (lit. half sleeve)	نُصّ كُم*
shout	صاح - يَصيح
sick (to become)	مرِض - يَمرَض
sick, ill, unwell	مَريض، عَيّان*
sickness	مَرَض
sign	لافِتة
since	مِن*، مُنذُ◆
to sing	II (غَنّى - يُغنّي)
singer	مُطرِب (ج. مُطرِبين)، مُغَنّي (ج. مُغَنّين)
sister	أخت (ج. أخوات)
to sit	جَلَس - يجلس◆، قعد، يقعُد*
situation	وَضع (ج. أوضاع)
size	مَقاس
skilled	ماهِر
sky, heaven	سَماء
to sleep, to go to sleep	نام - يَنام
sleeve	كُمّ (ج. أكمام)
small (MSA/ECA)	صَغير◆، صُغَيَّر*
smaller, younger	أصغَر
smart	ذَكي
smell	رائحة (ج. رَوائح)
smoke	II (دَخّن - يُدخّن)
smoking	تَدخين
snow	ثَلج (ج. ثُلوج)
society	مُجتَمَع (ج. مُجتَمَعات)
some	بَعض
sometimes	أحياناً
son	إبن (ج. أبناء)
song	أُغنِية (ج. أغاني)
sorry	آسِف
sound, voice	صَوت (ج. أصوات)
south	جَنوب

- to speak, talk — V (تكلّم - يتكلّم)
- to speak to, talk to — II (كلّم - يُكلِّم)
- special — مَخصوص
- specialization, major (in college) — تَخَصُّص (ج. تَخَصّصات)
- sports — رِياضة
- to spread — VIII (انتَشَر - يَنتَشِر)
- spreading — نَشر
- spring — الربيع
- standing — واقِف
- star — نجمة (ج. نُجوم)
- to start — بدأ - يَبدأ
- state — وِلاية (ج. وِلايات)
- station, terminal — مَحَطّة (ج. مَحَطّات)
- status — مَكانة
- steering wheel — عَجَلة قِيادة
- still — لا زال ♦ لسه*
- to stop (by itself) — V (تَوَقف - يتوقَّف)
- to stop (someone) — II (وَقّف - يِوَقِّف)
- stop it please! enough already! — خَلاص بَقى! *
- store, shop — مَحَلّ (ج. مَحَلّات)
- story — قِصّة (ج. قِصَص)
- straight, straight away, all the way — على طول*
- strange, stranger — غَريب
- street — شارِع (ج. شَوارِع)
- student — طالِب (ج. طُلّاب)
- student hostel, dorm — بيت (ج. بُيوت) طَلَبة
- study — دِراسة (ج. دِراسات)
- to study — دَرَس - يِدرس
- to study at home, review at home — III (ذاكِر - يِذاكِر) *
- stuffed (food) — مَحشي
- subject — مادّة (ج. مَوادّ)، مَوضوع (ج. مَواضيع)
- subway, underground — مِترو
- succeed, pass an exam — نجَح - يَنجَح
- Sudan — السودان
- suitcase — شَنطة (ج. شُنَط)، حقيبة (ج. حَقائب)♦
- sum, amount — مَبلَغ (ج. مَبالغ)
- summer — الصيف
- sun — شَمس
- Sunday — الأحد
- sunrise — شُروق
- sunset — غُروب
- to support — دعَم - يَدعَم
- support — دَعم

surprise	مُفاجَأة (ج. مُفاجَآت)
to be surprised	VI (تفاجأ - يَتَفاجأ)
sweet	حِلو
to swim	عام - يعوم*، سَبَح - يسبَح♦
to symbolize	رَمَز - يَرمُز
Syria	سوريا

T

tabbouleh (name of a dish, typically Lebanese)	تَبّولة
table	تَرابيزة (ج. تَرابيزات) *، طاوِلة (ج. طاوِلات) ♦
take	أخذ - ياخُذ
to take out	IV (أخرَج - يخرِج) ♦
taxi	تاكسي
to teach	II (درّس - يدرّس)، II (عَلّم - يُعَلِّم)
teacher, instructor	مُدَرّس (ج. مُدرّسين)
teacher, professor	أستاذ (ج. أساتذة)
team	فَريق (ج. فِرَق)
teaching, instruction	تدريس، تعليم
tell, inform	IV (أخبَر - يخبِر) ♦
Temple Mount	جَبل الهَيكَل
tennis (lit. ground tennis)	تِنِس أرضي
test	امتِحان (ج. امتِحانات)
to thank	شَكَر - يشكُر
thank God!	الحمدُ لِلّه!
thank you (lit. may you have a lot!)	كَتّر خيرِك!
thank you	شُكراً
thank you (lit. may your hand be safe or sound)	تِسلم ايدَك*
thanks a lot	شُكراً جَزيلاً
that I	إنّني♦، إنّي
that she	إنّها
that (f.)	تِلك♦
that (m.)	ذلك♦
that, to	أنّ♦
that, which	اِللي*
that, which, who (m., f., pl.)	الذي، التي، الذين♦
theater	مَسرَح (ج. مَسارِح)
then, and then	بَعدين*، ثُمّ♦
there	هناك
there is, there are	فيه*، هُناك♦
there isn't, there aren't	ما فيش*
these	دول
thing	شَيء (ج. أشياء)، حاجة (ج. حاجات)*

to think, have an opinion	VIII (افتَكَر ـ يِفتِكِر) *، فكّر ـ يفكّر، ظَنّ ـ يظُنّ
third	ثالِث
thirsty	عَطشان (ج. عَطشانين)
this (m.)	ده*، هذا♦
this (f.), these	دي*، هذه♦
Thursday	الخَميس
thus, this way	كِده*، هكَذا♦
ticket	تَذكَرة (ج. تذاكِر)
time	زَمَن
time (an occurrence)	مَرّة (ج. مَرّات)
time, appointed time	مَوعد (ج. مَواعيد)
tired	تَعبان
title	لَقَب (ج. ألقاب)
to	إلى، لِ
to where?	عَلى فين*
to you	ليك*
today	النهار دَه
together, altogether	كُلّه عَلى بَعضه*
together	مَع بَعض
tomatoes	طماطِم
tomorrow	بُكرة*، غد/غداً♦
touristic	سِياحي

tower	بُرج (ج. أبراج)
tradition	تَقليد (ج. تقاليد)
traditional	تَقليدي
train	قِطار (ج. قِطارات) ♦، قَطر (ج. قَطرات)*
to travel	III (سافر ـ يسافِر)
travel	سَفَر
trip	رِحلة (ج. رِحلات)
Tripoli	طرابلس
truly, indeed	فِعلاً
truly, in reality, verily	إنّ
to try, try out, test out	II (جَرَّب ـ يُجَرِّب)
to try, attempt	III (حاوَل ـ يُحاوِل)
Tuesday	الثَلاثاء
tune	لَحن (ج. ألحان)
Tunis, Tunisia	تونِس
turn out to be	طلع
two months before my trip (lit. before my trips by two months)	قَبل رِحلتي بشهرين

U

Umm 'Ali (milk pudding, a dessert)	أُمّ عَلي
under the leadership of	بقيادة

understanding	فاهِم
the United Arab Emirates	الإمارات العَرَبيّة المُتَّحدة
the United States	الوِلايات المُتّحدة
university	جامِعة (ج. جامِعات)
unlucky, poor, unfortunate	مَسكين (ج. مَساكين)
until, even	حتّي
to use	X (استعمَل - يستَعمِل)
used	مُستعمَل
usually	عادةً

V

vegetables	خُضار
verb	فِعل
very	جِدّاً
viewing, watching	مُشاهَدة
to visit	زار- يزور

W

the Wailing Wall	حائِط المَبكى
to wait	X (استنّى - يِستَنّى) *
to wake up	صَحا - يَصحو◆
to want	IV (أراد - يُريد) ◆، عايِز*، نِفس . . . *
warm	دافِئ
to watch	V (تفرّج - يِتفَرَّج)
water	مَيّة*
watermelon	بَطّيخ
weak	ضَعيف
weaken	IV (أضعَف-يُضعِف)
to wear, put on	لبِس - يِلبِس
weather	جَوّ، طَقس
Wednesday	الأربعاء
week	أُسبوع (ج. أسابيع)
weight	وَزن
welcome!	أهلاً وسهلاً!
welcome to you (response to أهلا وسهلا)	أهلا بيك*، أهلاً وسهلاً بيكِ*
west	غَرب
what	إيه*، ما◆
what (with verbs MSA)	ماذا
whatever you say (lit. your requests are orders)	طَلباتِك أوامر
whatever, regardless of	مَهما
when?	متى◆؟ إمتى*
when (not a question ECA)	لمّا، عندما◆
whenever	كلّما
where	أيْنَ◆، فين*
white	أبيَض

who, which, that	إللي*
the whole time	طول الوَقت
why	ليه*، لِماذا◆
widespread	مُنتَشِر
will, shall	حَ*، س◆، سَوفَ◆
will be happy to (lit. from my eyes)	مِن عينيّ
will not	لَن◆
	مِش هـَ، مِش حَ*
win	فاز - يَفوز
win, to beat (someone)	غَلَب - يَغلِب
winning	فَوز
winter	الشِتاء
I wish!	يا ريت!
with	مَع
with sugar	بِسُكُّر
without	مِن غير*، بدون
wonderful, wonderfully (lit. like jasmine)	زَيّ الفُلّ*
wool	صوف
word	كلمة (ج. كلمات)
to work	VIII (اشتغَل - يِشتِغِل)
work	شُغل، عَمَل
worker	عامِل (ج. عُمّال)
world	عالَم
World War I	الحَرب العالميّة الأولى
wow!	يا سَلام
wow! O, Oh, what's the matter?	يا ه*
written	مَكتوب

Y

year	سنة (ج. سِنين،* سَنَوات◆)
yellow	أصفَر
Yemen	اليمَن
yes	أيوه*
yes/no question word	هَل◆
yesterday	إمبارح*، أمس◆
you (lit. your presence)	حَضرتِك
you (pl.) have, with you (pl.)	عِندكم، عندُكو*
you (f.)	انتِ
you (m.)	انتَ
young man	شابّ (ج. شَباب)
young woman	شابّة (ج. شابّات)

Grammar Index

Arabic Terms